CORPORATE OPPORTUNITIES

Despite the many open questions on how to interpret corporate opportunity rules, their relevance for the development of a corporation in its early stages is undoubtable. The traditional economic reading of corporate opportunity doctrines has ascribed the rules to the area of economic agency theory, and has stressed their function to contain agency costs. But corporate opportunity rules are surrounded by a far more complex set of variables in highly innovative environments.

On the one hand, the rules limit the mobility of corporate founders who sit on start-up boards – where founders represent the very building blocks and knowledge upon which technical innovation depends. On the other, they may limit venture capital intra-industry operativity – when the same general partner sitting on the boards of competing start-ups find themselves in a position of divided loyalty.

Far from being a systematic commentary on corporate opportunity rules, this book applies the law and economics method to the corporate opportunity legal paradigm, drawing normative examples from both the common law and civil law traditions. After presenting a simplified economic model for the analysis of bargaining over corporate opportunities, it identifies common patterns in corporate opportunity rules and potential legal and/or contractual solutions for their development, either by way of court innovation or private ordering. These patterns and adaptations may prove crucial to different economic realities, such as industrial districts, venture capital and corporate venture capital.

CONTEMPORARY STUDIES IN CORPORATE LAW

Corporate law scholarship has a relatively recent history despite the fact that corporations have existed and been subject to legal regulation for three centuries. The modern flourishing of corporate law scholarship has been matched by some broadening of the field of study to embrace insolvency, corporate finance, corporate governance and regulation of the financial markets. At the same time the intersection between other branches of law such as, for example, labour, contract, criminal law, competition, and intellectual property law and the introduction of new inter-disciplinary methodologies affords new possibilities for studying the corporation. This series seeks to foster intellectually diverse approaches to thinking about the law and its role, scope and effectiveness in the context of corporate activity. In so doing the series aims to publish works of high intellectual content and theoretical rigour.

Titles in this series

Working Within Two Kinds of Capitalism: Corporate Governance and Employee Stakeholding: US and EC Perspectives
Irene Lynch Fannon

Contracting with Companies
Andrew Griffiths

The Jurisprudence of the Takeover Panel
Tunde Ogowewo

The Law and Economics of Takeovers: An Acquirer's Perspective
Athanasios Kouloridas

The Foundations and Anatomy of Shareholder Activism
Iris H-Y Chiu

Corporate Governance in the Shadow of the State
Marc T Moore

Reconceptualising Corporate Compliance
Anna Donovan

Corporate Opportunities

A Law and Economics Analysis

Marco Claudio Corradi

•HART•

OXFORD • LONDON • NEW YORK • NEW DELHI • SYDNEY

HART PUBLISHING
Bloomsbury Publishing Plc
Kemp House, Chawley Park, Cumnor Hill, Oxford, OX2 9PH, UK
1385 Broadway, New York, NY 10018, USA
29 Earlsfort Terrace, Dublin 2, Ireland

HART PUBLISHING, the Hart/Stag logo, BLOOMSBURY and the Diana logo are trademarks of Bloomsbury Publishing Plc

First published in Great Britain 2021

A catalogue record for this book is available from the British Library.

Library of Congress Cataloging-in-Publication data

Names: Corradi, Marco, 1977- author.

Title: Corporate opportunities : a law and economics analysis / Marco Claudio Corradi.

Description: Oxford ; New York : Hart, 2021. | Series: Contemporary studies in corporate law | Based on author's thesis (doctoral – University of Oxford, 2016) issued under title: A law and economics analysis of corporate opportunities doctrines from a comparative perspective. | Includes bibliographical references and index.

Identifiers: LCCN 2021023998 (print) | LCCN 2021023999 (ebook) | ISBN 9781509917457 (hardback) | ISBN 9781509953226 (paperback) | ISBN 9781509917464 (pdf) | ISBN 9781509917471 (Epub)

Subjects: LCSH: Corporation law—Economic aspects.

Classification: LCC K1315 . C679 2021 (print) | LCC K1315 (ebook) | DDC 346/.066—dc23

LC record available at https://lccn.loc.gov/2021023998

LC ebook record available at https://lccn.loc.gov/2021023999

ISBN: HB: 978-1-50991-745-7
ePDF: 978-1-50991-746-4
ePub: 978-1-50991-747-1

Typeset by Compuscript Ltd, Shannon

To all the unsung heroes and heroines

Preface

THE TITLE OF this book refers to 'corporate opportunities' instead of the more traditional 'corporate opportunity doctrines'. Such semantic choice reflects an intent to refrain from providing a systematic account of corporate opportunity doctrines: this would be an extremely challenging task. Even in the Anglo-American legal systems, where such doctrines have existed for a long time, the content of these doctrines is still elusive and the ramifications of the rules rather tangled. But despite the many open questions on how to interpret corporate opportunity rules, their relevance for the development of the corporation since its early stages is undoubtable.

The traditional economic reading of corporate opportunity doctrines has ascribed them to the area of economic agency theory and has stressed their function to contain agency costs. Such a view may have been satisfying in a pre-high-tech world, which relied on relatively slow-paced innovation models, more substantially based on internalisation of R&D, as compared to the present one. Regardless of the former models' capability to reflect the innovation dynamics, research has found that innovation in high-tech districts relies upon a continuous recombination of knowledge building blocks, also achieved through an open system, based on contracting for innovation.

Corporate founders – often employed as corporate directors – are the very incarnation of such building blocks of knowledge. Corporate opportunity rules, while limiting more or less stringently founders' intra-corporate mobility, definitely affect the innovation process. As a matter of fact, the role of directors' mobility in facilitating knowledge spillovers has also been a well-documented phenomenon in non-high-tech industrial districts, such as in Italy and Spain. Accordingly, chapter one shows that the early absence of corporate opportunity rules in such industrial environments may have facilitated intra-corporate directors' mobility thus promoting spillovers. But, as shown in chapter two, the costs related to dynamic innovation are intertwined with other costs, such as those emerging from the traditional economic agency theory, also complemented by Goshen and Squire's recent principals' cost theory, together with 'traditional' hold-up costs.

Given that a rigid *ex ante* allocation of the entitlement to exploit business opportunities may represent a cost for society in the case of positive transaction costs, chapters three and four attempt to show the relationships between business opportunities allocation, corporate opportunity remedies and efficient bargaining. But nowadays the real arena where corporate opportunity doctrines are challenging economic efficiency is the one of innovative start-ups and venture capital, to which chapters five and six are dedicated, following a two-hats approach. Chapter seven is a policy conclusion to the economic analysis carried out in the previous chapters. Again, rather than being a rigorous analysis of the existing laws of corporate opportunities, chapter seven follows the comparative and functional approach already employed in the previous chapters. It aims to identify common patterns in corporate opportunity rules and potential legal and/or contractual solutions for moving the development of such rules forward, either by way of court innovation or private ordering.

As this book is mostly dedicated to the interaction between corporate opportunity rules and a rather complex set of costs, including those deriving from dynamic inefficiencies, I have limited my enquiry to misappropriations by corporate directors. The application of corporate opportunity rules to shareholders is of great interest in the context of groups of companies and is an underdeveloped topic in law and finance literature. I hope to be able to tackle this challenging problem in a future research.

Acknowledgements

THIS BOOK IS the fruit of one of the main research projects in my academic life. I met innumerable people while I was wandering through research institutions collecting comparative material, and it would be hard to include all those I am indebted to in this short acknowledgement. Firstly, I am filled with gratitude to the University of Oxford as a whole – and especially the Law Faculty – for the amazing opportunity I was offered to develop my MJur, MPhil and DPhil theses. Part of the content of this book is taken from or has been inspired by that research. Among the professorial staff, I am particularly thankful to Paul L Davies for his patience, for his dedication in introducing me to UK law and for his liberality in offering me many valuable suggestions; and to John Armour – in both his role of MJur supervisor and his role of DPhil examiner – for the quality of his comments, for his encouragement and for his generous engagement with all his students. Geneviève Helleringer discussed with me multiple times the directive lines of this research, provided me with priceless suggestions and greatly encouraged me to complete this book. She has also been of great help in retrieving bibliographical material. Birke Häcker constantly supported my research while I was visiting the Institute of European and Comparative Law. Luca Enriques meticulously corrected and commented on my article, published in the *Journal of Corporate Law Studies*, which forms the basis of chapter three of this book, and has been constantly available to answer all my queries. My MPhil and DPhil examiners – Christopher Hare, David Kershaw and Jennifer Payne – provided me with many noteworthy comments and much useful feedback. Wolf-Georg Ringe offered me valuable research and bibliographical suggestions, acting well beyond the scope of his role as MJur tutor. Dan Awrey provided me with very insightful comments on one of the chapters of my DPhil thesis. Julian Nowag discussed with me issues relating to competition policies and has provided me with several bibliographical suggestions. Ariel Ezrachi warmly encouraged me to write a monograph: a short meeting with him was crucial in building up my motivation and determination to start this undertaking. St Catherine's College and Jesus College kindly hosted me during the long time I spent at Oxford, and I cannot even imagine attempting to compile a list of all the wonderful staff members and amazing people I met there, for whose companionship I am very grateful. Last but not least, the Bodleian Law Library played a crucial role in helping me to retrieve the research material for this book, and I would like to thank their dedicated and wholehearted service; in particular, Margaret Watson has been a constant point of reference for all my queries, and Ronald Richenburg greatly helped my understanding of the functioning of the US legal citation system.

During my visits to non-UK research institutions, many professors generously helped me to retrieve research material and/or understand their legal systems. In particular, I would like to thank: Katharina Pistor, Zohar Goshen, Jeffrey Gordon and Charles Sabel at Columbia Law School; Martin Gelter, Barry Hawk and Richard Squire at Fordham Law School; Candido Paz-Ares, Isabel Saez, Jesus Alfaro and Antonio Perdices at Universidad Autonoma de Madrid; François-Xavier Lucas at Centre Affaire Sorbonne, Paris I; Klaus Hopt, Patrick Leyens and Rehinard Zimmermann at the Max Planck Institute for Comparative and International Private Law; Gerhard Dannemann and Christiane Eisenberg at Humboldt University; Emmanuel Slautsky, Arnaud Nuyts and Alain-Charles Van Gysel at UBL; and Pierre-Henri Conac and Isabelle Corbisier at the University of Luxembourg.

I am also grateful to all the participants of the seminars and conferences at which I presented parts of this work. In particular, Virgina Harper Ho sent me several insightful written notes on one of my papers.

I had the honour to receive very insightful research suggestions on the British and Italian industrial environments, from Derek Morris and Romano Prodi respectively.

I also discussed parts of my project with Colin Mayer, Marco Becht, Edward Rock, Lorenzo Stanghellini, Jim Pressley, Ben Wolff, Byrial Bjørst, Suren Gomtsian, Cédric Argenton, Mauro Zamboni, Tiziana Sardiello, Panagiotis Delimatsis, Hugues Bouthinon-Dumas, Kristin van Zwieten, Bert Willelms, Jens Prufer, Michel Baroni, Jose-Miguel Gaspar, Alexandra Andhov, Adam Green, Peter Freeman, Francesco Vella, Giuliana Scognamiglio, Marco Saverio Spolidoro, Marco Lamandini, Renzo Costi, José Miguel Mendoza, Cyril Lin, Per Samuelsson, Michael Bogdan, Markus Kotzur, William Lazonick, Arad Reisberg, Dominik Wanner, Thomas Cheng, Thomas Papadopoulos, Uriel Procaccia, John Lowry, Justine Pila and Timo Minssen. I am very grateful to all of them. James Goudkamp, Jessica Östberg, Charles Graves, Keith Arundale, Michael Graff, Marco Palmieri, Alessandro Pomelli, Beatrice Colette, Henrik Gildehaus provided me with invaluable bibliographical material. My dear friend Marco Sgalaberni has been instrumental in providing me with reality checks – both at the time when I worked for his start-up and later when I went back to academia.

I developed chapters two and four on the basis of the tuition I received during the first year of my PhD in law and economics at the University of Siena, and my gratitude for that tuition goes to all the professorial staff involved.

I am also highly indebted to the Ragnar Söderbergs Stiftelse, not only for providing me with very generous funding while I was carrying out research in Sweden, but also for the extremely warm, truly caring and approachable attitude of the staff and of the Söderberg Styrelse, with their big 'research family'. I am also extremely grateful to my parents, Bruna and Corrado, for constantly and generously supporting me during the long period when I had no research funding.

I started this work in Sweden, but it was severely delayed, chiefly because of the onset of a sudden and life-threatening health condition. I am incredibly thankful that I survived the experience, and my infinite and wholehearted gratitude goes to the amazing staff of the Akutmottagning of the Malmö University Hospital. I will never forget their professionality, warmth and kindness, nor how they helped me to recover my strength over the following year. Last but not least, I would like to thank ESSEC Business School Paris and Singapore, its staff and its students. This work would have never been completed so smoothly without the welcoming, cooperative and transparent working environment they all have created.

A special thanks goes to the wonderful Hart Publishing editorial team: Christopher Bruner and Marc Moore provided me with extremely insightful comments on three different versions of my research project; and Roberta Bassi and Rosemarie Mearns supported me wholeheartedly and unconditionally throughout the hurdles of my recovery, constantly encouraging me to finalise the manuscript.

Walter Kluwer and Taylor and Francis have kindly authorised me to reuse parts of two articles of mine on corporate opportunities, respectively published in the *European Business Law Journal* (2016) and in the *Journal of Corporate Law Studies* (2018). All errors are my own.

Marco Corradi
10 April 2021

Table of Contents

1

Corporate Opportunity Legal Paradigms and Industrial Development: From Localised Business to Trade and Financial Globalisation

I. INTRODUCTION

CORPORATE OPPORTUNITY RULES prevent directors (and in certain jurisdictions, controlling shareholders and senior executives too) from appropriating business opportunities that are deemed to belong to the corporation. Before the 1970s, corporate opportunity rules were peculiar to common law jurisdictions.[1] They were introduced in Germany at the end of the 1970s,[2] but it was only around the year 2000 that they became part of many other continental European legal systems, including France,[3] Italy[4]

[1] Seminal cases are for the US *Lagarde v Anniston Lime & Stone Co*, 126 Ala 496, 28 So 199 (1900); *Guth v Loft Inc*, 5 A 2d 503 (Del Ch 1939). For the UK, see *Regal (Hastings) v Gulliver* [1942] UKHL 1; *Boardman v Phipps* [1966] UKHL 2. For Canada, see *Canadian Aero Services Ltd v O'Malley* (1973) 40 DLR (3d) 371. For later developments outside the UK, see, in Australia, *Paul A Davies (Aust) Pty Limited v Davies* [1983] 1 NSWLR 440; in New Zealand, *Pacifica Shipping Co Ltd v Anderson* (1985) 2 NZCLC 99.

[2] BGH WM 1977, 361. The German debate on corporate opportunities rules had already started in the 1950s with E-J Mestmäcker, *Verwaltung, Konzerngewalt und Recht der Aktionare* (Müller, 1958) 166ff.

[3] Cass com 18 December 2012, *Revue des Sociétés* 2013, 262. Note that in France there is no allocation of business opportunities to the corporation. Nonetheless, courts punish with damages the lack of disclosure of corporate opportunities by directors to their corporation. For comments on the recent introduction of corporate opportunity doctrines in France, see M Gelter and G Helleringer, 'Opportunity Makes the Thief. Corporate Opportunities vs Private Profits in Comparative Perspective (US, UK, Germany and France)' (2018) 15 *Berkley Business Law Journal* 134.

[4] Italian Civil Code, Art 2391, para 5, introduced in 2003. For comments, see for instance F Barachini 'L'Appropriazione delle Corporate Opportunities' in P Abbadessa and G Portale (eds), *Il Nuovo Diritto delle Società, Liber amicorum Gian Franco Campobasso* (UTET, 2006) 654; M Corradi, 'Le Opportunità di Affari all'Ultimo Comma dell'Art. 2391 cc: Profili Interpretativi tra "Società" ed "Impresa"' [2011] *Giurisprudenza Commerciale* 597. In continental Europe, an exception to the delay in the adoption of a corporate opportunity doctrine is represented by the Netherlands, where a corporate opportunity doctrine has been progressively created at least since the 1980s. See A Verdam, 'Corporate Opportunities: The Appropriation by Company Officers

and Spain.[5] By contrast, in some very economically advanced European countries, such as Sweden, the introduction of corporate opportunity rules has been suggested by academics with no effect on law-making.[6]

The widespread introduction of corporate opportunity rules in continental Europe has created debate about their legal interpretation.[7] By contrast, research on their economic function is surprisingly sparse in Europe.[8] Continental European case law on corporate opportunities is not particularly copious either.[9] This contrasts with the fact that overseas corporate opportunity doctrines are well developed in theory and in practice. In the United States of America (US), there is a significant debate on the economic role of such rules for business activity[10] and on their importance for the venture capital (VC) industry.[11] Nowadays, technological innovation has increased the availability of business information, which multiplies the probability of new takings of corporate opportunities. Technological innovation itself is also an increasing source of myriad business opportunities.[12] Given the steadily more globalised and cross-border dimension of business and of innovation, more than ever a comparative analysis of corporate opportunity rules and of their economic function can offer interesting insights on the relationships between corporate law and economic growth.

of Business Opportunities Belonging to the Company' (1998) 45 *Netherlands International Law Review* 233, 240ff.

[5] Spanish *Ley de Sociedades de Capital*, Art 228. A reform of that rule followed in 2015. See C Paz-Ares, 'Anatomía del Deber de Lealtad' (2015) 39 *Actualidad Jurídica Uría Menéndez* 43.

[6] J Östberg, *Styrelseledamöters Lojalitetsplikt – Särskilt om Förbudet att Utnyttja Affärsmöjligheter* (Jure AB, 2016) 329–431.

[7] nn 3–6.

[8] A couple of attempts to fuel the debate on the economic function of such rules can be found in M Corradi, 'Securing Corporate Opportunities in Europe – Comparative Notes on Monetary Remedies and on their Potential Evolution', (2018) 18 *Journal of Corporate Law Studies* 439; M Corradi 'Corporate Opportunities' Tested in the Light of the Theory of the Firm – a European (and US) Comparative Perspective' (2016) 27 *European Business Law Review* 755.

[9] See for instance in France, Cass com 18 December 2012, [2013] *Revue des Sociétés* 262. In Germany, BGH WM 1977, 361; BGH WM 1983; 140 BGH NJW 1986; 140 BGH WM 1989, 1335. In Spain, Audiencia Provincial de Madrid (Sección 28a) Sentencia num 104/2013 of 8 April AC\2013\1431; Audiencia Provincial de Barcelona (Sección 15a) Sentencia num 10/2009 of 13 January AC\2009\1601; Audiencia Provincial de Álava (Sección 1a) Sentencia num 225/2009 of 27 May AC\2009\1580. Of these cases, only one reached the Supreme Court: see Tribunal Supremo (Sala de lo Civil, Sección 1a) Sentencia num 502/2012 of 3 September RJ\2012\9007.

[10] M Whincop, 'Painting the Corporate Cathedral: The Protection of Entitlements in Corporate Law' (1999) 19 *Oxford Journal of Legal Studies* 19; E Talley, 'Turning Servile Opportunities into Gold: A Strategic Analysis of the Corporate Opportunities Doctrine' (1998–99) 108 *Yale Law Journal* 277.

[11] See T Woolf, 'The Venture Capitalist's Corporate Opportunity Problem' (2001) *Columbia Business Law Review* 473.

[12] Note that the development of the 'Internet of Things' has entailed not only an increase of the business opportunities within the high-tech markets, but also a disruption of the business models within the low-tech markets and therefore a wealth of new business opportunities across most of the industries. See V Krotov, 'The Internet of Things and New Business Opportunities (2017) 60 *Business Horizons* 831, 832.

New corporate opportunity rules appeared in Europe within the historical context of a significant number of reforms to EU Member States' corporate laws,[13] some of which were under the aegis of the European Community and later the European Union.[14] The debate about 'convergence versus divergence',[15] 'form and function',[16] institutional and political complementarities[17] and varieties of capitalism (VOC)[18] has become more and more

[13] See for instance, in Italy, Decreto Legislativo 6/2003; in Spain, the Real Decreto Legislativo 1/2010.

[14] Most of EU company law is now systematised in the Directive (EU) 2017/1132 of the European Parliament and of the Council of 14 June 2017 relating to certain aspects of company law. For directors' conflict of interest, the last important EU reforms are in the Directive (EU) 2017/828 of the European Parliament and of the Council of 17 May 2017 amending Directive 2007/36/EC as regards the encouragement of long-term shareholder engagement, [2017] OJ L 132/1. Art 9(c) of the directive introduces new rules on related party transactions, a field which is strictly related to corporate opportunity doctrines from a functional perspective. In general, it is highly debatable whether such a dense proliferation of European rules has had any substantial effect on Member States' company laws. See for instance L Enriques, 'EC Company Law Directives and Regulations: How Trivial Are They?' (2006) 27 *University of Pennsylvania Journal of International Economic Law* 1. For a critical approach, see J Armour, 'Who Should Make Corporate Law? EC Legislation versus Regulatory Competition' (2005) 58 *Current Legal Problems* 369, developing the view that corporate law should be legislated at EU level only in the unlikely (according to Armour) event that regulatory competition developed pathologically.

[15] See J Coffee Jr, 'The Future as History: The Prospects for Global Convergence in Corporate Governance and its Implications' (1999) 93 *Northwestern University Law Review* 641; R Gilson, 'Globalizing Corporate Governance: Convergence of Form or Function' (2001) 49 *American Journal of Comparative Law* 329; D Branson, 'The Very Uncertain Prospect of "Global" Convergence in Corporate Governance' (2001) 34 *Cornell International Law Journal* 321; M Siems, 'Convergence in Corporate Governance: A Leximetric Approach' (2009) 35 *Journal of Corporation Law* 729.

[16] See Gilson, 'Globalizing Corporate Governance' (2001).

[17] Note that the concept of institutional complementarity is polysemic and it does not necessarily refer to binary variables. See C Crouch et al, 'Dialogue on 'Institutional Complementarity and Political Economy' (2005) 3 *Socio-Economic Review* 359, 359–60; and at 378 for the complementarity between corporate governance and industrial relations. The literature on institutional and political complementarities has been developed with a higher degree of technicality by Anglo-American corporate lawyers, for instance A Shleifer and R Vishny, 'A Survey of Corporate Governance' (1997) 52 *Journal of Finance* 737; R Schmidt and G Spindler, 'Path Dependence and Complementarity in Corporate Governance' in J Gordon and M Roe (eds), *Convergence and Persistence in Corporate Governance* (Cambridge University Press, 2004) 114; M Gelter, 'Taming or Protecting the Modern Corporation? Shareholder–Stakeholder Debates in a Comparative Light' (2011) 7 *New York University Journal of Law and Business* 641. Because of obvious cultural differences, the debate is particularly strong in relation to employees. See for instance W Carlin and C Mayer, 'How Do Financial Systems Affect Economic Performance?' in J McCahery et al (eds), *Corporate Governance Regimes: Convergence and Diversity* (Oxford University Press, 2002) 325; M Roe, *Political Determinants of Corporate Governance* (Oxford University Press, 2003) 27–61, 71–82, 98–105, 125–49; P Gourevitch and J Shinn, *Political Power and Corporate Control* (Princeton University Press, 2005) 132; M Gelter, 'The Dark Side of Shareholder Influence: Toward a Holdup Theory of Stakeholders in Comparative Corporate Governance' (2009) 50 *Harvard International Law Journal* 129. On political theories see M Roe, *Strong Managers, Weak Owners* (Princeton University Press, 1994).

[18] The literature on VOC is extremely wide and it also encompasses areas that are not directly related to corporate governance. See for instance B Hancké, M Rhodes and M Thatcher (eds), *Beyond Varieties of Capitalism: Conflict, Contradictions and Complementarities in the European Economy* (Oxford University Press, 2007); B Hancké (ed), *Debating Varieties of Capitalism* (Oxford University Press, 2009); W Friedman and G Jones, *Business History and Varieties of Capitalism* (Cambridge University Press, 2010).

intense – and has also been enriched by substantial development of empirical research.[19]

Corporate opportunity rules should try to contain agency costs,[20] transaction costs and hold-up costs, thus promoting productive and dynamic efficiency.[21] In other words, measures directed to protect financial investors, as well as rules for the defence of specific investments and of industrial complementarities, all appear to coexist within the scope of corporate opportunity doctrines.[22] Also, the promotion of technological innovation can be a core objective pursued by corporate opportunity rules, especially when such innovation is produced by corporate founders who sit on the board of directors.[23] The overall set of economic incentives surrounding corporate opportunity rules is extremely complex in theory. Such complexity is enriched by further variables if we consider the diversity of the industrial, political and social contexts to which it is applied. Only by keeping in mind such complexity can the debate about corporate convergence and divergence be fully understood.

II. A CONCISE OVERVIEW OF THE DEBATE ON CORPORATE LAW CONVERGENCE AND DIVERGENCE

Since the beginning of the twenty-first century, the debate on corporate law convergence has been particularly lively. A provocative article by Hansmann and Kraakman solemnly announced the 'end of the history of corporate law'.[24] According to its authors, the process of convergence of different national corporate laws was already remarkably advanced by the end of the twentieth century.[25] Despite a general convergence in relation to some core corporate law functions, the extreme diversification of corporate legal rules was a reality

[19] See J Armour et al, 'How Do Legal Rules Evolve? A Cross-Country Comparison of Shareholder, Creditor and Worker Protection' (2009) 57 *American Journal of Comparative Law* 579; J Armour et al, 'Law and Financial Development: What We are Learning from Time Series Evidence' (2010) *Brigham Young University Law Review* 1435; J Armour et al, 'Private Enforcement of Corporate Law: An Empirical Comparison of the UK and US' (2009) 6 *Journal of Empirical Legal Studies* 701; J Armour et al, 'Shareholder Protection and Stock Market Development: An Empirical Test of the Legal Origins Hypothesis' (2009) 6 *Journal of Empirical Legal Studies* 343.

[20] See text at ch 2.III and accompanying notes.

[21] See text at ch 2.IV–V and accompanying notes.

[22] See text at ch 2.VII and accompanying notes.

[23] See text at ch 5.I and accompanying notes.

[24] H Hansmann and R Kraakman, 'The End of the History of Corporate Law' (2000–01) 89 *Georgetown Law Journal* 439. This title interestingly echoes the political essay by F Fukuyama, *The End of History and the Last Man* (Penguin, 1992).

[25] Hansmann and Kraakman, 'The End' (2000–01) 439. In fact, according to the authors, at that time all the corporate laws of economically developed countries already reflected businesses structured in the form of corporations, and sharing the following common features: '(1) full legal personality …; (2) limited liability for owners and managers; (3) shared ownership by investors of capital; (4) delegated management under a board structure; and (5) transferable shares'.

throughout different jurisdictions up until the past decade. Diversification has manifested itself in several ways, among which is the different weight granted to various stakeholders' interests.[26] Nonetheless, faced with the asserted failure of most of the stakeholder-oriented models, competitive pressure towards a long-term shareholder-oriented model would be inevitable.[27] According to the authors, such pressure would stem from scholars' persuasive arguments ('force of logic'),[28] from the allegedly superior results achieved by the US economy ('force of example')[29] and, finally, from the asserted competitive advantages in terms of access to capital and industrial organisation displayed by the US model ('force of competition').[30] Hansmann and Kraakman also acknowledge the presence of potential obstacles to such convergence, especially within those jurisdictions that adopt a model that is radically different from the Anglo-American one. Those obstacles would basically be the extraction of private benefits of control by controlling shareholders[31] and empire-building by families and other block-holders. In fact, block-holders are viewed as maintaining quasi-feudal relationships with their local communities.[32] Despite the presence of such obstacles, the authors strongly believe that the low profitability of the non-shareholder models and changes in social values (ie the decline of a quasi-feudal mentality) will bring about the erosion of old models and the triumph of the shareholder-oriented model.[33]

Despite the plausibility of some of the arguments advanced by Hansmann and Kraakman, the phenomenon that they predicted has not yet taken place. Maybe, as the reality is more complex than previously thought, additional or different variables will emerge than those suggested by the authors. Without any doubt, the global challenges that we are now facing, such as that of sustainability, have contributed to shifting the focus of the corporate debate towards stakeholder-oriented theories.[34] Therefore, the convergence of corporate laws towards the model depicted by Hansmann and Kraakman appears to be at least questionable.

Regardless of the accuracy of their predictions, Hansmann and Kraakman's article has enriched and stimulated a debate that already existed in relation to these topics. As already noted, their thesis is largely based upon the idea that the transition of all the corporate law models of developed countries towards the shareholder-oriented model is driven by at least two forces: first, changes in social values; and second, market mechanisms. Market mechanisms would be

[26] ibid 440.
[27] ibid 449.
[28] ibid.
[29] ibid 450.
[30] ibid 450.
[31] ibid 460.
[32] ibid 461.
[33] ibid 468.
[34] C Mayer, *Prosperity: Better Business Makes the Greater Good* (Oxford University Press, 2018).

the primary and prevalent propulsive force and would be triggered by the low profitability of non-Anglo-American models of corporate law (hence this theory can be defined as 'market-based').

Corporate lawyers and economists have provided analyses of the present divergence of corporate laws that offer alternatives to the market-based theory. Not all are founded on such an optimistic view of the efficiency of a single corporate law system (ie the Anglo-American one) as that of Hansmann and Kraakman. Although several nuances are likely to be noticed within each single doctrinal contribution, one may distinguish at least two main streams of alternative theories: one based on a legal origins argument and the other mostly relying on explanations based on political determinants. These theories, especially the latter, are connected to the cited area of institutional economics literature known as varieties of capitalism (VOC) theory.[35]

As will be seen, it might be difficult to understand the situation existing before the recent evolution of corporate opportunity rules without reverting to the variables highlighted by VOC theory. In fact, the theory is based upon the idea of 'institutional complementarity'; that is, on the idea that legal rules complement extra-legal variables found in the same economic system. In turn, the idea of institutional complementarity is extremely complex and often difficult to manage from a theoretical perspective. One might say that the concept of institutional complementarity has been introduced to explain the results of the social and political embeddedness that exists within each economic system and which creates path dependencies in its evolution. Social and political embeddedness also explains the large variety of solutions that may be adopted when facing the same economic problem.[36] In fact, each different solution would correspond to a different complex set of social, political and economic equilibria that become deeply intertwined throughout time.[37]

The concept of institutional complementarity may encompass a diversified set of explanations. First, literature has identified different kinds of institutional complementarities: natural complementarity (ie deriving from scientific laws of nature and at times observable in industry); technical complementarity and complementarity by design (ie when the source of efficiency is produced by a man-made conjunction of two inputs); ex post discovered complementarity (ie understood through a process of trial and error); and functional complementarity (ie the relationship between duties and rights of individuals).[38]

[35] See n 18.

[36] The beneficial side of such an embeddedness have been conceptualised as 'increasing returns' or 'system scale economies.' See J Beyer, 'The Same or not the Same-on the Variety of Mechanisms of Path Dependence' (2010) 5 *International Journal of Social Sciences* 1, 2.

[37] For a detailed description of the theories that employ the concept of institutional complementarity see the highly theoretical study by R Boyer, 'Coherence, Diversity, and the Evolution of Capitalisms – The Institutional Complementarity Hypothesis' (2005) 2 *Evolutionary & Institutional Economic Review* 43, 44ff.

[38] ibid 53.

When analysing corporate law as applied to different social, industrial and economic realities, several institutional complementarities occur.

Second, the causality link between the sets of variables highlighted by the concept of complementarity looks particularly important. There might be attempts to provide a clear law of causation when a given variable (social, economic, political) has influenced another. However, it is sometimes necessary to refer to the concept of co-evolution: 'the joint occurrence of two institutions or organizations might be the unintended outcome of a selection process mechanism, operating via the succession of stochastic shocks and possibly major events such as crises'.[39] From a practical perspective, this also means that it is extremely difficult to introduce successfully a given complementarity into an existing system. This depends on the difficulties inherent in calculating the impact of an innovation and the trajectory that such an innovation will follow within that economic system, given that every economic system is characterised by an extremely complex set of variables. This is why institutional complementarities are usually found ex post instead of being introduced *ex ante*.[40] The idea of institutional complementarity is probably a better tool for carrying out positive analysis.[41] Corporate lawyers have chosen to employ this concept from a positive perspective. This is clear in both the legal origins theory and the political theory.

According to the legal origins theory, the divergences observed nowadays within national corporate laws are because of cultural differences determined by various historical events in different areas of the world. The correlation is between history, the development of institutions and the law, and economic growth.[42] The extremely rich and sophisticated set of arguments found at the heart of the legal origins theory has been rationalised in a very popular article by La Porta, Lopez-de-Silanes and Shleifer.[43] The authors do not point to the superiority of common law over civil law or vice versa; they simply try to highlight some relevant differences. They depict common law as promoting market mechanisms and civil law as mostly based on centralised and policy-oriented

[39] ibid 52.

[40] ibid 60.

[41] For the distinction between normative and positive analysis see for instance F Parisi, 'Positive, Normative and Functional Schools in Law and Economics' (2004) 18 *European Journal of Law and Economics* 259.

[42] R La Porta, F Lopez-de-Silanes and A Shleifer, 'Corporate Ownership around the World' (1999) 54 *Journal of Finance* 471; 'Government Ownership of Banks' (2002) 57 *Journal of Finance* 265; 'What Works in Securities Laws?' (2006) 61 *Journal of Finance* 1; R La Porta et al, 'Legal Determinants of External Finance' (1997) 52 *Journal of Finance* 1131; R La Porta et al, 'Law and Finance' (1998) 106 *Journal of Political Economy* 1113; R La Porta et al, 'The Quality of Government' (1999) 15 *Journal of Law Economics and Organization* 222; R La Porta et al, 'Agency Problems and Dividend Policies around the World' (2000) 55 *Journal of Finance* 1; S Claessens and L Laeven, 'Financial Development, Property Rights, and Growth' (2003) 58 *Journal of Finance* 2401.

[43] R La Porta, F Lopez de Silanes and A Shleifer, 'The Economic Consequences of Legal Origins' (2008) 46 *Journal of Economic Literature* 285.

interventions (therefore at times risking restraining market activity). This article provides no prognosis as to whether the civil law or the common law model will prevail. Nonetheless, it stresses the presence of cross-contamination and the capacity of legal systems to adopt 'foreign' solutions when to do so would be efficient (eg, the increasingly frequent use of statutory law within common law systems).

According to the political theory, the main determinants that shape corporate governance are political in nature. Mark Roe identifies several connections between political variables, ownership structure and corporate governance. According to him, ownership concentration in continental Europe would have been useful to create a counterbalance to the industrial strength and political power enjoyed by trade unions.[44]

All these contributions express different points of view about the evolution of corporate law. Some postulate the superiority of a given model.[45] Others have a more inclusive attitude towards different cultural experiences. In that sense, they neither predict nor predicate the necessity to identify a winner in the interplay of constantly evolving corporate laws.[46] Within this second set of theories, the central concept is the one of institutional complementarities. Roe's ideas are clearly in line with this. The set of variables highlighted in these theories is so complex that different legislative outcomes can be found in jurisdictions that have followed completely different historical and cultural paths – namely the UK and Italy.[47] In fact, this divergence in legislation is also present between Italy and Spain, which have some similarities in terms of business culture and recent history.[48] In turn, recent Spanish law reforms seem to echo rather closely UK law, despite their cultural and historical divergences.[49] Such complexity should always be considered when trying to design corporate opportunity rules on the basis of a limited series of economic variables.

III. THE EVOLUTION OF CORPORATE OPPORTUNITY RULES IN LIGHT OF THE VARIETIES OF CAPITALISM THEORY – A COMPARISON BETWEEN BRITISH AND ITALIAN LAW

Of the many components of a social and economic system, the legal system is perhaps the most visible and apparently ordered one.[50] Therefore, legal variables

[44] M Roe, *Political Determinants* (2003).
[45] See for instance the cited article by Hansmann and Kraakman (n 24).
[46] See for instance Gilson (n 15).
[47] See text at section VI and accompanying notes.
[48] See text at section VII and accompanying notes.
[49] ibid.
[50] See for instance T Parsons, *Social System* (Routledge, 2005) 15ff; and see also T Parsons, 'An Outline of the Social System' in C Calhoun (ed), *Classical Sociological Theory* (Blackwell, 2007) 435: 'Because of the problems involved in the use and control of force, the political organization

influence and are influenced by a potentially infinite series of factors that are usually the subjects of different human sciences, such as economics, sociology and political science in general.[51] Those variables may be employed to trace the reasons for different normative paths across different legal systems. They may also be essential for understanding the chances of success of a transplant of 'foreign' normative elements into a given legal system.[52]

In this section, I show that, from a historical perspective, different corporate opportunity rules might have displayed similar efficiencies, reached through different complex points of equilibrium. Moreover, some models were more adaptable to changes in the world economy, while others needed substantial reforms and are still struggling to find the best way to keep pace with globalisation.[53] Nowadays, we are going through a historical period in which also some (relative) deglobalisation tendencies exist on the global scene[54] and these seem to be reinforced by the Covid-19 emergency, at least in certain areas of the globe.[55] Therefore, it is extremely difficult to calculate an exact balance of costs and gains deriving from reforms. The comparative case study that I propose, involving the UK and Italy, shows the complexity of the embeddedness of corporate opportunity rules in non-legal variables.

A. Historical Notes on the Evolution of the Corporate Opportunity Legal Paradigm

It has to be acknowledged that the origins of both the UK and the Italian corporate opportunity paradigm can be traced back at least to Roman times. An interesting fragment of the Roman imperial age deals with the following legal

must always be integrated with the legal system, which is concerned with administering the highest order of norms regulating the behavior of units within the society'.

[51] For economic analysis of the law, see R Cooter and T Ulen, *Law and Economics* (Harper Collins, 1988); T Miceli, *Economics of the Law* (Oxford University Press, 1997). See also N Mercuro and S Medema, *Economics and the Law* (Princeton University Press, 1997). For recent developments, see R Cooter and F Parisi (eds), *Recent Developments in Law and Economics* (Edward Elgar, 2009). Recent approaches to sociology of the law tend to focus on social forms, structures and processes, unlike the classical 1960s American school that is mostly based on the study of inequality. From that perspective this new approach is particularly versatile and also applicable to phenomena that are not characterised by conflict. For a description of the emerging approach, see S Liu, 'Law's Social Forms: A Powerless Approach to the Sociology of Law' (2015) 40 *Law and Social Inquiry* 1.

[52] See O Kahn-Freund, 'On Uses and Misuses of Comparative Law' (1974) 37 *Modern Law Review* 1.

[53] See text at sections VI–VII and accompanying notes.

[54] Such tendencies seem to be strongly related to a re-emergence of populism in politics. See H James, 'Deglobalization: The Rise of Disembedded Unilateralism (2018) 10 *Annual Review of Financial Economics* 219. Nonetheless, it has also been claimed that the populist vote is actually part of the globalisation trend. See M Martin, 'Keeping it Real: Debunking the Deglobalization Myth, Brexit and Trump: "Lessons" on Integration' (2018) 17 *Journal of International Trade Law and Policy* 62.

[55] H Lee and D Park, '*Post-Covid Asia: Deglobalization, Fourth Industrial Revolution, and Sustainable Development* (World Scientific, 2020).

case: two money changers (*argentarii*) were conducting their business in partnership while one of them was also carrying out a separate activity. Emperor Severus was asked whether the gains from that separate activity were to be considered as belonging to the partnership. The emperor replied that, despite the existence of a partnership between the two *argentarii*, there was no reason why the profits from one of their separate activities had to be conveyed to the partnership.[56] Apparently, at that time the freedom of each of the partners prevailed over the legal partnership bond between them.

How this principle evolved over time is perhaps difficult to understand completely. Nevertheless, there is evidence in medieval sources of a legal principle diametrically opposed to the one stated by Emperor Severus. In fact, about 1,000 years after the time of Emperor Severus, when northern Italy was perhaps the most economically and financially advanced area in Europe,[57] the legal perception of the appropriation of business opportunities changed. When there was a bilateral partnership, the members in charge of its administration were strictly banned from exercising any economic activity (not only competing activities). The remedy for the breach of that strict ban was a disgorgement of all profits to the partnership.[58] Interestingly, both in Roman times and in the Italian medieval period, economic activities were exercised under the supervision of extremely powerful business associations.[59] That being so, one could hardly try to justify those normative differences as a consequence of the more or less cooperative environment to which the entrepreneurs belonged. What matters is that, from a theoretical perspective, the concept of a lenient or strict corporate opportunity paradigm is neither a creation of civil law nor of common law. Awareness of the previously mentioned normative options has existed since ancient times, when the distinction between different families of law was not all that clear and when the legal concept of 'corporate opportunity' had not yet been made explicit.

[56] Dig Pro socio, book 17, 2, fragment 52, 5 (Ulpianus) now in T Mommsen and P Kruger, *The Digest of Justininan*, vol II (University of Pennsylvania, 1985) 504: '*Cum duo erant argentarii socii, alter eorum aliquid separatim quaesireat, et lucri senserat, quaerebatur, an commune esse lucrum oportet; et Imperator Severus Flavio Felici in haec verba rescripsit: etiam si maxime argentariae societas inita est, quod quisque tamen socius non ex argenteria causa quaesiit, id ad communionem non pertinere, explorati iuris est.*'

[57] A Greif, 'The Study of Organizations and Evolving Organizational Forms Through History' in G Carroll and D Teece (eds), *Firms, Markets and Hierarchies* (Oxford University Press, 1999) 338 reports that just the assets of the Bardi firm were valued at about four and a half times the English King's net income a century later.

[58] Piacenza, Stat Merc (1321), 145; Firenze, Stat Calimala (1332) I 67, as reported in A Lattes, *Il Diritto Commerciale nella Legislazione Statutaria delle Città Italiane* (Hoepli, 1884) 160 and footnote 65. Similar provisions were introduced through contract until at least the fifteenth century. See Greif, 'The Study of Organizations' (1999) 355ff.

[59] For accounts of the Roman organisational system, see F Wallbank, 'Trade and Industry under the Later Roman Empire in the West' in C Postan, M Postan and E Miller (eds), *The Cambridge Economic History of Europe*, 2nd edn (Cambridge University Press, 1987) vol 2, 74. With reference to the medieval Italian system, see R Lopez, 'The Trade of Medieval Europe: The South' in Postan and Miller (eds) *The Cambridge* (in this footnote) 306.

Therefore, the reasons for the diverging paths that characterise our jurisdictions in more recent times cannot be justified on the basis of a lack of awareness or an absence of theoretical models.

B. The Evolution of the Corporate Opportunity Paradigm Explained through Economic Variables

The enquiry about further institutional variables, such as the economic one, seems particularly relevant when looking for more plausible explanations. The difference in the economic and industrial environments of the two countries thus appears a very interesting starting point for understanding the recent history of the development of corporate opportunity rules and of their functional equivalents.

It is worth remembering that the economies of both the UK and Italy are characterised by a high degree of diversification. This is particularly true for Italy, where several industrial models coexist within the same geographical area. The diversities, especially in the Italian economic and industrial environment, should make us aware of potential difficulties encountered when trying to analyse business organisational models (ie, corporations in this discussion) as applied to the Italian economic environment as a whole.

Italian firms that are organised as public companies, *società per azioni* (SpA), traditionally are of many different dimensional and industrial types.[60] That fragmentation on the side of potential users of the same company type could become relevant from a comparative perspective. In fact, it could potentially distort the assessment of the efficiency of the related company rules. However, such a problem did not seem to arise, at least until very recently, with reference to the UK/Italy comparison, given the traditional absence of corporate opportunity rules in Italy and, conversely, the presence of corporate opportunity rules in the UK both for limited companies and public limited companies (plc).[61]

[60] In fact, as we will see, it is not only listed companies that adopt this form; small or medium businesses in district environments may often become SpA. See further section V. For a historical perspective on the development of Italian industry, see N Crepax, *Storia dell'Industria Italiana* (Il Mulino, 2002).

[61] In this context, I am analysing firms belonging to different industrial contexts (industrial/finance) in both countries. In Italy, in both contexts there is widespread use of the SpA form, whereas in the UK, family-owned businesses are often run through private limited companies, while banking companies are often plcs. Nevertheless, such a divergence within the UK does not alter the analysis. In fact, the UK corporate opportunity doctrine originates mainly in relation to private limited companies or trusts and is extended to directors of plcs in general, both in view of the nature of their duties and in relation to the rules contained in the CA 2006. For the origins of UK corporate opportunity doctrine in the law of trust, see J Lowry and R Edmunds, 'The Corporate Opportunity Doctrine: The Shifting Boundaries of the Duty and its Remedies' (1998) 61 *Modern Law Review* 515, 517.

The UK and Italian economies have both been characterised not only by the existence of heavy industry, but also by the industrial districts phenomenon, although the development of such districts has been much more intensive in the Italian economic environment than in the UK. In the UK, industrial districts are mainly (although not only) those with the surviving activities of an ancient and distinguished productive tradition dating back to the first Industrial Revolution, when the Italian economy was mostly an agricultural one.[62] Clearly, both countries have a certain degree of banking activity, even though again the UK is nowadays a far larger banking centre than Italy (and conversely, the Italian banking sector was far more prominent in medieval and Renaissance times).[63]

Despite the presence of different kinds of activities within both countries, it is true that the two economies do not necessarily employ the same company model for companies carrying out the same kind of activity. Different situations must be distinguished. For instance, the public company or its Italian equivalent, the SpA, is the prevalent model adopted for banking activities in both countries. In contrast, the same does not occur in relation to those industrial activities carried out within industrial districts.

Let us consider a few examples; first, the North Staffordshire ceramic district. The most important and internationally renowned ceramic manufacturers of this district include Aynsley, Minton, Royal Doulton, Spode and Wedgwood. All these companies were pre-eminent in the history of British and international pottery. Nevertheless, it looks as though none of them were ever organised as a public company. In fact, most started as partnerships and then became limited companies (with the exception of Wedgwood, which was transformed into a public company in 1940).[64] This is probably because most of these manufacturing concerns were privately owned. The limited liability form – limited company (Ltd) – is the model usually employed for this kind of business in the UK. To this day, these ceramic manufacturers preserve that form, despite having been acquired mostly by Irish groups.

In contrast with firms operating in British industrial districts, firms active in Italian industrial districts are often organised in the form of SpA. For instance, in the renowned Italian ceramic district of Sassuolo, most of the leading firms – Sil, Sichenia, Marca Corona, Panaria and Gresmalt – are SpA.[65] Moreover, in

[62] D Sassoon, *Contemporary Italy: Politics, Economy and Society Since 1945* (Routledge, 2014).

[63] See for instance R de Roover, *The Rise and Decline of the Medici Bank* (Beard Books, 1999).

[64] For the history of most of these companies, one can refer to www.potteryhistories.com; more specifically, for Aynsley, see antique-marks.com/aynsley-china.html; for Minton, see Museum Victoria, 'Mintons, Potters & Tile Manufactures, Stoke-upon-Trent, England, 1790s–1960s', collections.museumvictoria.com.au/articles/2802; for Royal Doulton, see Pottery Histories, 'Royal Doulton', www.potteryhistories.com/doultonhistory.html; for Spode, see Famous Potters, 'The History of Spode', www.thepotteries.org/potters/spode.htm; for Wedgwood, see Pottery Histories, 'Wedgwood (Josiah Wedgwood & Sons Ltd)', www.potteryhistories.com/page99.html.

[65] The example proposed in this section is clearly based on industrial variables. In absolute terms, data may well change. See E Wymeersch, 'Comparative Studies of the Company Types in Selected EU States' (2009) 6 *European Company and Financial Law Review* 71. Although this study is rather

several cases, firms operating in Italian districts can adopt the form of a listed company.[66]

Because of such a major organisational difference, it may sometimes be difficult to compare the effects of a given reform – that is, regarding corporate opportunity rules – on economic environments that at first glance might be perceived as similar. In fact, in addition to the differences regarding innovation and the conditions of employment, one should consider the fact that a UK corporate opportunity rules reform limited to public companies would probably not have such a significant impact on industrial districts (although non-high-tech industrial districts do not seem that relevant within the UK economy nowadays). Therefore, one has to keep in mind that potentially there can be many practical asymmetries within different economic environments. Such asymmetries may have consequences for the impact that a given reform has on the overall national economy of the relevant country. Nevertheless, this should not affect the importance of analysing the effects of corporate opportunity rules for each country, which should be done while simply keeping in mind the prevalence of different kinds of industries in the two countries that are the subject of this first comparison.

IV. THE UK CORPORATE OPPORTUNITY RULES AND THE SHIFT FROM AN INDUSTRIAL-BASED TO A FINANCIAL SERVICES-BASED ECONOMY

The UK was a pioneer in the Industrial Revolution.[67] The UK economy underwent a remarkable number of changes before it reached its present state of being centred on banking and financial services.[68] One might well expect substantive

interesting in absolute terms, unfortunately it does not deal with industry. Therefore, it cannot be employed for the purpose of identifying institutional complementarities.

[66] For how listed companies are currently included in the algorithm employed for describing business groups operating in districts, see G Cainelli, D Iacobucci and E Morganti, 'Spatial Agglomeration and Business Groups: New Evidence from Italian Industrial Districts' (2007) 40 *Regional Studies* 507, 511. For a list of listed companies in empirical research limited to some of the Emilia-Romagna industrial districts, see F Brioschi, M Brioschi and G Cainelli, 'From the Industrial District to the District Group: An Insight into the Evolution of Capitalism in Italy' (2002) 36 *Regional Studies* 1037, 1050.

[67] For a general description of the Industrial Revolution from a historical perspective, see H Habbakuk and M Postan (eds), *The Cambridge Economic History of Europe* (Cambridge University Press, 1965), vol 4. For a detailed account of English industrial development from an industrial organisation perspective, see A Marshall, *Industry and Trade* (Macmillan, 1919) 32ff. For a wider perspective on industrial economic history, see D North, *Structure and Change in Economic History* (Norton, 1981) 158ff.

[68] For the changes before the beginning of the twentieth century, see Marshall, *Industry and Trade* (1919). For the following evolution, see A Chandler, *Scale and Scope* (Harvard University Press, 1990). For a history of the UK banking development process, see R Cameron, *Banking in the Early Stages of Industrialization* (Oxford University Press, 1967), 15ff. It goes without saying that the present emphasis on financial services and banking does not necessarily represent the end point for UK economic evolution.

changes in the legal rules aimed at regulating the allocation of business opportunities. In fact, developing economies may need to protect special classes of interests that are essentially different from those that emerge in a mature economic environment and, later on, in one that is mainly based on banking activities. Nonetheless, from a historical perspective, one cannot observe dramatic changes in the UK corporate opportunity provisions, despite the gradual modification of marginal rules.

UK corporate opportunity doctrines have been traditionally based on the no-profit rule; a rule which prevents directors from making any profit out of the taking of corporate opportunities, regardless of whether such takings are in conflict with the interests of the company.[69] The Companies Act 2006 (CA 2006) can be interpreted as granting UK courts the degree of freedom necessary to reform the no-profit rule and eventually to introduce a no-conflict test.[70] CA 2006, s 175(1) – on directors' duty to avoid conflicts of interests – also applies to 'potential conflicts'. Moreover, according to s 175(2), 'it is immaterial whether the company could take advantage of the property, information or opportunity'. Hence, s 175(1) and (2) seem to be in line with a no-profit rule. Nonetheless, s 175(4) states that 'The duty is not infringed if the situation cannot reasonably be regarded as likely to give rise to a conflict of interest', a statement that seems to refer to the possibility to apply a no-conflict test,[71] even though a 'reasonable likelihood' does not introduce a requirement for strong evidence of an actual conflict.[72] The possibility of introducing a no-conflict test granted by CA 2006, s 175(4) was not exploited by the UK courts in their most recent interpretation of CA 2006, a hermeneutic activity which is crucial under s 170(4).[73] However, in decisions such as the one taken in the *Wilkinson* case[74] UK courts have showed to be perfectly capable of refined business-aware interpretation of corporate opportunity rules,[75] an important recent decision[76] confirms the rigid no-profit approach already established in the *Regal (Hastings) v Gulliver* case.[77]

One may wonder how such an apparent lack of significant evolution can be justified from an economic efficiency perspective. Regardless of its eventual economic rationale, one may ask what the consequences of a lack of a significant evolution for the UK economic environment have been.

[69] *Regal (Hastings)* (n 1). See a clear statement of the principle by Lord Russell at 144ff.

[70] D Kershaw, 'Lost in Translation: Corporate Opportunities in Comparative Perspective' (2005) 25 *Oxford Journal of Legal Studies* 603.

[71] See comments in Davies and Worthington, *Principles of Modern Company Law* (2012) para 16–146ff.

[72] Corradi, 'Corporate Opportunities' (2016) 794.

[73] Section 170(4) concerns the scope and nature of general duties and states that 'regard shall be had to the corresponding common law rules and equitable principles in interpreting and applying the general duties'.

[74] *Wilkinson v West Coast Capital* [2005] EWHC 3009 (Ch).

[75] On the significance of the reasoning of Warren J over the line of business test, see Corradi (n 8) 796.

[76] *O'Donnell v Shanahan* [2009] EWCA Civ 751.

[77] *Regal (Hastings)* (n 1).

First, one should start by saying that dispersed share ownership is not a long-standing phenomenon in the UK economy, at least when compared with the US.[78] Now, in a concentrated ownership context (as the UK was, until the end of the 1950s), it looks as though corporate opportunity rules may mainly represent a source of power in the hands of industrial families. This is true, at least to the extent to which such rules exclusively address directors' misappropriations, leaving controlling shareholders' takings untouched – as is the case in UK law. In fact, in the *Ultraframe v Fielding* case, Lewison J stated that a shadow director does not owe fiduciary duties to the company because 'In contrast to a de jure or de facto director [she] does not undertake or agree to act in relation to the company in any such way'.[79] Such ruling is crucial for clarifying whether the provisions of CA 2006, Ch 2 apply to shadow directors – such as controlling shareholders. In fact, there is no express provision in this sense in Ch 2, in contrast with Ch 3, which expressly applies to shadow directors.[80]

A general fiduciary rule that was originally conceived for the purpose of protecting vulnerable parties (ie an orphan in *Keech v Sandford*)[81] became one of the instruments provided by the law for the purpose of protecting controlling shareholders against directors, while controlling shareholders already enjoyed a strong position within the corporation. In fact, families were the most relevant insiders in the British company before the dispersal of block-holdings took place. By contrast, the absence of a similar provision against misappropriations of corporate opportunities carried out by majority shareholders did not address the other substantive agency problem existing in this kind of company, that is, that between majority and minority shareholders.[82]

Corporate opportunity rules may well have started to carry out an efficiency-enhancing function in the economic environment that developed after the shift towards a dispersed ownership structure. They did not require any change because they were actually functional to the new economic environment.

[78] The precise moment of the change from family-owned companies to dispersed ownership is debatable, but it certainly took place after World War II. See B Cheffins, 'Does Law Matter? The Separation of Ownership and Control in the United Kingdom' (2001) 30 *Journal of Legal Studies* 459, 466. On the causes of ownership dispersion see also B Cheffins, 'The Rise and Fall of Shareholder Activism by Hedge Funds' (2012) 14 *Journal of Alternative Investments* 17.

[79] See *Ultraframe (UK) Ltd v Fielding* [2005] EWHC 1638 (Ch), 1284, where Lewison J stated that a shadow director does not owe fiduciary duties to the company because 'In contrast to a de jure or de facto director [she] does not undertake or agree to act in relation to the company in any such way'. Such ruling is crucial for clarifying whether Companies Act 2006, Ch 2 provisions apply to shadow directors – such as controlling shareholders. In fact, there is no express provision in this sense in the Companies Act 2006, in contrast with its Ch 3, which expressly applies to shadow directors.

[80] M Corradi, 'Agency Costs in the Shadow of the European Stock Exchanges: a Comparative Assessment of the British and Italian Law on Related Party Transactions and on Corporate Opportunities' (2012) *Journal of Comparative Law* 23, 45–46.

[81] (1726) EWHC Ch J76.

[82] See R Kraakman et al, *The Anatomy of Corporate Law* (Oxford University Press, 2009) 35ff.

Misappropriations of corporate opportunities are particularly likely to occur in a dispersed shareholders context, given the absence of a strong counterbalance to the corporate power of directors.[83]

It has been shown that the process of separation between ownership and control in the UK cannot be explained primarily by reference to corporate law. According to Brian Cheffins, tax law was one of the most important factors that led to the dispersion of shareholdings and to the emergence of institutional investors. Starting from the 1940s, UK tax policy created strong counterincentives to private investments in equity.[84] Despite the prevalence of extra-corporate law variables, one cannot ignore that corporate law contributed to the phenomenon of shareholdings dispersal.[85] This might be true not only from the previously mentioned agency costs perspective, but also in relation to the educative function of the corporate opportunity rules. The current rules may have instructed corporate directors to behave in a way that is economically functional in the contemporary economic environment.[86]

The creation of a category of directors exclusively committed to the company's success[87] and who are not interested in making side profits for themselves is considered by some to be a distinctive feature of larger corporations.[88] This behaviour may be particularly important in a financial environment that is essentially based on agency and where trust in the ethics of the agent is crucial. Despite this, one should remember that strict corporate opportunity rules also entail costs. In fact, directors who are prevented from appropriating the business

[83] See L Enriques, G Hertig and H Kanda, 'Related-party Transactions' in Kraakman et al, *Anatomy* (2009) 154.

[84] B Cheffins, *Corporate Ownership and Control: British Business Transformed* (Oxford University Press, 2008) 341ff.

[85] Although such a hypothesis does not correspond to Cheffins' thesis, which mostly points to rules on disclosure and to the development of the stock market.

[86] From a general perspective, see T Tyler, *Why People Obey the Law* (Oxford University Press, 2006) 23–26. The author suggests that internal moral norms, which are internalised by people, may be far more important than deterrence in determining the effectiveness of the law. In fact, according to Hoffman (as quoted by Tyler at 24), one has to acknowledge that 'Though the norms are initially external to the individual and often in conflict with his desires, the norms eventually become part of his internal motive system and guide his behaviour even in the absence of external authority'. For some important suggestions of relevant implications of the economic theory paradigm see G Akerloff, 'Loyalty Filters' (1983) 73 *American Economic Review* 54. Specifically, with reference to corporate law, it has been argued that altruism (ie selflessness) may play a very important role in the 'enforcement' of fiduciary duties: L Stout, 'On the Export of U.S. Style Corporate Fiduciary Duties to other Cultures' in C Milhaupt (ed), *Global Markets, Domestic Institutions* (Columbia University Press, 2003) 46. An extensive collection of studies related to managerial psychology is contained in Y Altman et al (eds), *Managerial Psychology* (Sage, 2008).

[87] As already stated, faithfulness was particularly encouraged in the UK's historical legal treatment of directors. According to Marshall, that trend was counterbalanced by an excessive indulgence of their ignorance about economic matters. On that point, see Marshall (n 67) 321.

[88] With reference to the necessity of taking this argument into consideration when drafting corporate opportunity rules, see V Brudney and R Clark, 'A New Look at Corporate Opportunities' (1980–81) 94 *Harvard Law Review* 997, 1022ff.

opportunities that they have discovered receive fewer incentives to make discoveries. Nonetheless, this problem could well be compensated for by long-term incentives to directors, in the form of performance bonuses (although this clearly entails costs for the corporation).[89] Those incentives might also be tied to the business opportunities discovered.[90] Interestingly, UK executives' compensation has included a long-term component in the period following share ownership dispersal, whereas this has not occurred in Italy at the same time.[91] Those differences might demonstrate the need to stimulate the business creativity of UK directors, because of the lack of personal incentives (ie the possibility of exploiting corporate opportunities). In fact, as we have seen, the unauthorised taking of corporate opportunities has never been allowed by UK company law, at least after the *Regal (Hastings) v Gulliver* case.[92]

Until recently, the City preserved and reinforced its position as the leading debt market in the world.[93] However, the majority of business opportunities that are available in the banking industry probably more closely resemble the one-off type (eg investing in a non-controlling equity stake) than those that are connected to setting up productive activities. In reality, it looks as though the rate of industrial innovation is not as high in banking as in other industrial sectors.[94] So, in this special sector of the economy, a very strict rule might be particularly efficient. It contributes to creating or reinforcing a halo of moral righteousness

[89] Although, clearly, this kind of incentive for directors entails costs for the company.

[90] For general issues concerning managers' remuneration, see K Murphy, 'Executive Compensation' in O Ashenfelter and D Card (eds), *Handbook of Labor Economics* (Elsevier, 1999) 2485. For an overview of the economic literature concerning directors' remuneration, see S Athey and J Roberts, 'Organizational Design: Decision Rights and Incentive Contracts' (2001) 91 *American Economic Review* (Papers and Proceedings) 200.

[91] J Abowd and M Bognanno, 'International Differences in Executive Managerial Compensation' in R Freeman and L Katz (eds), *Differences and Changes in Wage Structures* (University of Chicago Press, 1995) 67, 71ff.

[92] *Regal (Hastings)* (n 1).

[93] Despite the global financial crisis and the many scandals involving financial institutions, the City still attracts the majority of those working in finance, unlike other national models which look far more prone to decentralisation. This very centralised structure has attracted the attention of many researchers. See for instance D Wojciky and D MacDonald-Korth, 'The British and the German Financial Sectors in the Wake of the Crisis: Size, Structure and Spatial Concentration' (2015) *Journal of Economic Geography* 1.

[94] This does not mean that the banking sector is not interested in innovation: IT is extensively applied to banking innovation. However, clearly, the kind of corporate opportunity that involves the application of IT to banking usually belongs to IT companies and not to the bank itself. Financial institutions are thus usually those third parties to whom the fruit of the innovation is sold, because they are customers. On IT and banking, see C Jayawardhena and P Foley, 'Changes in the Banking Sector – The Case of Internet Banking in the UK' (2000) 10 *Internet Research* 19. For an industrial organisation perspective, see J Penning and F Harianto, 'The Diffusion of Technological Innovation in the Commercial Banking Industry' (1992) 13 *Strategic Management Journal* 29. This reasoning does not seem to have been impaired by the fact that, as to the *demand* for innovation, there has been a bilateral interaction between IT and banking. See R Barras, 'Interactive Innovation in Financial and Business Services: The Vanguard of the Service Revolution' (1990) 19 *Research Policy* 215.

that in turn may have the effect of reassuring investors.[95] Nonetheless, its cost in terms of diminished chances of efficient exploitation are likely to be quite low – corporate opportunities in this sector usually have no direct contact with the banking industry.[96]

Despite the attractiveness of the strict UK rules for large established companies, especially those operating in the banking sector, one may wonder whether the effects of such rules on medium-sized firms were similarly desirable. Economic literature shows that the decay in UK industrial manufacturing was mainly due to a difficult transition from family-owned businesses to corporations organised according to the US contemporary paradigm. They failed because they could not reorganise into modern public companies quickly enough.[97] It is an open question whether UK corporate opportunity rules had any role in such failure.

What is clear is that the inability of some countries (eg Italy) to reach dimensional levels comparable to those reached by US industry was at least compensated by the presence of extremely productive small and medium-sized companies. In contrast, this kind of environment did not develop in the UK after its main industrial crisis at the end of the 1960s.[98] The absence of strict corporate opportunity rules in the Italian system may well have been one of the determining factors for the quick development of highly specialised productive districts – based on knowledge spillovers. These strict UK corporate opportunity rules might have militated against a similar phenomenon in the UK, where the corporate opportunity doctrine also applies to limited companies, the prevalent form of family-run businesses.[99]

[95] With reference to the genesis and the traits of the UK financial environment, see Cheffins, 'Does Law Matter?' (2001).

[96] An exception may be represented by the Fintech market, in which some City banks manage their own incubators. An example is the one promoted by Barclays (see www.barclaysaccelerator.com/#). Nonetheless, such innovation is pursued by start-ups that have separate legal personalities from banking companies – hence potential corporate opportunities issues will not affect the company employed for managing the banking activities.

[97] See Chandler (n 68).

[98] See Chandler (n 68). Nevertheless, one has to acknowledge that the phenomenon of industrial districts is not completely unknown to the UK economy. For instance, the North Staffordshire district is one of the oldest British industrial districts. This kind of industrial district developed in a way that is not too dissimilar to many Italian districts. The only point where one may see a divergence pertains to innovation: such a district was characterised by the preservation of a high-quality industry, not necessarily by the mechanism of shop-floor innovation. By contrast, it looks as though in the North Staffordshire district different kinds of innovation techniques were allowed, such as those based on cooperation carried out by associations such as the North Staffordshire Association for Ceramic Training and Development, the British Ceramic Plant and Machinery Manufacturers' Association, CERAM Research and the Ceramic Industry Forum.

[99] Nonetheless, the British economic system is substantially different from the artisanal model that was found in districts for more than a century. According to Cheffins, *Corporate Ownership* (2008) 60, 'it was commonplace for the business that dominated lists of publicly traded firms earlier in the 19th century to be launched without the founders taking up a dominant equity stake'.

V. ITALIAN DIRECTORS' DUTY NOT TO COMPETE WITH THE COMPANY AND CORPORATE OPPORTUNITY RULES IN A DIVERSIFIED ECONOMIC AND INDUSTRIAL SYSTEM

According to some Law and Economics literature, Italy appears to have inefficient company law rules. This might be true to some extent.[100] Nonetheless, the success that the northern and central (and in limited geographical areas, also the southern)[101] Italian industrial economy displayed until a couple of decades ago cannot not be explained exclusively by extra-legal factors. It might be that hidden efficiencies lie precisely in the relationship between the law and that economic and industrial diversity. The importance of this relationship was progressively identified within corporate law literature. While it is true that some comparative corporate law literature has made a point of showing that the common law systems of corporate law can be regarded as optimal models in efficiency terms,[102] adjustments to such a radical interpretation have come from institutional economics literature, which tends to invalidate part of the previous interpretation.

It has been shown that, despite the presence of diverging rules, a functional convergence may occur between certain jurisdictions in which concentrated ownership prevails and those in which dispersed ownership is more widespread.[103] This also depends on the quality of controlling shareholders as well as the amount of private benefits of control that they are able to extract from the company.[104] All those improvements are extremely relevant to the explanation for diverging rules. Explanations tend to focus on jurisdictions as a whole. They do not consider that certain sets of national rules may apply to economic environments with a high degree of diversity; the same set of rules may be efficient or inefficient depending on the specific economic sub-environment. This is why, even before considering Italian business organisation models, it is necessary to take into consideration a few basic macroeconomic and industrial organisation variables. Italian industries are extremely diverse both from a productive and a geographical perspective.

Italian industries have been populated by at least two kinds of important private actors: first, large and heavy industry, and second, firms operating in

[100] See the proxies provided, with reference to the extraction of private benefits of control, by A Dyck and L Zingales, 'Private Benefits of Control: An International Comparison' (2004) 59 *Journal of Finance* 537.

[101] For instance, the so-called 'triangolo del salotto' (the 'sofa triangle') which is active in the production of high-quality furniture and is based in Bari and Matera. See www.csilmilano.it/mobili/s24.html.

[102] See F Easterbrook and D Fischel, *The Economic Structure of Corporate Law*, 2nd edn (Harvard University Press, 1996); R Romano, *The Genius of American Corporate Law* (American Enterprise Institute Press, 1993).

[103] R Gilson (n 15); R Gilson, 'Controlling Shareholders and Corporate Governance: Complicating the Comparative Taxonomy' (2006) 119 *Harvard Law Review* 1641.

[104] Gilson, 'Controlling' (2006) 1661ff.

industrial districts. From a historical point of view, industrial districts represent quite a recent alternative to those industrial environments that arose in the first industrialisation period. During the nineteenth century, the Italian economy was characterised by the growth of traditional 'heavy' industry, which provided primary goods and basic infrastructure (eg steel and railway industries). Those companies were often owned by a few investors from very wealthy, often land-owning, families. These affluent investors were rarely personally involved in the manufacturing process; they mostly acted as financiers.[105]

A subsequent phase of the industrialisation process (in the 1950s and 1960s) followed a completely different path. This intense industrialisation process found its fertile soil in those geographical areas where a strong artisanal tradition had been handed down through the generations. People working in those areas shared common values and were from a homogenous social environment, which usually specialised in a specific type of product. This formed the basis for the development of industrial districts. One must also remember the presence of the state as an entrepreneur, at both central and local levels. The involvement of the state has gone through several modifications, reaching its peak during Fascism and then being progressively dismantled, starting in the 1990s, by the so-called privatisation process.[106]

A. Italian Corporate Opportunity Rules and Industrial Diversification

The connection between types of firms and the kinds of business opportunities that affect their development seems clear. Here, the question relates to what kinds of corporate opportunity rules may be of economic interest for Italian companies in relation to diversification. Financially, diversification may be extremely difficult in small firms (ie there are no funds to develop new lines of business). By contrast, diversification may be possible and at times desirable for medium or large firms.[107] The necessity for diversification for larger firms may be connected to two different sets of reasons, that is, those related to industrial strategy or to financial strategy.[108]

Beliefs about its positive effects on industrial productivity led to the adoption of a diversification strategy and to the formation of conglomerates in the

[105] See V Zamagni, *The Economic History of Italy 1860–1990* (Clarendon Press, 1993) 349ff.

[106] See A Goldstein, 'Privatization in Italy, 1993–2003: Goals, Institutions, Outcomes and Outstanding Issues' in H Sinn and J Walley (eds), *Privatization Experiences in the European Union* (Massachusetts Institute of Technology Press, 2006).

[107] For an overview of the literature on that point and the later process of turning to a theory that is averse to diversification, see L Lang and R Stulz, 'Tobin's Q, Corporate Diversification and Firm Performance' (1994) 102 *Journal of Political Economy* 1248. See also J Roberts, *The Modern Firm* (Oxford University Press, 2007) 214ff.

[108] R Clarke, *Industrial Economics* (Blackwell, 1985) 206ff.

1970s and 1980s, principally in the US, but this was progressively abandoned, particularly in the Anglo-American world. Such a fundamental change in attitude is due, in particular, to the negative consequences of diversification on the stock markets' evaluation of a company's shares and consequently on equity financing.[109] The performance of conglomerates is extremely difficult to monitor due to their multiple activities. This renders them inefficient when their main source of financing is equity capital. One of the main problems for listed conglomerates is that complex industrial variables fail to be appropriately reflected in their listing price. In contrast, traditional reasons for industrial diversification have not been so extensively challenged and still seem to apply to non-listed corporations. Industrial diversification may still play a role in those organisations controlled by a block-holder.

Investors tend to minimise their risk by resorting to investment diversification, also known as 'portfolio strategy'.[110] Nonetheless, a controlling shareholder is usually unable to diversify their investment by resorting to a proper portfolio strategy – because most of their property is likely to be invested in just one business – so they may want to diversify their investment from an industrial perspective. This is possible as long as there are few economies of scale, as occurs in many sectors of Italian industry.[111] The necessity to diversify industrial investments may have emerged in Italian companies, which are usually dominated by an important block-holder.[112] In such situations, it might be suggested that medium and large Italian companies may have been interested in focusing on diverse business opportunities.

A way to favour a preference for industrial diversification could have been to provide protection to a wide set of business opportunities, as the traditional UK rules do. That would have allowed companies to keep opportunities that did not fall within their original line of business within their existing boundaries. However, this reasoning was not followed by the Italian lawmakers. In fact, the limited protection (both in terms of the scope and of the sanctions) offered by Article 2390 of the Italian Civil Code (directors' duty not to compete) seems to be in conflict with such an objective. Article 2390 of the Italian Civil Code does not target directors who resign,[113] but, in Italian law, they are

[109] See Roberts, *Modern Firm* (2007) 214ff.

[110] For general notions about investment management, see G Connor et al, *Portfolio Risk Analysis* (Princeton University Press, 2010).

[111] I am here referring particularly to industrial districts, which are normally populated by small producers. In this context, small producers may cooperate in order to avail themselves of economies of scale for certain stages of their economic activity, especially for their export activity. See L Becchetti and S Rossi, 'The positive effect of industrial district on the export performance of Italian firms' (2000) 16 *Review of Industrial Organization* 53.

[112] F Barca and M Becht (eds), *The Control of Corporate Europe* (Oxford University Press, 2001).

[113] cf the strict interpretation of the no-conflict principle provided by UK jurisprudence that forbids directors any unauthorised taking of business opportunities. Nevertheless, directors may have room for manoeuvre through a strategic resignation. See text at ch 7.VI and accompanying notes.

intrinsically limited to competing businesses. We can see that there is little correspondence between Italian companies' potential interest to diversify and Italian corporate law.

Despite the absence of a strong corporate opportunity paradigm, it is clear that, with the exception of industrial districts (in which firms are usually mono-product firms), diversification has been a recurrent phenomenon throughout the history of Italian industry.[114] In the Italian context, diversification also seems a very successful strategy, with very few failures.[115] The absence of appropriate rules for controlling diversification may either signal inadequacy of legal reform or the existence of institutional complementarities that somehow have allowed such diversification to take place regardless of the absence of appropriate corporate opportunity rules.

It is reported that in many cases the business opportunities *not* in the line of business of the corporation required massive investment.[116] Given the financial structure of the Italian economy at that time, it would have been unlikely that a director of a corporation not possessing personal resources and/or important political connections could exploit an important business opportunity.[117] Potential competition would have come from majority shareholders, that is, members of families who were well connected politically. As to the taking of corporate opportunities by majority shareholders, instead of a corporate opportunity doctrine there may well have been allocative mechanisms involving informal dispute resolution within families, eventually promoting cohesion within the company.[118] Alternatively, each member of the family was more likely to promote the success of the family business instead of their own individual ideas, knowing well that *l'union fait la force* ('unity makes strength'). There may have been no need to keep business opportunities within the corporation, given that family betrayals were unlikely to occur. This kind of family cohesion and its

[114] G Federico and P Toninelli, 'Business Strategies from Unification up to the 1970s' in R Giannetti and M Vasta (eds), *Evolution of Italian Enterprises in the 20th Century* (Physica-Verlag, 2006) 191, 203–05.

[115] ibid.

[116] ibid.

[117] For a description of the connections between banking and politics, see D Sassoon, *Contemporary Italy* (2014). More specifically, see F Barca and S Trento, 'State Ownership and the Evolution of Italian Corporate Governance' (1997) 6 *Industrial and Corporate Change* 533. The authors enumerate the 'Several factors [which] played a role in impeding turnover within the entrepreneurial establishment', including the financial obstacles to entrepreneurs, particularly new entrants, who lack the 'right connections'.

[118] That way of solving agency problems may constitute a millenary path dependency in the Italian business environment and has certainly been recorded since the Middle Ages. However, according to Greif (n 57) 341ff, family bonds only partially explain medieval Italian firms' success in mitigating the same agency problems that their wealthier Jewish and Arab competitors were not able to overcome. Bonds not only provided an agency-cost-free environment within the family, but also contributed to the formation of very strong alliances against potentially opportunistic behaviour. This might also have solved problems that could arise by the advent of new partners external to the corporation.

effect on the allocation of business opportunities may well have been strengthened by cultural values stemming from shared history.[119]

When analysing diversification and corporate opportunity rules from a perspective of reform, we should also consider Article 2391 of the Italian Civil Code (which applies only to directors and not to majority shareholders). The reformed version of this Article introduces corporate opportunity rules apparently based on a no-conflict test, somewhat similar to one of the possible formulations of the UK corporate opportunity rules.[120] In contrast to the duty not to compete, this might be seen as a possible way to favour diversification when properly applied. In fact, within such a strict legal framework, one might well support the idea that industrial diversification is an interest worth pursuing by a given corporation (ie the misappropriation of corporate opportunities that are not in the line of business represents a conflict of interest). Nonetheless, given that the industrial and financial environment in Italy has not significantly changed, such a rule would be more effective when applied also to majority shareholders. The absence of any case law suggests that there must be other complementarity mechanisms that still regulate this kind of case.

The fact that Italian companies have succeeded in implementing diversification policies seems to invalidate the potential arguments in favour of tolerating some degree of misappropriation of the private benefits of control. The impossibility of diversifying one's investments, from both a financial and an industrial perspective, should lead the large block-holders to avoid any extreme investment.[121] However, this is often compensated by the possibility of appropriating private benefits of control, for instance through tunnelling.[122] Such takings might be viewed as a survival strategy, but in international corporate literature, there is little doubt that the consequence of extracting private benefits of control is often connected to the under-development of financial markets. Therefore, the Italian situation (at least before the 2003 reforms) clearly shows another institutional complementarity, one which produces inefficiencies nonetheless.[123]

[119] See, for instance, the express declarations in this sense by the members of the most important Italian family-run company, Ferrero SpA, contained in the Ferrero Code of Ethics, 6–7 and 24–25, available at s3-eu-west-1.amazonaws.com/ferrero-static/globalcms/documenti/3710.pdf.

[120] At least in the most optimistic interpretation of *Wilkinson v West Coast Capital* [2005] EWHC 3009 (Ch). See Corradi (n 8) 796ff.

[121] For the problems relating to block-holders' inability to diversify their investments, see Cheffins (n 84) 64 and 67. For a comparative perspective, see W Bratton and J McCahery, 'Comparative Corporate Governance and the Theory of the Firm: The Case Against Global Cross Reference' (1999) 38 *Columbia Journal of Transnational Law* 213.

[122] For a definition of tunnelling, see S Johnson et al, 'Tunneling' (2000) 90 *American Economic Review* 22. The concept usually refers to the ability of majority shareholders to expropriate minority shareholders through several kinds of operations, among which is the appropriation of corporate opportunities.

[123] For an analysis of the benefits connected to control, see T Nenova, 'The Value of Corporate Voting Rights and Control: A Cross-country Analysis' (2003) 68 *Journal of Financial Economics* 325. See also Dyck and Zingales, 'Private Benefits of Control' (2004).

The presence of industrial diversification diluting investment risk also seems to invalidate the justifications that one might use to argue for the tolerance of some degree of misappropriation. In conclusion, it seems that Italian corporate law rules (Italian Civil Code, Articles 2390 and 2391) do not grant Italian corporations the ability to prevent misappropriations of corporate opportunities by insiders. This looks like a potential failure in Italian corporate legislation, which should have addressed especially the problem of misappropriations of corporate opportunities by majority shareholders, given the ownership structure of Italian corporations. Nonetheless, there is historical evidence of successful exploitation of an extremely diversified set of new business opportunities by incumbent Italian corporations. This suggests the presence of institutional complementarities that may have provided a substitute to (never introduced, but desirable) corporate opportunity rules addressed to majority shareholders. Among those institutional complementarities, one should certainly recall the importance of family bonds, which have been depicted as a peculiar trait of Italian entrepreneurial families and the control exercised by politics over industry.

B. Corporate Opportunity Rules in the Italian Industrial Districts

Northern and central Italian economies, especially, have usually been strongly supported by the presence of industrial districts (*distretti industriali*). Put in a very concise way, some of the most relevant characteristics of industrial districts are: cultural homogeneity; strong local identity; mutual trust among economic actors; tight social bonds; and prevalence of informal dispute settlement mechanisms.[124]

There are some specific features that look especially relevant to corporate opportunity rules. First, Italian industrial clusters have been characterised from the beginning by quick production and diffusion of technical innovation. In many cases this was not high-end innovation (as in Silicon Valley), but mechanical innovation aimed at improving the quality of the product or the performance of the productive process (ie, following an old classification system, 'incremental innovation').[125] At times, this kind of innovation was limited to the production of know-how,[126] even though cases of high-end, 'radical' or 'disruptive' innovation have also been recorded.[127]

[124] For literature on Italian districts, see A Quadrio Curzio and M Fortis (eds), *Complessità e Distretti Industriali. Dinamiche, Modelli e Casi Reali* (Il Mulino, 2002). For a recent publication in English, see I Paniccia, *Italian Districts: Evolution and Competitiveness in Italian Firms* (Edward Elgar, 2002); references to districts' common features can be found at 163ff.

[125] F Belussi and L Pilotti, 'Knowledge Creation, Learning and Innovation in Italian Industrial Districts' (2002) 84 *Geografiska Annaler* 125, 133.

[126] ibid 132.

[127] ibid 134. For an in-depth analysis of the different incentives related to the different kinds of innovation within district environments, see G Cainelli, S Mancinelli and M Mazzanti, 'Social Capital and Innovation Dynamics in District-based Local Systems' (2007) 36 *Journal of Socio-Economics* 932.

Second, the creation of new competing or industrially complementary firms by resigning directors has been a very common phenomenon.[128] One of the causes might also be found in the proximity between formal and real control,[129] which has rendered the extraction of private benefits by managers very difficult. In fact, district companies are mainly owned by families with a charismatic founder who normally sits on the board of directors. This leader usually retains a very strong influence over day-to-day decision-making. That being the case, managers may well have preferred to leave the original firm to set up a new one, rather than renegotiating their employment position with a very powerful blockholder and/or founder.[130]

Third, another common phenomenon is the one of the so-called *imprese motrici* – pioneers in certain technical sectors. After a short- or medium-term brilliant performance, *imprese motrici* were often overtaken by new entrants.[131] These could be active in the same market, as well as in new or partially new product markets.[132] Such a quick development process by new entries has also been traditionally characterised by a special form of internal solidarity. In fact, one of the main ways of financing in districts has always been personal credit by entrepreneurs operating in the same sector.[133]

Given the feature of Italian industrial districts, one may wonder whether it is possible to identify any form of connection between such an economic development process and the absence of a strong corporate opportunity provision. First, appropriation of business opportunities for the purpose of forming new firms may have become one of the normal ways former managers or new entrepreneurs start new businesses. The possibility for *resigned* directors to freely appropriate business opportunities, under the limited reach of directors' duty not to compete with the company (Italian Civil Code, Article 2390), may contribute to explaining both the decline of *imprese motrici* and the success of such an industrial development, based on new entries.[134] The development of

For a discussion of the specific relationship between high-end innovation and corporate opportunity rules, see extensively ch 5.

[128] See G Viesti, *Come Nascono i Distretti Industriali* (Laterza, 2000) 36.

[129] For this concept, see P Aghion and J Tirole, 'Formal and Real Authority in Organizations' (1997) 105 *Journal of Political Economy* 1.

[130] See F Azzariti, *I Percorsi di Crescita delle Piccole e Medie Imprese. Teorie, Modelli e Casi* Aziendali (Franco Angeli, 2002).

[131] Viesti, *Distretti Industriali* (2000) 36ff. For an effective depiction of the high entry and exit rates that characterised this kind of market, see B Invernizzi and R Revelli, 'Small Firms and the Italian Economy: Structural Changes and Evidence of Turbulence' in Z Acs and D Audretsch (eds), *Small Firms and Entrepreneurship: An East–West Perspective* (Cambridge University Press, 1993) 123, 142ff. Paniccia (*Italian Districts*, 2002) notes that this kind of initial entrepreneurship had three main background sources: former artisans, incubating industrial firms and pioneers.

[132] ibid.

[133] G Romeo, *La Finanza dei Distretti Industriali* (Franco Angeli, 2007) 27.

[134] A similar mechanism has been noticed in the US in industries such as semiconductors, disk drives, and lasers. See R Agarwal et al, 'Knowledge Transfer through Inheritance: Spin-out Generation, Development, and Survival (2004) 47 *Academy of Management Journal* 501. Note that the duty not to compete can be waived. See Cass n 3091, 31 October 1975.

new opportunities by former insiders would not have required such a long negotiation process as the one that might occur when a corporate opportunity rule is operating. However, frequent appropriations of business opportunities by insiders may have gradually impoverished *imprese motrici*, pushing them outside the market.

Second, given the districts' economic and financial solidarity, one might imagine that the presence of a corporate opportunity provision would have contributed to the disruption of the trust environment that has just been described (ie loyalty to the district more than loyalty to the company). In fact, the threat represented by the old employer recalling the whole stream of new profits resulting from the setting up of new firms could have strongly discouraged such a rapid growth by new entrants. This displays analogies with a legal phenomenon highlighted by Gilson[135] in relation to the development of the Silicon Valley economy, where the more lenient Californian rules concerning technology transfers may have contributed to the creation of an extremely competitive and innovative environment. It is worth remembering that the district structure seems somehow to mirror the fragmentation of production through vertical and horizontal disintegration observed in the Silicon Valley.[136] Moreover, the Silicon Valley's innovation system based on start-ups, often founded by the former employees or managers of other companies, seems to be comparable to the economic mechanisms of the Italian districts. This analogy prompts an additional set of arguments related to the labour structure in districts. I am not referring to the application of corporate opportunity rules to a company's employees, but to the impact of the presence or absence of corporate opportunity rules (as applied to directors) on the interests and on the incentives of a company's employees.

When considering employees, it has to be acknowledged that their exposure to the allocative effects of the business decisions related to the exploitation of new business opportunities can be particularly relevant from at least two different perspectives: those relating to new opportunities belonging to the line of business of the company but not entailing process innovation; and those relating to new opportunities (whether or not belonging to the same line of business) but entailing process innovation. These two kinds of opportunities can have opposite effects on employees.

On the one hand, experience has shown that employees usually make investments that are specific to the firms they work for.[137] That being the case, their

[135] R Gilson, 'The Legal Infrastructure of High Technology Industrial Districts: Silicon Valley, Route 128 and Covenants Not to Compete' (1999) 74 *New York University Law Review* 575. The explanation provided by Gilson is one of the many possible explanations for the success of Silicon Valley industries. For a radically different approach, see J Armour and D Cumming, 'The Legislative Road to Silicon Valley' (2006) 58 *Oxford Economic Papers* 596.

[136] D Rosenberg, *Cloning Silicon Valley* (Pearson Education, 2002) 10.

[137] On asset specificity, see O Williamson, 'Credible Commitments: Using Hostages to Support Exchange' (1983) 73 *American Economic Review* 519.

efforts can be adequately rewarded as long as their company allows them to make use of their acquired skills. Therefore, a company's commitment to secure opportunities that are in its line of business may usually appear as crucial to the stability of the pact between employer and employees. On the other hand, the exploitation of business opportunities entailing process innovation might harm employees when they are unable to acquire the specific skills for the company's new methods of production. This may happen because, the new process being more profitable, a large part of the company's financial resources may be shifted to the new process (for instance, introducing new IT), while employees who are not highly skilled turn out to be redundant. This may happen also in the service industry. For instance, this occurred in the 1990s within the Italian financial sector, where information and communication technologies displaced the least qualified employees.[138] Job losses are particularly significant in those sectors where product innovation and demand growth are lower.[139] Moreover, exploiting such an opportunity may require a working knowledge that is different from the original investments in specific human skills. Employees may look at that opportunity in an unfavourable way because they may be unable to acquire new skills cheaply.[140]

That said, one must remember that firms also employ another crucial set of productive factors that are involved in the exploitation of new opportunities, namely physical assets. Research shows that the optimal amount of asset-specific investments is closely related to a firm's industrial relations. In particular, when labour is strongly unionised, unions may be able to take advantage of the non-transferability of specific assets. They may ask for higher wages. Nonetheless, as a consequence, there will be reduced investment, which will cause a downward spiral in the firm's business.[141]

These ideas seem to fit into the Italian economic and legal environment and seem to specifically relate to company law rules for the allocation of business opportunities when they operate in districts. In relation to ownership structures, a traditional hypothesis stresses the functionality of Italian concentrated ownership in containing the high level of conflict between labour and employers.[142] However, usually this applies to large corporations. By contrast, such conflict

[138] R Evangelista and M Savona, 'The Impact of Innovation on Employment in Services: Evidence from Italy (2002) 16 *International Review of Applied Economics* 309, 316.

[139] See T Antonucci and M Pianta, 'Employment Effects of Product and Process Innovation in Europe' (2002) 16 *International Review of Applied Economics* 295, 303, 306.

[140] For an overview of the literature concerning the relation between innovations and employment, see C Edquist, L Hommen and M McKelvey, 'Product Versus Process Innovation: Implications for Employment' in J Michie and A Reati, *Employment, Technology and Economic Needs* (Edward Elgar, 1998) 128. Product innovation and process innovation are usually connected, respectively, to net employment gains and losses. However, former employees may be unable to obtain a placement in the newly created positions.

[141] J Cavanaugh, 'Asset-Specific Investment and Unionized Labor' (1998) 37 *Industrial Relations* 35, 36.

[142] See Roe (n 17) 83ff.

has been, traditionally, far weaker in smaller firms because of Italian legislative support for small entrepreneurs.[143] This has also been demonstrated in the analysis of the districts' environments. In some districts, left-wing political parties have traditionally identified small entrepreneurs with the working class.[144] As a consequence, class conflict and labour unrest has traditionally been lower.[145]

It may not be easy to identify the exact dimensional threshold that implies the disappearance of a favourable attitude of labour and unions towards entrepreneurs – that is, the point at which entrepreneurs expanding their activities over a certain size may be viewed as a union's antagonists. One has to acknowledge that district environments have traditionally been very favourable to asset investments (although fragmented among small- and medium-sized firms), for the reasons previously described (ie less conflict and a lower risk of asset expropriation). As a consequence, setting up a new firm may have been easier in such an economic environment, as long as the entrepreneur could be categorised as 'small', as usually happens with start-ups in the seed phase. An existing firm may have encountered increasing levels of labour conflict when expanding its activities through the internalisation of new business opportunities. In fact, an increasing degree of labour unrest would have corresponded to dimensional growth. In that sense, it is possible to say that lenient corporate opportunity rules, favouring fragmented small-scale production, may have helped to create a labour-friendly political environment.[146]

One may wonder whether employees were penalised by such a system. In fact, it seems that employees may go unprotected in an economic environment where firms find it difficult to secure new business opportunities. A possible response to that conundrum comes from the peculiarities of district labour. Research has shown at least two interesting points in relation to district employees. First, they operate in an industrial framework that has been organised according to flexible specialisation, in contrast, for instance, to the Fordist system. That means that employees have usually started working for firms after they have studied at technical schools and are able to successfully handle many different complex tasks.[147] Second, district employees are described as always struggling to improve their position and usually wanting to become entrepreneurs themselves.[148] That implies that if they have to find a new job because their existing firm fails, those

[143] G Orlandini, 'Diritto del Lavoro e Regolazioni delle Reti' in F Cafaggi (ed), *Reti di Imprese tra Regolazione e Norme Sociali* (Il Mulino, 2004) 281, 309.

[144] S Brusco and M Pezzini, 'La Piccola Impresa nell'Ideologia della Sinistra in Italia' in F Pyke et al (eds), *Distretti Industriali e Cooperazione tra Imprese in Italia* (Banca Toscana 1991) 155, 159. With reference to the role of politics in Italian capitalism from a general perspective, see F Barca, *Il Capitalismo Italiano: Storia di un Compromesso Senza Riforme* (Donzelli, 1999).

[145] ibid.

[146] On corporate opportunity rules and the firm's dimensional variable, see Corradi (n 8) 770ff.

[147] V Capecchi, 'Una Storia della Specializzazione Flessibile e dei Distretti Industriali in Emilia-Romagna' in Pyke et al, *Distretti Industriali* (1991) 35, 36.

[148] G Beccattini, 'Il Distretto Industriale Marshalliano come Concetto Socio-Economico' in Pyke et al (n 144) 51, 56.

employees would easily be able to adapt to a new position. That would render their specific investment in a given firm less crucial to their career. In other words, their investment can be described as industry-specific rather than firm-specific. Moreover, their personal objectives (becoming entrepreneurs) would contrast with life-long employment in one firm.

The relative independency of district employees from the company they work for is confirmed by the evidence that, in districts, a worker's mobility almost always depends on their choice rather than on their employer's decisions.[149] Also, from a wider perspective, the strategies for the allocation of new business opportunities are somewhat different from those in an environment that tends to promote the dimensional growth of established firms. In a district environment, business opportunities may have been viewed by employees and by non-family-member directors as a way to become independent entrepreneurs. That being so, one should not be surprised if company law has set up, at least for managers, a free appropriation regime with little reference to appropriation bans. Such a provision may be considered complementary to the overall social and economic environment.[150]

In conclusion, the absence of sound corporate opportunity rules in the Italian legal system may display institutional complementarities in the unique district environment. This looks particularly interesting from a political perspective. In fact, what has occurred in the district reality seems to contradict what Mark Roe has observed in relation to large Italian companies – that is, the necessity for entrepreneurs' families to build block-holdings to contain requests for improvements in salary and working conditions.[151] District employees did not perceive themselves to be in social conflict with (and somehow crushed by) their employer, but capable of significantly improving their situation by frequently changing jobs and often starting their own businesses. In turn, the possibility of changing employer frequently has been granted by the rather quick turnover of new entrants offering new employment opportunities.

C. State-Controlled Companies

Until the beginning of the 1990s, the Italian economy was dominated by public entrepreneurial activity; many companies were controlled by the state through

[149] Orlandini, 'Diritto del Lavoro' (2004) 310.

[150] Not surprisingly, the debate regarding the role of skill transferability inherent in employees' mobility has stimulated a debate in a neighbouring area of the law, ie the law of trade secrets. Also in this area, in terms of efficiency, an appropriate balance has to be struck between contrasting interests, ie the protection of a firm's interest versus regional development. See M Reder and C O'Brien, 'Managing the Risk of Trade Secret Loss Due to Job Mobility in an Innovation Economy with the Theory of Inevitable Disclosure' (2012) 12 *Journal of High Technology Law* 373.

[151] Roe (n 17).

its holding *Istituto per la Ricostruzione Industriale* (IRI).[152] The SpA rules would apply at least to some of them.[153] One thus has to consider the consequences if there is no effective ban against taking of corporate opportunities in such an economic environment.

Economic research has described companies controlled by the Italian state as inefficient in most cases.[154] In the light of corporate theory, part of that inefficiency may be explained by the absence of related party transactions rules[155] coupled with a generally uninterested owner.[156] Whatever the reason, misappropriation of private benefits may have been particularly easy in publicly owned companies. However, from a product market efficiency perspective, the absence of a ban on the taking of corporate opportunities might be considered to be at least unclear. In fact, assuring the conveyance of valuable business opportunities to an inefficient exploiter (ie a state-owned or mixed public/private ownership firm) cannot be considered to be an efficient norm. The appropriation of business opportunities by directors for founding efficient private firms should be considered a desirable practice, certainly one to be encouraged. That may have been true especially when the restructuring of publicly owned companies was not viable. Nevertheless, given the politics in the Italian industrial scene, it may well be that the previously described kinds of potentially efficient taking of corporate opportunities were marginal (unless the taker had 'the right political connections' which allowed them to develop a given corporate opportunity).

VI. CONCLUDING REMARKS ON THE COMPARISON BETWEEN THE UK AND ITALY

When institutional complementarities are taken into consideration, the comparison between two jurisdictions must be based on several variables, as in the case of Italy, where industrial districts exist alongside large family-owned companies and mixed state/private ownership corporations. Certain legal rules might have favoured specific industrial models (eg the district model). These may have benefited from a liberal approach to the directors' duty not to compete with the company (ie the only Italian business opportunities rule that existed before the

152 See R Petri, *Storia Economica d'Italia* (Il Mulino 2002) 97ff. For a detailed analysis of the economic activities exercised by the Italian State through IRI, see N Acocella, *L'impresa Pubblica Italiana e la Dimensione Internazionale: il Caso dell'IRI* (Einaudi, 1983).

153 On the evolution of this kind of company, see for instance A Rossi, 'Società con Partecipazione Pubblica,' in *Enciclopedia Giuridica* (Treccani, 1993) vol 29.

154 Acocella, *L'impresa Pubblica Italiana* (1983) 3 ff.

155 For the economic efficiency reasons in favour of a set of rules around related-party transactions, see La Porta Lopez, de Silanes and Shleifer, 'Economic Consequences' (2008).

156 See N Shapiro, 'Ownership and Management', in P Davidson and J Kregel (eds), *Employment, Growth and Finance* (Edward Elgar, 1994) 84: 'In economics the enterprise is efficiently operated when it is owner-operated'. However, in this case the interest of the owner (the state) can be particularly subject to political mutations that do not necessarily prioritise efficiency.

2003 reforms). Nevertheless, it would be hard to say that the Italian lawmaker adopted an equally lenient approach to corporate opportunities *for the purpose of* promoting innovation within districts. This may well be an unexpected occurrence. There is no mention of districts in the law relating to directors' duty not to compete with the company (districts were not even fully developed in 1942).[157] However, the lawmaker did not seem particularly interested in considering the efficiency implications of corporate opportunity rules or of their functional equivalent.

The possibilities for industrial diversification of Italian family-owned firms, through protection of non-competing activities, were not discussed by the lawmaker. Along the same lines, it would not make much sense to say that the UK's choice to concentrate most of its development efforts on its already well-developed banking sector was due to strict corporate opportunity rules or that those rules were put in place for that specific purpose. In fact, such rules were clearly pre-existent, and they emerged in a totally different context. Nonetheless, it might be the case that a series of phenomena, the causal correlation of which would be extremely difficult to prove, may have coexisted concomitantly.[158] The consequence of this might have been that a given path dependency developed in a given area of the law, to be applied to a given economic context, has facilitated the development of efficiencies within a different economic context. Therefore, connections between Law and Economics may become loose when we try to explain them through a strict causality nexus.

Perhaps the concept of culture should be employed to understand such correlations.[159] In other words, it might be that the UK's cultural inclination to promote transparency and its dedication to the interests of the principals, relying on the fair actions of a loyal agent, have promoted an environment in which banking activities find a particularly fertile ground. The culture of Italian districts, relying more on a generalised sense of duty towards the productive community than towards a specific principal, may have promoted an environment in which appropriations of corporate opportunities may have been seen as an expression of the continuation of the overall success of the district. Moreover, the interplay between existing and new firms founded on the taking of corporate opportunities may well have been accepted as one ingredient for the success of districts and of their social community.

Now, if we imagine transplanting the British rules into the Italian districts and transplanting the Italian rules into the British financial environment, we may well see that the rules do not fit in the other country, either culturally or

[157] See 'Relazione al Codice Civile – Libro V' (ie the official documents that accompanied the enactment of the Italian Civil Code in 1942) (Istituto Poligrafico dello Stato, 1943) 219, para 980.

[158] The concept of coexistence seems to be particularly important for explaining institutional complementarities. See Acocella (n 152) 50.

[159] L Harrison and S Huntington, *Culture Matters: How Values Shape Human Progress* (Basic Books, 2000).

from an economic perspective. In fact, the blurring of boundaries between agent and principal would be absolutely unacceptable within an established financial environment such as the one of the City.[160] It may well be the case that the traditional British no-profit rules would have suppressed part of the creative incentives of small and medium Italian industrial enterprises (especially those of their insiders) and the subsequent creation of new dynamic and successful companies through technological spillovers. Clearly, part of such an apparent contradiction may be because a model that looks equivalent from the point of view of its main legal characteristics (ie public company and SpA) was employed for completely different purposes and perhaps in the Italian environment in quite an indiscriminate way.[161]

Historically speaking, there may be several reasons for divergence in corporate opportunity rules in different European countries. Some of them may derive merely from cultural path dependency, and some from specific legal choices. Nevertheless, at times it is extremely difficult to reconnect these variables through a causality link. The complexity – and at times the circularity – of the interactions between culture, industry and the law renders the formulation of clear evolutionary laws quite uncertain.

A final consideration to be made is of the impact of financial and industrial globalisation on the described economic environments. Industrial globalisation and competition from products imported from countries with low labour costs has posed a severe threat to the survival of the industrial districts. This has led to several changes in the dynamics of those districts that have survived the global changes.[162] However, financial globalisation has increased the presence of investors demanding transparency and rules framed on the Anglo-American model, which is more able to control agency costs.[163] The UK model seems far more able to provide an efficient response to the challenge of financial globalisation. Nonetheless, any system is required to keep pace with the constant institutional changes. Spain may provide a good example of one of the potential reactions of non-Anglo-American corporate laws in the face of globalisation.

VII. CORPORATE OPPORTUNITY RULES AND THE DEVELOPMENT OF THE SPANISH ECONOMY FROM AUTARCHY TO INTERNATIONALISATION

The presence of institutional complementarities in Italy and the UK provides an argument against the 'end of the history of corporate law'.[164] In fact, the

[160] This is actually a foundational concept in finance. See M Jensen and W Meckling, 'Theory of the Firm: Managerial Behaviour, Agency Costs and Ownership Structure' (1976) 3 *Journal of Financial Economics* 305.

[161] See text at sections 5.II–III and accompanying notes.

[162] cf also the next section for an account of the recent developments on Spanish districts.

[163] La Porta et al, 'Legal Determinants' (1997).

[164] See text at section II and accompanying notes.

existence of institutional complementarities (in terms of ownership structure, industry and society at large) may be a strong point in favour of efficient diversification of legal rules.[165] A limitation in the VOC literature is that institutional variables other than the law are often employed in a static perspective, in their present form and without sufficient consideration of the time and the pace characterising their development. Such static analysis of institutional complementarities may turn out to be insufficient to explain differences in legal choices. For instance, given the similarities between the Spanish and Italian social, industrial and financial environments, we would imagine that Spanish and Italian (supposedly rational) lawmakers have made identical or at least very similar legal choices in relation to corporate opportunity doctrines.[166] Nonetheless, this is not the case.

Spanish corporate opportunity rules were subject to intensive attention by the lawmaker.[167] In fact, in the course of the last two decades those rules were reformed twice and were applied by Spanish courts in a few (albeit very meaningful) cases.[168] In contrast, Italian corporate opportunity rules were never applied after their introduction in 2003 and they were not subject to many in-depth studies by Italian jurisprudence.[169] This divergence in the Spanish and the Italian legal approaches to this topic may be interpreted as either that the extra-legal institutional variables previously mentioned are not relevant for the lawmaker or that it is necessary to refocus on Spanish and Italian social, economic, financial and industrial environments, employing further and more refined extra-legal variables.

Timing is an important variable that can be taken into consideration for better understanding the differences between Italian and Spanish normative choices. That means understanding markets (and economic reality at large) as phenomena embedded in temporal structures.[170] Temporal structures may determine profound variations in reactions to situations that present very similar substantive variables.

If one observes Spanish and Italian corporations and their functions within their respective current national economies, one might easily conclude that they present very similar features. Spanish *sociedad anónima* (SA) and Italian SpA

[165] Gilson (n 15).

[166] For a comparison of the Spanish and Italian business environments, in the last few decades, see V Binda and A Colli, 'Changing Big Business in Italy and Spain, 1973–2003: Strategic Responses to a New Context' (2011) 53 *Business History* 14.

[167] Corradi (n 8) 814–16.

[168] See n 8.

[169] Among the few studies available, see Barachini (n 4) and Corradi (n 4).

[170] Expression taken from C Eisenberg, 'Embedding Markets in Temporal Structures: A Challenge to Economic Sociology and History', in K Nathaus and D Gilgen (eds), Change of Markets and Market Societies: Concepts and Case Studies (Wandel von Märkten und Marktgesellschaften: Konzepte und Fallstudien) (2011) 36 *Historical Social Research (Historische Sozialforschung)* 55.

are both employed for setting up either large or medium-sized corporations.[171] Moreover, those corporations typically belong to distinct segments in their respective national economies. Both Spain and Italy have recently developed large corporations able to play a role in the international arena.[172] However, in terms of productivity and employment, both economies are strongly sustained by industrial districts.[173] Despite these similarities, Spanish and Italian corporations have their roots in social, industrial and economic developments, which, although similar, occurred at a significantly different pace. What is argued here is that the different pace (and intensity) in the economic development of the two countries – although leading to similar economic outcomes – might have led to different legal choices in terms of corporate opportunity rules. In fact, Spain experienced historical, political and economic contingencies that are very similar to those in Italy, but with a delay of around 10 years. This led Spain into a different social and economic situation in respect of the peaks in globalisation of trade, and especially of finance, that anticipated the 2007–08 crisis. This, in turn, might have determined a substantially different reaction to those global economic mutations faced by every developed economy. To see how these different reactions took place, it is necessary to compare the development of Spanish and Italian economies from a socio-political perspective.

First, both Italy and Spain went through a long period of dictatorship, under political systems engineered and led by Benito Mussolini (1922–45) and Francisco Franco (1939–75), respectively. Those regimes promoted long periods of autarchy, and rendered those countries unreceptive to foreign experiences, both in terms of business organisation and in terms of the law.[174] However, under those dictatorships, the state became a crucial player in economic arenas, mostly populated by small or medium-sized firms. This happened in Italy through the mediation of the *Istituto di Ricostruzione Industriale*, established in 1933, and in Spain, around a decade later, through the *Instituto Nacional de Industria*, established in 1944.[175]

Italian autarchy ended with the fall of fascism. By contrast, Spanish autarchy lasted at least until the end of the 1950s, when progressive reforms started the

[171] In fact, Spanish business adopts this form of SA not only in the case of national champions, but also medium-sized companies. For instance, if we consider a famous Spanish industrial district, the ceramic and tile district of Castellón de la Plana, we can notice that most companies are SA. See Tiles of Spain, 'Companies', available at www.tileofspainusa.com/companies/#sthash.xmCKGhcN.8SfzJrk1.dpbs.

[172] Binda and Colli, 'Changing Big Business' (2011).

[173] R Boix and V Galletto, 'Marshallian Industrial Districts in Spain' (2008) 7 *Scienze Regionali* 29. The authors stress the fact that compared to the UK, Spanish and Italian districts account for a far higher percentage of total jobs.

[174] For Italy, see D Baker, 'The Political Economy of Fascism: Myth *or* Reality, or Myth *and* Reality? (2006) 11 *New Political Economy* 227; for Spain, see S Payne, *The Franco Regime: 1936–1975* (University of Wisconsin Press, 1988) 384ff.

[175] See Binda and Colli (n 166) 16.

so-called Second Golden Age under General Franco's leadership, resulting in an economic boom at the end of the 1960s and the beginning of the 1970s. During that period, the Spanish economy witnessed a significant economic development, part of which may be attributable to the increase in foreign investment.[176] Comparatively, Italy had witnessed a similar economic boom around 10 years earlier, which peaked at the end of the 1950s and the beginning of the 1960s.[177] Therefore, internationalisation of trade and investment were well-established phenomena in Italy well before Spain had started to open up to foreign trade and investment.

A similar temporal gap between Italian and Spanish economic development occurred with a second economic boom. Whereas in Italy this took place throughout the 1980s and reached a brief peak in 1991,[178] the Spanish boom started around 1997 and ended around 2007.[179] Therefore, again, the temporal gap between two similar phenomena was of about 10 years. Spain needed to catch up with most Western European countries (especially with Italy, as explained above). This delay might be partially responsible for the intensity of Spanish policy in terms of corporate law in general and therefore also in relation to corporate opportunities.

The time variable, however, does not provide an effective explanation if it is not connected to substantive variables. Foreign direct investments seem crucial to understanding the different normative choices taken by the Spanish and Italian lawmakers and courts. Introducing sound corporate opportunity rules can be a winning strategy when there is a strong international component in a country's national economy, particularly when the foreign investors are Anglo-American. In fact, the Anglo-American legal context provides strong corporate opportunity and conflict of interest rules.[180] However, such a choice clearly entails a potential trade-off in terms of the vitality of the national industrial districts.

As already seen, strict corporate opportunity rules may limit the range of means by which technological spillovers occur. The idea of innovation based on shared knowledge and on spillovers, often determined by the setting up of new firms within districts, is well-established in industrial economic literature

[176] See S Lieberman, *Growth and Crisis in the Spanish Economy: 1940–1993* (Routledge, 1995) 62ff and 112ff.

[177] See Zamagni, *Economic History of Italy* (1993).

[178] The Italian newspapers celebrated 1991 as *il secondo sorpasso* (the second overtaking), meaning that the Italian economy had surpassed the French economy in terms of nominal GDP; *il (primo) sorpasso* (the (first) overtaking) referred to Italian economy surpassing the British economy. That occurred in 1987 (and for a very short period of time in 2009). See for instance M Clark, *Modern Italy: 1871 to Present* (Pearson, 2008) 472.

[179] See S Royo, 'After the Fiesta: The Spanish Economy Meets the Global Financial Crisis' (2009) 14 *South European Societies and Politics* 19, 20ff.; for a wider assessment in the light of the previous decade, see also G Tortella Casares, *The Development of Modern Spain: An Economic History of the Nineteenth and Twentieth Centuries* (Harvard University Press, 2000).

[180] See L Enriques and P Volpin, 'Corporate Governance Reforms in Continental Europe' (2007) 21 *Journal of Economic Perspectives* 117.

(although it does not necessarily represent the core of innovation literature).[181] Moreover, this kind of mechanism is specifically applicable to Spanish industrial districts, as noted by Spanish literature on industrial organisation.[182] It is also clear that strict corporate opportunity rules may somewhat disrupt Spanish industrial districts' innovation mechanisms, even though, through adequate reforms, such drawbacks might be corrected.

Having considered all these factors, one can easily see that signalling to foreign investors the alignment of Spanish corporate law with the Anglo-American rules may imply costs in terms of efficiency within national industrial districts, at least on a temporary basis. Therefore, one may ask why the Spanish lawmakers took several clear steps in that direction, whereas Italy introduced only a rather short and ambiguous norm that was never applied by the courts.[183]

Data on foreign direct investments net flows in Spain and Italy show that Spain had the incentive to take greater risks in terms of internationalisation of its corporate law, whereas Italy remained in a rather ambiguous position, perhaps because it was less able to attract foreign investments in general.[184] Clearly, at times it may be difficult to establish whether differences in foreign investments determined a different intensity in terms of law reforms or the reverse, that is, the presence of frequent law reforms had the effect of attracting more foreign investments. Some potential explanations might be found in the analysis of official data. Foreign direct investments in Spain were constantly higher than in Italy between 1988 and 2013. In Spain, foreign investment peaked in the years preceding the Spanish corporate law reform of 2003 (6.5 per cent in 2000, 4.5 per cent in 2001 and 5.7 per cent in 2002). There was then a substantial drop until 2012, the year of the most important decision in matters of corporate opportunities[185] (2.3% per cent in 2012), and then a substantial increase in 2013 (3.2 per cent). Clearly, as often is the case, foreign investments were probably driven to a large extent by extra-legal factors. However, it is interesting to note that the increase in foreign investments seems somehow to prompt Spanish lawmakers and courts to provide efficient solutions for corporate law issues related to conflict of interest. In 2014, one year after the last increase in foreign investments, the Spanish Government rapidly approved a corporate law reform,

[181] See text in the section VI and accompanying notes.

[182] See X Molina-Morales, 'Industrial Districts and Innovation: The Case of the Spanish Ceramic Tiles Industry' (2002) 14 *Entrepreneurship & Regional Development: An International Journal* 317.

[183] Not at least from research conducted on the officially published cases.

[184] The World Bank defines foreign direct investment as 'the net inflows of investment to acquire a lasting management interest (10% or more of voting stock) in an enterprise operating in an economy other than that of the investor. It is the sum of equity capital, reinvestment of earnings, other long-term capital, and short-term capital as shown in the balance of payments. This series shows net inflows (new investment inflows less disinvestment) in the reporting economy from foreign investors, and is divided by GDP.' Definition taken from the World Bank, 'Foreign Direct Investment, NetInflows (% of GDP)', available at data.worldbank.org/indicator/BX.KLT.DINV.WD.GD.ZS.

[185] Tribunal Supremo (Sala de lo Civil, Sección 1a) Sentencia num 502/2012 of 3 September RJ\2012\9007.

which seems to regulate directors' conflict of interest in a way that is somewhat similar to the UK law, at least in its structure.[186]

Given the strong commitment of the Spanish lawmakers to provide sound corporate opportunity rules, one may ask at least two questions. First, why Spain took such a strong signalling strategy (two reforms, very close together, and some policy relevant case law, affecting extremely important economic interests). Second, why the new Spanish corporate opportunity rules look so similar to the UK CA 2006.

As to the first question, there may be several explanations. First the two cited reforms send a signal of commitment to foreign investors. Second, the strength of such commitment may be due to at least two reasons. The Spanish transition from dictatorship to democracy (1974–78) was rather smooth and progressive, unlike that in Italy. Moreover, it occurred much more recently. Therefore, a strong signal in terms of being open to global law and finance theory and Anglo-American practice may be understood as a clear decision to leave behind the previous market-averse policies, which were heavily based on local tradition. This was probably not that necessary, at least in terms of signalling, in Italy, where the transition from dictatorship to democracy happened at a time of global political change. At that time, the Italian policy signal was strong both in political terms (Mussolini was executed) and in economic terms (the new 1948 Constitution clearly adopted a liberal model, tempered by some socialist nuances).[187] In fact, there was a clear demarcation between areas of Anglo-American influence and areas of Soviet influence. Therefore, belonging to the Western block would be, per se, an implicit policy signal. Moreover, these law and finance theories were not as mature as they are now. The temporal element surrounding a similar transition can be considered as crucial for determining different reactions in normative terms. The last Spanish economic boom (end of 1990s) happened on the verge of an acceleration of global financial investments worldwide, whereas the last Italian economic boom (1980s) took place in a moment of increasing trade globalisation that had not reached finance yet with the same intensity witnessed in the last two decades. Therefore, again, the temporal structure in which these changes were embedded might have determined different normative reactions.

As to the second question – why the Spanish lawmakers chose rules that seem structured in a way that looks so similar to the British rules – there may be several explanations. The similarities between Spanish and UK corporate opportunity rules is rather impressive, if not perhaps in function, at least in form. Article 227 of the *Ley de Sociedades de Capital* refers in general to the 'duty of loyalty' (*Deber de lealtad*). Article 228 of the *Ley de Sociedades de Capital* identifies

[186] See text preceding n 188.

[187] See Costituzione della Repubblica Italiana [Italian Republic Constitution], in particular 'Titolo III', arts 35–47.

directors' obligations deriving directly from their duty of loyalty (*Obligaciones básicas derivadas del deber de lealtad*), among which – in subsection 228(e) – is the duty to avoid conflicts of interest or conflicts of duties ('*Adoptar las medidas necesarias para evitar incurrir en situaciones en las que sus intereses, sean por cuenta propia o ajena, puedan entrar en conflicto con él interés social y con sus deberes para con la sociedad*'). Article 229(d) identifies the misappropriation of a corporate opportunity ('*A provecharse de las oportunidades de negocio de la sociedad*') as a violation of rules pertaining to directors' conflicts of interest. The systematisation of Spanish corporate opportunity rules interestingly mirrors the one of CA 2006, s 175. Even more interestingly, Article 227.2 of the *Ley de Sociedades de Capital* states that a breach of directors' duty of loyalty will be sanctioned not only through damages but also through a disgorgement of profits ('*La infracción del deber de lealtad determinará no solo la obligación de indemnizar el daño causado al patrimonio social, sino también la de devolver a la sociedad el enriquecimiento injustoobtenido por el administrador*).

Now, the UK has been an important player in the Spanish economy, representing 12 per cent of the total Spanish foreign market investment in 2018.[188] Therefore, Spanish lawmakers might have intended to show that Spanish corporate law is keeping pace with UK standards. However, this does not look the most plausible explanation. In fact, it may simply be that the 'conflict' test adopted by the Spanish lawmakers is much more in line with continental Europe's tradition of self-dealing. In addition, it may well be that Spanish lawmakers realised the greater flexibility of the 'conflict' test as compared to the 'line of business' test. Therefore, they may have adopted it merely for efficiency reasons.

Once one has identified possible explanations for the intense reform efforts undertaken by the Spanish lawmakers, it is necessary to look at their potential repercussions for Spanish industrial districts. When comparing the British and the Italian systems, I took into consideration a British and an Italian ceramic district (North Staffordshire and Sassuolo).[189] It is possible to extend the comparison to a Spanish industrial district that also produces ceramics and tiles, that is, Castellon de la Plana. According to industrial economics research, the Spanish tile district is characterised by the same features that are common to all industrial districts. As to those common traits, one should keep in mind that in the Spanish tile district the main 'mechanism [for innovation and especially for diffusion of knowledge] consists in new firms, mostly created by management and employees from a parent firm, which are located in the areas where the founders have lived and worked'.[190] Therefore, it is clear that rules that create

[188] See the OECD statistics as reported on Santander, 'Spain: Foreign Investment', available at santandertrade.com/en/portal/establish-overseas/spain/foreign-investment.

[189] See text at section V and accompanying notes.

[190] See Molina-Morales, 'Industrial Districts and Innovation' (2002) 321. This point was observed also by general research on industrial districts, in particular by A Bramanti and L Senn, 'Product Innovation and Strategic Patterns of Firms in a Diversified Local Economy: The Case of Bergamo' (1990) 2 *Entrepreneurship & Regional Development* 153.

obstacles for this kind of new activity are likely to be detrimental to the innovation dynamics within Spanish industrial districts. However, on closer inspection, it may be that the dynamics within industrial districts are also changing. It is clear that as to research and development-based innovation models (ie, not industrial district-based innovation, where the UK does not seem to be particularly strong), the UK is one of the most advanced European countries, whereas Spain lags behind.[191] Despite this, Spanish district innovation is particularly efficient, at least for specific production dynamics.

One may ask how the potential losses in district innovation were compensated by the new internationalisation dynamics. A partial reply to this conundrum might come from Spanish industrial organisation literature specialising in innovation. Recently, Anglo-Spanish industrial organisation theory has signalled the importance of internationalisation for Spanish innovation dynamics. In particular, industrial economic theory signals the possibility that foreign investment in this sector may promote the diffusion of new technology imported by foreign investors.[192] Therefore, the lawmakers might have some way to take into consideration the possibilities that part of the losses in local innovation spillovers are compensated by foreign investors. At least Spain, unlike Italy, seems to have taken a clear position in relation to the globalisation process and to the new opportunities coming from the increase in international investments.

VIII. CONCLUSION

The analysis of the development of the British, Italian and Spanish industries in relation to corporate opportunity rules has shown that, at least in this specific case, the interactions between different institutional variables cannot be explained simply through the law of cause and effect. Hence, there may be cases in which one finds a given kind of rule concomitantly with other institutional variables, without the possibility of demonstrating clearly which variables have influenced the others. This should not be considered as meaningless within a positive analysis. Where it is difficult to formulate a theory with the kind of empirical data available, it is still possible to identify a vast series of variables, which will eventually be combined through further qualitative and quantitative research. All the main theories that explain the convergence and divergence within different corporate laws may be very insightful when applied to corporate opportunities. In corporate opportunity doctrines, legal, industrial, and

[191] From a comparative perspective, see M Mate-Sanchez Val and R Harris, 'Differential Empirical Innovation Factors for Spain and the UK' (2014) 43 *Research Policy* 451.

[192] J Rosell-Martınez and P Sanchez-Sellero, 'Foreign Direct Investment and Technical Progress in Spanish Manufacturing' (2012) 44 *Applied Economics* 2473; I Alvarez and J Molero, 'Technology and the Generation of International Knowledge Spillovers: An Application to Spanish Manufacturing Firms' (2005) 34 *Research Policy* 1440.

political variables may be deeply intertwined. Although globalisation tends to push towards efficiency, such a goal is likely to be reached by different paths. Moreover, globalisation tends to favour the circulation of different legal models that will inevitably facilitate the possibility of finding alternative efficient solutions to the main economic problems raised by corporate opportunity doctrines. The complexity of variables found in different industrial environments is also an important reminder for those engaged in economic analysis of corporate opportunity rules. Corporate opportunity rules are crucial both to finance and to industrial production, so any analysis based on a limited set of variables must be carefully assessed against the wider context in which these rules operate.

An analysis that is merely based on costs may tend to simplify its theoretical framework, in order to work with a limited number of well-quantifiable variables. It may exclude many sociological 'soft' variables that are difficult to quantify, such as the value of a set of extremely heterogeneous and mutable family bonds or the effects of the social cohesion that exists within certain industrial environments and its transformation throughout time. Even more, it may ignore the complex set of almost invisible threads that connect each individual to their peers, beyond their interests for an economic profit. However, a cost analysis, though imperfect, may help to reorder ideas and to provide a (rough) estimation of the costs connected to different institutional equilibria – an estimation which can contribute to informing policy-making, along with a wider set of considerations.

2

A Cost-Based Analysis of Corporate Opportunity Doctrines

I. INTRODUCTION

AN ANALYSIS OF the corporate opportunity paradigm from a historical, sociological and political perspective would need to consider so many variables that its findings could not be employed for normative purposes. Whilst an approach to analysis that narrows the meta-legal perspective therefore needs to be taken, this does not necessarily mean sticking to a purely exegetic approach, limited to the grammatical, systematic and teleological aspects of the legislation. In the last few decades, and especially after the 1960s, many legal scholars have progressively abandoned a purely exegetic method and have approached legal problems from a multidisciplinary perspective.[1] Economic analysis of the law represents one of the ways in which academics have questioned the status quo of existing legislation and have prompted lawmakers to consider potential avenues of reform with the aim of enhancing economic efficiency.[2] Nonetheless, the indiscriminate use of economic analysis has been subject to criticisms by scholars following different approaches[3] and also by some of the founders of the Law and Economics school.[4] Among other criticisms, scholars have increasingly pointed at the unrealistic nature of the *homo economicus* rationality assumption,[5] showing that human beings tend to behave irrationally in many situations[6] – although the presumed irrationality of

[1] Such an increased interest in a multidisciplinary approach may have derived from younger generations' disappointment with the status quo – a widespread sentiment during the cultural revolution movements of the 1960s and 1970s. See B Tamanaha, *On the Rule of Law: History, Politics, Theory* (Cambridge University Press, 2006) 73ff.

[2] Law and Economics was also employed for contrasting left-wing interventionist politics, supported by welfare economics in the 1960s. See M Horwitz, 'Law and Economics: Science or Politics?' (1980) 8 *Hofstra Law Review* 905, 906.

[3] J Baron and J Dunoff, 'Against Market Rationality: Moral Critiques of Economic Analysis in Legal Theory' (1995) 17 *Cardozo Law Review* 431.

[4] R Posner, 'Some Uses and Abuses of Economics in Law' (1979) 46 *University of Chicago Law Review* 281.

[5] R Korobkin and T Ulen, 'Law and Behavioral Science: Removing the Rationality Assumption from Law and Economics' (2000) 88 *California Law Review* 1051.

[6] C Jolls, C Sunstein and R Thaler, 'A Behavioral Approach to Law and Economics' (1998) 50 *Stanford Law Review* 1471.

corporate agents has been questioned by corporate theorists.[7] The integration of behavioural arguments in Law and Economics analysis can be understood more as a chance to provide a more complete perspective on the economics variables than as a demonstration of the groundlessness of economic analysis of the law. Law and Economics critics have also pointed to the inability of the mainstream Law and Economics scholarship to learn from mistakes and to incorporate criticism, thus pointing out the unreasonable attitude of some Law and Economics scholars more than to the general inaccuracy of the arguments promoted by such scholarship per se.[8]

When it comes to corporate law, an economic approach may seem narrow and exclusively focused on private contracting and on profits.[9] Nowadays, it is highly doubtable that the contractarian paradigm alone can justify corporate legislation.[10] One of the alternatives to the contractarian paradigm is one based on a political approach. It focuses on the public dimension of the corporation and on its connection to political action – hence on a wider set of interests[11] that in 'classic' contractarian narrative can be viewed as 'externalities'.[12]

Economic analysis of corporate law is not monolithic. In fact, the set of interests on which it focuses can vary to a large extent. For instance, the so-called stakeholder theory[13] – also based on economics arguments[14] – focuses on a vast set of beneficiaries. It promotes welfare maximisation in a different way to traditional finance-based theories.[15] In fact, the debate on whether interests outside those of shareholders should be addressed by corporate law is far older than the economic analysis of the law.[16] A Law and Economics analysis seems to offer

[7] J Arlen, M Spitzer, and E Talley, 'Endowment Effects within Corporate Agency Relationships' (2002) 31 *Journal of Legal Studies* 1.

[8] M Nussbaum, 'Flawed Foundations: The Philosophical Critique of (a Particular Type of) Economics' (1997) 64 *University of Chicago Law Review* 1197.

[9] F Easterbrook and D Fischel, *The Economic Structure of Corporate Law*, 2nd edn (Harvard University Press, 1996). For criticisms, see L Kornhauser, 'The Nexus of Contracts Approach to Corporations: A Comment on Easterbrook and Fischel' (1989) 89 *Columbia Law Review* 1449.

[10] M Moore, 'Private Ordering and Public Policy: The Paradoxical Foundations of Corporate Contractarianism' (2014) 34 *Oxford Journal of Legal Studies* 693.

[11] D Ciepley, *Beyond Public and Private: Toward a Political Theory of the Corporation* (2013) 107 *American Political Science Review* 139. The political theory of the corporation is particularly flourishing with reference to multinationals. C Dörrenbächer and M Geppert, *Politics and Power in the Multinational Corporation* (Cambridge University Press, 2011).

[12] M Moore, *Corporate Governance in the Shadow of the State* (Hart Publishing, 2013).

[13] M Blair and L Stout, 'A Team Production Theory of Corporate Law' (1999) 85 *Virginia Law Review* 247; M Gelter, 'The Dark Side of Shareholder Influence: Managerial Autonomy and Stakeholder Orientation in Comparative Corporate Governance' (2009) 50 *Harvard International Law Journal* 129.

[14] L Stout, *The Shareholder Value Myth: How Putting Shareholders First Harms Investors, Corporations, and the Public* (Berrett-Koehler, 2012).

[15] F Easterbrook and D Fischel, 'The Corporate Contract' (1989) 89 *Columbia Law Review* 1416.

[16] The debate between 'contractualistes' and 'institutionalistes' in continental Europe legal doctrine dates back to the beginning of the twentieth century; see P Didier, 'La Théorie Contractualiste de la Société' (2000) II *Revue des sociétés* 95; P Jaeger, *L'Interesse Sociale* (Giuffre, 1964). The stakeholder-oriented statements by the German politician Walther Rathenau prompted a fierce discussion also

several alternative routes for introducing within corporate theory discourse the consideration of interests other than those of the shareholders.

According to the residual claimant argument, 'focusing principally on the maximisation of shareholder return is, in general, the best means by which corporate law can serve the broader goal of advancing overall social welfare'.[17] Nonetheless, to put it in the words of *The Anatomy of Corporate Law*, 'the corporation – and, in particular, its shareholders, as the firm's residual claimants and risk-bearers – have a direct pecuniary interest in making sure that corporate transactions are beneficial, not just to the shareholders, but to all parties who deal with the firm'.[18] This is reflected, for instance, in the concept of 'enlightened shareholder value' adopted by the UK Companies Act 2006 (CA 2006), s 172(1), which regulates the director's duty to promote the success of the company. In promoting the success of the company, the director is supposed to have regard to, among other things, 'the interests of the company's employees ... the need to foster the company's business relationships with suppliers, customers and others' and 'the impact of the company's operations on the community and the environment'.[19]

If protecting the interests of constituencies different from shareholders is often in the interest of shareholders, also a Law and Economics analysis of corporate opportunity rules can benefit from taking into consideration non-shareholders' along with shareholders' interests. I have already shown that historical and political analysis of corporate opportunity rules, as embedded in a complex set of institutional variables, often shows that certain normative equilibria end up satisfying the interests of more than one stakeholder group and of large segments of an economy as a whole.[20] Therefore, although the agency costs framework can still be considered to be a primary way to address corporate opportunity rules, a more complex set of considerations than the one merely pertaining to the economic theory of agency can provide a more complete picture. Even within the narrower analysis of the costs surrounding

outside Germany. D Vagts, 'Reforming the Modern Corporation: Perspectives from the German' (1996) 80 *Harvard Law Review* 23, 39: Rathenau 'taught that the corporation should be run as an institution for its own sake and that the public interest would be injured by the failure to provide for self-financing and growth and especially by the utilization of the legal right of shareholders to liquidate concerns of great public interest'. In Italy, many corporate lawyers debated the function of corporate law in the light of Rathenau statements with very successful publications. See A Asquini, *I battelli del Reno* (Giuffre, 1959) and F d'Alessandro, 'Il Diritto delle Società da i «Battelli del Reno» alle «Navi Vichinghe»' (1988) 111 *Il Foro Italiano* 47. See also text at ch 7.I and accompanying notes.

[17] R Kraakman et al, *The Anatomy of Corporate Law: A Comparative and Functional Approach* (Oxford University Press, 2017) 23.

[18] ibid.

[19] A Keay, 'Tackling the Issue of the Corporate Objective: An Analysis of the United Kingdom's Enlightened Shareholder Value Approach' (2007) 29 *Sydney Law Review* 577, 594ff, according to whom the legal concept of enlightened shareholders' value bears similarities to the American States 'constituencies statutes', without any further intention to embrace the stakeholder theory.

[20] See text at ch 1.V.B and accompanying footnotes.

the relationships between a company and its insiders, the agency costs paradigm has proven to be unsatisfactory.[21] The need to develop new perspectives without throwing away the insights given to us by agency theory seems to be an important objective for modern corporate scholarship.

Finally, one cannot ignore the recent debate on sustainability. This debate has reignited the 'shareholder versus stakeholder' debate, by offering new points of view on the role of the corporation within society at large. Under the aegis of privatisation, European companies have found themselves delivering to the public goods and services that were previously offered by the state.[22] It is debatable whether they have been capable of delivering such goods and services in a better way than the state.[23] In such a new context, the Milton Friedman corporate rationale consisting of maximising shareholder value has been depicted as inadequate for representing the business paradigm of the twenty-first century.[24] According to Colin Mayer, a better business could be founded on the recognition that 'a corporation is an employer, investor, consumer, producer and supplier all rolled into one'[25] and that '[t]he repositioning of corporations, capital and control' would have 'fundamental implications for business, economics and public policy as the Copernican revolution had for astronomy'.[26]

Colin Mayer's analysis – of the failure of traditional shareholder theories to depict how corporations really work – goes well beyond a mere re-evaluation of the role of stakeholders. The author explains that many companies do not operate according to value-maximising logics but instead aim to serve society in the best way possible by providing solutions to people's problems.[27] In his view, the effort to satisfy the needs of society at large in multiform ways may become the aim of the twenty-first-century corporation.[28]

A recent policy document by the British Academy, 'Principles for Purposeful Business', sets general principles and introduces the idea that 'Regulation

[21] Z Goshen and R Squire, 'Principal Costs: A New Theory for Corporate Law and Governance' (2017) 117 *Columbia Law Review* 767.

[22] D Bös, 'Privatization in Europe: A Comparison of Approaches' (1993) 9 *Oxford Review of Economic Policy* 95.

[23] K Schmidt, 'The Costs and Benefits of Privatization: An Incomplete Contracts Approach' (1996) 12 *Journal of Law, Economics, and Organization* 1; For the distributional consequences of privatisations, see N Birdsall and J Nellis, 'Winners and Losers: Assessing the Distributional Impact of Privatization' (2003) 31 *World Development* 1617.

[24] C Mayer, *Prosperity: Better Business Makes the Greater Good* (Oxford University Press, 2018) 2. Mayer's theses were criticised by Bebchuk and Tallarita (L Bebchuk and R Tallarita, 'The Illusory Promise of Stakeholder Governance' (2020), available at papers.ssrn.com/sol3/papers.cfm?abstract_id=3544978), to whom Mayer reacted with a further paper: C Mayer, 'Shareholderism Versus Stakeholderism – A Misconceived Contradiction. A Comment on "The Illusory Promise of Stakeholder Governance" by Lucian Bebchuk and Roberto Tallarita', European Corporate Governance Institute-Law Working Paper 522 (2020).

[25] ibid 4.

[26] ibid 5.

[27] C Mayer, 'The Future of the Corporation and the Economics of Purpose', ECGI Finance Working Paper 710/2020.

[28] ibid.

should expect particularly high duties of engagement, loyalty and care on the part of directors of companies to public interests where they perform important public functions'.[29] It is not clear from the document whether in so doing there was any intention at all to take into account the directors' duty of loyalty. Although the view of the corporation advanced in the document is likely to allow the pursuit of sustainability and in general better serve the world, it is not necessarily easy to translate such a vision into regulations adopting a so-called stakeholder theory. What the debate on sustainability certainly provides us with is a consciousness of deep interconnections – both between all individual human beings and between humans and the planet on which they live. This is definitely a wider window on the position of the corporation in the world than the one traditionally offered by law and finance scholarship. A cost-based analysis of corporate opportunity rules, a fundamental component of the directors' duty of loyalty, may still serve to find reason-based guidelines to instruct what some wish to be manifested as a corporate revolution, in pursuance of the collective welfare, beyond individual profit.

II. THE ECONOMIC EFFECTS OF CORPORATE OPPORTUNITY DOCTRINES AND THEIR CONNECTION TO THE DUTY OF LOYALTY OF DIRECTORS

One may attempt to describe and explain the costs involved in the allocation and exploitation of corporate opportunities with a simple mathematical equation.[30] However, a simple summation of different costs may fall short in accurately describing the economic reality. The reason for this inadequacy is that the above-mentioned costs exist in varying relationships to each other. They also need to be understood within a bargaining context because they tend to affect each other in a dynamic way, with a series of potential mirror effects. Therefore, they cannot be described exhaustively with a simple arithmetical formula, which works better for approaching a static phenomenon.

Considering such costs and highlighting the multiplicity of ways in which they interact may constitute a more effective approach to understanding the economic effects of the rules that allocate business opportunities. The theoretical possibility of writing a meaningful equation for describing the complex interaction among such costs cannot be excluded. Nonetheless, such an equation would either include an almost infinite number of variables – and hence turn out to be unfeasible – or would exclude so many variables as to become of little practical use.

[29] The British Academy, 'Principles for Purposeful Business' (2019), www.thebritishacademy.ac.uk/publications/future-of-the-corporation-principles-for-purposeful-business.

[30] M Corradi, 'Corporate Agency Costs in the Shadow of the European Stock Exchanges: A Comparative Assessment of British and Italian Law on Related Party Transactions and Corporate Opportunities' (2012) 6 *Journal of Comparative Law* 23, 29–30.

The first set of costs that corporate law literature ascribes to the misappropriation of corporate opportunities is agency costs.[31] In systems dominated by equity market financing, protecting the corporation from misappropriations of corporate opportunities is normally viewed as an investor-friendly policy measure.[32] Nonetheless, if we expand the reach of our reasoning outside the boundaries of economic agency theory, we can notice at least two sets of additional costs.

First, there may well be costs deriving from a strict application of corporate opportunity rules, ie an application that provides harsh sanctions for misappropriations. This depends simply on the fact that each party's valuation of a business opportunity depends on many factors which are difficult for a lawmaker to predict *ex ante* and which vary case by case (examples are sunk costs and hold-up costs). An *ex ante* allocation by the lawmaker cannot effectively predict which party (the corporation or the insider) will value the opportunity more. Therefore, such a lack of predictability may easily result in an inefficient allocation, when remedies associated to the breaches of such rules do not facilitate bargaining.[33]

As a matter of fact, the de jure allocation of business opportunities to the corporation may derive more from the moral imperative underlying the company directors' duty of loyalty than from a full understanding of its economic consequences.[34] A potential misallocation – eg to the incumbent corporation while its insider values the opportunity more – may come at a cost both for the parties and for society as a whole. Of course, such a misallocation may be corrected through transactions between company and insider.[35] Nonetheless, we cannot predict *ex ante* whether in the presence of positive transaction costs bargaining will always lead to a Pareto efficient allocation of the business opportunities at issue.[36]

A misallocation produced by poorly designed legal rules can negatively affect the development of very simple business opportunities (eg information concerning a given piece of real estate sold at a given price) and/or more economically complex ones (eg information concerning the possibility of developing an innovative sophisticated technology, or information concerning the possibility of acquiring a given corporation). If the business opportunity at stake is a

[31] R Sitkoff, 'The Economic Structure of Fiduciary Law' (2013) 91 *Boston University Law Review* 1039, 1040ff.

[32] R La Porta et al, 'Legal Determinants of External Finance' (1997) 52 *Journal of Finance* 1131.

[33] See text at ch 4.II and accompanying notes.

[34] L Jacobs, 'Business Ethics and the Law: Obligations of a Corporate Executive' (1972) 28 *Business Law* 1063. To some extent, I agree that the application of a fully contractarian paradigm to this situation ends up being at least unclear, as suggested in general by Mark Moore when considering the different hypothetical bargaining hypothesis to be employed for drafting efficient rules. See Moore, *Corporate Governance* (2013) 258 ff.

[35] See text at ch 4.I–II and accompanying notes.

[36] And this is why the post-bargaining phase is important in case of failure to reach an agreement. See text at ch 4.VI and accompanying notes.

productive one – for instance, a technological innovation to be implemented or a going concern that can be reorganised in a more efficient way – the costs may be higher than in the case of a misallocation of a simpler corporate opportunity.

A possible scenario is that a business opportunity consisting of a technological innovation is allocated to a company, and the company values it less than the insider does. Such a lower valuation may derive from the fact that the company will face organisational and strategic hurdles when trying to integrate the new technology in its production process.[37] For instance, this could occur because an incumbent company may face sunk costs, deriving from previous specific investments incompatible with the new investment opportunity.[38] Unless corrected through bargaining, such a misallocation may produce a further stream of inefficiencies. For instance, the final good or service may reach the market later in time, or it may be produced and marketed in smaller quantities and/or sold at a higher price per unit, or a poorer exploitation may result in a lower quality (dynamic inefficiency).

It is easy to underestimate how crucial dynamic efficiency is for consumer welfare. The Covid-19 crisis illustrates the importance of the time variable; the creation of an effective vaccine was a priority for the whole of the world's population and needed to be achieved quickly. When a given good or service is expected to solve a global issue, even a small acceleration in the progress towards delivering a solution can be of the utmost importance, because of the impacts it has on the whole world population. This is why the fundamental importance of the time variable is notable in broader contexts, especially in relation to this phase of our development as a human species living on Planet Earth: one more decade of carelessness for the environment and the situation may degenerate completely, assuming that this is not already inevitable. Although traditional economic analysis of the duty of loyalty has particularly focused on agency theory, the hypothesis recalled above shows that over-constraining agents' behaviour may mean refraining from achieving dynamic efficiency.[39] Achieving dynamic efficiency today looks indispensable for the future of Planet Earth, for the protection of the environment and for the enhancement of productive efficiency – which may mean less wasting of resources.[40] Whatever facilitates the efficient allocation of business opportunities, especially those directed to the

[37] Of course, this is not always the case. See C Hill and F Rothaermel, 'The Performance of Incumbent Firms in the Face of Radical Technological Innovation' (2003) 28 *Academy of Management Review* 257, 260–61.

[38] M Corradi, 'Corporate Opportunities Doctrines Tested in the Light of the Theory of the Firm – a European (and US) Comparative Perspective' (2016) 27 *European Business Law Review* 755, 772.

[39] See text at ch 5.VIII and 5.IX and accompanying notes.

[40] OECD, 'Towards a Green Growth' (2011), www.oecd.org/greengrowth/48012345.pdf. However, not everyone sees technological innovation as a source of solutions to environmental problems: M Cohen, 'Ecological Modernization and its Discontents: The American Environmental Movement's Resistance to an Innovation-driven Future' (2006) 38 *Futures* 528. A balanced and careful approach may represent a potential way forward. A Grunwald, 'Diverging Pathways to Overcoming the

improvement of the planet, may mean lesser effort is needed to correct certain downsides of capitalism, which are usually understood as negative externalities (such as, for example, pollution).[41]

The cost profiles of corporate opportunity rules may also be regarded from a competition perspective. They may end up reinforcing competition by protecting the innovative efforts of an incumbent company to introduce costly product and process innovation:

> This is what happened in the famous case of Standard Oil. At the beginning of its ascent in 1870, the price of refined kerosene was 26 cents a gallon, and Standard Oil's cost to produce it was 3 cents a gallon. At the height of its market power in 1885, the price of refined kerosene was 8 cents a gallon, and Standard Oil's cost to produce it was .452 cents a gallon … The evidence on Standard Oil suggests that Rockefeller was able to greatly improve the production process, allowing both great profits for himself, and substantially lower prices for consumers.[42]

Or, on the contrary, an incumbent company may not always be ready or may not find it economically convenient to adopt a certain technological innovation; it may be that only the insider will be ready to do so.[43] Apart from the most dramatic cases cited above (elaborating a vaccine for Covid-19; innovating for protecting the environment), when investment opportunities are related to technological innovation, whether they are implemented or not in a timely and productively efficient manner will affect consumer choice – hence dynamic efficiency. Again, it is crucial to enable inventive opportunities to be allocated to the party that is willing and able to exploit them in the most efficient way possible.

In the worst hypothetical scenario, corporate opportunity rules may be employed in a way similar to that of the so-called killer mergers. As Motta and Peitz explain: 'The main force behind the so called "killer acquisitions" … consists of the well-known Arrow replacement effect, whereby an incumbent has less incentive to develop an innovation because it would cannibalise (part of) its current profits'.[44] Following a similar rationale, an incumbent corporation – once it has understood that exploiting the innovation would be particularly costly, given its ongoing concern – may decide not only that it will not pursue the business opportunity, but that it will also prevent the insider from exploiting it, in order to stop dynamic competition.[45]

Environmental Crisis: A critique of Eco-modernism from a Technology Assessment Perspective' (2018) 197 *Journal of Cleaner Production* 1854.

[41] A Le Kama and D Ayong, 'Sustainable Growth, Renewable Resources and Pollution' (2001) 25 *Journal of Economic Dynamics and Control* 1911.

[42] A Diamond Jr, 'Schumpeter's Creative Destruction: A Review of the Evidence' (2006) 22 *Journal of Private Enterprise* 120, 124.

[43] See text at ch 5.VII and accompanying notes.

[44] M Motta and M Peitz, 'Big Tech Mergers' (2020) 'Information Economics and Policy', CEPR Discussion Paper No DP14353, ssrn.com/abstract=3526079.

[45] M Corradi and J Nowag, 'Enforcing corporate Opportunities Rules: Antitrust Risks and Antirust Failures' (2018), www.law.nyu.edu/sites/default/files/upload_documents/Corradi%20AND%20 Nowag.pdf.

To conclude this brief overview of at least some of the costs surrounding the enforcement of corporate opportunity rules, it can be noted that the set of variables we may be prompted to consider is rather complex. The genesis of corporate opportunity doctrines is connected to a simple request to a corporate insider who is a fiduciary to act ethically, ie in a purely disinterested way. The economic implications of this request have become apparent over time and have also emerged in various ways throughout the development of individual countries' industries.[46] Nowadays, the agency costs paradigm falls short in its ability to depict the economic dynamics surrounding these rules.

III. DETERRING MISAPPROPRIATIONS AND CONTAINING AGENCY COSTS

The Anatomy of Corporate Law refers to three main categories of conflict of interest[47] among the constituencies of a corporation 'which all have the character of what economists refer to as "agency problems" or "principal-agent" problems':[48] the one between shareholders and directors ('owners and managers' in the words of *The Anatomy*),[49] the one between controlling and noncontrolling shareholders ('owners who possess the majority or controlling interest in the firm and ... the minority or noncontrolling owners' in the words of *The Anatomy*)[50] and the one between 'the firm ... and the other parties with whom the firm contracts, such as creditors, employees, and customers'.[51]

The economic theory of agency is not necessarily limited to corporate law.[52] In general terms, it applies to situations where there is, on one hand, a so-called principal, who owns certain assets and, on the other hand, a so-called agent, who manages those assets on behalf of the principal. The agent is non-observable

[46] See text at ch 1.IV and accompanying notes.

[47] Note that in civil law, 'conflict of interest' is the term usually employed in statutory law not only for describing but also for regulating agency problems. For instance, Italian Civil Code, Art 2373 refers to 'conflitto di interessi del socio di societa' per azioni' (conflict of interest of the shareholder of a public company). Common law is often mostly descriptive – as the main categories employed for regulating specific conflicting conducts are self-dealing and the taking of corporate opportunities. See M O'Connor, 'How Should We Talk about Duty – Directors' Conflict-of-Interest Transactions and the ALI's Principles of Corporate Governance' (1992) 61 *George Washington University Law Review* 954. Note also that the statutory and jurisprudential categories employed in common law for regulating directors' fiduciary duties are of recent use in civil law. See K Pistor and C Xu, 'Fiduciary Duties in Transitional Civil Law Jurisdiction: Lessons from the Incompleteness of Law Theory' in C Milhaupt (ed), *Global Markets, Domestic Institutions: Corporate Law and Governance in a New Era of Cross-Border Deals* (Columbia University Press, 2003) 77.

[48] J Armour, H Hansmann and R Kraakman, 'Agency Problems and Legal Strategies' in Kraakman et al, *The Anatomy of Corporate Law* (2017) 29.

[49] ibid.

[50] ibid 30.

[51] ibid.

[52] B Mitnick, 'The Theory of Agency' (1975) 24 *Public Choice* 27: 'Examples include worker-boss, physician-patient, adviser-administrator, and parent-child relations'.

or limitedly observable by the principal. This entails an information asymmetry: the agent might manage the assets of the principal in a way that is not in line with the interests of the principal – hence in a conflicted way.[53] It is not that surprising that the economic agency theory has been successful in legal sciences. In fact, the situation described by this economic theory is one which often occurs in cases that are regulated by the law of trusts – or by other rules that historically derive from the law of trusts, as is the case with the duties of corporate directors.[54]

Jensen and Meckling provided the most notorious application of this theory to corporate law, developing a model that has capital structure implications.[55] According to Jensen and Meckling, hypothetically, in order for the managers not to shirk their duties, they should completely own the firm. Hence outside equity should be banned.[56] However, such a solution would entail several drawbacks. First, managers would be unable to diversify their investments.[57] Second, because of capital constraints, they would need to revert to debt financing, which in turn would introduce agency problems, as normally owners' and creditors' interests are likely to diverge.[58]

More recent reconstructions of the principal–agent relationship describe the interactions between the two in a far more sophisticated way: instead of depicting only one category of costs (ie costs deriving from an agent's disloyalty), they introduce the additional concept of competence costs.[59] Such costs are not a product of self-interest; they are simply the consequence of a lack of skills, information or intelligence[60] – failures that (especially in the case of the latter) often cannot easily be amended. Therefore, different corporate governance arrangements can be understood as attempts to minimise the sum of four kinds of costs, ie those deriving from the principal's disloyalty, the principal's incompetence, the agent's disloyalty and the agent's incompetence.[61] Although the taking of corporate opportunities normally has to do with a director's disloyalty, when it comes to a corporate opportunity's evaluation, the concept of competence will

[53] See for instance, as explained by S Ross, 'The Economic Theory of Agency: The Principal's Problem' (1973) 63 *The American Economic Review* (1973) 134. Note that this is a rather original way to look into the relationships between a corporation and its managers. Managers' 'fidelity' was already questioned by J Mill, *Principles of Political Economy* (Longmans, 1909) 139ff. Like Adam Smith, Mill thought that managers' cooperative spirit with the cooperation would prevail on their greed. A modern reinterpretation of Mill's work is provided by L Stout, 'On the Export of U.S. Style Corporate Fiduciary Duties to Other Cultures' in C Milhaup (ed), *Global Markets, Domestic Institutions* (Columbia University Press, 2003) 46.

[54] L Sealy, 'The Director as Trustee' [1967] *Cambridge Law Journal* 83.

[55] M Jensen and W Meckling, 'Theory of the Firm: Managerial Behaviour, Agency Costs and Ownership Structure' (1976) 3 *Journal of Financial Economics* 305.

[56] ibid 312ff.

[57] ibid 349.

[58] ibid 334ff.

[59] Goshen and Squire, 'Principal Costs' (2017) 785.

[60] ibid 795, table 1.

[61] ibid 770.

nonetheless turn out to be extremely useful for understanding the effectiveness of different kinds of arrangements.[62]

The most frequent manifestation of conflict of interest that is regulated by the duty of loyalty is self-dealing.[63] Self-dealing consists of a transaction between a corporation and one of its insiders (director or controlling shareholder). Hence it can be a manifestation of the first two types of conflict of interest identified in *The Anatomy* (ie directors/shareholders and controlling/non-controlling shareholders). By contrast, the taking of a corporate opportunity may involve all of the three kinds of conflict of interest outlined in *The Anatomy* (ie also the one between shareholders and constituencies such as creditors and employees).

The paradigmatic case of a director misappropriating a corporate opportunity is a classic example of the first type of conflict of interest identified in *The Anatomy*.[64] Corporate opportunities may also be appropriated by controlling shareholders when the corporate ownership structure is concentrated or in group contexts. For instance, there can be cases of a member of an entrepreneurial family and block-holder who – although not sitting on the board of the company – is aware of a given corporate opportunity, such as the possibility of acquiring a large amount of real estate at a convenient price, and decides to make the acquisition for themselves.[65] Takings by majority shareholders may also occur in corporate group contexts, where a corporate opportunity discovered within a subsidiary may be exploited by the parent company or by another subsidiary.[66] Additionally, stakeholders other than directors and majority shareholders may be involved in corporate opportunities cases. Firstly, they may be takers; such as in the case of an employee who seizes a business opportunity discovered whilst working for the company. This kind of taking is usually regulated by employment law rules[67] and/or by the contract between the company and the employee.[68]

Creditors, employees and customers may also experience the indirect consequences of a misappropriation of a corporate opportunity despite not being involved in the taking nor having any claim on the corporate opportunity arising from corporate law. For instance, the decision by a company to exploit a new technology that is also a corporate opportunity may have adverse consequences for creditors in the case where the introduction of that new technology increases

[62] See text at ch 4.V and accompanying notes; and text at ch 7.IV and accompanying notes.

[63] L Enriques, 'The Law on Company Directors' Self-Dealing: A Comparative Analysis' (2000) 2 *International and Comparative Corporate Law Journal* 297.

[64] For instance, *Guth v Loft* 5 A 2d 503 (Del 1939); see Easterbrook and Fischel, 'The Corporate Contract' (1989) 90ff.

[65] See text at ch 1.V.A and accompanying notes.

[66] *Sinclair Oil Corporation v Levien* 280 A.2d 717, 721 (Del 1971), where Sinclair had taken corporate opportunities away from Sinven.

[67] For instance, for Germany see the German Employees' Invention Act dated 25.07.1957, Bundesgesetzblatt I, 756.

[68] See text at ch 5.IV and accompanying footnotes.

the level of risk taken by the company or requires it to resort to other lenders.[69] The same kind of opportunity may also be detrimental to the interests of some incumbent employees, if they do not possess the skills necessary for managing a newly introduced technology and are therefore at risk of dismissal.[70] This kind of employee may be happy to see the corporate opportunity go elsewhere, although that may not be a long-term solution to their problem. It will be then only a matter of time before their employer goes out of the market or resolves to update its technology. Consumers may be negatively affected in terms of choice if, for example, a given corporate opportunity goes unexploited, as this has dynamic (in)efficiency consequences. Hence, if we take a broad stakeholder approach, we can understand that in many cases the taking of a corporate opportunity consisting of an invention affects in various ways different constituencies which have interests that are in conflict or are misaligned with those of the shareholders.

Given that corporate opportunity misappropriations affect different stakeholders in various and complex ways, a bright-line rule that assigns business opportunities by default to the corporation, can be seen as an optimal solution. In fact, the allocation of the entitlement to exploit business opportunities to the corporation is a linchpin around which potential negotiations between different parties can develop.[71] But since we cannot know *ex ante* who is the best exploiter of each business opportunity, a well-considered system should be based on two core principles: it should force disclosure of new business opportunities; and it should not over-deter efficient misappropriations.[72]

Claiming the centrality of deterrence with reference to corporate opportunity rules does not mean downplaying the importance of compliance and its capability of affecting corporate behaviours, especially when employed in the sense of building integrity through persuasion.[73] Empirical research has shown that compliance can be an extremely effective tool for containing agency costs.[74] Nonetheless, it has also been argued that corporate compliance may work in a suboptimal way when directed towards serving a system based on deterrence: at least in the United States of America (US), internal corporate compliance programs can be seen as 'the instrumentalities of hard law'.[75] For this reason, in the present moment, deterrence can be seen as the main function incarnated

[69] J Armour, G Hertig and H Kanda, 'Transactions with Creditors' in Kraakman (n 17) 109ff, 111ff.

[70] T Zwick, 'Employee Resistance against Innovations' (2002) 23 *International Journal of Manpower* 542.

[71] See text at ch 4.II and accompanying notes and text at ch 3.I and accompanying notes.

[72] See text at ch 4.III and accompanying notes.

[73] D Langevoort, 'Monitoring: The Behavorial Economics of Corporate Compliance with Law' (2002) 71 *Columbia Business Law Review* (2002) 71, 104ff.

[74] D Henry, 'Agency Costs, 'Ownership Structure and Corporate Governance Compliance: A Private Contracting Perspective' (2010) 18 *Pacific-Basin Finance Journal* 24.

[75] M Baer, 'Governing Corporate Compliance' (2009) 50 *Boston College Law Review* 949, 955.

by corporate opportunity rules and compliance as a way to prevent breaches *ex ante* or reveal breaches ex post. When a breach occurs, remedies not only address the problem on a general basis but also carry out a function of specific prevention – and offer the means to restore the position of the company in cases of misappropriation.[76]

Even if the agency costs paradigm, as applied to corporate opportunity rules, seems solid and its mechanisms are well-understood in corporate law theory and practice, one should be aware of the unprecedented challenges brought by the evolution of our globalised world. Many emerging variables are shaping our new world, and they may require the rethinking of traditional categories of analysis. Among such new variables, we can cite the modifications in ownership structure of many important global players;[77] the increasing pace and the unprecedented transformative effects of technological innovation, in particular of artificial intelligence[78] (both crucial to sustainability);[79] and, despite such evolution, a slowing of economic growth.[80] The last chapter of *The Anatomy* prompts us to prepare for corporate agency problems to be reinterpreted in potentially completely new ways.[81]

Besides the tight relationship between corporate opportunity rules and innovation,[82] what may in future shake the fundamental variables employed by today's scholars are the changes in ownership structure. Nowadays, in terms of ownership structure, we can observe an increasing heterogeneity across the globe. The US, which was renowned for its example of corporate environments characterised by the prevalence of dispersed ownership, is now witnessing a progressive concentration of corporate ownership in the hands of indexed funds.[83] Indexed funds have totally different features than the kind

[76] I am borrowing the term 'specific prevention' from criminal theory. See L Mazerolle and J Roehl, *Civil Remedies and Crime Prevention* (Criminal Justice Press, 1998), although normally breaches of corporate opportunity rules have no criminal consequences.

[77] See text to nn 82–85 and 89–91.

[78] M Haenlein and A Kaplan, 'A Brief History of Artificial Intelligence: On the Past, Present, and Future of Artificial Intelligence' (2019) 61 *California Management Review* 5. And for some environmental applications see, among many others, A Kaab et al, 'Combined Life Cycle Assessment and Artificial Intelligence for Prediction of Output Energy and Environmental Impacts of Sugarcane Production' (2019) 664 *Science of the Total Environment* 1005; H Nguyen and X-N Bui, 'Predicting Blast-induced Air Overpressure: a Robust Artificial Intelligence System Based on Artificial Neural Networks and Random Forest' (2019) 28 *Natural Resources Research* 893.

[79] See text at section V and accompanying notes.

[80] R Gordon, 'Declining American Economic Growth Despite Ongoing Innovation' (2018) 69 *Explorations in Economic History* 1.

[81] J Armour et al, 'Beyond the Anatomy' in Kraakman (n 17) 267.

[82] See text at ch 5.VIII–IX and accompanying notes.

[83] J Fichtner, E Heemskerk and J Garcia-Bernardo, 'Hidden Power of the Big Three? Passive Index Funds, Re-concentration of Corporate Ownership, and New Financial Risk' (2017) 19 *Business and Politics* 298: 'the Big Three in the United States and find that together they constitute the largest shareholder in 88 percent of the S&P 500 firms. In contrast to active funds, the Big Three hold relatively illiquid and permanent ownership positions'.

of block-holder that has characterised the continental European environment before and after privatisation.[84] Although things have changed recently, indexed funds have rarely been active investors. Normally, they neither possess nor exercise any strategic decisional power over the destiny of the corporations in which they invest.[85]

At the moment, it does not seem possible to predict whether investment funds will become strict enforcers of corporate opportunity rules against directors. It is equally difficult to foresee whether they will become so deeply involved in a corporation's decision-making process that they will be interested in reallocating corporate opportunities among investees, thus furthering their own interests – as may be happening in the context of venture capital.[86] Recent research highlights the function of indexed funds in promoting the adoption of good corporate governance practices, ie their stewardship function, instead of engaging in a detailed intervention in a company's decision-making.[87] Competition and corporate lawyers together are seeking answers to questions around the evolution of the role of indexed funds in corporate governance, while debating these issues in the very controversial research arena represented by parallel holding literature.[88] This part of the history still has to be written and it is premature even to dare to advance a prediction on the exact role that will be played by indexed funds in corporate governance.

Whilst the ownership structure of US corporations has been shaken by the parallel holding phenomenon, one cannot say the same with reference to Europe. In continental Europe, the traditional model based on controlling shareholders still seems to be prevalent, although there are differences between legal families, with the highest degree of ownership concentration found in the French family of legal systems and the lowest degree found in the Scandinavian family.[89]

In the People's Republic of China (PRC), the new competing economic superpower on the global scene, private corporations are often under PRC Communist Party monitoring.[90] Moreover, in the PRC, state-owned corporations are still

[84] F Barca and M Becht, *The Control of Corporate Europe* (Oxford University Press, 2002).

[85] J Fisch, A Hamdani and S Solomon, 'The New Titans of Wall Street: A Theoretical Framework for Passive Investors' (2019) 168 *University of Pennsylvania Law Review* 17, 50ff recall the traditional underdevelopment of indexed funds in terms of staff dedicated to governance matters, which may have rendered them unable to intervene systematically in the investees' corporate life. Nonetheless, the authors are also recording a progressive increase of such indexed funds' governance staff.

[86] See text at ch 6.IV.D and accompanying notes.

[87] Fisch, Hamdani and Solomon, 'The New Titans of Wall Street' (2019) 52ff.

[88] The debate was started by J Azar, M Schmalz and I Tecu, 'Anticompetitive Effects of Common Ownership' (2018) 73 *The Journal of Finance* 1513. For an effective criticism of the theory, see E Rock and D Rubinfeld, 'Common Ownership and Coordinated Effects (2020) 83 *Antitrust Law Journal* 201. For a refined study on the role of the governance variable within this debate, see S Hemphill and M Kahan, 'The Strategies of Anticompetitive Common Ownership' (2019) 129 *Yale Law Journal* 1392.

[89] G Aminadav and E Papaioannou, 'Corporate Control around the World' (2020) 75 *The Journal of Finance* 1191, 1216.

[90] X Yan and J Huang, 'Navigating Unknown Waters: The Chinese Communist Party's New Presence in the Private Sector' (2017) 17 *The China Review* 37.

very important economic players.[91] Corporate opportunity problems in the PRC might therefore have some similarities with those present in Europe before privatisation – although Chinese legislation in this area seems to be in its early stages.[92]

Given the heterogeneity of ownership structures across the globe, and given the emergence of previously unknown issues – such as the issue of a double layer of agency costs – traditional agency theory may need to include a much larger number of financial and institutional variables.[93] In particular, the observation of corporate governance and consequently corporate opportunity rules through the lenses of globalisation poses extremely complex questions, to which it would be hard to find a unitary reply. Nonetheless, if we refocus on a set of less ambitious questions, we can be reassured that understanding the different economic effects of corporate opportunity rules at a micro level can open a window also on the larger picture. Hence, the rationale and the logic pertaining to bargaining on corporate opportunities (which triggers a set of costs deriving from the specific investment in tangible and intangible assets that characterise the life of most businesses) seems still worth enquiring about.

IV. PROTECTING THE LONG-TERM BUSINESS DEVELOPMENT OF THE CORPORATION AND REDUCING HOLD-UP COSTS

Corporate opportunities may significantly affect the growth potential of a corporation. This is true not only with reference to those business opportunities that consist of a ground-breaking innovation. It is equally true for that myriad of less notable business opportunities thanks to which the corporation ends up concluding ordinary transactions with third parties for the purpose of carrying out its day-to-day business. Any kind of trade information may be valuable to the corporation: information on a stock of raw materials sold at particularly convenient price, on a piece of real estate that may be employed for building a new plant in the vicinity of the existing one, or simply on a possible new deal with a potential trade partner.

From a public policy perspective, we may be tempted to assume that a corporation's growth potential is a value that deserves to be protected per se – not least because of the abundance of management studies that attempt to find the

[91] C Zhang, 'How Much Do State-Owned Enterprises Contribute to China's GDP and Employment?' (2019), openknowledge.worldbank.org/bitstream/handle/10986/32306/How-Much-Do-State-Owned-Enterprises-Contribute-to-China-s-GDP-and-Employment.pdf?sequence=1.

[92] F Ma, 'Business Integrity v. Business Efficiency: The Corporate Opportunity Doctrine in China (2015) 23 *Journal of Financial Crime* 201.

[93] While an agency cost approach faces already many challenges even considering a more limited set of variables. See text at ch 1.VI and accompanying notes.

magic formula for rapid corporate growth.[94] Nonetheless, even from a mere legal point of view, this assumption may not be valid. If we consider antitrust law, we can see that corporate growth has never been considered desirable per se from a policy perspective – especially under the light of the structure–conduct–performance paradigm.[95] In various ways, antitrust and competition laws were conceived to prevent monopolisation[96] and abuse of dominant positions, and attached a special responsibility to super-dominant firms[97] – although the US and EU paths have taken different approaches.[98] Although the antitrust aversion to corporate growth originated as a political concern,[99] the aversion seems in line with the tenets of neoclassical economics, or at least is consistent with its assumptions. In fact, one of the assumptions of perfect competition is the existence of multiple firms which act as price-takers – a condition diametrically opposed to that of a monopoly.[100] From a theoretical perspective, we need to wait until the advent of the Chicago antitrust school – with its valorisation of economies of scale, economies of scope and network effects – for an understanding of the industrial value embedded in corporate growth.[101]

The development of the more lenient Chicago antitrust attitude towards corporate growth was anticipated by the work of several economists, including Ronald Coase. Unlike most of his colleagues, Coase was interested in seeing firms first-hand.[102] He formulated his theory of the firm while observing

[94] See for instance C Fombrun and S Wally, 'Structuring Small Firms for Rapid Growth' (1989) 4 *Journal of Business Venturing* 107; M Hay and K Kimya, 'Small Firm Growth: Intentions, Implementation and Impediments' (1994) 5 *Business Strategy Review* 49.

[95] L Weiss, 'The Structure-Conduct-Performance Paradigm and Antitrust' (1979) 127 *University of Pennsylvania Law Review* 1104.

[96] Sherman Act, s 2: 'Every person who shall monopolize, or attempt to monopolize, or combine or conspire with any other person or persons, to monopolize any part of the trade or commerce among the several states, or with foreign nations, shall be deemed guilty of a [felony]'. And see H Hovenkamp, 'The Monopolization Offense' (2000) 61 *Ohio State Law Journal* 61 1035.

[97] TFEU, Art 102. See in particular *Compagnie Maritime Belge Transports v Commission*, Joined Cases T-24–26 & 28/93, [1996] ECR II-1201, [106]–[07].

[98] M Schinkel and P LaRouche, 'Continental Drift in the Treatment of Dominant Firms' in R Blair and D Sokol, *The Oxford Handbook of International Antitrust Economics* (Oxford University Press, 2014) vol 2.

[99] G Stigler, 'The Origin of the Sherman Act' (1985) 14 *The Journal of Legal Studies* 1.

[100] The definition of 'perfect competition' is the fruit of a stratification of contributions by Smith, Walras and Cournot, and also by Italian economists such as Pareto and Barone. For an analysis of the origins of such concept in economics literature, see M Mosca and M Bradley, 'Perfect Competition According to Enrico Barone' (2013) 64 *Cahiers d'économie politique/Papers in Political Economy* 9, 11ff.

[101] On economies of scope, see D Teece, 'Economies of Scope and the Scope of the Enterprise' (1980) 1 *Journal of Economic Behavior & Organizations* 223; on economies of scale, see R Bade and M Parkin, *Foundations of Economics* (Pearson Education, 2011). On network effects, see M Katz and C Shapiro, 'Systems Competition and Network Effects' (1994) 8 *Journal of Economic Perspectives* 93.

[102] R Coase, '1991 Nobel Lecture: The Institutional Structure of Production' in O Williamson and S Winter (eds), *The Nature of the Firm* (Oxford University Press, 1993) 227, 228. Coase recalls as most of his colleagues at the time were interested in continuing the work of formalisation of Adam Smith's intuition on the coordination of the economy by way of a system of prices.

multiple plants[103] and seeking to understand why business reality, based on centralisation processes (ie on the firm), was so distant from the one depicted by the theory of perfect competition, based on organisational disintegration and arm's length transactions. Coase noted that setting up a firm implies replacing market transactions with the coordination of the different productive assets by the entrepreneur.[104]

According to Coase, 'The main reason why it is profitable to establish a firm would seem to be that there is a cost of using the price mechanism'.[105] Among the costs incurred while using the price mechanism, Coase identifies information costs,[106] negotiation costs, and contracting costs.[107] All such costs are reduced by way of setting up a firm.[108] Coase sees the relationships between the market-based and the firm-based models as totally flexible. In fact, he states that if the entrepreneur fails to contain costs, 'it is always possible to revert to the open market'.[109] Hence, he does not express a preference for a firm-based model. In contrast, he is well aware of the risks entailed by monopolies.[110]

Coase's enquiry goes beyond the prejudice against monopoly and tries to understand why production is not organised in one big firm. He explains that with the increased complexity of the organisation, and the multiplicity of transactions carried out within it, mistakes would inevitably increase – and this would entail further costs.[111] Coase foresees mistakes as one consequence – among others – of the 'dissimilarity of the transactions' carried out by the enlarged firm.[112]

Summing up Coase's ideas on the growth of firms, we can say that Coase explains it as a result of a temporary equilibrium between transaction costs incurred on the market and organisational costs occurring within firms.[113] If corporate opportunities are considered as mere assets, Coase does not provide us with a solution regarding their allocation. It seems that, like any other asset, they could either be the object of arm's length transactions or internalised within the firm. The only potential and loose indication as to which opportunities may be difficult to integrate within the firm is that pertaining to the 'dissimilarity of the transactions', which is in some ways similar to the idea of operations out of the line of business of the corporation, for which the integration process may be particularly costly.

[103] R Coase, 'The Nature of the Firm: Origin' in Williamson and Winter, *Nature of the Firm* (1993) 34.
[104] R Coase, 'The Nature of the Firm' (1937) 4 *Economica* 386, 390.
[105] ibid.
[106] ibid.
[107] ibid.
[108] ibid 391.
[109] ibid 392.
[110] ibid 394.
[111] ibid 397ff.
[112] ibid.
[113] ibid 404.

If Coase's theory of the firm does not provide a clear answer as to which would be the most efficient allocation of business opportunities, not even the 'Coase Theorem' helps us to find a correct solution.[114] In fact, given that transaction costs are always higher than zero, in general we should be concerned about the *ex ante* allocation of the entitlement to exploit business opportunities – in order to approximate allocative efficiency. Nonetheless, it is hard to predict how that could be done effectively. In a business reality characterised by positive transaction costs, Guido Calabresi suggests that 'The resource allocation aim is to approximate, both closely and cheaply, the result the market would bring about if bargaining actually were costless'.[115] Nonetheless, approximating the market result through *ex ante* allocation should be considered as a default option, once the attempt to bring transaction costs as close to zero as possible has failed.

Trying to predict how the parties would have bargained over a given business opportunity may be extremely challenging. Mark Moore has identified the challenges both in employing a weak hypothetical bargaining theory and in employing a strong one,[116] as first identified by Charny.[117] A weak bargaining hypothesis (one identifying the actual bargaining parties and the specificities of the case) cannot inform a general policy view.[118] Conversely, a strong bargaining hypothesis (a very abstract one, assuming rational actors and a clear bargaining context) may have a very limited normative relevance, because it would collide with 'its extreme counter-factuality in relation to the circumstances at hand'.[119]

Some substantiation of the corporate opportunity rules' function of protecting the corporation's growth potentials comes from Oliver Williamson. Williamson develops Coase's intuitions on the 'dissimilarity of transactions' and formulates his theory of 'idiosyncratic conditions of bilateral monopoly',[120] which is a way to describe specific investments. The core concept underlying Williamson's theory is that the value of a given investment has a relational component, which varies depending on the way it is combined with other factors (which can be intrinsic to the asset, or locational, or human).[121] For instance, if a company operates in the tile industry, a technological innovation tailored to its

[114] R Coase, 'The Problem of Social Cost' (1960) 3 *Journal of Law and Economics* 1.

[115] G Calabresi, 'Transaction Costs, Resource Allocation and Liability Rules – A Comment' (1968) 11 *Journal of Law and Economics* 67, 69.

[116] Moore (n 12) 248ff.

[117] D Charny, 'Hypothetical Bargains: The Normative Structure of Contract Interpretation (1991) 89 *Michigan Law Review* 1815.

[118] Moore (n 12) 241ff.

[119] ibid.

[120] O Williamson, 'Transaction-Cost Economics: The Governance of Contractual Relations' (1979) 22 *Journal of Law and Economics* 233, 242ff.

[121] Williamson identifies cases of asset-specific investments, location-specific investments and human capital-specific investments. For an analysis of these concepts see Corradi, 'Corporate Opportunities Doctrines' (2016) 772ff.

productive activity may be more valuable for that firm than for a firm operating in another sector.[122]

The 'varieties of capitalism' literature has stressed the diversity in the intensity of specific investments in different economic and political environments.[123] Nonetheless, it is clear that almost any firm will commit to a minimum level of specific investments – that is, it will locate its activity somewhere (unless it is purely internet-based), it will hire specialised employees, and it will have some (even minimal) assets, which can be either material or immaterial.[124] As a consequence of that, its productive efficiency may depend on its ability to keep on attracting investments that are specific to those environments it has already invested in. Corporate opportunity rules may be seen as a way to protect such specific investments – especially when they cover opportunities in the line of business of the corporation. This is the case with Delaware law, with its line of business rule.[125]

Similarly, civil law jurisdictions have protected such idiosyncrasies through the directors' duty not to compete with the corporation.[126] Even several civil law corporate opportunity rules based on the notion of 'interest' – such as the Italian one – may reach a comparable result.[127] This connection between industrial economics theory and corporate opportunity rules may even be employed for refining law-making in the future, because industrial organisation has refined such concepts to a higher degree than corporate law.[128]

A further argument that is antecedent to Williamson's research, but which carries similar policy implications, is the one developed by Harold Malmgrem. A company may have committed to specific investments that go well beyond physical assets or immaterial assets such as those protected by intellectual property (IP) law. In a world of imperfect information, a company's managers as a team acquire, through experience, the capability to collect and analyse business information.[129] In that sense, they may be able to easily contain costs incurred in contracting with third parties and deriving from poorly informed choices. In fact, in those domains in which they are experienced – that is in the line of business of the corporation – they may be able to reach the right business decisions

[122] For a discussion on innovation in the tile industry, see text at ch 1.VII and accompanying notes.

[123] See P Hall and D Soskice (eds), *Varieties of Capitalism* (Oxford University Press, 2001); B Hancke (ed), *Debating Varieties of Capitalism* (Oxford University Press, 2009); B Hancke, M Rhodes and M Thatcher (eds), *Beyond Varieties of Capitalism: Conflict, Contradiction and Complementarities in the European Economy* (Oxford University Press, 2007).

[124] Corradi (n 38) 773.

[125] *Guth v Loft*, 5 A 2d 503 (Del 1939); *Broz v Cellular Info Sys, Inc*, 673 A 2d 148 (Del 1996).

[126] Corradi (n 38) 810ff.

[127] Italian Civil Code, Art 2391(5) states that 'directors are also liable for damages they caused to the company by the use, for their own benefit or for the benefit of third parties, of data, information or business opportunities they became aware of in the exercise of their duties'.

[128] Corradi (n 38) 811.

[129] H Malmgren, 'Information, Expectations and the Theory of the Firm' (1961) 75 *Quarterly Journal of Economics* 399, 401.

with little cost and time expenditure. This may well be one more reason for allocating the entitlement to exploit business opportunities in the line of business to the corporation – as the team that will make decisions over their exploitation will do so efficiently.[130]

V. NON-PATENTABLE TECHNOLOGICAL INNOVATION AND A CORPORATE OPPORTUNITY DOCTRINE DILEMMA: THE COSTS OF PROTECTING v DIFFUSING INNOVATION

From an agency costs perspective, the analysis of corporate opportunities consisting of innovative ideas and/or technological innovations may not significantly differ from that of other corporate opportunities. Also, innovative business opportunities are assets of the corporation; they have an economic value, and they require legal protection against unauthorised misappropriations. They can also be sold to a third party – when efficient bargaining is possible. But if we approach the problem of investment opportunities in the field of innovation from a wider welfare perspective, encompassing allocative, productive and dynamic efficiency, overall perception of the most adequate policies in terms of protection of corporate opportunities may change significantly. A cost-based analysis that considers a full set of efficiency implications may need to refer to many more policy objectives than the mere need for a company to have its proprietary boundaries fully protected.

With reference to innovative corporations, the closest policy objective to the protection of corporate boundaries played by corporate opportunity rules may be the protection of innovation when IP rights protection is not available – for instance because a given invention is not patentable.[131] To put it into the words of Samila and Sorenson:

> Although companies can often protect inventions – discrete, codifiable entities – with patents, much innovation comes in the form of tacit knowledge: routines and practices that are not easy to codify. This knowledge can contribute crucially to the efficiency of firms and may serve as a source of competitive advantage. Yet, its tacit nature means that firms cannot easily separate it from the individuals in which it resides.[132]

The protection offered by corporate opportunity rules, in this case, is limited to potential misappropriations by insiders. Outsiders may always attempt to acquire information on the new technology and exploit it by way of setting up a

[130] Corradi (n 38) 777–78.

[131] J Golden, 'Patentable Subject Matter and Institutional Choice' (2010) 89 *Texas Law Review* 1041. And see also L Ouellette, 'Patentable Subject Matter and Nonpatent Innovation Incentives' (2015) 5 *University of California Irvine Law Review* 1115.

[132] S Samila and O Sorenson, 'Noncompete Covenants: Incentives to Innovate or Impediments to Growth' (2011) 57 *Management Science* 425, 427.

competing firm. Corporate opportunity rules could not be employed to prevent them from doing so.

The idea of protection of innovation from insiders' misappropriations is still consistent with the economic agency paradigm. Nonetheless, the economic agency paradigm may not provide sufficient explanations of the implications of corporate opportunity rules for technological innovation. The idea that any invention by a company's directors needs to be allocated to the company may miss several incentive dynamics which affect the innovation process within and outside the corporation. Such dynamics may be organisational, technological and/or financial, and they may open a window on the tangles represented by the different costs of intra-corporate technological innovation.

First, from an organisational perspective, in many cases complex innovations can be the fruit of a team effort.[133] Moreover, it may or may not happen that in such a team, one or more members offer a particularly significant contribution to the innovation at issue. In other cases, the invention is not the fruit of a team effort.[134] The invention skills may be concentrated in one founder who is endowed with diagonal thinking capabilities and who propels paradigm-shifting changes in a given product market or who creates new product markets – as in the case of many Silicon Valley innovations.[135]

Second, from a technological perspective, a given innovation may be developed for the purpose of starting up a new firm or it may be developed within an already operative firm. In the case where it is developed within an already operative firm, the innovation can be complementary to the firm's ongoing business activity or it can have little to do with it.

Third, certain innovations may require extremely significant research and development investments before they can even be started, as is the case for many patented pharmaceutical products.[136] In contrast, there are innovations that are the fruits of almost solitary work in garages and where the main investment is in human effort.[137]

The reason why I cite so many hypotheticals is that, from an innovation perspective, there may be different costs involved in allocating corporate opportunities *ex ante* depending on which of these variables occurs. In terms of incentives, it makes sense to assign – at least in part – the corporate opportunities

[133] A Drach-Zahavy and A Somech, 'Understanding Team Innovation: The Role of Team Processes and Structures' (2011) 5 *Group Dynamics: Theory, Research, and Practice* 111.

[134] See text at ch 5.II and accompanying notes. See also the criticism of the idea that sole inventors have ever existed in M Lemley, 'The Myth of the Sole Inventor' (2012) 110 *Michigan Law Review* 709, according to whom invention is also a social phenomenon in the cases of those we call 'sole inventors'.

[135] See text at ch 5.II and accompanying notes.

[136] Although this traditional view is increasingly criticised: D Light and R Warburton, 'Demythologizing the High Costs of Pharmaceutical Research' (2011) 6 *BioSocieties* 34.

[137] And a good number of social relationships. See P Audia and C Rider, 'A Garage and an Idea: What More Does an Entrepreneur Need?' (2005) 48 *California Management Review* 6.

to those who contribute to their invention. If the opportunity is the fruit of the creative efforts of an individual founder/director, then that individual is likely to be incentivised if they can reap at least a portion of the fruits of their efforts – as would occur without a corporate opportunity rule or in the case of a Solomonic division of the entitlement.[138] In the opposite case, if the opportunity is the fruit of a team effort of several founders/directors, a strict corporate opportunity rule may protect the team against opportunistic behaviours by members of the team.[139] At times, nevertheless, a strict corporate opportunity rule that allocates the business opportunity to the corporation may fail to compensate those members of the team that contribute the most to the innovation.[140]

Besides the problem of incentives to innovate provided to the innovator(s) who is/are active within the corporation, it is important to remember that it will be the corporation that exploits the innovation. The innovative skills and efforts of corporate directors and employees are intertwined with further assets, ie the productive assets employed for exploiting the innovation. These may be things, such as the machinery hosted in a productive plant, but also may be human skills, such as producers' intellectual and manual skills. This roughly corresponds to the idea of idiosyncrasy advanced by Williamson.[141] The complementarity of an innovation to the specific investments of a company may constitute an argument in favour of the allocation of such a corporate opportunity to the company that has committed to such investments, as a way to contain hold-up costs.[142]

Finally, in most cases, a technological innovation has only been realised thanks to the support of financers. When financing is provided in the form of equity, corporate law and corporate opportunity rules may play an important role in protecting and incentivising investments in innovation.[143] Again, the level of protection of the above-mentioned investment in innovation is likely to be higher with the increasing level of specificity. If a company is set up by an entrepreneur and a venture capital fund with the purpose of funding a specific product, we cannot expect to incentivise this kind of financing if we leave the entrepreneur free to run away with the projected innovation without repaying their funder's investments.[144]

Cost analysis becomes even more complex if we take a wider perspective, based on consumer welfare – ie if we consider the cost of such rules for the

[138] See text at ch 4.V and accompanying notes.

[139] See text at ch 5.IV and accompanying notes for similar reasoning with reference to employees' invention.

[140] See text at ch 4.V.

[141] O Williamson, 'Transaction-Cost Economics: The Governance of Contractual Relations' (1979) 22 *Journal of Law and Economics* 233, 242ff.

[142] Corradi (n 38) 772.

[143] Easterbrook and Fischel (n 9) 90ff.

[144] Therefore, venture capitalists revert to several legal tools to protect their investment from entrepreneurs' opportunism, among which corporate opportunity rules. See text at ch 6.IV.D and accompanying notes.

community at large. From this point of view, we can identify a potential trade-off between productive and dynamic efficiency. This may be seen in the light of a further trade-off; that is, the one between innovation spillovers – which are easier in a situation where the innovation freely circulates – and innovation incentives, which depend on protection of the innovation from free exploitation by third parties.[145] As already shown, in certain industries, it might be that benefits from spillovers of non-patentable, inexpensive and incremental innovation may be higher than those deriving from the protection of such technological innovation through corporate opportunity rules.[146]

As a conclusion, the costs connected to protection of non-patentable innovation through corporate opportunity rules can be very difficult to assess *ex ante*, as they can be connected to an extremely complex set of variables. This creates an argument in favour of a well-considered effort to increase the viability of bargaining on corporate opportunities.[147] Apart from bargaining, a set of different legal tools can be employed to adjust corporate opportunity doctrines to the vast set of relevant policy variables. These tools include well-considered drafting of corporate opportunity waivers (where allowed),[148] modulation of the different tests adopted for identifying corporate opportunities,[149] and special attention devoted to the legal treatment of resigning directors.[150]

VI. BARGAINING OVER CORPORATE OPPORTUNITIES, SETTING APPROPRIATE REMEDIES AND REDUCING TRANSACTION COSTS

From an economics point of view, the core objective of corporate opportunity rules should be to achieve allocative, productive and dynamic efficiency. As the set of variables that comes into play with reference to different kinds of corporate opportunities is extremely complex, I believe that bargaining is the most useful tool for allowing the different interests of the parties to emerge and to be traded on. Nonetheless, for bargaining to occur and to bear fruit, the normative system surrounding bargaining must both force disclosure of corporate opportunities by insiders and contain transaction costs so that bargaining is effective.[151]

With 'simpler' corporate opportunities, such as the opportunity to buy a residential estate at a given price, the main economic objective pursued by the system may be limited to allocative efficiency – ie the good should simply be

[145] See text at ch 1.VII and accompanying notes.
[146] ibid.
[147] See text at ch 4.I and accompanying notes.
[148] See text at ch 7.V and accompanying notes.
[149] See text at ch 7.III and accompanying notes.
[150] See text at ch 7.VI and accompanying notes.
[151] See text at ch 4.III–IV and accompanying notes.

allocated to the party who values it more. In other cases, when a corporate opportunity is the starting point for the production of goods or services, productive efficiency should be the core objective to be pursued: the subject entitled to exploit the business opportunity at issue should be the one who is able, through such exploitation, to produce the maximum quantity of good or services at the lowest costs possible.

As already said, there can be corporate opportunities which consist of inventions, and in this case the efficiency calculation becomes even more complex because it involves several dynamic variables that influence each other as well as a high degree of uncertainty. An invention might introduce efficiency in the industry where it applies. It might also create a completely new product. If the incumbent company is not technically able to implement the invention in its productive process, the invention may be implemented by one of its directors, who will eventually resign from the board.[152] Not only is the future success of such an invention uncertain, but the relationship between the newly founded corporation and the incumbent one is also covered in question marks. Once the invention is ready to be marketed, will the new product be a perfect substitute for the presently traded one? Or will it be differentiated in some aspects? Or will it be complementary to the existing one? Will the newly founded corporation support the incumbent one? Or will it become its fiercest competitor? All such considerations may occupy the minds of the parties in such a bargain and may be instrumental in defining their preferences.

Certainly, in the case of an innovative business opportunity, the ideal outcome is that it is allocated to its best exploiter; the second best outcome is that it is allocated to the less efficient exploiter. What should definitely be avoided is the third possible outcome, ie that the opportunity is held by the incumbent, who will deliberately not make use of it in order to avoid potential competition by its insider and a potential new entrant. Of all the possible outcomes, this last would produce the greatest welfare loss. This is one of the reasons why corporate opportunity rules have a crucial position within an economic environment based on technological innovation.

VII. CONCLUSIONS

The Covid-19 pandemic has made it clear that today's world is highly interconnected and integrated – both for good and for ill. Human existence in its traditional biosphere is threatened on multiple sides. This requires all human beings to take their share of responsibility in ensuring our planet is one where life is possible and hopefully pleasurable for both present and future generations.

[152] As happens at times with disruptive innovation. See text at ch 5.VII and 5.IX and accompanying notes.

There is an even greater responsibility upon corporations, which are today's major actors in the transformation of our world, to adapt their actions in order to pursue balance and harmony with the ecosphere. The improvement of the environmental situation and of our health both depend to a large extent on the development of technology. Therefore, drafting rules that facilitate or direct human efforts towards sound technological developments can be seen as an important contribution to the pursuit of sustainability.

Although certain areas of regulation, such as IP law, may seem to provide a more visible stimulus to innovation, corporate law is also often involved in setting incentives to innovate. Beyond traditional economic agency theory, corporate opportunity rules provide the corporation with a sort of homeostatic mechanism. While they ensure that all the necessary tangible and intangible assets for a corporation's development are kept within its proprietary boundaries, by allowing a degree of appropriation of business opportunities by corporate insiders, they grant communication of the insiders' knowledge and experience to the business environment that lies outside a particular corporation's boundaries. Such movement of knowledge building blocks may take the form of technological spillovers or simply contribute to knowledge recombination, even by way of a legal structure known as 'contracting for innovation'.[153]

To some extent, when it comes to corporate founders, it is often their business purpose and vision that moves with them and keeps them directing their energy and enthusiasm towards creating a better society – meaning they are operating well beyond the classic profit logic. This is why within the dynamics surrounding corporate opportunity rules we can often find opposing forces; on one hand, the need for protection of boundaries, and on the other hand, the need for the opening of such boundaries. Only a delicate balancing of such forces – and an accurate understanding of the trade-offs between different sets of costs – can ultimately achieve a harmonious dance between these forces; a dance which moves in the direction of the improvement of our society. The remedial system, affecting both the allocation and the bargaining over corporate opportunities, plays a crucial role in the balancing of the above-mentioned forces.

[153] See text at ch 5.V and accompanying notes.

3

An Economic Analysis of the Remedies for the Misappropriation of Corporate Opportunities

I. AN INTRODUCTION TO DETERRENCE FROM A PHILOSOPHICAL AND ECONOMIC PERSPECTIVE

A SET OF well-considered and policy-effective legal remedies may work as a linchpin around which a bargaining activity over corporate opportunities between a company and its directors can be organised.[1] Whichever way the entitlement to exploit business opportunities is allocated, the law will eventually provide a response to the breach of such legal entitlement – a response which we call legal sanction. Hence, the allocation of a business opportunity, which contains an obligation to abstain from misappropriations, and the connected legal sanctions operate interconnectedly.[2] They represent a comprehensive set of policy tools employed not only to distribute resources but also to affect economic actors' behaviours through incentives and counter-incentives, by way of creating costs and/or rewards for the parties in a transaction.[3] Knowledge of the remedial systems is crucial not only for understanding their capability to channel and orient the bargaining activity of economic actors, but also for appreciating the evolution of legal systems at large from a political and sociological perspective.

Since the dawn of civilisation, sovereigns and lawmakers have employed a variety of policy tools to encourage their subjects or citizens to abide by the law. In the Age of Enlightenment, Cesare Beccaria, in his *Dei Delitti e delle Pene*, opened his considerations on the 'proportion between crime and punishment' with the following statement: 'If pleasure and pain are the motors of sensitive

[1] See text at ch 4.II and accompanying notes.

[2] R Schwartz and S Orleans, 'On Legal Sanctions' (1967) 34 *The University of Chicago Law Review* 274: 'Sanctions are officially imposed punishments aimed at enforcement of legal obligations'.

[3] Or at least they are designed to achieve such objectives, although they are not necessarily successful, especially when there are strong countervailing pressures. See P Jones, 'Sanctions, Incentives, and Corporate Behavior' (1985) 27 *California Management Review* 122.

beings, if the invisible lawgiver of humanity has decreed rewards and punishments as one of the motives to impel men to even their noblest endavour'.[4]

Beccaria focuses on the profound 'spiritual' motivation instilled by remedies in the depth of the psyches of human beings who live in a society. From a more modern perspective and from the point of view of a state's citizens, the psychological perception of the remedial policy tools may boil down to two emotional dimensions: fear of punishment; and/or desire to adopt the above-mentioned behaviours out of acknowledgment of their (relative or absolute) benefits for the individual and for the society as a whole, besides any possible religious or philosophical motivation.[5] Nowadays, such an emotional dimension can also be observed through the scientific lenses of evolution and neurobiology. Pleasure and pain may be imprinted in our most primitive instincts.[6] Actually, from a neurobiological perspective, these two neuronal reactional paths seem to be extremely closely related – instead of being 'opposite' as they may be in the common cultural perception of emotional states.[7] This might contribute to explain why both have been successfully employed for ensuring that citizens abide by the law.

From the point of view of our cultural evolution, our civilisation, especially in the version which is most respectful of human rights, is clearly not in line with the 'an eye for an eye and a tooth for a tooth' principle – and not with the idea of inflicting pain in general – not even for a 'higher' purpose.[8] Apart from Gandhi's picturesque but truthful suggestion that a strict enforcement of the 'an eye for an eye' principle would quickly turn everyone blind,[9] there has been thorough scientific investigation on the limits of criminal deterrence.[10] Moreover, it is

[4] C Beccaria, *Dei Delitti e Delle Pene*, ch XXIII, trans by J Farrer, *Crimes and Punishment, Including a New Translation of Beccaria's Dei Delitti e delle Pene* (Chatto and Windus, 1880) 196. In the most ancient systems of law it would seem that a regulated and attentively calibrated imposition of pain was employed far more frequently than pleasure rewards. It is sufficient to take a quick look to the Hammurabi Code to see how easy it was to end up being put to death; see R Harper (ed), *The Code of Hammurabi* (University of Chicago Press, 1904) 11, paras 1–3 of the Code; 13–15, paras 6–11 of the Code; 17, paras 14–16 of the Code.

[5] Fear and desires have also been employed as categories for the meta-legal analysis of specific legislations. See for instance J-Y Son, 'Out of Fear or Desire? Toward a Better Understanding of Employees' Motivation to Follow IS Security Policies' (2011) 48 *Information & Management* 296, which also employs the categories of extrinsic versus intrinsic motivation, although such classifications of fear as extrinsic and desire as intrinsic (ibid 297) are surely questionable.

[6] Although the association of punishments with pain and of rewards with pleasure is not always that straightforward. S Leknes and I Tracey, 'Pain and Pleasure: Masters of Mankind' in M Kringelbach and K Berridge (eds) *Pleasures of the Brain* (Oxford University Press, 2010) 320.

[7] S Leknes and I Tracey, 'A Common Neurobiology for Pain and Pleasure' (2008) 9 *Nature Reviews Neuroscience* (2008) 314.

[8] Art 5 of the 'The Universal Declaration of Human Rights' proclaimed by the United Nations General Assembly in Paris on 10 December 1948. 'No one shall be subjected to torture or to cruel, inhuman or degrading treatment or punishment.'

[9] I Alli, *101 Selected Sayings of Mahatma Gandhi* (eBookIt, 2013) fn 8: 'an eye for an eye will only make the only world blind'.

[10] J Braithwaite, 'Minimally Sufficient Deterrence' (2018) 47 *Crime and Justice* 69: 'The evidence for the power of deterrence in reducing crime is thin, after all'.

easy to agree with Niccolò Machiavelli on the fact that the 'principe' (the ruler) would benefit more from having their orders obeyed out of love than out fear.[11] Love for those behaviours that are beneficial to the society as a whole may be one of the possible motors of compliance programmes.[12] Certainly, compliance with corporate opportunity rules should be explained and encouraged. In the words of Thomas More, the lawmaker 'should curb crime and, by educating his people properly, prevent it rather than allow it to increase and then punish it'.[13]

Unfortunately, it is equally understandable that a world without remedies – where humans have internalised all those principles that benefit both themselves and their fellow human beings – is perhaps utopic, and it has not been created yet.[14] While it is worth keeping alive the aspiration towards that ideal world and take relentless action to pursue it, one may consider the deterrence aspects embedded in legal remedies as a less desirable but a temporarily necessary aspect of legislation while the world is in an imperfect state – even though, clearly, they are not and they should not be its end point.[15]

I am clearly not advocating for the usefulness of imprisonment or even harsher penalties, and especially not in relation to breaches of corporate law. I am simply saying that the law – and also corporate law – should be ready to consider in a rational way a full range of tools for pursuing its objectives, beyond compliance. Therefore, when I refer to deterrence further on in the text, I normally refer to the idea of rendering a potentially detrimental behaviour not useful and not economically desirable for the perpetrator. I am not arguing in favour of inflicting any additional form of physical or moral pain. I also believe that the Law and Economics of optimal deterrence, as explained by Cooter and Freedman, can perfectly accommodate positions of dislike for the infliction of suffering as a way of advancing the promotion of legal values and the enhancement of our society as a whole.

[11] N Hochner, 'Machiavelli: Love and the Economy of Emotions' (2014) 32 *Italian Culture* (2014) 122. This clearly is an unconventional reading of Machiavelli's work. Nonetheless, Hochner has illustrated in detail that in Machiavelli's political thought love (intended as non-sexual love), and especially manifested as love for freedom, is prevalent over fear (ibid 128 ff).

[12] Although it has been empirically proven that, in different contexts (such as for instance the tax one), targeted messages trying to sensitise the addressees of tax regulations in relation to their civic duties has a modest effect on their compliance. M Chirico et al, 'An Experimental Evaluation of Notification Strategies to Increase Property Tax Compliance: Free-riding in the City of Brotherly Love' (2016) 30 *Tax Policy and the Economy* (2016) 129.

[13] T More, *Utopia* (Yale University Press, 2014) 42.

[14] ibid 42: 'he should curb crime and, by educating his people properly, prevent it rather than allow it to increase and then punish it; he should not be hasty to revive laws which are customarily ignored, especially those which are long disused because they were never desirable'.

[15] As a purely cultural notation, in the view of a recognition of the archetypes that have influenced Western civilisation, I think it is worth observing that perhaps not by pure chance the biblical *Book of Proverbs* mentions the fear of the Lord as the *beginning* of wisdom (and possibly righteousness as a by-product of wisdom) and not its end point (*Proverbs* 9:10). Clearly, this is a merely Western perspective, while wisdom has been viewed by different civilisations as rooted in many different sources. See J Birren and C Svensson, 'Wisdom in History' in R Sternberg and J Jordan, *A Handbook of Wisdom: Psychological Perspectives* (Cambridge University Press, 2005) 3.

From a fiduciary law perspective, the idea of rendering a given behaviour not desirable may also be understood as removing an unfair advantage. Such a viewpoint has been challenged by Golash:

> If we consider 'unfair advantage' in the context of all social advantages, it will be difficult to show that the typical criminal offender has more than his share. With respect to better-situated offenders, we would have a better chance of making the case that, as a result of crime, they had more than their fair share of advantages … To the extent that this is true, however, we can easily redress their unjust enrichment by repossessing their wrongful gains and give them back to the victims, thus reducing the victims' unfair burdens.[16]

Golash's pessimism is probably less justified with reference to situations that occur within the corporate context, such as the misappropriation of corporate opportunities. In fact, the monetary sums that represent the unfair advantage for the taker can well be employed for compensating the victims. However, the potential negative externalities which may derive from the misallocation of corporate opportunities (eg lower productive or dynamic efficiency) remain to some extent less easily addressed by the remedial system.[17] Nonetheless, such a misallocation cannot be considered as a pure consequence of the remedial system, which is only one of the factors that contribute to drive the allocation of business opportunities. The allocation itself is normally a consequence of bargaining.

To conclude, a Law and Economics approach to remedies, at least in this context, does not necessarily need to be seen as a dry operation, deprived of any ethical consideration. Ethical considerations, such as the repulsion for inflicting pain to others, should work as fundamental guiding principles when the lawmaker sets sanctions. This is why I seek to address here the problem of effectively containing the taking of corporate opportunities by rendering it economically inconvenient. Therefore, when I discuss punitive damages, I also refer to them as a tool for rendering misappropriations that are non-advantageous for the taker and not as properly 'punitive' remedies, as their denomination would suggest.

II. THE DISMISSAL OF A COMPANY'S DIRECTOR AS A CONSEQUENCE OF A MISAPPROPRIATION OF A CORPORATE OPPORTUNITY

Hypothetically, there are a number of models that regulate the removal of directors from their office as a consequence of a misappropriation of a corporate opportunity: no possibility of removal; removal *ad nutum* (ie without any justification)

[16] D Golash, *The Case Against Punishment: Retribution, Crime Prevention, and the Law* (NYU Press, 2005) 82–83. *cf* R Cooter and B Freedman, 'The Fiduciary Relationship: its Economic Character and Legal Consequences' (1991) 66 *New York University Law Review* 1045.

[17] See text at ch 5.VIII and accompanying notes.

upon a decision of the shareholders' assembly; removal by the shareholders' assembly, but where the decision to remove has to be specifically justified in relation to a misappropriation of a corporate opportunity; removal upon a decision of the board of directors or by the supervisory board in the dualistic model (again *ad nutum* or to be specifically justified); removal by court order; and automatic removal once misappropriation is ascertained.[18]

At times, the sanction of removal may have no or little deterrence effect per se, as in the case of a director who intends to resign voluntarily for the purpose of setting up an independent business activity that they could practically not run while being a director of their current company. In this case, it does not usually matter whether they are still in charge as a director in their old corporation or not at the moment of the taking of a corporate opportunity. If the purpose of such taking is setting up a new, incompatible business activity, sooner or later the director will resign and therefore will not be affected by the dismissal to any significant extent. Even if we assume that the director in our example has no intention to resign, their eventual removal might not be interpreted as a very effective sanction. The former insider will now have a new and (presumably) more lucrative business activity.[19]

As a consequence of the above, the removal of directors will presumably be effective as a remedy only in those cases in which the misappropriations at issue are small and repeated and they are carried out over a long time span (eg several acquisitions of a given merchandise at a particularly favourable market price) and the director intends to hide their wrongdoing, where possible, and continue working for the company. In such a case, there would be a trade-off between the earnings generated by the taking and the loss resulting from the dismissal (with consequent potential difficulties for the dismissed director in finding a new, similar position). However, the loss stemming from the dismissal would not be compensated for by the possibility of appropriating further corporate opportunities in future. The insider would no longer be working for the company after their dismissal; that is, they would no longer be able to appropriate corporate opportunities. The outcome of such a trade-off would clearly depend on the value of the opportunity. If the corporate opportunity at stake grants the taker an important profit that can be invested elsewhere with higher expected returns, it may well be that the trade-off plays in favour of the taking.[20] Therefore it may

[18] Note that in this context we focus on dismissal as a sanction for a breach of a duty of loyalty, ie as a way to contain agency costs. In alternative theoretical reconstructions, dismissal is seen as a remedy to the lack of competence of the agent. See Z Goshen and R Squire, 'Principal Costs: A New Theory for Corporate Law and Governance' (2017) 117 *Columbia Law Review* 767, 800. Note that for Goshen and Squire, ibid 802, 'If the managers are self-seeking but otherwise competent, the optimal solution might be more monitoring and better pay-based incentives'.

[19] One may also consider the alternative hypothesis that the insider wants to keep working for their corporation to use corporate resources to exploit a continuing corporate opportunity. Such a case would be easily detectable and would trigger immediate sanctions.

[20] Here I am not considering the possibility for the company to obtain a declaration of a proprietary constructive trust – I am separately analysing each remedy. See text at section III and accompanying notes.

well be said that such a trade-off can only be calculated on a case-by-case basis. As to the losses generated by the dismissal at issue, one has to take into consideration not only the monetary losses, but, clearly also the social ones; that is, the eventual adverse consequences in terms of loss of the social prestige connected to one's role in the corporation.

A specific but still very important point concerns the extent to which the dismissal affects the remuneration plan of the director, in particular with reference to benefits payable on loss of their office. If the misappropriation of a corporate opportunity is considered a breach of contract, it may well be that losing the benefits is perceived as a strong deterrent against misappropriations.

The hypothetical model where it is impossible to remove a director does not require comment, except for its lack of potential deterrence, regardless of the type of corporate opportunity at stake. When one considers the other earlier-cited legal models, such as those based on a decision to be taken by the shareholders' assembly or by the board of directors, the usual considerations that are advanced with reference to different constituencies apply also to these contexts. Therefore, where the board of directors has the choice of whether or not to remove the taker of a corporate opportunity, the decision may well be not to remove them in order to encourage the same amount of 'tolerance' of the perpetrator, if other board members find themselves in similar positions (so-called mutual back-scratching).[21] However, when the decision is made by disinterested shareholders, mutual back-scratching is unlikely to occur, unless all the directors are also shareholders of the corporation in question.

In terms of costs, the overall procedure, when entrusted to the shareholders' meeting, will usually be costlier than when entrusted to the board of directors. Calling and holding a shareholders' meeting is usually far more expensive than holding a board meeting.[22] Additionally, the procedure for calling a shareholders' assembly is more time-consuming than that for calling a board meeting; timing may be a very important factor in relation to business opportunities that require quick action.[23] Quick action is likely to be required any time the third party offering the opportunity at issue is ready to contract with parties other

[21] The phenomenon of mutual back-scratching is renowned especially with reference to directors' compensation. See I Brick, O Palmon and J Wald, 'CEO Compensation, Director Compensation, and Firm Performance: Evidence of Cronyism?' (2006) 12 *Journal of Corporate Finance* (2006) 403, 404.

[22] A shareholders' meeting will still have to take place, with personal participation or the use of proxies. Either way, the meeting has to be held in a given place, with actual people in attendance. Despite efforts to create the possibility for shareholders to digitally exercise their rights, several problems seem to stand in the way of such a system. See D Zetzsche, 'Shareholder Passivity, Cross-Border Voting and the Shareholder Rights Directive' (2008) 8 *Journal of Corporate Law Studies* 289.

[23] Moreover, a higher or lower degree of interaction usually anticipates the meeting within different countries which may in turn influence the outcome of the meeting in different ways. See D Zetzsche, 'Shareholder Interaction Preceding Shareholder Meetings of Public Corporations – A Six Country Comparison' (2012) 2 *European Company and Financial Law Review* 105.

than the company or its insider (in fact, this would clearly deprive the company of any corporate opportunity claim).

An important distinction between the case of the empowerment of the shareholders' meeting and the case of the involvement of the board of directors concerns the conditions that are required to remove the director who has misappropriated a corporate opportunity. If the legislation sets no condition for removal (ie, any director can be removed *ad nutum*), the fact that a director misappropriated a corporate opportunity will not necessarily appear to the public as the reason for such removal. By contrast, if proof of the misappropriation by the director is required, it goes without saying that that will entail further costs (and eventual difficulties) related to obtaining this proof.[24]

An alternative to a decision by shareholders or directors is recourse to the courts. In this case, there are several factors that determine the effectiveness of such a remedy; in particular, who is entitled to bring proceedings, where the burden of proof lies, and whether the judges are competent in terms of being able to understand the business situation underlying the misappropriation.[25]

A final potential model is one that automatically connects the judicial verification of the facts pertaining to the misappropriation of a corporate opportunity to the removal of the culpable director; that is, the corporation is not required to ask for removal. Recourse to the courts may preclude reconciliations unless the law does not forbid the reinstatement of the director in their position.

In civil law countries the model based on the shareholders' meeting competence prevails (with the exception of Germany, where the supervisory board is competent to decide removals).[26] However, there are some differences, at least in form, within the countries opting for removal by shareholders, as to whether or not the sanction of removal is expressly granted as a consequence of the violation of a director's duty. For instance, Article 2390, paragraph 2 of the Italian Civil Code expressly states that the director who has violated their duty not to compete with the corporation can be dismissed. By contrast, provisions on corporate opportunities do not include any specific reference to the removal of directors for eventual misappropriations (see Article 2391, paragraph 5 of the Italian Civil Code). In such cases we will need to refer to the general provisions on removal of directors.

An important point to be taken into consideration may be the necessity to prove that the dismissal is caused by the misappropriation of a corporate opportunity. Some jurisdictions grant directors who have been dismissed without

[24] See the Alarm.com case as explained in the text at ch 6.IV.E and accompanying notes.

[25] For a thorough analysis of all the implications deriving from the burden of proof, see R Posner, 'An Economic Approach to the Law of Evidence' (1999) 51 *Stanford Law Review* 1477. An example of an empirical analysis of the role of judges in shaping corporate law in Italy is provided by L Enriques, 'Do Corporate Law Judges Matter? Some Evidence from Milan' (2002) 3 *European Business Organization Law Review* 765.

[26] *Aktiengesetz*, para 84(3).

objective justification (for instance, Article 2383, paragraph 3 of the Italian Civil Code requires *giusta causa*, ie a 'good' or 'just' cause) the right to claim damages against the company. Italian jurisprudence shows that a violation of fiduciary duties (such as the misappropriation of corporate opportunities) would be an objective justification for a director's dismissal.[27] Similarly, in a case of a breach of *Aktiengesetz* (AktG) paragraph 88 (directors' duty not to compete with the corporation), German law allows dismissal without notice.[28] When it is difficult to prove such misappropriation, whether it is possible for the director to ask for compensation may significantly affect the deterrence element of the dismissal. In Spanish law, according to Article 224 of the *Ley de Sociedades de Capital*, a breach of directors' duties is a special cause for dismissal, that can be asked by any shareholders (*a solicitud de cualquier accionista*).

In UK law, in sharp contrast with pre-1948 British law, according to the Companies Act 2006 (CA 2006), s 168, a director can now be removed by ordinary resolution of the shareholders' meeting at any time, regardless of any contrasting agreement contained in a company's bylaws.[29] Moreover, the articles of the association may contain further specific grounds for the removal of directors (such as providing the board with the right to remove directors *ad nutum*).[30] Therefore, at a first glance, it may be said that the British system has significantly converged towards continental European models. Regardless of whether a misappropriation of a corporate opportunity can be proved, a disloyal director can be removed. Moreover, when, according to the company's bylaws, the board is competent to remove the director, the procedure will be even quicker compared to the one given to the shareholders' meeting.

It is particularly important to consider the financial consequences of such a removal. If a director is able to save themselves through 'golden parachutes', removal will hold no deterrence. First, the component of the remuneration of company directors in the UK that is set by contract is usually the larger source of income for executive directors.[31] Therefore, it will be necessary to consider how this component is affected by evidence or absence of evidence of the misappropriation of a corporate opportunity.

Normally, the CA 2006 preserves the right of directors to compensation for breach of contract in relation to removal.[32] However, in case of a serious breach

[27] M Aiello, 'Gli Amministratori di Società per Azioni' in P Rescigno (ed), *Trattato di Diritto Privato*, 2nd edn (UTET, 2013) tomo 6, vol 16, 1ff; more specifically, this has always been very clear with reference to the breach of directors' duty not to compete. See M Spolidoro, 'Il Divieto di Concorrenza per gli Amministratori di Società di Capitali' [1983] *Rivista delle Società* 1314, 1372.

[28] K Schmidt and M Lutter, *Aktiengesetz Kommentar*, 3rd edn (Ottoschmidt, 2015) vol 1, comment to para 88, 1353, 1360, point 14.

[29] P Davies and S Worthington (eds), *Gower and Davies' Principles of Modern Company Law*, 9th edn (Sweet & Maxwell, 2012) paras 14.49 ff.

[30] ibid 400.

[31] ibid 400.

[32] ibid 413.

of contract by a director, such protection will not operate.[33] A serious violation of the duty of loyalty, such as the misappropriation of a corporate opportunity, would clearly amount to a serious breach of contract. But such a violation would need to be proved. In the UK, given the higher remuneration enjoyed by directors, such evidence looks even more important than in continental Europe.[34] However, it is also true that if the company did not pay the director the benefits that were agreed by contract, the director would have to initiate litigation in order to recover their contractual termination benefits. If the director has some skeleton hiding in their closet, an attempt to recover their benefits may go very wrong.[35]

Regardless of the possibility of a contractual remedy, praxis seems to be to try to let the director go quietly in order to avoid scandal.[36] Therefore, contractual matters will usually be settled out of court, but this will not necessarily enable the director to receive all of their contractual entitlements. The proportion of the benefits they succeed in recovering will depend on the strength of their bargaining position (and this in turn will depend to a large extent on the risks they may run into if they decide to litigate). This shows that at times, institutional complementarities that exist beside legal rules may exert significant influence on the way remedies are applied within a given jurisdiction.[37] By contrast with the UK's praxis to attempt to avoid scandal, German praxis seems to refer to the possibility of including in executive managers' employment contracts further penalties for the violation of the directors' duty not to compete.[38]

Under Delaware law, directors are elected by default every year by a majority of shareholders, unless otherwise specified in the constitutional document.[39] Any director, or the entire board of directors, may be removed, with or without cause, by the majority of shareholders who are entitled to vote at an election of directors.[40] Contrary to what the default rules may lead one to think, an analysis of the Delaware corporate praxis suggests that directors are usually entrenched by the practice of so-called staggered boards.[41] Although that

[33] ibid 415.

[34] For comparative studies on the remuneration of directors, see M Conyon and K Murphy, 'Stock-Based Executive Compensation' in J McCahery et al (eds), *Corporate Governance Regimes* (Oxford University Press, 2002) 625ff and R Crespi, C Gispert and L Rennebog, 'Cash-Based Executive Compensation in Spain and in the UK', ibid 677ff. See also A Cahn and D Donald, *Comparative Company Law* (Cambridge University Press, 2010) 416ff.

[35] In *Bairstow v Queens Moat Houses* [2001] EWCA Civ 81, this strategy went spectacularly wrong: the director sued the company for damages for breach of contract. He ended up liable for the company's counterclaim and was ordered to repay many millions to the company for unlawful distributions.

[36] Davies and Worthington, *Principles of Modern Company Law* (2012) para 16.186.

[37] On the concept of institutional complementarity, see ch 1.II and accompanying notes.

[38] Schmidt and Lutter, *Aktiengesetz Kommentar* (2015) para 14.

[39] Delaware General Corporation Law (DGCL), ss 211(b) and 216(3).

[40] DGCL, s 141(k).

[41] See L Bebchuk, J Coates IV and G Subramanian, 'The Powerful Antitakeover Force of Staggered Boards: Further Findings and a Reply to Symposium Participants' (2002) 55 *Stanford Law Review* 885. For the relevance of staggered boards within the debate on private ordering see M Moore, *Corporate Governance in the Shadow of the State* (Hart Publishing, 2013) 103ff.

practice has apparently declined recently, it still plays a role in Delaware corporate governance practice.[42] Nevertheless, directors who are elected to staggered boards can be removed with cause. Therefore, in the US (Delaware) case, the possibility of proving any misappropriation looks particularly important. Absence of cause, unlike in most European jurisdictions, will make the early removal *ad nutum* of directors impossible. A further obstacle to the removal of directors derives from the fact that shareholders can only vote to remove the director in question at the annual meeting. In fact, there seems not to be any other stockholder meetings apart from the annual meeting.[43] Stockholders are not entitled to call a special meeting, unless the certificate of incorporation or the bylaws expressly authorise one or more shareholders to call the meeting.[44]

To conclude, there is a certain degree of homogeneity in relation to directors' removal in European corporate laws. This means that the possibility of removing a director *ad nutum* always exists. Moreover, the possibility of proving a violation of fiduciary duties may make a difference to the possibility of the director claiming damages for a dismissal without cause. By contrast, Delaware corporate law does not allow removal *ad nutum*. Therefore, the possibility to prove the existence of a misappropriation is even more crucial than in European jurisdictions. In some specific contexts, especially those of small and repeated takings, the dismissal of a director may be very effective, and most jurisdictions seem to provide for this course of action. Moreover, loss of contractual employment benefits or the imposition of contractual penalties connected to the dismissal may have further deterrence effects.

III. GAIN-BASED REMEDIES IN COMMON LAW: ACCOUNT OF PROFITS AND DISGORGEMENT OF PROFITS ASSISTED BY A PERSONAL OR PROPRIETARY CONSTRUCTIVE TRUST

CA 2006, s 178 provides that 'the consequences of a breach (or threatened breach) of ss. 171 to 177 are the same as would apply if the corresponding common law rule or equitable duty applied'. In other words, unlike other national laws, CA 2006 does not codify the remedies for breach of directors' duties.[45]

[42] Research has shown a staggered board can reduce firm value. See L Bebchuk and A Cohen, 'The Costs of Entrenched Boards' (2005) 78 *Journal of Financial Economics* 409. See also R-J Guo, T Kruse and T Nohel, 'Undoing the Powerful Anti-Takeover Force of Staggered Boards' (2008) 14 *Journal of Corporate Finance* 274.

[43] DGCL, s 211(b).

[44] DGCL, s 211(d).

[45] R Nolan, 'Enacting Civil Remedies in Company Law' (2001) 1 *Journal of Corporate Law Studies* 245, 249. According to Nolan, the main challenge would be the codification of proprietary remedies in equity, given the doctrinal divergencies in this subject matter.

An account of profits assisted by a constructive trust is the most frequent UK equitable remedy against a misappropriation of a corporate opportunity.[46] This kind of remedial constructive trust is not a general remedy.[47] Nonetheless, it is worth remembering that a company director is regarded as being a trustee in relation to the company's asset, even beside any breach of their duties to the company. Therefore, if a director, as a result of a violation of their duty of loyalty to the company, receives assets which should have instead been offered to the company, a constructive trust can be declared. This is not regarded as a remedial constructive trust.[48]

A remedial constructive trust, instead, is a means through which a court can impose an account profit. Depending on its formulation, it can be interpreted either as a proprietary or as a personal remedy. The distinction between proprietary and personal remedies affects two main areas: the legal treatment of the creditors of insolvent directors and the tracing of the assets following a misappropriation of a corporate opportunity.[49]

With reference to the case of insolvency, a proprietary remedy grants the constructive beneficiary priority over the creditors of the trustees. By contrast, such priority is not granted in the case of a personal remedy. As to tracing, a proprietary remedy allows the tracing of all the profits derived from subsequent reinvestments. In contrast, a personal remedy provides only the disgorgement of the immediate profits of the misappropriation.

When an account of profits/constructive trust is administered in the form of a proprietary remedy, it can have the effect of rendering the legal condition of the taker extremely uncertain – hence triggering a strong psychological reaction which traditional Law and Economics might fail to consider to its full extent.[50] In other words, there may be a deterrent potential in this remedy which goes beyond the mere quantum of the disgorgement.

Say, for instance, that a young director of a rather small company who has great entrepreneurial skills seizes a corporate opportunity and subsequently develops a series of business activities over time. Each time the new company is sold through an initial public offering (IPO) or to a private acquirer, our entrepreneur and director reinvests their profits in a new venture. This is not uncommon for those very creative entrepreneurs who operate in an innovative start-up environment.[51] Now, from a policy perspective, although the original

[46] See, for UK law, Davies and Worthington (n 29) paras 16.184ff, and for US law, E Orlinsky, 'Corporate Opportunity Doctrine and Interested Director Transactions: A Framework for Analysis in an Attempt to Restore Predictability' (1999) 24 *Delaware Journal of Corporate Law* 451, 472 and 475.

[47] See Lord Browne-Wilkinson in *Westdeutsche Landesbank Girozentrale v Islington London Borough Council* [1996] AC 669, 714–16.

[48] *FHR European Ventures LLP and others v Cedar Capital Partners LLC* [2014] UKSC 45.

[49] Such different results are very clear in *A-G for Hong Kong v Reid* [1994] 1 AC 324, where one can read the main features of a proprietary conception of constructive trust.

[50] J Rachlinsky, 'New Law and Psychology: A Reply to Critics, Skeptics, and Cautious Supporters' (1990–2000) 85 *Cornell Law Review* 739, 741–43.

[51] See text at ch 5.VIII and accompanying notes.

misappropriation may require deterrence, it would also seem efficient to incentivise the subsequent reinvestments and the creative activity connected to them. Under a proprietary remedy, any subsequent reinvestment can be traced by the courts, which can then declare a constructive trust functional to the disgorgement of the profits to the corporation that was originally deprived of its corporate opportunity. Such a remedy may have at least two adverse consequences. First, it may discourage not only one-shot takings, but also the entire set of subsequent activities carried out by the original insider. Second, it may generate a sort of adverse selection effect. In fact, only those directors who are less confident in their ability to gain out subsequent reinvestments will risk being subject to this sanction.[52]

Nonetheless, if we consider the proprietary version of the constructive trust/account of profits sanction from the mere point of view of deterrence, it may approximate better efficient deterrence. It is true that the deterrent effects of uncertainty are difficult to quantify. However, they may constitute a significant drawback for successful directors/entrepreneurs who are willing to leave the corporation and set up their own business. The presence of such a remedy may simply suggest that they should offer full disclosure of the corporate opportunity, in order to leave with a clean pair of hands.

One may wonder whether UK courts grant to companies a personal or proprietary version of the constructive trust/account of profits against a director who has misappropriated a corporate opportunity. This has not always been clear.

Often, UK courts have applied an account of profits to corporate opportunity cases,[53] but they have not specified whether the remedy was personal or proprietary. In those cases where they have applied the remedy also to third parties, it can be deduced that they have intended the remedy as proprietary[54] – but what about the other cases? The uncertainty around the nature of the constructive trust/account of profits remedy in corporate opportunity contexts has raised an intense debate both in doctrine and in jurisprudence.[55]

[52] M Corradi, 'Securing Corporate Opportunities in Europe – Comparative Notes on Monetary Remedies and on the Potential Evolution of the Remedial System' (2018) 18 *Journal of Corporate Law Studies* 439, 451–52.

[53] *Regal (Hastings) v Gulliver* [1942] UKHL 1; *Boardman v Phipps* [1966] UKHL 2; *Industrial Development Consultants Ltd v Cooley* [1972] 1 WLR 443; *Bhullar v Bhullar* [2003] EWCA Civ 424.

[54] *Cook v Deeks* [1916] AC 554 as explained by Lewison LJ in *FHR v Mankarious* [2013] EWCA Civ 17, para 45: 'The Privy Council did not make any declaration of trust but ordered the taking of an account. On the face of it this would appear to be a personal remedy. But the account was ordered not only against Deeks and his co-directors but also against the Dominion Construction Company. Since the Dominion Construction Company was not itself a fiduciary, the order against it could only be justified on the basis that it was in knowing receipt of trust property. Thus, the principal must have had a proprietary interest in the contract'.

[55] R Goode, 'Proprietary Liability for Secret Profits – A Reply' (2011) 127 *Law Quarterly Review* 493; A Hicks, 'The Remedial Principle in *Keech v Sandford* Reconsidered' (2010) 69 *Cambridge Law Journal* 287; G Virgo, 'Profits Obtained in Breach of Fiduciary Duty: Personal or Proprietary Claim?' (2011) 70 *Cambridge Law Journal* 502; P Watts, '*Tyrrell v Bank of London* – an Inside

Lord Neuberger, in the Supreme Court's decision *FHR v Mankarious*,[56] attempted a clarification of the principle. He stated that

> at least in some cases, where an agent acquires a benefit which came to his notice as a result of his fiduciary position, or pursuant to an opportunity which results from his fiduciary position, the equitable rule ('the rule') is that he is to be treated as having acquired the benefit on behalf of his principal, so that it is beneficially owned by the principal. In such cases, the principal has a proprietary remedy in addition to his personal remedy against the agent, and the principal can elect between the two remedies.[57]

Lord Neuberger based his final ruling also on corporate opportunity cases.[58] He confirmed that the fiduciary position of a company's director attracts the rule he previously formulated in rather general terms, bypassing the law of trusts:

> The agent owes a duty of undivided loyalty to the principal, unless the latter has given his informed consent to some less demanding standard of duty. The principal is thus entitled to the entire benefit of the agent's acts in the course of his agency … The agent's duty is accordingly to deliver up to his principal the benefit which he has obtained, and not simply to pay compensation for having obtained it in excess of his authority. The only way that legal effect can be given to an obligation to deliver up specific property to the principal is by treating the principal as specifically entitled to it.[59]

In *FHR v Mankarious*, Lord Neuberger expressly cited *Chan v Zacharia*,[60] a corporate opportunity case – which may induce us to think with that, according to Lord Neuberger's doctrinal orientation, a proprietary remedy will normally be applied to misappropriations of corporate opportunities.[61]

If at present the constructive trust/account of profits remedy is intended as proprietary, it may display some punitive element. This means that it cannot be conceived as a mere restitution for subtractive unjust enrichment – because otherwise it would be limited to the profits that were made out of the first exploitation of the business opportunity taken from the corporation. The idea that the remedy at issue is not a mere parasitic category of unjust enrichment had already been proposed by Sarah Worthington before Lord Neuberger's decision in *FHR v Mankarious*.[62] Worthington has highlighted the different

Look at an Inside Job' (2013) 129 *Law Quarterly Review* 527; W Swadling, 'Constructive Trusts and Breach of Fiduciary Duty' (2012) 18 *Trust & Trustees* 98; D Hayton, 'Proprietary Liability for Secret Profits' (2011) 127 *Law Quarterly Review* 487; S Worthington, 'Fiduciary Duties and Proprietary Remedies: Addressing the Failure of Equitable Formulae' (2013) 72 *Cambridge Law Journal* 720.

56 [2014] UKSC 45.

57 ibid para 7.

58 ibid para 14.

59 ibid para 33.

60 *FHR v Mankarious* (n 56) [45], reporting *Chan v Zacharia* (1984) 154 CLR 178: 'any benefit obtained in circumstances where a conflict … existed … or … by reason of his fiduciary position or of opportunity or knowledge resulting from it … is held by the fiduciary as constructive trustee'.

61 Corradi, 'Securing Corporate Opportunities in Europe' (2018) 451.

62 S Worthington, 'Reconsidering Disgorgement for Wrongs' (1999) 62 *Modern Law Review* 218, 219ff.

function played by equitable remedies, which is prophylactic and not merely restorative or compensatory.[63] In fact, in this context, fiduciary law is concerned with proscribing certain activities, not with precluding particular outcomes. The appropriate remedial response for breaches of these equitable obligations is disgorgement because this is the remedy which best supports the legal obligation being enforced.[64]

If it is true that the constructive trust/account of profit remedy is prophylactic and aims to preserve the effectiveness of certain fiduciary duties, one may wonder whether we shall abstract this function from the nature of this specific remedy. If it is the function that matters, that is providing enough deterrence for preventing the violation of the duty of loyalty, one may also ask whether we should consider – at least from a policy perspective – remedies with the same deterrence power as a potential way forward for engineering an efficient remedial system.[65] This seems to happen in Canadian Law, as it results from the words of Chief Justice McLachlin, in *Strother v 3464920 Canada Inc*:

> Underlying this debate is the tension between the need to deter fiduciaries from abusing their trust on the one hand, and the goal of achieving a remedy that is fair to all those affected, on the other where extra deterrence is required, it is better achieved by remedies such as exemplary damages, which unlike account [of profits], can be tailored to the particular situation.[66]

Common law evolves through (often slow and progressive) erosion of past doctrinal orientations, leaving a degree of freedom to the creative skills of courts. Recent reforms brought to the corporate laws of many civil law countries seemed to represent a great chance to embrace a clear policy line in terms of corporate opportunity rules – that is, a policy line also reflecting the awareness matured in common law jurisdictions in the same areas of the law. One may wonder whether the evolution of the civil law remedial systems offers a chance to pursue such a policy line effectively.

IV. GAIN-BASED REMEDIES IN CIVIL LAW JURISDICTIONS: THE SPANISH 'ENRIQUICIMIENTO INJUSTO' AND THE GERMAN 'EINTRITTSRECHT'

Directors may devote a large amount of time and effort to the pursuance of a given opportunity. This may well happen outside their employment time and/or

[63] Note how this is in line also with the ideas advanced by M Conaglen, *Fiduciary Loyalty* (Hart Publishing, 2010) on the prophylactic function of fiduciary duties.

[64] Worthington, 'Reconsidering disgorgement' (1999) 237ff.

[65] J Berryman, 'Equitable Compensation for Breach by Fact-Based Fiduciaries: Tentative Thoughts on Clarifying Remedial Goals' (1999) 37 *Alberta Law Review* 95. Nonetheless, note that not everyone agrees with the deterring function of fiduciary remedies. See for instance S Bray, 'Fiduciary Remedies' in E Criddle, P Miller and R Sitkoff (eds), *The Oxford Handbook of Fiduciary Law* (Oxford University Press, 2019) 449, 467: 'Fiduciary remedies, by and large, do not punish. They are not what one would expect of a set of remedies designed for optimal deterrence'.

[66] *Strother v 3464920 Canada Inc*, 2007 SCC 24, [2007] 2 SCR 177.

may encompass activities far beyond what their duties to the corporation require them to do. This has to be kept in mind when we focus on unjust enrichment, because the line between what is just and unjust may be difficult to trace in the context of corporate opportunities.

From a wider remedial perspective, one has to acknowledge that the absence of equitable remedies in civil law renders unjust enrichment – at least potentially – a far more precious legal tool in civil law than in common law. The legal development of the doctrine of unjust enrichment has followed often winding paths. 'While under the common law the principle of enrichment has endured a long struggle for recognition, in civil systems it has been acknowledged for centuries.'[67] A few significant differences still exist between the civil law and the common law approach, but I would argue that there is no superiority of civil law over common law or vice versa in this field of the law.[68]

'Unjust enrichment', or, in most Latin countries, 'enrichment without cause',[69] has a common root in Roman law. The most-cited source on its origins is attributed to Pomponius, as reported in the *Corpus Iuris*: 'Iure natura aequum est neminem cum alterius detrimento et iniuria fieri locupletiorem'.[70] As Reinhard Zimmermann notes, the core difference between the law of delicts and the law of unjust enrichment is that the first looks at the condition of the plaintiff, whereas the second focuses on the condition of the defendant – it being immaterial whether the plaintiff has suffered a loss or not.[71] Hence, as the name suggests, the rules at issue pertain to 'a law of unjustified enrichment and not of unjustified loss'.[72] From a taxonomical perspective, and following Zimmermann, the kind of unjust enrichment that could be employed in corporate opportunity cases would not be an 'enrichment-by-transfer claim' but an 'Enrichment-in-any-other-way' claim.[73] A director who has exploited a corporate opportunity for their own benefit, on top of having deprived the corporation of the profits deriving from such exploitation, has enriched themselves 'without cause'.

Even though, in practice, restitution for unjust enrichment may look similar to constructive trust and account of profits, there is at least one important distinction between the two which is worth stressing. Whereas in some of the jurisprudential and doctrinal interpretations recalled in the previous section,

[67] B Dickson, 'Unjust Enrichment Claims: A Comparative Overview' (1995) 54 *Cambridge Law Journal* 100.

[68] G Dannemann, *The German Law of Unjustified Enrichment and Restitution: A Comparative Introduction* (Oxford University Press, 2009) 179ff.

[69] V Gomes and J Manuel, 'Unjust Enrichment: A Few Comparative Remarks' (2001) 9 *European Review of Private Law* 449.

[70] Justinianus D 50, 17, 206. R Zimmermann, 'Unjustified Enrichment: The Modern Civilian Approach' (1995) 15 *Oxford Journal of Legal Studies* 403, prefers to cite the original version by Pomponius, Pomp D, 12,6,14, which does not refer to 'iniuria'.

[71] Zimmermann, 'Unjustified Enrichment' (1995) 403.

[72] ibid 404.

[73] ibid 417.

an account of profits may incorporate a punitive element, unjust enrichment has not been traditionally interpreted in such a sense.[74] This means that all the speculations on the functional continuity between equitable remedies such as the account of profits and the punitive damages cannot be applied automatically to unjust enrichment. I cannot exclude the possibility that if we look to the way unjust enrichment has recently been applied as a remedy for the breach of the duty of loyalty, we may see that the underlying policy reason is punitive. Nonetheless, this should be confirmed by further jurisprudential studies, and such teleological interpretation should be coordinated with the general law of unjust enrichment within each jurisdiction.

The law system that seems to have made the most effective use of the potentials of unjust enrichment as a remedy against the misappropriations of corporate opportunities is the Spanish one. The 2014 reform of Spanish company law[75] has introduced a new provision stating that '[l]a infracción del deber de lealtad determinará no solo la obligación de indemnizar el daño causado al patrimonio social, sino también la de devolver a la sociedad el enriquecimiento injusto obtenido por el administrador' (a breach of the duty of loyalty will determine not only the obligation to the company for damages, but also the obligation to return to the company the unjust enrichment obtained by the director).[76]

A similar provision has already been contained in Spanish partnership law since 1885.[77] It mandated a cumulative application of the remedies of unjust enrichment together with damages.[78] Hence, although the Spanish explicit application of unjust enrichment rules to the misappropriation of corporate opportunities in the case of a public company is unique among European civil law systems, one has to acknowledge that it derives from a path dependency first established in an adjacent area of Spanish organisational law.

Ex ante a set of laws cannot decide which remedy will be the most effective for the purpose of preventing misappropriations of corporate opportunities. In fact, if the insider values the opportunity more than the corporation does, then a disgorgement of profits will represent a higher sum than the one the company could have made thanks to exploitation of the investment opportunity at issue.[79] This latest sum would correspond to the amount of damages paid by the insider to compensate the company's loss. By contrast, if the corporation values the corporate opportunity more than the insider does, the sum corresponding to the

[74] P Gallo, 'Unjust Enrichment: A Comparative Analysis' (1992) 40 *American Journal of Comparative Law* 431; Dickson, 'Unjust Enrichment Claims' (1995) 111ff.

[75] Law 31/2014, 3d of December 2014.

[76] 'Ley de Sociedades de Capital' (Spanish Company Act, introduced by Real Decreto Legislativo n1 of the 2nd July 2010), Art 227(2).

[77] 'Código de Comercio' (Spanish Commercial Code, introduced by Real Decreto of the 22nd August 1885), Art 136.

[78] C Paz-Ares, 'La Sociedad Colectiva: Posicion del Socio y Distribucion de Resultados' in R Uria and A Mendez, *Curso de Derecho Mercantil*, 2nd edn (Civitas, 2006) 639, 645.

[79] See text at ch 4.VI and accompanying notes.

company's losses consequent to that misappropriation will be higher than the profits made by the insider.[80] Hence, a cumulative remedy as the one established by Spanish law will deter misappropriations regardless of the parties' relative evaluations of the corporate opportunity. Given that equitable remedies, which are peculiar to common law jurisdictions, were not available in Spanish law, the Spanish lawmaker did its best to approximate the degree of deterrence displayed by common law jurisdictions.

In Italian partnership law, a specific remedy based on unjust enrichment for misappropriations of corporate opportunities is unknown. This is not surprising, given that the action for unjust enrichment in Italian law[81] cannot be sought 'when the injured party can exercise another action to be compensated for the damage suffered'.[82] The fact that there is a remedy for breach of the rules on the misappropriations of corporate opportunities – namely damages[83] – may constitute a severe obstacle to a claim based on the action for unjust enrichment. Clearly, the unavailability of the action for unjust enrichment in Italian law for misappropriations of corporate opportunities is more the fruit of a legal path dependency than of a conscious policy line.[84] The awareness within Italian jurisprudence of the limited availability of remedies against the misappropriation of corporate opportunities has prompted speculation over the possibility of applying remedies pertaining to the protection of intellectual property and/or to unfair competition in the context of misappropriations.[85] Nonetheless, this additional remedial system might be applicable only in very exceptional cases – that is, cases of explicit violation of unfair competition rules.[86]

In principle, and from a mere reform perspective, French law would seem rather well-positioned in terms of the introduction of a remedy similar to the disgorgement of profits. In fact, French law has successfully experienced such a remedy for intellectual property law violations.[87]

Italian law may encounter many more limitations than Spanish law when it comes to providing a remedial system for the misappropriation of corporate

[80] ibid.

[81] 'Azione generale di arricchimento' (General Enrichment Action), regulated by Italian Civil Code, Art 2041.

[82] Italian Civil Code, Art 2042 states that 'L'azione di arricchimento non è proponibile quando il danneggiato può esercitare un'altra azione per farsi indennizzare del pregiudizio subito' (the unjust enrichment claim can be proposed when the plaintiff cannot exercise any other action to claim indemnity for the injury suffered).

[83] See text at the following section and accompanying notes.

[84] The origins of the limits to the use of the unjust enrichment remedy in certain civil law jurisdictions such as Italy is explained by Zimmermann (n 70) 410ff.

[85] F Barachini, 'L'Appropriazione delle *Corporate Opportunities*' in P Abbadessa and G Battista Portale (eds), *Il nuovo diritto delle società, Liber amicorum Gian Franco Campobasso* (UTET, 2006) 654.

[86] A Pomelli, Commento all'Articolo 2391 CC, in A Maffei Alberti, *Commentario Breve al Diritto delle Società* (CEDAM, 1997) 744.

[87] M Sejean, 'The Disgorgement of Illicit Profits in French Law' in E Hondius and A Janssen, *Disgorgement of Profits* (Springer, 2015) 121–38.

opportunities based on unjust enrichment. If we consider the German remedies against the breach of the director's duty not to compete with the corporation (*Wettbewerbsverbot*, *Aktiengesellscahft* (AktG) §88), we can see that German law provides two alternative remedies: a claim for damages, or a so-called *Eintrittsrecht* (translated roughly as 'subrogation right'.[88] The *Eintrittsrecht* does not seem to have any equivalent in other civil law jurisdictions, and it closely resembles an account of profits granting the company the right to seek full disgorgement of profits.

An *Eintrittsrecht* is assisted by a company's full right to access the competing undertaking's accounts in order to retrieve information about its profits.[89] Moreover, it targets not only material profits, but also immaterial ones, such as know-how or a customer list.[90] German jurisprudence envisaged the applicability by analogy of the *Eintrittsrecht* to the misappropriation of corporate opportunities.[91] Nonetheless, such an extensive interpretation was rejected by the *Bundesgerichtshof*, adducing as a justification the derivation of a German corporate opportunity doctrine from the *Treuepflicht*, the duty of loyalty, and not from the prohibition of competing activities.[92] Although this might not be the last word from the *Bundesgerichtshof*, it is regrettable that a system endowed with many viable remedial alternatives does not make full use of them in the case of corporate opportunity rules violations. Nonetheless, one cannot exclude that in future German courts may emulate the Spanish example, extending this remedy to the misappropriation of corporate opportunities.

A final and still relevant point is worth making with reference to the case where a given jurisdiction decides to apply the unjust enrichment remedy to corporate opportunity cases. It is possible that an insider unlawfully exploits in an extremely successful way a corporate opportunity they have previously misappropriated. Conversely, it can also occur that their newly founded business turns out to be a total failure. In the latter case, would the claimant be granted the value of the corporate opportunity at the moment when it was misappropriated, or the value at the moment of the claim? The answer to such a question may be difficult to determine. First, it may depend on how this kind of unjust enrichment is theoretically constructed. If we pose ourselves the same question with reference to enrichment-by-transfer claims, the reply is not uniform across civil law jurisdictions – especially when the taking cannot be considered *mala fide*. Now, there may be cases of bona fide corporate opportunity takings, where the opportunity at issue may look not to be in the line of

[88] See H Hirte, P Mülbert and M Roth, *Grosskommentar zum Aktiengesetz*, vol 1 (paras 76–91), 5th edn (DeGruyter, 2015) para 88, ss 7–8, paras 62ff.

[89] See T Wachter, *Kommentar zum Aktiengesetz*, 2nd edn (RWS, 2014) comment to AktG § 88, s 3.3.

[90] Hirte, Mülbert and Roth, *Grosskommentar* (2015) § 88, s 8, para 4(d).

[91] ibid s 17, para 199. See Dannemann *German Law of Unjustified Enrichment and Restitution* (2009) 134ff.

[92] BGH 4.12.2012, II ZR 159/10, DStR 2013, 600 = NZG 2013. 216.

business of the corporation and where it therefore may be uncertain whether the insider had to disclose or not. As Reinhard Zimmerman reminds us, 'The European legal systems do not agree on the basic principle to be adopted'.[93] For instance, the German system is usually rather defendant-friendly, as the defendant is considered to be 'liable only for his actual "enrichment" at the time of litispendence'.[94]

The interpretation reached by each jurisdiction concerning the quantification of the enrichment to be refunded may be a very relevant issue to solve before reverting to such a remedy. Even in those civil law systems where unjust enrichment law could be used as a remedy against misappropriations of corporate opportunities, the possibility to revert to a claim based on damages may turn out to be crucial in situations involving this kind of breach. From this perspective, once again, the Spanish system anticipates the solution of potential problems of this kind which might arise in doctrine and in jurisprudence, as it cumulates the possibility to claim damages and unjust enrichment.[95]

To conclude, gain-based remedies against the misappropriations of corporate opportunities in civil law jurisdictions seem to be different not only in nature, but also in function, because they are not assisted by profit-tracing as in the common law systems.

V. DAMAGES AWARDS FOR THE MISAPPROPRIATION OF CORPORATE OPPORTUNITIES IN COMMON LAW AND IN CIVIL LAW JURISDICTIONS

Whereas lawmakers might have conceived the constructive trust/account of profits remedy also with a look to their potential for deterrence (among other policy objectives), the same cannot usually be said about compensatory damages. Scott Hershovitz has claimed that there may be a subjective revenge component in certain claims for compensatory damages.[96] Nonetheless, this does not automatically imply that there is a deterrence policy underlying the legal permissibility of compensatory claims. Revenge is an ex post way to look to tort – not an *ex ante* one as is deterrence. Moreover, the ordinary perspective adopted by the lawmaker is not one of general or specific prevention.[97]

[93] Zimmermann (n 70) 412.

[94] ibid.

[95] See n 78.

[96] S Hershovitz, 'Tort as a Substitute for Revenge' in J Oberdiek (ed), *Philosophical Foundations of the Law of Torts* (Oxford University Press, 2014) 86, 88: 'I do not doubt that tort can serve as an outlet for vindictive motives, and I think that true even when punitive damages are not in play'.

[97] J Goudkamp, 'Exemplary Damages' in G Virgo and S Worthington (eds), *Commercial Remedies: Resolving Controversies* (Cambridge University Press, 2016).

Nowadays, corrective justice is mostly understood from an Aristotelian allocative perspective.[98] To put it in the words of John Gardner:

> Something has shifted between … two parties. The question of corrective justice is not the question of whether and to what extent and in what form and on what ground it should now be allocated among them full stop, but the question of whether and to what extent and in what form and on what ground it should now be allocated back from one party to the other, reversing a transaction that took place between them.[99]

From a functional perspective, the effects of a remedy consisting in compensatory damages may be said to be similar in common law and in civil law jurisdictions. Nonetheless, whereas the law of civil law damages is usually codified, in common law it is subject to the usual dualism determined by the existence of equitable remedies.

First, it must be remembered that in principle also a UK company can seek equitable compensation or common law damages.[100] Equitable compensation or common law damages may prove to be more suitable than disgorgement of profits in certain cases.[101] In fact, in those cases where the insider proves to be an inefficient exploiter of the investment opportunity that she misappropriated, a mere account of profits will cover only part of the damages for loss of profits caused to the corporation. The corporation may have been far more efficient than the director in such a case. Equitable compensation is a monetary personal remedy whose function is compensating the claimant.[102] Common law damages are a more general alternative to equitable compensation.[103]

In contrast, while there is no substantial difference between common law damages and equitable compensation in the case of the duty of loyalty, this is

[98] Hershovitz, 'Tort' (2014) 89.

[99] J Gardner, 'What is Tort Law For? Part I. The Place of Corrective Justice' (2011) 30 *Law & Philosophy* 1, 9–10. And see further comments on this assumption in Hershovitz (n 96) 90ff.

[100] On equitable compensation, see I Davidson, 'The Equitable Remedy of Compensation' (1982) 13 *Melbourne University Law Review* 349; L Aitken, 'Developments in Equitable Compensation: Opportunity or Danger?' (1993) 67 *Australian Law Journal* 596; D Davies, 'Equitable Compensation: "Causation, Foreseeability and Remoteness"' in D Waters (ed), *Equity, Fiduciaries and Trusts* (Carswell, 1993) 297; C Rickett and T Gardner, 'Compensating for Loss in Equity: The Evolution of a Remedy' (1994) 24 *Victoria University of Wellington Law Review* 19; Berryman, 'Equitable Compensation' (1999); C Rickett, 'Compensating for Loss in Equity – Choosing the Right Horse for Each Course' in P Birks and F Rose (eds), *Restitution and Equity* (Informa Law, 2000) 173; J Getzler, 'Equitable Compensation and the Regulation of Fiduciary Relationships' in P Birks and F Rose (eds), *Restitution and Equity* (Informa, 2000) 235; A Burrows, 'We Do This at Common Law but That in Equity' (2002) 22 *Oxford Journal of Legal Studies* 1; P Davies, 'Remedies for Breach of Trust' (2015) 78 *Modern Law Review* 681.

[101] Berryman (n 65) 99. J Lowry and R Edmunds, 'The Corporate Opportunity Doctrine: The Shifting Boundaries of the Duty and its Remedies' (1998) 61 *Modern Law Review* 515, 527ff cite a series of cases of breach of a fiduciary duty in Anglo-Commonwealth jurisdictions where the remedy sought by the plaintiff was equitable compensation because the breach had not resulted in the insider making a profit.

[102] A Burrows, *English Private Law*, 3rd edn (Oxford University Press, 2013) para 21.133.

[103] Davies and Worthington (n 29) paras 16–181.

not the case when there is a breach of the duty of care.[104] What is still remarkable in UK law is that there are several alternatives to a constructive trust/account of profits, which cover all the possible cases of divergent evaluations of the same investment opportunity by the company and the potential takers.

Whilst limited to a narrower set of remedies, such an alternative exists also in certain civil law jurisdictions. For instance, as already stated, Article 227(2) of the Spanish *Ley de Sociedades de Capital* refers to damages where the final quantification can also take into consideration the unjust enrichment resulting from additional profits. Directors' liability for damages resulting from a breach of the duty of loyalty – hence also of corporate opportunity misappropriations – results as well from the general rule contained in Article 236 of the *Ley de Sociedades de Capital*. Spanish jurisprudence on corporate opportunities antecedent to the 2014 Spanish corporate law reform also claimed that directors may also be liable to pay 'moral damages' to the company, where there the breach of the duty of loyalty has repercussions on the market value of the company, as this can be viewed as affecting the company's reputation.[105]

Nowhere in French law is it clearly stated that business opportunities are allocated *ex ante* to the corporation, as no corporate opportunity doctrine or general fiduciary law has been developed in French case law.[106] Nevertheless, directors have a duty to disclose such opportunities to the corporation. Therefore, it is difficult to define a given business opportunity as 'corporate' under French law, given the absence of a clear corporate right to exploit business opportunities.[107] Nonetheless, French case law has introduced directors' liability for damages in cases where directors fail to disclose the existence of a corporate opportunity to their company.[108]

Once a corporate opportunity has been disclosed, it looks like the company has no right to any preferential exploitation. The opportunity will be appropriated by the economic actor (company or insider) who successfully bargains for the acquisition of those rights from the third party who can dispose of them. If the company has no right to the exploitation of the opportunity, one may wonder what damages it can seek in case of no disclosure. Thibaut Massart has not only clearly excluded the idea of a disgorgement of profits,[109] but has also clarified that courts must not allow a plaintiff to seek damages for the full

[104] See *AIB Group (UK) plc v Mark Redler & Co Solicitors* [2014] UKSC 58 and comments by Davies, 'Remedies' (2015) 681. For the main differences between the two remedies, see Burrows, *English Private Law* (2013) para 21.134.

[105] P Portellano Diez, *Deber de Fidelidad de los Administradores de Sociedades Mercantiles y Oportunidades de Negocio* (Civitas, 1996).

[106] M Gelter and G Helleringer, 'Opportunity Makes a Thief: Corporate Opportunities as Legal Transplant and Convergence in Corporate Law' (2018) 15 *Berkeley Business Law Journal* 92, 134.

[107] ibid 138, the authors stress that besides the existence of a growing case law that introduce some general principles for the protection of business opportunities, there are many open questions.

[108] See for instance Cass Com 18 December 2012, [2013] *Revue des Sociétés* 262, 266.

[109] See T Massart, 'Note to Cass Com 12 March 2013' [2013] *Revue des Sociétés* 689, 692.

loss of chances.[110] The final result is very likely to depend on a discretionary evaluation by the judge. Nonetheless, it is also worth stressing that the *Cour de Cassation* has discussed cases where there may have been a concomitant breach of a duty of loyalty[111] together with a violation of rules on unfair competition and awarding expectation damages.[112]

Liability for breach of the rules on directors' interests and for breach of the duty not to compete with the corporation are also expressly imposed by Articles 2390 and 2391 of the Italian Civil Code.[113] Moreover, Article 1226 of the Italian Civil Code provides a flexible way to calculate damages, that is to say, damages can be determined in an equitable way (*via equitativa*) when it is difficult to quantify the exact value.[114] Article 1226 may turn out to be particularly helpful in corporate opportunity cases. In fact, an actualisation of the hypothetical profits earned by the company in the case where it had been allowed to exploit the business opportunity (ie absent any misappropriation) may be an extremely difficult calculation in practice.[115] Finally, also in the case of violation of a director's duty not to compete with the company, the company is granted a claim for damages (Article 2390 of the Italian Civil Code).[116] Nonetheless, practice has highlighted the probation difficulties underlying this kind of action.[117]

A remedial alternative between *Eintrittsrecht* and damages is expressly acknowledged in German law for the *Wettbeverbsverbot*. In fact, German courts have also allowed a claim for damages, even in the form of loss of profit (*lucrum cessans*).[118] Nonetheless, evidential difficulties in German law render in practice the *Eintrittsrecht* the main remedy for the *Wettbeverbssverbot*.[119] Unfortunately, given the cited orientation of the *Bundesgerichtshof* (BGH) in matters of corporate opportunities and *Eintrittsrecht*,[120] the same remedy alternative does not exist for the breach of the *Geschäftschancenlehre* in present German law.

[110] See ibid 266.

[111] For the progressive emergence of the duty of loyalty within French law, see Gelter and Helleringer, 'Opportunity Makes a Thief' (2018) 134ff.

[112] Cass Com 15 November 2011. See comments by G Helleringer, 'Le Dirigeant à l'Epreuve des Opportunités d'Affaires' (2012) 24 *Recueil Dalloz* 1560, fn 3.

[113] For a comment, see for instance M Ventoruzzo, 'Commento all'Articolo 2391 del Codice Civile' in P Marchetti et al (eds), *Commentario alla Riforma delle Societa*' (Giuffre, 2006) 490, 495.

[114] Cass 8 February 2005, n 2538 [2005] *Giurisprudenza Italiana* 1637.

[115] Note that here the meaning cannot be interpreted in the context of the law of equity and that there is no intention by Italian lawmakers to refer to that context. For some ideas on the potential complexity of this calculation under Italian law, see Ventoruzzo, 'Commento all'Articolo 2391' (2006) 499.

[116] See Spolidoro, 'Il Divieto di Concorrenza' [1983] 1372ff.

[117] ibid.

[118] See Schmidt and Lutter (n 28) vol 1, comment to para 88, s 3, para 2. Moreover, in some cases conditions may be present for an action in tort (Bürgerliches Gesetzbuch (BGB) para 823). See on this point Hirte, Mülbert and Roth (n 88), comment to AktG § 88, s 15.2.

[119] See U Noack and W Zöllner (eds), *Kölner Kommentar zum Aktiengesetz* (Carl Heymanns, 2010) vol 2, pt 1, paras 76–94 AktG comment to AktG § 88, s 7.1.

[120] See n 92.

It is precisely the difficulties in providing evidence as to the *quantum* of the compensation that prompt some further consideration *de lege ferenda* – given the present absence of remedies for the misappropriations of corporate opportunities, beside damages, within most civil law jurisdictions (with the notable exception of the Spanish one). In fact, there may be a way to solve the probational difficulties together with increasing the potential for deterrence of compensatory damages. This would simply consist of creating a rebuttable presumption of equivalence between the damage inflicted on the corporation by an insider misappropriation of a corporate opportunity and the profits the insider has gained thanks to the exploitation of the corporate opportunity.[121] If a court could argue the necessity of such a presumption on the basis of evidentiary difficulties, this mini-reform could go through without requiring the intervention of the legislative power – and it would be a significant improvement in the effectiveness potential of compensatory damages.

VI. PUNITIVE (OR 'EXEMPLARY') DAMAGES FOR THE MISAPPROPRIATION OF A CORPORATE OPPORTUNITY

'Punitive' or 'exemplary' damage were often referred to as 'vindictive' in the nineteenth century – as if courts were taking charge of a vindictive desire or a right to revenge of the victim.[122] Nowadays, the term 'punitive' clearly hints at an element of punishment.[123] The term 'exemplary' suggests an element of general prevention by way of deterrence. Nonetheless, it is still debated whether punitive damages are intended to punish and/or to deter. At least two well-renowned jurists[124] have advanced the idea that in certain cases punitive damages are restitutionary[125] or substitutionary in nature.[126] Both theories have encountered severe criticisms.[127] Nowadays, in the light of Article 6 of the European Convention on Human Rights, it has been suggested that their imposition equates to a criminal charge.[128]

[121] This solution has been suggested to me by Professor Gerhard Dannemann in an email exchange about this topic.

[122] Hershovitz (n 96) 88 ff.

[123] Hershovitz (n 96) ibid claims that punishment is nothing but the modern term for vindictive and that formally they are the same, apart from revealing a different attitude to the role of the law when applying such remedy.

[124] R Stevens, *Torts and Rights* (Oxford University Press, 2007); E Weinrib, *The Idea of Private Law* (Harvard University Press, 1995).

[125] Weinrib, *Idea of Private Law* (1995) 135ff.

[126] Stevens, *Torts and Rights* (2007) 85ff.

[127] Goudkamp, 'Exemplary Damages' (2016) 335 and 336.

[128] R Meurkens, *Punitive Damages* (Kluwer, 2014) 185 suggests that: 'it is also defensible to label the imposition of punitive damages as a *criminal charge*'.

Whether punitive damages discharge a function or deterrence or not from a philosophical perspective is of limited relevance from the point of view of the Law and Economics of damages. In fact, what matters is whether they can be employed in order to obtain perfect disgorgement – regardless of how they are labelled. This idea is expressed very clearly in the words of Cooter and Freedman:

> The severity of punishment can be measured by the amount that the sanction exceeds perfect disgorgement. To capture this idea, the 'punitive multiple,' denoted *m*, is defined as the ratio of the total sanction to perfect disgorgement. Thus a punitive multiple of one (m = 1) indicates perfect disgorgement and no punishment; in contrast, a punitive multiple of two (m = 2) indicates that the sanction is twice as large as perfect disgorgement and therefore embodies punishment.[129]

It can be noted that the ideal of 'perfect disgorgement' is hard to achieve when an account of profits is the remedy applied to a misappropriation of a corporate opportunity. In fact, perfect disgorgement could be achieved if the investment opportunity at stake is valued exactly the same by company and insider. In case of diverging valuation, the disgorgement will be imperfect. In particular, it will be punitive when the insider values the opportunity more because of her higher exploitation capabilities – unless the court grants an allowance to the insider to mitigate the punitive element.

From a practical perspective, it may not be important to reach perfect disgorgement. Instead, 'perfect deterrence' against non-disclosure of corporate opportunities and/or misappropriations should be the core reason for employing punitive damages. The calculation of the expected sanction, including the probability of detection, as explained by Cooter and Freedman, may be considered as the best way to achieve such an objective. Punitive damages look particularly interesting from this point of view. In fact, as they are not quantified as a compensatory damage, nor as a profit, *in principle* they could be employed in a very flexible way to deter behaviours. This would be possible through the application of the Cooter and Freedman formula, once a correct estimate of the probability of detection is provided. The quantum of damages would be inversely proportional to the probability of detection.

Despite their suitability for pursuing deterrence objectives, punitive damages have not been introduced in many jurisdictions. Where they have been introduced, their use is often subject to severe limitations. Even in the US, where punitive damages have found the most fertile ground, they still go through limitations and significant jurisprudential criticism for many reasons.[130] One of the reasons why punitive damages are constantly in the crosshairs of jurisprudence is the lack of predictability of their quantification.[131] This aspect is already rather

[129] Cooter and Freedman, 'The Fiduciary Relationship' (1991) 1052.

[130] See D Owen, 'Punitive Damages Overview: Functions, Problems and Reform' (1994) 39 *Villanova Law Review* 363.

[131] See D Dobbs, 'Ending Punishment in "Punitive" Damages: Deterrence-Measured Remedies' (1988) 40 *Alabama Law Review* 831. See also T Eisenberg, 'The Predictability of Punitive Damages'

questionable within the US legal system. If punitive damages had to be qualified as criminal sanctions within European systems, such unpredictability would result in even more severe obstacles.[132] Aside from the general criticism brought to this remedy, the spare use of punitive damages with reference to corporate opportunity rules is a reality even in the US, where they have been employed only in a few exceptional cases by Texan courts.[133]

Despite all the caveats that may exist within the European legal systems – which are bound by increasing requirements created by human rights laws – some doctrinal evolutions within the law of several European countries might make us think optimistically about the future of punitive damages. One of the consequences of globalisation is the circulation of legal models. This is not true only within academia, but also in practice. Nowadays, it is a frequent occurrence for a breach of a given duty to take place in one country and be sanctioned in a different country. This is why many EU Member States' courts have been confronted with the problem of granting recognition in Europe to punitive damages awarded by a US court.

Given the integration of the EU internal markets, the issue of recognition of foreign punitive damages awards has a European reach. Nonetheless, EU Member States' courts have not taken a homogenous position. The fiercest opposition to the recognition of a US punitive damages award has come from the German courts.[134] In France, the courts' position towards the recognition of punitive damages awards has not been so neat. In 2010, a *Cour de Cassation* decision overruled a decision by the *Cour d'Appel de Poitiers* that had denied exequatur to a Californian decision applying punitive damages on the basis of a conflict with French public policy. The Supreme Court held that punitive damages are contrary to French public interest only when they are disproportionate to the

(1997) 26 *Journal of Legal Studies* 623. Attempts at rationalising the quantum have been made, with questionable applicability to practice. See K Viscusi, 'The Challenge of Punitive Damages Mathematics' (2001) 30 *Journal of Legal Studies* 313. For a general economic approach, see M Polinsky and S Shavell, 'Punitive Damages: An Economic Analysis' (1997–1998) 111 *Harvard Law Review* 869.

[132] That criminal sanctions have to be fully predictable is common tradition in civil law countries, usually expressed through the brocard '*nullum crimen, nulla poena, sine praevia lege poenali scripta et stricta*', which contains indications both as to the non-retroactivity of the criminal sanction and to its predictability.

[133] See, for instance, *United Teacher's Associates v MacKeen & Bailey*, 847 F Supp 521 (WD Tex 1994), although it is not clear whether in this case punitive damages derived from a concurrent cause of action.

[134] BGH, IXth Civil Senate, 4 June 1992, Docket No IX ZR 149/91 [1992]. Nevertheless, as a matter of domestic law, German law seems to have evolved in the direction of recognising the preventative function of the law of damages in the past two decades. See U Magnus, 'Punitive Damages in German Law' in L Meurkens and E Nordin (eds), *The Power of Punitive Damages – Is Europe Missing Out?* (Intersentia, 2012) 245–82. The literature also tends to acknowledge that despite a formal opposition by German courts to the concept of punitive damages, there are cases of damages awards of a punitive nature. See V Behr, 'Punitive Damages in American and German Law – Tendencies Towards Approximation of Apparently Irreconcilable Concepts' (2003) 78 *Chicago-Kent Law Review* 105, 126.

injury suffered by the victim or to the breach of the debtor's contractual obligations, because they would cause an unjust enrichment to the benefit of the claimant.[135]

The cited French Supreme Court decision was published on the verge of an incipient debate on the introduction of a punitive system within the French legal system. This debate culminated in proposals for the reform of the second part of Article 1266 of the French Civil Code, which eventually was unsuccessful.[136] Although the quantification of punitive damages in the event of a reform remained an open question,[137] the French Supreme Court openings and the existence of legal reform proposals on this topic shows that it is not impossible to talk about punitive damages in Europe, even in a country with a very strong legal tradition such as France.

As in the case of the remedies for corporate opportunity misappropriations, the biggest surprise in continental Europe came from Spain. In the *Alabastres Alfreda* case, the Spanish Supreme Court gave exequatur to an American treble damages award imposed on a Spanish company for unauthorised use of intellectual property, violation of a registered trademark, and unfair competition.[138] This award by the Supreme Court acknowledged the punitive and preventative function of punitive damages – thus showing no intent to try to fit this remedy into a compensatory framework. It also has to be noted that, without any official reform proposals in this sense, Spanish courts have progressively started to introduce punitive elements in tort law.[139] A similar tendency has been noted in Italian doctrine,[140] although such internal evolutions seem to contradict the denial of exequatur of US punitive damages awards by the Italian Supreme Court.[141]

If the attitude towards punitive damages seems to be changing in some continental European countries, such a wind of change seems to be absent within UK law in recent times, even though the UK legal system is precisely where

[135] Cass Civ 1 December 2010 [2010] *Bulletin* I, no 248.

[136] The approved version of the reform of French Civil Code did not introduce punitive damages. See Ordonnance n 2016-131 du 10 février 2016 portant réforme du droit des contrats, du régime général et de la preuve des obligations, JORF, no 0035 du 11 février 2016 texte no 26.

[137] See M Parker, 'Changing Tides: The Introduction of Punitive Damages into the French Legal System' (2013) 41 *Georgia Journal of International and Comparative Law* 390. And see also C Mahe, 'Punitive Damages in the Competing Reform Drafts of the French Civil Code' in Meurkens and Nordin, *Power of Punitive Damages* (2012) 261–82. N Rias, 'L'Amende Civile: une Fausse Bonne Idée' [2016] *Receuil Dalloz* 2072, explains that punitive damages might be incompatible with French legality and *ne bis in idem* principles.

[138] *Miller Import Corp v Alabastres Alfredo, SL*, Sentencia del Tribunal Supremo, 13 November 2001 (Exequátur No 2039/1999).

[139] M Otero Crespo, 'Punitive Damages under Spanish Law: A Subtle Recognition?' in Meurkens and Nordin (n 134) 283–310.

[140] Tribunale di Torre Annunziata, Sez Stralcio, 24 February 2000 [2000] *Danno e Responsabilità*, 11, 1121; Tribunale di Torre Annunziata, Sez Stralcio, 14 March 2000, [2000] *Danno e Responsabilità*, 11, 1123.

[141] Cass, 19 January 2007, n 1183 [2007] *Giustizia Civile*, 10, I, 2124.

punitive damages originated.[142] In fact, there seem to be difficulties in overcoming the tripartition proposed by Lord Devlin in the landmark case *Rookes v Barnard*, limiting punitive damages to: (1) cases of oppressive, arbitrary or unconstitutional actions by servants of the Government; (2) situations where the defendant's intentional attempts to make a profit exceed the compensation available to the plaintiff; and (3) cases of express statutory provisions.[143] The situation where a defendant's intentional attempts to make a profit exceed the compensation available to the plaintiff resemble very closely corporate opportunity cases where the insider values the business opportunity more highly than the company. Nonetheless, there would be two significant obstacles to the use of this sanction in a corporate opportunity claim. In fact, this would entail the breach of a director's contract, whereas the remedy is limited to tort claims. Second, it is unclear whether evidence should be provided of a director's precise calculation of their exceeding profits – which would be very difficult *ex ante*, given all the uncertainties connected to a business activity.[144]

Given that the present situation seems to restrict the use of punitive damages to a very limited range of cases, one may ask whether reforms are foreseeable in the near future. Despite such reforms having been advocated,[145] the negative reply seems to prevail in jurisprudence.[146] This is somewhat disappointing, as the UK system would be in a far better position than continental European legal systems to reform this area of the law efficiently.

In continental Europe there still are theoretical obstacles to the introduction of punitive damages. First, in civil law jurisdictions tort law is usually conceived as compensatory.[147] Hence, if the orientation that considers punitive damages as non-compensatory is correct, it may be difficult to frame such a sanction in the present tort law system. Moreover, in civil law the punitive function usually pertains to criminal law or administrative law. Such branches of the law are viewed as dogmatically separated from civil law.[148] Civil law jurisdictions impose

[142] *Wilkes v Wood* (1763) 98 ER 489 (CP) – a case of defamation against the King.

[143] *Rookes v Barnard* [1964] AC 1129 (HL) 1225–28.

[144] S Deakin, C Johnston and B Markesinis, *Markesinis and Deakin's Tort Law*, 7th edn (Oxford University Press, 2012) 800.

[145] Goudkamp (n 97).

[146] Deakin, Johnston and Markesinis, *Markesinis* (2012) 803.

[147] Meurkens, *Punitive Damages* (2014) 146ff. But see also H Koziol, 'Comparative Conclusions' in H Koziol (ed), *Basic Question of Tort Law from a Comparative Perspective* (Jan Sramek Verlag, 2015) 685, Par 8/163: 'all the arguments against deterrent function of "Schadenersatzrecht" – the law of compensation – in the Continental European sense are directed solely against the idea of primary or even only deterrent function, but not against a secondary function … it is broadly accepted that tort law also – as a side effect – has a deterrent function'.

[148] Meurkens (n 128) 168ff. In fact, in the civil law tradition, the criminal law is deeply embedded in rigid constitutions that limit the possibility of employing criminal sanctions and that require a detailed description of the cases in which they can be employed and the level of penalty that can be imposed (or precise criteria for the calculation of that amount). See further explanations in H Koziol, 'Punitive Damages – A European Perspective' (2007–2008) 68 *Louisiana Law Review* 741, 751ff.

a complex series of safeguards for the application of criminal law – which would be bypassed if a court had to award punitive damages in a civil law trial.[149] On top of that, in civil law jurisdictions prosecution policy usually cannot be exercised by private citizens.[150] In fact, in continental European jurisdictions it is only the state that has competence for law enforcement.[151]

Even though the theoretical obstacle to the introduction of punitive damages in Europe suggests that a generalised transplant of the US system in Europe is not likely to be an easy thing, one cannot exclude more targeted policy interventions introducing punitive damages in specific areas of the law. For instance, the European Commission has already manifested interest for this remedy *de lege ferenda*.[152] Therefore, I believe that understanding the potentials of this remedy in corporate law settings may help also to propel reforms in this direction.

VII. CRIMINAL SANCTIONS FOR THE MISAPPROPRIATIONS OF CORPORATE OPPORTUNITIES: NOTES WITH A VIEW TO THE FUTURE LAW

Were punitive damages to be introduced as an alternative remedy against the misappropriation of corporate opportunities, they might be considered, at least in certain jurisdictions, as criminal or quasi-criminal sanctions.[153] If that were the case, one could wonder whether a reform introducing punitive damages could be justified in point of criminal law theory. Even beyond this, one could ask whether criminal sanctions other than punitive damages could be considered as adequate ways to deter directors from misappropriating corporate opportunities.

To my knowledge, in the sample of jurisdictions I am analysing, there are no cases of misappropriations of corporate opportunities punished by criminal law.[154] Nonetheless, lawmakers have adopted criminal sanctions for behaviours that are substantially similar in their nature to those occurring in cases of breach of corporate opportunity rules. There are at least two competing criminal

[149] Such as the *ne bis in idem* principle and heightened standards of proof. Meurkens (n 128) 174ff.

[150] ibid 172ff.

[151] ibid 189ff.

[152] See Green Paper on Damages Actions for Breach of the EC Antitrust Rules Brussels, 19.12.2005 COM (2005) 672 final; White Paper on Damages Actions for Breach of the EC Antitrust Rules, Brussels, 2.4.2008 COM (2008) 165 final. And see comments by Meurkens (n 128) 224ff.

[153] B Zipursky, 'A Theory of Punitive Damages' (2005) 84 *Texas Law Review* 105, 106.

[154] Unless we consider the Texan exception awarding punitive damages and cited in n 132, bordering with criminal law as intended in European systems. Under UK law, one *might hypothetically* apply the Fraud Act 2006, s 3, on 'fraud by failing to disclose information', to some corporate opportunity cases (i.e. when this is evident). Section 3 states: 'A person is in breach of this section if he – (a) dishonestly fails to disclose to another person information which he is under a legal duty to disclose, and (b) intends, by failing to disclose the information – (i) to make a gain for himself or another, or (ii) to cause loss to another or to expose another to a risk of loss'. Nonetheless, consider that so far there is no evidence of applications of s 3 to corporate opportunity cases.

sanctioning models. The first one targets the misuse of corporate assets and/or the harm consequent to a conflicted operation. The second one focuses on the absence of disclosure of certain categories of relevant information.

Examples of rules targeting the misuse of corporate assets are the ones contained in Articles L241-3(4) and L242-6(3) of the French Code of Commerce, and in Article 2634 of the Italian Civil Code, on *infedeltà patrimoniale*. The French rule punishes – with imprisonment for a period of up to five years – directors who have used corporate assets in bad faith and for their interests or for the interests of a company in which they are interested. This rule may not apply that easily to corporate opportunities unless it is proven that business opportunities are 'assets' ('immaterial assets'?).[155] Article 2634 of the Italian Civil Code, on *infedeltà patrimoniale*, provides administrative and criminal sanctions in cases where a director has voted in conflict of interest and by doing so has harmed the company. In this rule, as well as in the French rule, the focus is on the harm of the conflicted behaviour to the assets of the corporation.

An alternative sanctioning model, one based on disclosure, is perhaps more interesting for the case of a misappropriation of corporate opportunities. If bargaining is central to corporate opportunity doctrines, optimal disclosure is the necessary condition for bargaining to occur. With reference to self-dealing cases, CA 2006, s 182 states:

> Where a director of a company is in any way, directly or indirectly, interested in a transaction or arrangement that has been entered into by the company, he must declare the nature and extent of the interest to the other directors in accordance with this section.

Section 183 provides for the sanctions for the breach of such an obligation, and states that 'A director who fails to comply with the requirements of section 182 … commits an offence' punishable with imprisonment. This is clearly a rule that is aimed at removing information asymmetry in the interests of one of the parties of the transaction. Nonetheless, it is clear that ss 182 and 183 would not apply to corporate opportunities because there is no 'transaction' or 'arrangement' which the company has entered into.[156] Article 2629-bis of the Italian Civil Code contains a criminal rule that also targets lack of disclosure of a director's interest in a transaction with the company if damage follows therefrom. This rule applies only to listed companies and to companies whose shares are 'widely diffused among the public'.[157]

A criminal rule sanctioning absence of disclosure in the case of takings of a corporate opportunity would clearly be formulated in a different way from the British and the Italian ones mentioned above. It should aim at forcing disclosure

[155] See M Corradi, 'Les Opportunités d'Affaires Saisies par les Administrateurs de la Société en Violation du Devoir de Loyauté' [2011] *Bulletin Joly Sociétés* 157.
[156] Davies and Worthington (n 29) para 16.111 and 16.116.
[157] As defined in Art 2 bis of Regolamento Consob n 11971/1999 (Regolamento Emittenti).

of the corporate opportunity and not of the interest of the director. In fact, it is self-evident that if a director intends to exploit the investment opportunity at issue, they also have an economic interest in the opportunity.

Whenever a criminal sanction is introduced in a given legal system, it must be the object of extremely attentive scrutiny, given the social and administrative costs that will follow its introduction. Not only must there be a cost–benefit analysis, but also a thorough criminological understanding of the behaviours it aims at deterring.

A starting point for understanding white-collar crimes from a criminological perspective is often Sutherland's work. Sutherland stresses the special role of white-collar crimes as class crimes[158] and addresses the commonly distorted perception of white-collar crimes as respectable crimes. He believes they should be perceived and treated in the same way as street crimes. Sutherland's work has formed the basis of Friedrichs and Shapiro's research on white-collar crimes. Friedrichs adds the concept of risk to the respectability and trust variables identified by Sutherland.[159] Shapiro identifies breach of trust, already present in Sutherland's and Friedrichs' analysis, as the core criminological feature present in white-collar crimes.[160] Wilson highlights the outdated concept of 'respectable crime' as needing to be reviewed in the light of modern society.[161] According to Wilson, the current reaction to the criminalisation of corporate behaviours in response to recent financial scandals was shaped by the public attitude that developed during Victorian times.[162]

Intertemporal awareness is also present in Friedrichs' recent work, and this shows that Sutherland's analysis of white-collar crimes is still valuable today.[163] Considering Sutherland's focus on respectability of the violator and breach of trust, Friedrichs also stresses the significant emotional insulation of directors from the extremely harsh consequences of their decisions for employees and investors.[164] Friedrichs highlights several elements of concern in the behavioural variable emerging from corporate directors' individual greediness[165] without dismissing it as irrelevant. Conversely, he also shows that such behaviours are embedded in certain conflicted situations that are structural within corporations.[166] Therefore, he warns that 'Criminologists have

[158] E Sutherland, *White-Collar Crime* (Holt, 1949).

[159] D Friedrichs, *Trusted Criminals: White-Collar Criminals in Contemporary Society* (Belmont, 1996).

[160] S Shapiro, 'Agency Theory' (2005) 31 *Annual Review of Sociology* 263.

[161] S Wilson, *The Origins of Modern Financial Crime: Historical Foundations and Current Problems in Britain* (Routledge, 2014).

[162] ibid 101ff.

[163] D Friedrichs, 'Enron Et Al.: Paradigmatic White-Collar Crime Cases for the New Century' (2004) 12 *Critical Criminology* 112, 115.

[164] ibid 116.

[165] ibid 121.

[166] ibid 118–19.

to attend to the various ways in which these networks, interlocks, inherent conflicts of interest, and inadequate forms of oversight promote a criminogenic environment'.[167]

The seriousness and the breadth of the harm caused by certain directors' misconduct can be of particular concern, and it is sensible to believe that this kind of crime should not be treated more leniently than street crime. Nonetheless, there is no agreement on the usefulness of criminal sanctions, and the warnings against overcriminalisation should be given appropriate consideration.[168] First, because of the irrationality of human beings, the deterrence potential of criminal sanctions may end up being far more limited than expected.[169] This might not apply to white-collar criminals, though, given that they usually commit crimes while discharging their duties as directors – activity for which they necessarily engage in rational calculations. Second, from a comparative perspective, research on US white-collar crimes has shown a certain degree of inconsistency in courts' decisions, despite many federal attempts to govern the process through guidelines.[170] Third, even when criminal sanctions may be considered as a tool for containing white-collar crimes, criminalisation should not be confused with imprisonment.

Apart from its impact as a deterrent having been questioned by empirical research,[171] imprisonment entails many further policy drawbacks. For instance, it has been shown that there exists a risk of prosecution of non-harmful conducts by rent-seeking and self-interested prosecutors.[172] Moreover, when the verdict of imprisonment involves a short period of detention, it is often not executed. The fact that it is not executed may have the reverse effect of signalling the lesser gravity of the conduct instead of stigmatising the wrongdoer.[173] Richard Posner has also provided economic arguments against imprisonment and in favour of alternative sanctions, such as fines, for white-collar crimes.[174] When an individual can afford to pay a high fine, such a remedy will increase revenues and lower

[167] ibid 119.

[168] D Friedman, 'Why not Hang Them All?' (1999) 107 *Journal of Political Economy* 259.

[169] P Robinson and J Darley, 'Does Criminal Law Deter? A Behavioural Science Investigation' (2004) 24 *Oxford Journal of Legal Studies* 173.

[170] K Strader, 'White-Collar Crime and Punishment: Reflection on Michael, Martha, and Milberg Weiss' (2007) 15 *George Mason Law Review* 45.

[171] C Jonson, 'The Effects of Imprisonments' in F Cullen and P Wilcox, *The Oxford Handbook of Criminological Theory* (Oxford University Press, 2013) 672. However, for a different interpretation of empirical data, see I Ehrlich and Z Liu, 'Sensitive Analysis of the Deterrence Hypothesis: Let's Keep the Econ in Econometrics' (1999) 42 *Journal of Law and Economics* 455.

[172] Friedman, 'Hang Them All?' (1999).

[173] R Alexander, *Insider Dealing and Money Laundering in the EU: Law and Regulation* (Ashgate, 2007) 232–33. The author notices that only in the UK is imprisonment for insider dealing for a sufficiently long time taken seriously.

[174] See R Posner, 'Optimal Sentences for White Collar Crimes' (1979–1980) 17 *American Criminal Law Review* 409. Posner also states: 'for every prison sentence there is some fine equivalent; if the fine is so large that it cannot be collected, then the offender should be imprisoned. How then are the rich favored under such a system?'.

costs (ie running prisons) for society as a whole.[175] Moreover, where stigma proves to be a desirable component of a remedial system,[176] Posner hypothesises that 'the stigma or moral revulsion that attaches to certain conduct does so because of the nature of the conduct rather than the fact that it is labelled criminal or proceeded against by the criminal process'.[177] In a more general way and in light of what has already been discussed, imprisonment tends more towards inflicting harm than promoting socially desirable behaviours and should therefore be avoided.

Clearly, one does not necessarily need to think in a binary way – that is, imprisonment versus fines. To provide a couple of examples of some alternative ways forward in terms of policy, reparative and restorative approaches are emerging as very effective policy tools.[178] Remedies such as unpaid community work mean that directors who have caused harm to a large number of citizens can be confronted with, in the words of Friedrichs, 'the painful human costs of these decisions'.[179]

If lawmakers were to decide that criminal sanctions – in their various forms – are the most appropriate response to the necessity of raising the deterrence against misappropriations of corporate opportunities, the question is raised of how easy this approach would be to implement in practice.

The criminalisation of corporate opportunities would probably encounter a series of problems – rooted both in criminal law and in criminology – that would prove difficult to overcome. First, it would be necessary to identify exactly the conduct that is to be subject to criminal sanctions. If the essence of an efficient corporate opportunity doctrine is granting efficient bargaining, a major risk of inefficiency would derive from lack of disclosure of corporate opportunities.[180] Therefore, it would be unadvisable to punish misappropriations per se.[181] In fact, a criminal sanction against a (disclosed) misappropriation of a corporate opportunity may come at the cost of deterring efficient breaches of the duty of loyalty.[182] Instead, it would be appropriate to grant criminal

[175] For the catastrophic US imprisonment rate increase and the associated cost for the US budget, see L Wacquant, 'The Great Penal Leap Backward: Incarceration in America from Nixon to Clinton' in J Pratt et al (eds), *The New Punitiveness* (Willan, 2005) 3ff.

[176] Stigma can be an effective criminal deterrent. See P Funk, 'On the Effective Use of Stigma as a Crime-deterrent' (2004) 48 *European Economic Review* 715. Nonetheless, it also entails social costs, such as increased recidivism and lower future employment perspective. See E Rasmusen, 'Stigma and Self-fulfilling Expectations of Criminality' (1996) 39 *Journal of Law and Economics* 519.

[177] Posner, 'Optimal Sentences' (1979–1980) 417. However, the stigma significantly depends on cultural variables. Therefore, Posner's idea may not apply outside the US context.

[178] G McIvor, 'Reparative and Restorative Approaches' in A Bottoms, S Rex and G Robinson, *Alternatives to Prison* (Willan, 2004).

[179] Friedrichs, 'Enron Et Al' (2004) 116.

[180] See text at ch 4.I and accompanying notes.

[181] Corradi (n 52) 463.

[182] On the concept of efficient breach of duty, see D Markovits, 'Sharing Ex Ante and Sharing Ex Post: The Non-Contractual Basis of Fiduciary Relations' in A Gold and P Miller (eds), *Philosophical Foundations of Fiduciary Law* (Oxford University Press, 2014) 210.

sanctions against a lack of disclosure. Such a criminal sanction would be also in line with criminological research on white-collar crimes, as it is a manifestation of that breach of trust described by most criminologists as the core of this kind of crime.[183] Therefore, a model based on the criminalisation of the absence of disclosure followed by harm to the corporation may be the most advisable one.

As a conclusion, I restate my personal aversion to criminal sanctions for breaches of corporate opportunity rules. Were criminal sanctions ever to be employed, emphasis should be on re-education and restitution to society, which would certainly help to promote more responsible corporate behaviours.

VIII. THE VIABILITY OF TEMPORARY REMEDIES: INJUNCTIONS AND *ASTREINTES*

The possibility of asking the court for an order that the director does not compete against the corporation (or does not take a corporate opportunity) is likely to be of very limited use from a practical perspective. This should not be a source of particular concern. The economic effects of temporary relief should be perceived at least as controversial. In fact, an injunction not to carry out an economic activity will per se damage the economic system. Hence – in case it proves indispensable – it is crucial that this kind of remedy is imposed only for in the short term, in order not to damage the going concern of the firm. Otherwise, damage may be inflicted not only to the firm's productive assets, but also (and especially) to the firm's employees who are ordered not to carry on their activities. This is why, in general, remedies that target profits but leave the activities of the corporation untouched (eg. constructive trust with subsequent transfer order)[184] may be considered more efficient, as they leave the going concern unaffected.

Where Anglo-American systems are able to grant equitable proprietary protection for misappropriations of corporate opportunities, a court order to the director 'not to continue misappropriating the opportunity' is not likely to be the first remedy thought of by an Anglo-American lawyer. An injunction may assist temporarily as part of the procedure, but does not seem to be a central part of the Anglo-American system.[185]

In civil law, the availability of an *astreinte* against a misappropriation of a corporate opportunity is uncertain. For instance, in Italian law it may be granted against a director who is breaching her duty not to compete with the corporation – under the condition that the director has not resigned from

[183] See text corresponding to n 164.

[184] See text corresponding to n 46ff.

[185] W Schaller, 'Corporate Opportunities and Corporate Competition in Illinois: A Comparative Discussion of Fiduciary Duties' (2012) 46 *John Marshall Law Review* 1, 28.

the corporation.[186] Hence a director could easily bypass the rule just by resigning their position. In fact, Italian company law has no equivalent to CA 2006, s 170(2)(a), which states that:

> A person who ceases to be a director continues to be subject – (a) to the duty in section 175 [duty to avoid conflicts of interest] as regards the exploitation of any property, information or opportunity of which he became aware at a time when he was a director.

In Italian law, there may be further obstacles to the introduction of *astreintes* against the misappropriation of corporate opportunities, deriving from the jurisprudential debate on whether such a remedy is typical or atypical.[187] In fact, *astreintes* against misappropriations of corporate opportunities are not explicitly regulated by the Italian lawmaker, though the debate is ongoing.[188] Although the debate is still young,[189] there seem to be progressive openings in the direction of granting this remedy also when it is not explicitly contemplated in statutory law.[190] If nonetheless the thesis according to which the remedy is typical had to prevail in court applications – hence it were to be awarded only in a *numerus clausus* of situations – the remedy would be precluded in this context. In contrast with Italy, Germany law seems far less problematic with reference to *astreintes* for breaches of directors' duty not to compete with the company, as its application has been recorded in practice.[191]

A final point concerns the legal consequences of a director's failure to comply with a court injunction to desist from competing with the company or misappropriating a corporate opportunity. Apart from the possibility for the company to claim damages, criminal provisions for behaviour in contempt of court resembling those applied for in the US[192] and in the UK[193] are available also in civil law jurisdictions (for example Article 650 of the Italian Criminal Code). However, under the Italian courts' interpretation, the above-mentioned criminal provisions are not always applied to injunctions.[194]

[186] See for instance V Calandra Buonaura, 'Potere di Gestione e Potere di Rappresentanza degli Amministratori' in GE Colombo and GB Portale (eds), *Trattato delle Società per Azioni*, vol 4 (UTET, 1991) 237.

[187] See L Querzola, *La Tutela Anticipatoria fra Procedimento Cautelare e Giudizio di Merito* (Bononia University Press, 2006) 222.

[188] See Querzola, *La Tutela Anticipatoria* (2006) 222ff. With specific reference to corporate opportunities, the most articulate comment on this subject expressly denies the possibility for the court to grant an injunction. See Barachini, 'L'appropriazione' (2006).

[189] Querzola (n 187) ibid.

[190] See A Bellelli, 'L'Inibitoria come Strumento Generale di Tutela contro l'Illecito' [2004] *Rivista di Diritto Civile* (I) 607.

[191] See Noack and Zöllner, *Kölner Kommentar* (2010) comment to AktG para 88, s 7, para 4. Similarly, no problem seems to arise in Spanish law; see Portellano Diez, *Deber de Fidelidad* (1996) 123–24.

[192] See J Beale Jr, 'Contempt of Court: Criminal and Civil' (1908) 21 *Harvard Law Review* 161; D Dobbs, 'Contempt of Court: A Survey' (1971) 56 *Cornell Law Review* 183.

[193] C Miller, *Contempt of Court*, 3rd edn (Oxford University Press, 2000).

[194] See Cass 11 December 2014 n 51668 [2014] *Diritto & Giustizia* 12 December 2014, 40.

IX. REPUTATIONAL SANCTIONS AS A CONSEQUENCE OF THE MISAPPROPRIATION OF A CORPORATE OPPORTUNITY AND THE DIFFICULTIES OF QUANTIFICATION

In order to understand the reach of reputational sanctions, one must first remember the main distinction between ethics and culture and consequently between the different sources of constraint generated by ethical and cultural considerations. Whereas ethics pertains to the sphere of the internal consciousness of each individual, culture relates to the interaction between individuals in a given social context. Therefore, ethics can be depicted as an endogenous source of constraint, and culture is better described as an exogenous one.[195]

It may be that ethics is an important determinant as to how directors act (or do not act) in relation to the taking of corporate opportunities. As has been noted, because being ethical is an internal dimension, it is very difficult to investigate. Therefore, the effects of ethics are hard to measure.[196] Even if we were able to measure in some way the impact of ethics on directors' behaviour, a discussion on ethics should not be conducted in a chapter devoted to remedies. The idea of 'remedy' is clearly connected to the interaction of an individual with an external source of constraint to their conduct. By contrast, what may matter in the present framework of analysis is 'culture'. In fact, culture is crucial to understanding reputational sanctions.[197] Cultural components that are not derived from the legal system are extremely difficult to monitor because of their complexity. Moreover, they form a system that is parallel to the legal one and that, to some extent, cannot be discussed within this research. By contrast, cultural components that derive from the law are directly relevant to the present discussion and therefore they deserve to be taken into consideration.

The underlying idea of an approach to reputational sanctions based on culture is how the imposition of a given sanction on those who break a given rule will be perceived by the community within which they operate and/or by the general public. This perception will eventually entail a reaction by those who judge the behaviour at stake as culturally acceptable or unacceptable. If such a behaviour is considered unacceptable, the consequent reaction should be detrimental to those who misbehave. Moreover, it should go beyond mere disapproval in order to carry some deterrence function. To understand the effective operability of the cultural reaction mechanism, we have to take into consideration at least the following factors: the amount of social stigma connected to each type of sanction; the effective implementation of the sanction; and the availability of information about the imposition of the sanction to the community in which wrongdoers operate and/or to the public.

195 D Awrey, W Blair and D Kershaw, 'Between Law and Market: Is There a Role for Culture and Ethics in Financial Regulation?' (2013–2014) 38 *Delaware Journal of Corporate Law* 191, 205ff.

196 ibid.

197 Or, in other words, understanding the interaction between ethics and culture, or 'ethical culture'. For this approach, see Awrey, Blair and Kershaw, 'Between Law and Market' (2013–2014) 205ff.

As to legal sanctions, we can imagine an increasing amount of social stigma, from damages to disgorgement of profits, and from administrative sanctions to criminal sanctions.[198] Administrative sanctions (such as the disqualification of directors) and criminal sanctions do not apply to the taking of a corporate opportunity.[199] Therefore, highly stigmatic measures are clearly excluded from the range of remedies available to courts for corporate opportunity misappropriations. Consequently, the 'cultural' meaning connected to misappropriations of corporate opportunities is not likely to be particularly strong in relation to the type of sanctions available at law. Nevertheless, in order to have a better understanding of the potential reputational consequences of an unauthorised taking of a corporate opportunity, other factors have to be considered.

Firstly, we have to consider whether there is a frequent, consistent and significant application of the corporate opportunity doctrine. Within our sample jurisdictions we find diverse situations. There are countries – such as the US and the UK – where the corporate opportunity doctrine has been applied consistently for more than a century.[200] In these countries, we imagine that legal, and also popular, culture is much more likely to consider any unauthorised taking as generally dishonest. This is likely to be connected not only to the long-term existence of a corporate opportunity doctrine, but also to the doctrine's derivation from and/or similarity to basic rules in trust law.[201] In other words, in the US and in the UK, one does not need to be a corporate director to have a general understanding of the concept of conflict of interest within a fiduciary relationship, because knowledge of the behaviour expected from a fiduciary has been circulating in the business environment for centuries.

In addition to the business environment, the concept of the fiduciary has been in the public domain in the law of trust as applicable to family situations for several centuries, as the landmark case *Keech v Sanford* shows.[202] By contrast, in most civil law countries, with the exception of Germany, corporate opportunity rules have been introduced more recently, and therefore the possibility of creating a 'fiduciary culture' has only just started. Within the civil law countries, we can distinguish between those in which there is an effective application of the

[198] See M Cheh, 'Constitutional Limits on Using Civil Remedies to Achieve Criminal Law Objectives: Understanding and Transcending the Criminal-Civil Law Distinction' (1990–1991) 42 *Hastings Law Journal* 1325, especially 1353ff, for a comparison of civil and criminal law sanctions. For an economic analysis of the aforementioned concepts, see E Iacobucci, 'On the Interaction between Legal and Reputational Sanctions' (2014) 43 *Journal of Legal Studies* 189. According to Iacobucci, there is a strong connection between the gravity of the punishment and the degree of reputational sanction.

[199] Although the UK Company Directors Disqualification Act 1986, Sch 1, Pt 1, para 1 refers to 'Any misfeasance or breach of any fiduciary or other duty by the director in relation to the company', and is referred to in s 9 of the same Act, on matters for determining the unfitness of directors of an insolvent company.

[200] See text at ch 2.III–V and accompanying notes.

[201] See text at ch 2.III and accompanying notes.

[202] *Keech v Sandford* [1726] EWHC J76.

doctrine, such as Germany, France and Spain, and those, such as Italy, in which, unfortunately, the rule has never been applied, despite having been introduced more than a decade ago. It is clear that in Italy, the total absence of judicial efforts in this direction risks rendering it unlikely that public opinion will agree on the necessity to respect this rule.

A final note concerns the relationship between reputation and the business and financial press. It is well known that the business and financial press is very specialised. Therefore, its staff tend to be extremely professional and, in most of cases, are well aware of the important role that information about corporate governance plays. This turns out to be particularly important for institutional investors.[203] One may well imagine that it would be possible to create a general understanding in the business community about the misappropriation of corporate opportunities. However, whether the financial press is interested in such news is likely to depend to a large extent on the importance of the violations that occur. Currently, this kind of information is likely to circulate more often in Spain, in relation to listed companies, than in the UK or in France, where most of the case law is confined to smaller corporations.

One must also consider the existence of conditions for potential reputational repercussions on those who have breached corporate opportunity rules, as well as the probability that such a breach is followed by reputational sanctions. In that case, we would need to specify what those sanctions would be. Firstly, it may be said that such a breach may be perceived as a manifestation of a certain degree of dishonesty in relation to one's principals. Such information would be extremely interesting for potential new principals. Therefore, it could negatively affect the chances for the person in breach to be hired in a similar position (ie as a director). Nonetheless, if the director sets up a new company that they own, such reputational sanctions will not significantly touch them. Secondly, such an action might demonstrate the individual's talents as an efficient taker/entrepreneur. Economic operators may well appreciate such brave, though legally questionable, behaviour. The effectiveness of this kind of sanction must be considered in relation to the social environment in which the sanction is applied. As Kahan reminds us:

> Individuals are much more likely to commit crimes when they perceive that criminal activity is widespread. In that circumstance, they are likely to infer that the risk of being caught for a crime is low. They might also conclude that relatively little stigma or reputational cost attaches to being a criminal; indeed, if criminal behavior is common among their peers, they may even view such activity as status enhancing. Finally, in a community in which crime is perceived to be rampant, individuals are less likely to form moral aversions to criminality.[204]

[203] D Tambini, 'What are Financial Journalist for?' (2010) 11 *Journalism Studies* 158.
[204] ibid 350.

As a final remark, the potential reach of reputational sanctions is likely to be greater for a specific kind of director – that is, for an independent director, who is likely to accept several appointments in different companies. This hypothesis is also in line with the general literature on reputational sanctions, which usually depicts independent directors as those who are more likely to be affected in the board of directors, in view of the spillover effects of reputational sanctions.[205]

X. CONCLUSIONS

In *Bhullar v Bhullar*, Lord Justice Parker discussed the applicability of the *Boardman v Phipps* rule to the case of a company's director, and concluded that 'As Lord Upjohn made clear in *Phipps v Boardman*, flexibility of application is of the essence of the rule'.[206] It is true that such flexibility is also reflected in the existence of the equitable remedies and in the possibility of applying them in different circumstances and in a pragmatic way. This renders Anglo-American jurisdictions able to provide not only 'static' efficiency, but also 'dynamic' efficiency, through constant adaptation to the needs arising in the business community. Such an option is clearly a 'bonus' that Anglo-American courts can employ for furthering efficiency in a changing business world.

Certain remedies in all the jurisdictions considered in this chapter are comparable, for instance, dismissal of directors (although with a less efficient rule in the US than in other jurisdictions) and *astreinte* (albeit an unclear situation in Italian law). Dismissal and *astreinte*, in addition to being alternatives, are not likely to be the most effective remedies in cases of misappropriations of corporate opportunities. As to pecuniary remedies against misappropriation, the Anglo-American jurisdictions display the highest variety of remedies, also thanks to the availability of remedies which derive either from common law or from equity law.

There may also be differences in the effects of reputational sanctions across countries. The absence of criminal provisions in all the countries analysed, the fact that at least in some countries, such as the UK and France, corporate opportunity cases have rarely been in financial press (since they usually do not concern listed companies), and the exiguous amount of case law in other countries may render this kind of sanction unlikely to be a source of serious concern for directors, at least at present.

To conclude, it appears that Anglo-American corporate laws have a far more effective set of legal remedies against the misappropriation of corporate

[205] E Kang, 'Director Interlocks and Spillover Effects of Reputational Penalties from Financial Reporting Fraud' (2008) 51 *Academy of Management Journal* 537.

[206] *Bhullar* (n 53) [27]–[28].

opportunities – which may also be due in part to their capability to constrain insiders' behaviour in the long run, for instance through profit-tracing. Such a difference in the effectiveness of legal remedies seems to be the real divide between common law and civil law jurisdictions. Such a great divide between jurisdictions is likely to be a source of very important consequences for both disclosure and efficient negotiation over corporate opportunities, as I consider in the next chapter.

4

Bargaining Over Corporate Opportunities as the Central Objective of Corporate Opportunity Doctrines

I. INTRODUCTION: LEAVING BEHIND THE PROPERTY VERSUS LIABILITY RULES DEBATE – A DESTRUCTURED APPROACH TO BARGAINING

THE ECONOMIC VALUE of corporate opportunities, especially those that consist of ideas that might be transformed into future technological innovations, can be extremely difficult to determine. At times, one may not even know whether a given technological innovation will generate any profit at all, given the extremely high rate of failure within start-ups.[1] Therefore, bargaining can be considered an extremely precious tool that allow different evaluations to emerge within a negotiation context. This in turn may help the parties to clarify their ideas on a given business opportunity. Ultimately, bargaining can lead to an allocation of business opportunities that is efficient both from a productive and a dynamic perspective – which in turn can contribute to the maximisation of social welfare.[2]

In traditional corporate law literature, the taking of corporate opportunities by insiders can be characterised as 'tunnelling',[3] or as an 'appropriation of private benefits' of control[4] or simply as 'misappropriation'.[5] Such terms stress

[1] M Cantanessa et al, 'Startups' Road to Failure' (2018) 10 *Sustainability* 2346; E Skawińska and R Zalewski, 'Success Factors of Startups in the EU – A Comparative Study' (2020) 12 *Sustainability* 8200.

[2] F Bator, 'The Simple Analytics of Welfare Maximization' (1957) 47 *The American Economic Review* 22. Note that there is a distinction between productivity and efficiency: a firm can be technically efficient but still able to enhance its productivity by exploiting economies of scale. T Coelli et al, *An Introduction to Efficiency and Productivity Analysis* (Springer, 2005) 3–4. It may well be that an incumbent company, despite holding a larger market share than a new entrant, incurs higher costs in adapting quickly to technological changes and is therefore actually less able to exploit a business opportunity consisting in groundbreaking technology on a large scale in the short and medium run.

[3] See S Johnson et al, 'Tunneling' (2000) 90 *American Economic Review* 22. Although the original definition of tunneling usually refers to majority shareholders, this term is also often applied to directors.

[4] A Dyck and L Zingales, 'Private Benefits of Control: An International Comparison' (2004) 59 *Journal of Finance* 537.

[5] For instance, R Cassim, 'Post-resignation Duties of Directors: The Application of the Fiduciary Duty not to Misappropriate Corporate Opportunities' (2008) 125 *South African Law Journal* 731.

the fact that such activity is detrimental to the company. The normative consequence of a perspective that considers the taking of corporate opportunities by insiders as a breach of directors' duty of loyalty is deterrence for the purpose of minimising misappropriations[6] – ie, as a way to contain agency costs.[7] Nonetheless, opportunities to develop a given business may well be an object of efficient bargaining between the company and its insider over the rights to exploit the opportunity at issue. Such bargaining, in turn, may ultimately lead to the allocation of the business opportunity to a company insider.[8] On this basis, Michael Whincop has developed a sophisticated Law and Economics analysis that discusses the degree of protection to be granted to corporate opportunities for the purpose of furthering efficient bargaining.[9] Whincop's analysis is based on the traditional distinction between property rules and liability rules.

Since the 1960s, Law and Economics literature has enquired into the efficiency profiles connected with the choice between property and liability rules.[10] Basing their views on Coase's intuitions about the irrelevance of the allocation of entitlements to allocative efficiency in the case of zero transaction costs, several scholars have provided insights into the efficiency profiles of the allocation of entitlements in the case of positive transaction costs.[11] This discussion was originally confined to property law. Nevertheless, as this paradigm was based on the idea of bargaining over an entitlement, it was also developed in contract law theory and subsequently in corporate law theory.[12]

Calabresi and Melamed, who posed the basis for the distinction between property rules and liability rules in normative terms (or *de lege ferenda*), introduce that distinction by stating that 'the categories are not, of course, absolutely distinct'.[13] Calabresi and Melamed's refusal of a strict dogmatic distinction between the two kinds of rules may reveal to us that 'property rules'

[6] On deterrence, see text at ch 3.I and accompanying notes.

[7] See F Easterbrook and D Fischel, *The Economic Structure of Corporate Law* (Harvard University Press, 1996).

[8] This approach is found in E Talley, 'Turning Servile Opportunities into Gold: A Strategic Analysis of the Corporate Opportunities Doctrine' (1998–1999) 108 *Yale Law Journal* 277.

[9] M Whincop, 'Painting the Corporate Cathedral: The Protection of Entitlements in Corporate Law' (1999) 19 *Oxford Journal of Legal Studies* 19.

[10] On property rules and liability rules, see G Calabresi, 'Transaction Costs, Resource Allocation and Liability Rules – A Comment' (1968) 11 *Journal of Law and Economics* 67; G Calabresi and D Melamed, 'Property Rules, Liability Rules, and Inalienability: One View of the Cathedral' (1972) 85 *Harvard Law Review* 1089; I Ayres and J Balkin, 'Legal Entitlements as Auctions: Property Rules, Liability Rules, and Beyond' (1996) 106 *Yale Law Journal* 703; I Ayres and R Gertner, 'Strategic Contractual Inefficiency and the Optimal Choice of Legal Rules' (1992) 101 *Yale Law Journal* 729; I Ayres and E Talley, 'Solomonic Bargaining: Dividing an Entitlement to Facilitate Coasean Trade' (1995) 104 *Yale Law Journal* 1027.

[11] See M Polinsky, *An Introduction to Law and Economics* (Walter Kluwers, 2011) 15: 'If there are positive transaction costs … the preferred rule is the rule that minimizes the effects of transaction costs'.

[12] See Z Goshen, 'The Efficiency of Controlling Corporate Self-Dealing: Theory Meets Reality' (2003) 91 *California Law Review* 393.

[13] Calabresi and Melamed, 'Property Rules, Liability Rules, and Inalienability' (1972).

and 'liability rules' are simply the extreme manifestations of a continuum of remedies. Therefore, normative conclusions may be granted a higher degree of precision, without the need to make a proposed rule necessarily fit into one definition or the other. In other words, Calabresi and Melamed created the property/liability distinction as a way to reflect different degrees of intensity of protection granted to a given entitlement and not for the purpose of encapsulating normative solutions in a rigid binary structure. Subsequent literature has made use of the above-mentioned flexibility for the purpose of proposing a similar economics discussion within different theoretical frameworks.

One of the best examples of a very flexible interpretation of the above-mentioned terms is provided by Ayres and Balkin. They start their analysis by stating that 'the only difference between liability and property rules is the price of exercising the option – the damages to be paid for the nonconsensual taking'.[14] This supposition looks particularly relevant in normative terms. In fact, once the liability and property rules categories are completely destructured from a normative perspective, more potentially efficient solutions may emerge than the one suggested by a binary approach – which, incidentally, may not reflect adequately the nuances characterising each kind of remedy.

I will also take such a destructured view, for the purpose of identifying an optimal degree of protection for corporate opportunities. I will not adopt any dogmatic distinction between property and liability rules. Instead, and so as not to confuse the reader, I will refer to different levels of protection of the entitlement. In fact, the only eventual qualitative difference in remedies might be the effects of a constructive trust on negotiation, especially in a case of failed negotiation. In fact, a constructive trust followed by a transfer order is not a purely monetary remedy, because it compels the transfer of specific assets. Moreover, when such a transfer is not possible, if the accounting of profits assisted by the constructive trust is proprietary in nature, it is also assisted by profits tracing.[15]

On the basis of the above-mentioned destructured perspective, I discuss the effect on bargaining of punitive damages; the constructive trust (in its proprietary and personal versions) that usually assists the disgorgement of profits (or the account of profits, in the UK);[16] the full liability of the insider (ie *damnum emergens* and *lucrum cessans*) in its civil law form or as equitable compensation; and partial liability of the insider (ie something less than full liability). To those remedies can be added – exclusively for the situation where corporate opportunities have been taken but the insider/taker does not resign as a result – the dismissal of a director. I will leave aside the reputational sanctions cited in chapter three because they are rather difficult to analyse from a comparative

[14] Ayres and Balkin, 'Legal Entitlements as Auctions' (1996) 705.

[15] See text at ch 3.III and accompanying notes.

[16] Account of profits (for past profits) and constructive trust (for future profits) are usually cumulative in Anglo-American law, as is one component of damages, ie *lucrum cessans* (lost chance of profits). See text at ch 3.III and accompanying notes.

perspective, given the paucity of the discourse currently available in literature on the point.

Although my view is that liability and property rules are categories that do not bring very clear heuristic or normative benefits, I am still employing them when describing the models of those authors who have found the Law and Economics distinction useful and have therefore applied it to their research.

II. MODELS FOR THE ANALYSIS OF BARGAINING OVER CORPORATE OPPORTUNITIES

Whincop's and Talley's models of bargaining on corporate opportunities present different hypotheses and different solutions. Whincop's model involves progressive reasoning; several hypotheses are added to his original assumptions one at a time. He starts from the hypothesis of perfect information and perfect verification by courts, in which he finds that both a property and a liability rule turn out to be efficient, although with different distributive outcomes.[17] He then adds the hypothesis of strategic bargaining; that is, the idea that, in a repeated game, parties may behave aggressively, holding out for a larger stake in the gain from trade in order to increase their reputation as tough negotiators.[18] This idea may be correct in the light of negotiation theory only when the parties opt for the negotiation approach described by Whincop (which is clearly neither the only nor prevalent one in modern negotiation practice).[19] Firstly, the longevity of the relationship between a company and its insider may well determine a cooperative attitude on both sides, unless there has been some particular recent disagreement between the two.[20] Secondly, one has to remember that the takings of some of the most valuable corporate opportunities, especially the one consisting of technological innovation, may also be one-offs. In fact, such a taking may allow the taker to set up a new firm and therefore resign from their position as an insider.[21] In these cases, there will be no further interactions between insider and corporation once the opportunity has been taken; that is, there will be no

[17] Whincop, 'Painting the Corporate Cathedral' (1999) 36.

[18] Whincop (n 9) 37. S Özyurt, 'Bargaining, Reputation and Competition' (2015) 119 *Journal of Economic Behavior & Organization* 1.

[19] See R Korobkin, *Negotiation Theory and Strategy* (Aspen Publishers, 2009). Alan Stitt, who is one of the most renowned experts in negotiation, often stresses the drawbacks of so-called competitive bargaining, to which cooperative bargaining or principled negotiation is often preferred. The many drawbacks of competitive bargaining include the risks of ending a commercial relationship, the limited creativity of the approach, and the frequent creation of deadlock situations – see A Stitt, *Mediating Commercial Disputes* (Canada Law Book, 2003) 35ff. Apart from those identified above, there is a further disadvantage in playing the tough bargainer, especially if a 'tough seller' is planning to become a buyer in future. In fact, a tough buyer can be strategically employed in by the seller when there are several prospective buyers. See Özyurt, 'Bargaining' (2015).

[20] A Goldman and J Rojot, *Negotiation Theory and Practice* (Kluwer, 2003) 34–35.

[21] See for instance *Can Aero v O'Malley* [1974] SCR 592.

repeated game of the kind described by Whincop. In fact, the insider will be likely resigning from their position within the corporation. By contrast, in light of the theory on open innovation and on contracting for innovation, it may well be that the incumbent company is interested to preserve good relationships with the resigning director.[22]

The potential differences between one-off and repeated misappropriations do not necessarily affect the rest of Whincop's analysis, once Whincop introduces further assumptions; that is, he assumes that information is imperfectly verifiable because the parties know their own reservation price but not the counterparty's, and that the court is unable to verify the value of the opportunity. In such a case, Whincop stresses the dangers of a different kind of strategic bargaining – that is, the one depending on each party's wrong evaluation of their counterparty's reservation price.[23] This kind of behaviour is also likely to occur in a one-period game. In this case, imperfect verification will not allow a correct allocation when bargaining is not successful. In relation to such situations, Whincop stresses the special disadvantages deriving from fixing the level of liability lower than the company's reservation price and the consequent need for the company to bribe the insider not to take the opportunity.[24]

Whincop's position is in stark contrast to the findings of Ayres and Talley on Solomonic bargaining. For the general case of contracting over an entitlement, Ayres and Talley support an untailored liability rule. Untailored liability is an order to the taker of the entitlement to pay a fixed sum to the owner, as compensation for the taking, regardless of the owner showing actual loss (this is the reason it is called 'untailored'). Among different levels of untailored liability rules (ie corresponding to lower or higher levels of liability), Ayres and Talley seem to stress the efficiency-enhancing properties of a weak untailored liability rule – that is, one that fixes a lower sum than the one that would be necessary for the full protection of the interests of the owner. The reason that Ayres and Talley prefer such a rule is that it would force bilateral disclosure, solving the problems often generated by a strategic hold-up on the part of an owner protected by a property rule.[25]

By contrast, in the case of corporate opportunities, Whincop derives from a tailored, 'weak' (ie certainly lower than the company's reservation price) liability rule a series of adverse consequences, both in terms of distribution and in terms of efficiency. First, Whincop finds such a rule unjust in terms of distribution, given that the insider would derive their gain from the breach of a fiduciary duty.[26] Second, the rule would be inefficient because one may presume that the

[22] See text at ch 5.VIII.

[23] Whincop (n 9) 38.

[24] ibid.

[25] Ayres and Talley, 'Solomonic Bargaining' (1995).

[26] Whincop (n 9) 38. It is worth noting that this kind of reasoning is heavily influenced by Whincop's Australian legal background. A lawyer coming from a jurisdiction where the director's

company has built up specific competences for exploiting the business opportunity more efficiently.[27] Therefore, according to Whincop, corporate opportunities should be allocated to the company *ex ante* and should be strongly protected. Third, when many insiders are interested in taking the opportunity, the company would need to bribe all of them, exponentially increasing its transaction costs and consequently rendering the taking impossible.[28] Therefore, in such a case, Whincop concludes that a property rule would work better both on distribution and efficiency grounds.

Finally, Whincop maintains his previous conclusions, even when he changes his assumptions in order to mirror more closely his ideas about the informational structure that surrounds, in his view, the aforementioned bargaining. For Whincop, there is, on one side, an insider who knows both their reservation price and the corporation's and, on the other side, a number of shareholders who know none of the reservation prices; that is, they do not even know the value of the opportunity for the company.[29] This would occur because Whincop assumes that it is the shareholders who will ultimately be competent to authorise takings by insiders. In this case, Whincop adds to the previously mentioned reasons for imposing a property rule further reasons based respectively on shareholders' protection and on the need to provide incentives for disclosure by insiders. Whereas the first reason is intuitive, the second argument claims that the insider under a property rule will disclose their reservation price immediately. In fact, the insider may need to be quick to propose their offer. The need to be swift would be a consequence of potential misappropriations of the business opportunity by third parties once the information on the opportunity starts circulating.[30] This may well be one of the situations described in negotiation theory through the general concept of 'cost of impending negotiations'.[31]

When discussing property rules versus liability rules, Whincop shows a very flexible approach to semantics. On one hand, he expressly states that a full liability rule (ie one that fixes liability at the company's reservation price or higher) equals a property rule.[32] On the other hand, it is also clear throughout the whole

duty of loyalty to the corporation does not exist or has recently been introduced would probably reason divergently.

[27] ibid 39. Whincop is quite vague and does not expand on this point or quote literature on specific investments as he could have done. It might be that by 'specific competences' he refers to a semantic field that is wider or narrower than the one covered by the term 'specific investment'. On specific investments, see B Klein, R Crawford and A Alchian, 'Vertical Integration, Appropriable Rents, and the Competitive Contracting Process' (1978) 21 *Journal of Law and Economics* 297; O Williamson, 'Transaction-Cost Economics: the Governance of Contractual Relations' (1979) 22 *Journal of Law and Economics* 233.

[28] Whincop (n 9) 39.

[29] ibid 41.

[30] ibid 42.

[31] Goldman and Rojot, *Negotiation Theory* (2003) 66ff.

[32] Whincop (n 9), at fn 100, expressly refers to the concepts developed by Ayres and Balkin in their article on auctions (n 11).

discussion that there is no such thing as a predetermined value for a liability rule, the court being free in Whincop's model to determine any level of liability.

We can derive from Whincop's approach at least two provisional conclusions. First, on an analytical plane, it is clear that there is a full range of different levels of protection of entitlements, and the decision to set the division between property and liability at a given level is to some extent discretionary (here, property rules correspond to a higher (but how high?) level of protection of the entitlement). Second, on a normative plane, Whincop concludes that a property rule is more desirable both from a distributive and from an efficiency perspective. Even if we assume that his conclusions are correct, Whincop does not tell us what kind of property rule we should apply to corporate opportunity cases. In fact, property rules may also correspond to different levels of protection, provided that, by Whincop's definition, they are set at a level equal to or higher than the value of the business opportunity for the company.[33]

The Law and Economics framework proposed by Talley[34] is more sophisticated in its economic analysis than that proposed by Whincop. It is based on ideas about the information system underlying bargaining activity over corporate opportunities and introduces some industrial organisation variables. Talley assumes that the rationale for not imposing a total ban on the taking of corporate opportunities is that a company and its insiders may have different specialisations.[35] Each of them is able to exploit more efficiently those opportunities that fall within the area in which they are specialised.[36] Directors are the usual messengers through which the company is informed about the existence of new corporate opportunities.[37]

The company will usually be presented with roughly three kinds of business opportunities: those that fall too far from the company's technical competence (but fall within the insider's technical competence); those that perfectly match the company's technical skills (and fall far from the insider's personal specialisation); and those that are in the middle (ie that could be exploited efficiently by both the company and its insiders).[38] Assuming that there is information asymmetry as to the specificities of the opportunity, the insider will be tempted to misrepresent the specific features of those opportunities that fall within the third category in order to make them look unattractive to the company.[39] By contrast, insiders will be uninterested in the second category and they will also be the only party interested in the first category.

[33] Whincop (n 9).

[34] Talley, 'Turning Servile Opportunities into Gold' (1998–1999).

[35] V Brudney and R Clark, 'A New Look at Corporate Opportunities' (1981) 94 *Harvard Law Review* 997.

[36] Talley (n 8) 311ff.

[37] ibid 312.

[38] ibid 313.

[39] ibid 317.

According to Talley, an optimal corporate opportunity rule should force maximum disclosure by insiders.[40] Talley does not employ the distinction between property rules and liability rules (not nominally, at least), perhaps because he is very much aware of the difficulties inherent in the use of those terms. Nevertheless, he clearly refers to different levels of protection of the entitlement.[41] He stresses that a high level of protection will force disclosure-even though in his words it is not that clear how it will force disclosure of the specific information that is necessary to identify the kind of opportunity at stake-but he also explains that the same high level of protection may have an adverse effect by preventing efficient breach by the insider of their duty.[42] He then concludes that an ideal rule should be aware of the above-mentioned trade-off. According to Talley, protection of the company should prevail over a marginal sacrifice of the insiders' potential efficient breach of contract.[43]

Talley's ideas are insightful from many perspectives. They can be further expanded by analysing the effects of different levels of protection throughout the different phases of bargaining. Talley's analysis is purely based on Law and Economics. From the point of view of negotiation theory, bargaining is embedded in a temporal framework; ie it is preceded by a pre-negotiation phase, which in the case of corporate opportunities must be preceded by disclosure, and is followed by the outcome of the negotiation. It may well be that the parties do not reach an agreement, and therefore parties' post-bargaining behaviour in the case of failed agreement can open some insights from a normative perspective.[44]

III. ASSUMPTIONS UNDERLYING THE ANALYSIS OF BARGAINING OVER CORPORATE OPPORTUNITIES

The effects of legal rules on bargaining is a far-reaching one, encompassing the several steps undertaken by the parties towards reaching a mutual agreement. Bargaining on corporate opportunities can be analysed by focusing sequentially on different phases – that is, the disclosure of a corporate opportunity, then the

[40] ibid 328. Note that a disclosure-forcing effect can be attributed not only to corporate opportunity remedies, but also the underlying test, ie for instance a no-profit versus no-conflict test. See J Armour, 'Corporate Opportunities: If in Doubt, Disclose (but how?)' (2004) 63 *Cambridge Law Journal* 33, 35.

[41] Talley mostly writes about damages awarded by the court. However, it is clear that he refers to a vast range of remedies, at least in quantitative terms.

[42] Talley (n 8) 328.

[43] According to Talley, in this situation an essential role is also played by the distributive preferences connected to the necessity to maximise shareholders' value. For this discussion, see Talley (n 8) 324.

[44] An analysis of the interactions among the different phases of the negotiation process is offered by C Patton and S Balakrishnan, 'The Impact of Expectation of Future Negotiation Interaction on Bargaining Processes and Outcomes' (2010) 63 *Journal of Business Research* 809.

bargaining over it, and finally the situation resulting from failure to reach an agreement.

I will preface the following discussion by noting that this model does not delve into the intricacies of the personal and emotional relationships between the parties. While in certain cases such psychological factors may have a significant impact on negotiation,[45] consideration of this would require development of a framework that is different from the Law and Economics one that I am proposing here. It would be hard, if not impossible, to predetermine the nature of the personal relationships between the parties in the context of a negotiation on corporate opportunities, not least because changes in the parties' attitude can be triggered by the negotiation process itself. If, on the one hand, a long-term relationship is predictive of a cooperative style,[46] on the other hand, the absence of alternatives to negotiation may determine the adoption of a more competitive style.[47] In any case, each situation will be unique, and will depend on the history of the relationships between the two parties and on how the negotiation process improves or worsens the relationship. This is not to understate the relevance of what behavioural economics has described as 'bounded self-interest'. Nonetheless, contrary to the hypotheses of supporters of behavioural economics theory applied to the law, I do not think that in this context 'bounded self-interest' could be described as one of the 'systematic (rather than random or arbitrary) departures from conventional economic models'.[48]

On top of that, one should also consider that the parties' attitude towards negotiation can be asymmetric. In the simplest of the cases, an insider trying to appropriate a business opportunity may be motivated simply by their desire to start up a new and independent business. On the other side of the negotiation table, the sets of incentives driving the person who negotiates for the incumbent company may be rather complex. The representative of the company at the negotiating table may simply want to act in the best interests of the company, but their attitude could be affected by a desire to enhance their position within the company through boosting their reputation.[49] This may introduce a series of biases, both in the assessment of the business opportunity and in the final decision. For instance, if the person in charge of the negotiation wants to impress the board and build up a reputation of being a tough negotiator, they may actually behave more aggressively and/or refuse a rational deal which is favourable for both the incumbent company and the insider.[50]

[45] Goldman and Rojot (n 20) 34.

[46] ibid.

[47] ibid.

[48] C Jolls, C Sunstein and R Thaler, 'A Behavioral Approach to Law and Economics (1998) 50 *Stanford Law Review* 1471–1477.

[49] A Trask and A De Guire, *Betting the Company: Complex Negotiation Strategies for Law and Business* (Oxford University Press, 2013) 32.

[50] In a corporate context, the risk is particularly high in so-called 'open door bargaining', where the agent's negotiation process is observable by the principal. See J Fingleton and M Raith, 'Career Concerns of Bargainers' (2005) 21 *Journal of Law, Economics, and Organization* 179.

Turning back to the triphasic negotiation framework proposed above (disclosure, proper bargaining, post-bargaining), given that information is asymmetric and transaction costs are positive, different degrees of protection provided to corporate opportunities are likely to produce different effects in each of the cited stages. I will make a few necessary assumptions in my analysis.

The first assumption I make is that there is a test for identifying a 'corporate opportunity' which is clearer than the one resulting from the analysis of US corporate laws.[51] Here, 'corporate opportunities' are those business opportunities that fall within the line of business of the corporation and that the director learns about while discharging their duties to the corporation. This assumption depends on the fact that the popular Delaware rule, first formulated in *Guth v Loft*,[52] has become a sort of legal benchmark in academic literature. Moreover, a functionally similar, although not identical, way of reasoning seems to be common to the conflict test adopted by most European corporate opportunity rules[53] and also occasionally in UK doctrine and jurisprudence,[54] although in the UK the prevalent test remains based on the 'no profit' rule.[55]

Obviously, the US law does not display homogeneity as to the tests adopted for the identification of a corporate opportunity.[56] Nevertheless, the 'line of business' rule has been highly influential within US corporate laws, either alone or, in most of the cases, combined with further tests.[57] Embracing this rule means also acknowledging the existence of different nuances with reference to the definition of 'line of business'. In fact, that term may refer to the present line of business, to the foreseeable future line of business and also to business functionally related to the main line of business.[58] As explained later, such flexibility in the interpretation of line of business (which is useful in practical terms) is also connected to the idea of variable degrees of protection to be granted to corporate opportunities in normative terms.[59]

[51] See E Orlinsky, 'Corporate Opportunity Doctrine and Interested Director Transactions: A Framework for Analysis in an Attempt to Restore Predictability' (1999) 24 *Delaware Journal of Corporate Law* 451. Clearly, the legal framework would be far more complex if we needed to introduce the different features of some of the corporate laws cited in this book, ie British, French, Italian and Spanish.

[52] *Guth v Loft Inc*, 5 A2d 503 (Del Ch 1939).

[53] See text corresponding to fns 61 and 62.

[54] This is clearly an extremely controversial topic in UK company law. Nevertheless, parts of the case law are based on a general no-conflict rule that is logically close to the line of business test. The test applied by British courts can at times be even more refined than the tests employed by US courts. See for instance the tests adopted by Warren J in *Wilkinson v West Coast Capital* [2005] EWHC 3009 (Ch). Nevertheless, it is important to remember again that in UK law it does not matter whether the director discovered the opportunity while discharging their duties or not. The opportunity will be deemed as corporate in any case. On this point, see for instance *Bhullar v Bhullar* [2003] EWCA Civ 424.

[55] The inherent intricacy of the codification process has been described by E Lowry, 'The Codification of Directors' Duties: Capturing the Essence of the Corporate Opportunity Doctrine' (2006) 2 *Ownership and Control* 22, 27ff.

[56] See Orlinsky, 'Corporate Opportunity Doctrine' (1999).

[57] See ibid.

[58] See Talley (n 8).

[59] See text at section VII and accompanying notes.

As to European civil law legislations, there is no widespread adoption of the line of business test.[60] Nonetheless, the conflict test looks functionally similar. In fact, companies are usually interested in business opportunities that are in their line of business, and opportunities that are in the line of business of the corporation tend to be those that are connected to its industrial interests. The interest test is per se flexible with reference to those business opportunities that fall within the potential line of business of the corporation (ie any opportunity may be in the interest of the company if an appropriate justification is provided).[61]

A second assumption is that allocative efficiency corresponds to productive efficiency, as it usually occurs when markets are perfectly contestable. By contrast, if we assume that product markets are not contestable, things may change. In fact, especially in those markets where there is significant stagnation, there may well be situations in which the party who values the opportunity more is the one that is less productively efficient – perhaps the incumbent company, provided that it is able to extract oligopolistic rents from the opportunity on a reasonably stable basis.[62] The introduction of more efficient technology (when eventually invented) in a stagnating market can clearly alter the game. However, technological change is not likely to occur all the time and in every market. Moreover, assuming that technological change actually occurs, such occurrence might not be reflected in the reservation price expressed at the time the negotiation takes place.[63] Therefore, I assume a contestable market at the time in which the negotiation takes place, in order to exclude any significant variation in the reservation prices of the parties that might reflect the possibility of extracting oligopolistic rents from trade on a reasonably stable basis.[64]

[60] M Corradi, 'Corporate Opportunities Doctrines Tested in the Light of the Theory of the Firm – a European (and US) Comparative Perspective' (2016) 27 *European Business Law Review* 755, 814. But note that recently the French Supreme *Court de Cassation* has reasoned on the basis of what seems to be a version of the 'line of business' test. See Cass Com, 5 Juillet 2016 – no 15-15.868, involving an aesthetic clinic organised as a 'société par actions simplifiée', whose shadow director had acquired a piece of real estate, while such an acquisition was not in the line of business of the company.

[61] ibid 818.

[62] This is not necessarily the case, according to J Azar, 'The Common Ownership Trilemma' (2020) 87 *The University of Chicago Law Review* 263, 273–74; in fact, 'with market power, the Fisher Separation Theorem does not apply, and shareholders may not agree on how to use that power. Prosocial shareholders may want to use that power in a way that does not lead to the highest possible level of profits, even in the long-term'. Although this seems plausible in principle, I am not convinced that most shareholders would behave in a 'prosocial' way on every possible topic. In other words, whereas subjects such as the environment may attract prosocial activism, extracting oligopolistic rents (unless conducted in breach of antitrust law) may be a kind of conduct that is not even understood by the average shareholder.

[63] As the introduction of a new technology requires time. See M Plaza, O Ngwenyama and K Rohlf, 'A Comparative Analysis of Learning Curves: Implications for New Technology Implementation Management' (2010) 200 *European Journal of Operational Research* 518.

[64] M Corradi and J Nowag, 'Enforcing Corporate Opportunities Rules: Antitrust Risks and Antirust Failures' (2018), www.law.nyu.edu/sites/default/files/upload_documents/Corradi%20AND%20Nowag.pdf.

A third assumption concerns distribution of the gains from trade. In the present analysis, focus is on efficiency profiles. As to distribution, I assume that the dominant rule is that of 'maximising shareholders' value'.[65] Therefore, I do not discuss the validity of this paradigm and possible alternatives involving more complex distribution arrangements benefiting other stakeholders. Nonetheless, I acknowledge the fact that different distribution arrangements may affect *ex ante* incentives of parties to disclose information and the willingness of parties to commit to different levels of investment to exploit the corporate opportunity at stake. Therefore, at times, there will be a trade-off between efficiency and predetermined distribution objectives to be taken into consideration.

A fourth assumption concerns information that is assumed to be to some extent incomplete and asymmetric. I will provide further details when discussing the different kinds of information at stake in disclosure and negotiation; that is, information about the existence of a corporate opportunity, information about its technical nature and information about its value.

A fifth assumption is that there is no repeated game between company and insider; that once the opportunity is taken, the insider will leave the corporation and set up a new firm. It is worth noting that there may be cases in which the opportunity at stake is not a productive one (such as, for instance, a piece of real estate that is not connected to any specific business development). The taking of such an opportunity may not be a reason for a director to leave a company. I will present separately a few comments on the case of opportunities that may not imply that directors leave the company. In fact, they may follow different modalities and they may be subject to different sets of incentives, given that they imply the occurrence of a repeated game.

A final important note concerns behavioural economics. It has been proposed that Law and Economics analysis may benefit from a reconsideration of the *homo economicus* assumption, because 'people can be said to display bounded rationality, bounded willpower, bounded self-interest'.[66] I have already commented on bounded self-interest.[67] As to bounded willpower, I do not see any particular connection with the appropriation of corporate opportunities by insiders. Instead, with reference to bounded rationality, one may enquire about the possible presence of an endowment effect[68] and the potential use of rules of thumb.[69] As to a possible endowment effect, one may wonder whether a business opportunity is perceived as a 'token' or as a 'mug', to recall a famous analogy derived from an empirical experiment on the endowment effect.[70]

[65] *cf* Talley (n 8), who assumes liquidity constraints on the insider.
[66] Jolls, Sunstein and Thaler, 'A Behavioral Approach' (1998) 1476.
[67] See text corresponding to n 48.
[68] Jolls, Sunstein and Thaler (n 49) 1488.
[69] ibid 1477.
[70] D Kahneman, J Knetsch and R Thaler, 'Experimental Tests of the Endowment Effect and the Coase Theorem' (1990) 98 *Journal of Political Economy* 1325, 1329ff.

According to Arley, Spitzer and Talley, directors may perceive a business opportunity more as a token than as a mug, at least if we apply to this context their general observation:

> [A]gents might not manifest an endowment effect if a sense of loyalty or obligation to the firm mutes their sense of entitlement ('shared entitlement' hypothesis). In particular, agents might not endow if entering into an agency relationship causes them to feel the firm is entitled to the assets implicated in the relationship, resulting in a sense of shared or incomplete entitlement. This would be particularly likely to mute the endowment effect where an agent's decision whether to keep the asset affects the firm's welfare.[71]

Nonetheless, it may be that the 'sense of loyalty' the authors refer to may be less perceived in non-Anglo-American jurisdictions, where such duties have been introduced more recently. Moreover, if the corporate opportunity consists of an invention and it has been developed outside the corporation, such a sense of endowment may be present, at least if we make an analogy with what has been found in intellectual property (IP) theory.[72] Although such an endowment effect might occur in certain cases, I also think that when it occurs its main effect may be to lower incentives to disclose. I propose that in any case, disclosure is the core objective of a sound corporate opportunity doctrine, and lack of disclosure should be deterred with rather harsh sanctions. Therefore, I do not think that such a possible endowment effect should alter my analysis.

IV. THE PROTECTION OF ENTITLEMENTS TO EXPLOIT CORPORATE OPPORTUNITIES AND DISCLOSURE

There can be no bargaining without disclosure. In fact, even though I usually refer to business opportunities in the line of business of the corporation as 'corporate', it is equally true that, although they belong *in principle* to the corporation, the corporation cannot exploit them until the board of directors of the corporation is informed about their existence.[73] Therefore, corporate opportunity remedies must also be considered in relation to this important factor.

Here I refer to disclosure of the *existence* of a corporate opportunity and of the traits of that opportunity that are crucial for its assessment. Those who

[71] J Arlen, M Spitzer and E Talley, 'Endowment Effects within Corporate Agency Relationships' (2002) 31 *Journal of Legal Studies* 1, 9.

[72] C Buccafusco and C Sprigman, 'Valuing Intellectual Property: An Experiment (2010) 96 *Cornell Law Review* 1. Their findings and their policy prescriptions are strongly criticized by O Tur-Sinai, 'The Endowment Effect in IP Transactions: The Case against Debiasing' (2011) 18 *Michigan Telecommunication & Technology Law Review* 117.

[73] M Corradi, 'Corporate Agency Costs in the Shadow of the European Stock Exchanges: A Comparative Assessment of British and Italian Law on Related Party Transactions and Corporate Opportunities' (2012) 6 *Journal of Comparative Law* 23, 35.

usually discover business opportunities are the corporation's insiders. Therefore, the ability of a corporation to effectively appropriate a corporate opportunity mostly depends on an act of disclosure by an insider (who, to simplify, I assume is a director of the corporation). The act of disclosure may be also connected to positive and negative incentives, that is, the classic carrot and stick.[74] Carrots may be advancements in career and/or eventual rewards that benefit the insider, in return for them disclosing the existence of a corporate opportunity. Sticks, employed for deterrence, may be different kinds of remedies against misappropriations.[75]

Advances in career and possible rewards related to disclosure of corporate opportunities are usually contractual and may depend on the policy of each corporation. Nonetheless, they might negatively affect the corporation from a distributional perspective (especially when the company has to pay a price to the insider). In other words, when the same level of disclosure can be obtained by deterrence, such an approach will be more consistent with the idea of maximising shareholders' value. Therefore, deterrence is crucial, for it is thanks to deterrence that opportunities come to light.

When one tries to understand deterrence, it is useful to recall the Cooter and Freedman formula, according to which, for deterrence to be effective, sanctions have to be higher than the product of expected gains from misbehaviour and the probability of detection and enforcement.[76] Earlier, I provided an overview of the remedies that may potentially be awarded in relation to misappropriations of corporate opportunities.[77] Here I focus primarily on those remedies that have been adopted by courts. I do not consider criminal sanctions. In fact, nowadays no jurisdiction in the sample I am analysing has a clear criminal policy against misappropriations of corporate opportunities.[78]

When predicting the deterrent effect of non-criminal sanctions, the first important consideration pertains to the probability of detection, which is always lower than one.[79] When the opportunity is exploited after the director has resigned their position in the company, the doctrine requires evidence that the ex-director received the information pertaining to that corporate opportunity

[74] See text at section II and accompanying notes.

[75] Of course, this is one of the ways to read directors' psychology and it accounts for only part of their reasoning. See L Stout, 'On the Proper Motives of Corporate Directors (or, Why You Don't Want to Invite Homo Economicus to Join your Board)' (2003) 28 *Delaware Journal of Corporate Law* 28 (2003) 1, 3–8.

[76] See R Cooter and B Freedman, 'The Fiduciary Relationship: Its Economic Character and Legal Consequences' (1991) 66 *New York University Law Review* 1045.

[77] See text corresponding to section I and accompanying notes. And see also ch 3 delving into each type of remedy.

[78] See text at ch 3.VII and accompanying notes.

[79] I assume there is no perfect jurisdiction. Moreover, it is also true that absence of disclosure decreases the chances of detection. Absence of disclosure requires increasing the harshness of legal sanctions.

while they were a director. This may often be difficult to prove.[80] The third party who dealt with the insider has no interest in disclosing information pertaining to those facts, especially when the insider has become a good business partner. Because the probability of detection is always lower than one, it is necessary to look for remedies that are stronger than the insider's gains from misappropriation. Otherwise, there will not be any disclosure-forcing effect.

Next, two cases can be considered; first, the case in which the company values the opportunity more than the insider does and, second, the reverse situation. In the first case, full damages will usually amount to a higher sum than pure disgorgement of profits and therefore this remedy may force disclosure because, when multiplied by the probability of detection, full damages still provide a higher sum than any profits from misappropriation. By contrast, in the case in which the insider values the opportunity more than the company does, the disgorgement of profits will better force disclosure than full damages, but probably not in an optimal way. In fact, profits multiplied by a figure lower than one will always be lower than plain profits.[81]

Given that the lawmaker cannot know *ex ante* the party who values the opportunity more, neither of the main rules usually employed against misappropriations (full damages or disgorgement of profits) can be considered as fully suitable to force disclosure in *every* possible situation. Therefore, in order to understand how remedies can be combined for forcing full disclosure, one has to introduce further considerations. Apart from reputational sanctions, which are extremely hard to quantify,[82] one has to consider at least the dismissal of directors,[83] punitive damages[84] and, possibly, the constructive trust in its proprietary version.[85]

In this context, we focus on the hypothesis of a one-off misappropriation for the purpose of setting up a new business. In such a case, the insider may have already calculated the trade-off between leaving their position in the company and starting their new business. Therefore, the dismissal of directors may have some deterrent effects, but those are likely to be limited to a loss of part of the director's contractual benefits. Those remedies that look more interesting from the point of view of obtaining further deterrence are the constructive trust and punitive damages.

As to the constructive trust, its deterrent effect may depend on whether it is interpreted as a personal or a proprietary remedy. If it is interpreted as a personal remedy, its effects do not go beyond those that have already been described with

[80] Some jurisdictions may also require evidence that directors discovered the opportunity at issue while in charge, but this is not necessary in UK law. See, for instance, *Bhullar* (n 54). The UK view is that executive directors are *always* discharging those duties while in charges.
[81] See text at ch 3.IV and accompanying notes.
[82] See text at ch 3.IX and accompanying notes.
[83] See text at ch 3.II and accompanying notes.
[84] See text at ch 3.VIII and accompanying notes.
[85] See text at ch 3.III and accompanying notes.

reference to the disgorgement of profits (or account of profits).[86] This remedy provides access to the profits deriving from the exploitation of the corporate opportunity at issue but not to those further profits connected to subsequent investments made with the profits or proceeds of the sale of the first investment. However, if it is interpreted as a proprietary remedy, things may change significantly. In this case, the remedy will allow tracing of all the profits deriving from subsequent investments.[87]

Now, going back to Cooter and Freedman, one may say that regardless of the way a constructive trust operates, it will never allow optimal deterrence. Again, one will need to compare two sums, that is, the expected sanction (future profits also from subsequent investments multiplied by a figure lower than one) against the expected profits (the same sum but simply multiplied by one). Therefore, again, the expected profits will amount to a higher sum than the expected sanction. However, in order to understand the constructive trust's full deterrent potential, one has to consider the degree of psychological uncertainty it produces in the mind of the insider. In other words, the insider may be very successful or very lucky, and they will probably not appropriate the opportunity at hand if they do not have confidence in their business acumen. Once they have misappropriated a corporate opportunity, they may engage in further investments and, in some cases, be extremely successful.[88]

Such a motivated insider has high psychological expectations regarding their business success. Now, because of the risk of declaration of a constructive trust, the insider will – regardless of their success – always be subject to the threat that the company will use tracing to recoup all the profits from their further activities. On the basis of these long-term and long-reaching effects, the remedy at issue puts a very strong psychological pressure on the insider.[89] One may say that potentially this remedy may have an extremely strong disclosure-forcing function. In fact, the insider may want to guarantee their business freedom in future instead of living with the threat of losing all the fruits of their business efforts.

This kind of deterrent effect transcends the borders of neoclassical economics. Therefore, it requires further studies grounded in behavioural economics. Intuitively an insider who misappropriates a corporate opportunity is constraint-averse and therefore, in general, they will probably not like the possibility that the company can continue to trace the fruits of their efforts for a long time after the misappropriation has occurred.[90]

[86] ibid.

[87] ibid.

[88] ibid.

[89] It is well known that not only uncertainty in detection (discountable as probability of detection) but also uncertainty on the amount of the sanction produces a deterrent effect. See T Baker, A Harel and T Kugler, 'The Virtues of Uncertainty in Law: An Experimental Approach' (2003) 89 *Iowa Law Review* 443.

[90] Note that there is a voice of strong disagreement with what is hypothesised here. In fact, it has been stated that fiduciaries are unlikely to know in detail the effects of a constructive trust and subsequent tracing in practice. See A Hicks, 'Do Constructive Trusts Deter Disloyalty?' (2018) 69

The kind of reasoning that can be applied to another kind of remedy – punitive damages – is far less behavioural and much more grounded in neoclassical economics. In fact, optimal deterrence can be achieved with punitive damages, through that simple mathematical calculation exemplified by Cooter and Freedman. Punitive damages should be raised to a level that, when multiplied by the probability of detection, produces a figure that is higher than the insider's expected gains from misappropriation. Punitive damages may be difficult to quantify.[91] However, I believe that, with reference to deterrence, one should not be overly concerned about setting a higher threshold of damages. In fact, it is true that optimal deterrence is not directed towards harming the addressee of the sanction. The threshold should be high because the objective of forcing disclosure is connected to the achievement of optimal efficiency. Disclosure is crucial for bargaining to take place. And bargaining is fundamental for an efficient allocation of corporate opportunities. The welfare of society depends significantly on such efficient allocation, which in turn will also benefit the potential taker. Moreover, again from a welfare perspective, Posner's arguments against imprisonment do not apply to punitive damages, because usually punitive damages do not entail additional costs for society.[92] In other words, punitive damages should be high enough to pass the Cooter and Freedman test and therefore force disclosure.

V. NEGOTIATION AND THE PROTECTION OF ENTITLEMENTS TO EXPLOIT CORPORATE OPPORTUNITIES

We now turn to bargaining proper, which is possible only once disclosure has taken place. Property and liability rules are often depicted in Law and Economics literature as having different qualities in terms of promoting efficient bargaining. The classic solution proposed by Posner is built on the idea that, when transaction costs are low, a so-called property rule is more likely to induce efficient bargaining.[93] The most frequent explanation is that the prospective buyer will need to deal with the proprietor to buy the entitlement. In other words, the owner will provide their authorisation to the taking only when the prospective buyer offers a price that is higher than the owner's reservation price (hence here there is no consideration of strategic behaviours).[94] Conversely, a liability rule would be optimal when transaction costs are high but where courts can easily verify the value of the entitlement for each party.[95]

Northern Ireland Legal Quarterly 147, 168. I believe that nowadays a corporate director is likely to be educated in legal matters and therefore know about such consequences. Of course, this also depends on their educational background and therefore cannot be taken for granted.

[91] See text at ch 3.VI and accompanying notes.

[92] ibid.

[93] R Posner, *Economic Analysis of Law*, 9th edn (Aspen, 2014) chs 3 and 4.

[94] ibid.

[95] ibid.

Ayres and Talley offer a different perspective, according to which a liability rule represents a way of splitting an entitlement and therefore forcing bilateral disclosure (ie a manifestation of the so-called Solomonic bargaining).[96] For a liability rule to be put in place, courts are not required to be able to 'tailor' liability (ie to verify the exact value of the entitlement for both parties). Ayres and Talley extol the virtues of an untailored liability rule precisely because it works as an entitlement-splitting rule.[97] In this case, both parties, especially those plaintiffs for whom Cosean trade has the highest return, are forced to disclose their reservation price. Neither of them can be sure they will receive the full entitlement in the end (again because the entitlement is split by the law).[98]

Although both of the aforementioned perspectives may, plausibly, be considered as efficiency-enhancing rules, approaching the problem of setting the most efficient remedies with reference to the breach of corporate opportunity rules requires some important additional discussion. It may well be the case that not all the aforementioned findings apply equally to the theoretical framework on which the present analysis is based. The variables occurring in cases of bargaining over corporate opportunities may differ from those occurring in cases of bargaining over a different good or right because of the peculiarities of the entitlement to exploit corporate opportunities. In particular, in the case of corporate opportunities, one may need to focus on (at least) the following variables: the qualities and personal skills of the parties; the information structure found within the negotiation context; and the different levels of protection of the entitlement available at law.

The qualities and personal skills of the parties represent an important element in the negotiation because they directly affect the information structure and the capacity to assess the value of the opportunity. For example, Whincop assumes that shareholders or the shareholders' meeting (or assembly) is competent to authorise the taking of corporate opportunities by insiders.[99] He proposes a model in which an insider negotiates with shareholders or with a fictitious entity represented by a majority of the shareholders. He then identifies a series of problems that are directly connected to shareholders' lack of technical skills to evaluate corporate opportunities.[100] He assumes that shareholders are unaware not only of the counterparty's reservation price, but also of their own. On this specific point, Whincop's argument is perhaps oversimplified, at least to the extent to which it does not take into consideration different kinds of shareholders and/or different authorisation models. Even if it is assumed that shareholders are called to authorise insiders' takings, the outcome would significantly depend on the quality of shareholders; that is, on whether they

[96] Ayres and Talley (n 10).
[97] ibid.
[98] ibid 1056–57.
[99] Whincop (n 9).
[100] ibid.

are block-holders, institutional shareholders or dispersed shareholders.[101] Moreover, it is unlikely that in modern corporate law systems shareholders are those who provide authorisation for takings. In fact, authorisation provided by a majority of disinterested directors looks like the emerging model, at least in Anglo-American countries where these rules are more often applied.[102] Therefore, in this section, to simplify discussion, I will assume that the board of directors is in charge of the authorisation. Of course, I am not affirming that this is the only possible model. As Goshen and Squire have thoroughly demonstrated, the (relatively) best way to engineer efficient corporate law rules is to focus both on costs born both by principals and agents.[103] Whereas agency costs are well-known in corporate theory, principals' costs refer in most cases to principals' incompetence.[104]

A second point concerns information. I assumed above that information about the characteristics of the business opportunity at issue is not likely to be complete.[105] I now describe more precisely how information is likely to be distributed among parties. First, insiders are likely to know more about a corporate opportunity they present to the company than those who decide for the company (ie the other directors). In fact, insiders may have at their disposal the whole set of relevant information – both the technical details of the corporate opportunity at issue and commercial information about the third parties who presented the business opportunity to the insider and with whom the deal will possibly be concluded. Whether an insider discloses all the information available to them or not depends on how rules on disclosure are formulated; that is, whether they require full disclosure, and whether there is adequate deterrence in case of failed disclosure.[106]

If rules that mandate disclosure are accurately formulated and applied, we can presume that the company will receive an adequate level of information

[101] It is well known that some shareholders are particularly renowned for being active. See J Armour and B Cheffins, 'The Rise and Fall of Shareholder Activism by Hedge Funds' (2012) *Journal of Alternative Investments* 17; J Armour and B Cheffins, 'The Past, Present and Future of Shareholder Activism by Hedge Funds' (2011) 37 *Journal of Corporation Law* 5; T Briggs, 'Corporate Governance and the New Hedge Fund Activism: An Empirical Analysis' (2007) 31 *Journal of Corporation Law* 681. For a recent analysis of the investment techniques adopted by hedge funds, see G Ringe, 'Hedge Funds and Risk-Decoupling – The Empty Voting Problem in the European Union' (2013) 36 *Seattle University Law Review* 1027.

[102] In certain civil law countries – Spain, for instance – there is also such a trend. See *Ley de Sociedades de Capital* (Spanish Stock Company Law) Art 230, para 2, allowing for board authorisation for operations below or equal to the value the value of 10% of the company's assets.

[103] Z Goshen and R Squire, 'Principal Costs: A New Theory for Corporate Law and Governance' (2017) 117 *Columbia Law Review* 767.

[104] ibid 771.

[105] See text at section IV and accompanying notes.

[106] Again, along the lines of what has been demonstrated by Goshen and Squire (n 103), disclosure of all material information will not necessarily be the panacea to all transaction costs. There may be cases in which a principal is incompetent to understand the disclosed information. Nonetheless, if the business opportunity is in the line of business of the company, hopefully its directors are able to assess its value once given all the relevant information.

that will allow its directors – if competent – to price the opportunity. Likewise, the insider is likely to price the opportunity correctly for themselves because they are the party that collects and disposes of the information. By contrast with the previously cited set of information, what is likely to differ between the parties is the correctness of the information regarding the counterparty's reservation price. The insider is likely to be able to evaluate the company's reservation price. In fact, evaluation on behalf of the company is likely to be part of the insider's ordinary tasks as a director. In other words, the insider is usually familiar with the ongoing concern of the company, its present technical barriers, the labour constraints related to possible changes in technology and all the other relevant factors that play a role in an industrial strategy decisions.[107] Conversely, the company may be far less aware of the insider's reservation price, because it might not know of the way the insider wants to exploit the opportunity.

In an attempt to understand what happens when company and insider try to negotiate over the allocation of a given corporate opportunity we need to consider the two opposing hypotheses regarding the value of the corporate opportunity which were presented above in the discussion of disclosure.[108] According to the first hypothesis, the opportunity is more valuable to the company than to the insider, whereas according to the second hypothesis, the opportunity is more valuable to the insider.

This way of analysing bargaining over corporate opportunities is counterintuitive from the perspective of the lawmaker. A remedial system could not differentiate *ex ante* based on the variables mentioned above. Nevertheless, it remains useful to consider these two cases separately for analytical purposes. In fact, this way of dissecting the problem will reveal that it is necessary to rethink some classic Law and Economics clichés based on the distinction between so-called property and liability rules as applied to corporate opportunities. In my discussion of each of the two hypotheses, I will consider and assess several different levels of legal protection and the effects of each level on entitlement. These levels are: punitive damages; constructive trust, together with disgorgement of profits (or account of profits); full liability (ie *damnum emergens* and *lucrum cessans*); and partial liability (ie something less than full liability).

A. Remedies when the Company's Reservation Price is Higher than the Insider's

When the opportunity is more valuable to the company than to the insider, there should be no negotiation, at least if we approach the problem by keeping the 'maximising shareholders' value' rule for distributional purposes.

[107] This was noted by Whincop (n 9).

[108] See text at section IV and accompanying notes.

Therefore, an ideal corporate opportunity rule should be formulated with the primary purpose of discouraging takings, as such takings would be inefficient. All the stronger levels of protection previously mentioned look capable of discouraging takings and therefore look more desirable than the weakest form of protection – that is, partial liability. In fact, partial liability would force the company to bribe the insider.[109]

I also need to highlight the fact that, when the opportunity is more valuable to the company than to the insider, full damages will amount to a greater sum than disgorgement of profits. In fact, if one assumes that the value of the opportunity for the insider is lower than for the company, it is a logical consequence that the opportunity is less profitable for the insider. Therefore, profits made by the insider will be lower than the ones hypothetically made by the company if it had been allowed to exploit the opportunity at issue. Hence, mere disgorgement will not be sufficient restitution. As a consequence, an optimal choice could be full damages (or, potentially, punitive damages).

Full damages would allow the company to recover the higher profits it would have made had it exploited the opportunity itself. In this case, lawyers might perceive the choice of full damages as a remedy as problematic. In fact, once common law remedies such as disgorgement of profits and the constructive trust are discarded, there would be no transfer of property in the goods acquired in exploitation of the company's corporate opportunity. In terms of economics, this should not be at all problematic from a distributive perspective (full damages do grant that the shareholders' value is maximised, because they would be a sum that is higher than disgorgement of profits). However, this might to some extent seem unusual reasoning to lawyers who attach to proprietary remedies a stronger symbolic connotation. Such a legalistic reasoning would not be consistent with basic economics tenets.

What has been said so far in relation to the choice between full damages and a constructive trust where the corporate opportunity is more valuable to the company than to the insider is true only from a numerical/mathematical perspective. It is necessary to add at least one important consideration that derives from the fact that the insider/director may face financial difficulties in paying damages. Whereas a constructive trust, at least in its proprietary form, will grant the company a priority claim on the goods acquired through the exploitation of the business opportunity, this may not be true with reference to full damages, which do not grant any proprietary claim (and therefore any of its legal effects).[110] Therefore, it may be that *in practice* a constructive trust better secures the rights of the corporation; but much depends on the insider's financial constraints and debt exposure.

[109] See text at section III and accompanying notes.
[110] See text at ch 3.III and accompanying notes.

B. Remedies when the Company's Reservation Price is Lower than the Insider's

The case of the opportunity being more valuable to the insider than to the company does not lead to an immediate clear-cut solution either. When the insider values the opportunity more, it is clear that they should be put in a position to appropriate it through bargaining. Here we see how granting too high a level of protection to corporate opportunities might prevent efficient allocation. Whenever the quantum of recovery by the company is higher than the profits the company will make from the exploitation of the opportunity (such as in the case of punitive damages or disgorgement of profits) the company will face incentives to behave strategically. In other words, in such a case we can well understand that the company's behaviour may be particularly aggressive when trying to appropriate most of the share of the gains from trade. Indeed, the fact that a director proposes to take the corporate opportunity in question and is ready to resign may be perceived as a very strong signal; at least, it may signal that the director is planning to make greater profits out of the opportunity than out of their position within the company (even though the director might be valuing non-monetary components such as independence, creativity, personal risk-taking and so on). In an ideal negotiation context, to put it in Goldman and Rojot's words:

> [B]ounded rationality reminds us that everybody behaves rationally in their own eyes, according to their own set of goals … Although the other person may have a more or less clear understanding of the objectives being sought, certainly that understanding exceeds our own awareness of the other's decisional criteria. Accordingly, rather than assume that perplexing behaviour is irrational, we should recognise that its rationality might be revealed, and thereby addressed, if we gain more information about that person's information, values, objectives, expectations, analysis.[111]

Nonetheless, it may well be that such additional information does not emerge through negotiation. The director's interest in the corporate opportunity in question may then create a sort of mystery around their valuation of the opportunity, and this may induce further strategic behaviour by the incumbent company, which may try to extract a component of the overall surplus that is hard to quantify/actualise (such as the emotional attachment of the insider to their creation, or their confidence in their future success).[112] This in turn may cause a complete failure in the transaction. Therefore, in such a case, from an efficiency perspective, it might be more advisable to impose a full liability rule,

[111] Goldman and Rojot (n 20) 29.

[112] The value of such an emotional attachment may be easier to evaluate (and therefore employed rationally in a negotiation context) when the actors have interacted repeatedly in transactions concerning the goods they are attached too. See for instance M Kim and S Stepchenkova, 'Examining the Impact of Experiential Value on Emotions, Self-connective Attachment, and Brand Loyalty in Korean Family Restaurants' (2018) 19 *Journal of Quality Assurance in Hospitality & Tourism* 298.

which would approximate the idea of maximising shareholder value (at least, that is the way shareholder value would have been maximised through the ordinary activity of the company, if one excludes preying on the insider's success).

It is also clear that there is a potential argument against the solution I have just proposed: if one had to be fully consistent with a shareholders' maximisation objective, a constructive trust/disgorgement of profits would be preferable and, in this case, efficiency could be sacrificed. This would also be in harmony with Talley's ideas as previously described.[113] However, from an economics perspective, the operation of enlarging the pie to be shared clearly comes first.[114] Therefore, one should first privilege an efficient allocation of the entitlement to exploit the opportunity at stake. Under the conditions discussed in this section, full damages seem the best way to maximise allocation efficiency.

We also have to consider the potentially detrimental effects of the further equity remedy usually coupled with disgorgement of profits – that is, constructive trust.[115] If the insider perceives that there is a risk of a court order that transfers the fruit of their investment in their integrity to the incumbent firm, they may decide to underinvest in the exploitation of their opportunity, even when the opportunity is particularly promising. The risk of underinvestment may be particularly high when the constructive trust is interpreted as being a proprietary remedy; that is, when it allows tracing of the profits of the subsequent reinvestments following the exploitation of the corporate opportunity in question. Such a remedy, although potentially functioning to force disclosure, may have a paralysing effect on negotiation for the acquisition of a corporate opportunity.[116]

The potential problems raised by constructive trusts, according to the hypothesis in which the opportunity is more valuable to the insider than to the shareholders, are not necessarily unavoidable. If one can think of corrections to such a strong rule that may temper a company's strategic behaviour, such a rule may be maintained and may become efficient overall. Rules that, for example, grant allowances to the insider who has made good use of the opportunity may temper their counterincentives to an efficient breach of contract.[117]

In conclusion, there is no incontrovertible evidence regarding what may be the best rule to facilitate bargaining. From a mere numerical point of view, full liability looks like the best rule to achieve efficiency. However, once we try to understand how rules work in a real bargaining context, it may well be that

[113] See text at section II and accompanying notes.

[114] I am aware that in wider social contexts, the paradigm consisting of enlarging the pie first has been criticised by lawyers. See recently M McCluskey, 'Defining the Economic Pie, Not Dividing or Maximizing It' (2018) 5 *Critical Analysis of the Law* 78.

[115] See text at ch 3.III and accompanying notes.

[116] As a matter of fact, it may overcomplicate an already difficult calculation carried out for an investment that is already subject to so many uncertainties, such as one pertaining to technological innovation. For a general theory, see A Dixit and R Pindyck, *Investment under Uncertainty* (Princeton University Press, 1994) 1–5 and 135ff.

[117] See next section, text corresponding to nn 132 and 133.

the constructive trust, as conceived by Anglo-American courts, is in practice an efficient rule. This is particularly true if courts are able to provide incentives to efficient breach of contract by the insider through allowances or other legal correctives. In turn, this depends greatly on the size of the allowance awarded in such a case.

VI. RESIDUAL POST-NEGOTIATION EFFICIENCY PROFILES AND THE PROTECTION OF ENTITLEMENTS TO EXPLOIT BUSINESS OPPORTUNITIES

Now that I have attempted to describe the effects of different levels of protection of corporate opportunities in the disclosure and negotiation phases, I need to examine what issues the negotiation process might eventually leave unresolved. It is clear that the negotiation and the post-negotiation phases are deeply intertwined. When negotiating, the parties should have ex post scenarios firmly in mind. This is known as the best alternative to negotiated agreement (BATNA)[118] or the best alternative to proposed agreement (BAPA).[119] In the context of a negotiation over corporate opportunities, the idea of separating the two phases is mostly for the purpose of stressing the possibility of strategic behaviours during negotiation and their consequent detrimental effects.

As a preliminary remark, we first have to understand what will happen once negotiation has eventually failed. In this case, it is likely that one of the parties will appropriate the opportunity; that is, either simply implement the idea or technology or reach out to the third party whose participation is necessary for the exploitation of the business opportunity. It may be that either the company or the insider succeeds in securing the opportunity for themselves. Once the opportunity is contractually secured, one of the main problems is that, regardless of who the taker is, they should commit to investing enough resources for the purpose of developing the opportunity. An important investment is safe only when there is a clear and stable allocation of entitlements.[120] In fact, none of the parties will be likely to invest in the opportunity unless they know that they are legally entitled to appropriate the fruits of their efforts. The situation following a failed bargaining is complex, and its analysis can benefit from the two hypotheses previously considered for deterrence and bargaining.

[118] R Pinkley, M Neale and R Bennett, 'The Impact of Alternatives to Settlement in Dyadic Negotiation' (1994) 57 *Organizational Behavior and Human Decision Processes* 97.

[119] Goldman and Rojot (n 20) 64–65.

[120] Empirical research has demonstrated that weak protection of property rights is the major cause of underinvestment. S Johnson, J McMillan and C Woodruff, 'Property Rights and Finance' (2002) 92 *American Economic Review* 1335. See also how technology and property rights are often viewed as two variables that coupled together tend to boost economic development: A Asoni, 'Protection of Property Rights and Growth as Political Equilibria' (2008) 22 *Journal of Economic Surveys* 953.

First, let us consider again the case in which the opportunity is more valuable to the company than to the insider. Strong protection of the entitlement (and in this case full damages are higher than disgorgement of profits) is consistent both with the idea of allocative and productive efficiency and with the distributional assumption I previously made (I assumed that the desired distribution policy is the maximising of shareholder value).[121] Nevertheless, one should not necessarily dismiss remedies such as the constructive trust as inefficient per se. In fact, it depends on how quickly these remedies are administered. If a constructive trust is declared quickly enough, provided that the company is still able to exploit the opportunity, the damages will amount to a small sum. The company will soon have the opportunity back and will therefore be able to exploit it efficiently. Therefore, the efficiency and swiftness of a court's intervention will determine the desirability of one remedy (constructive trust when courts are swift) or the other (damages when courts are slow).[122]

The reverse hypothesis looks extremely problematic and requires a careful analysis. The existence of rules, such as the Anglo-American ones, that require the declaration of a constructive trust and the disgorgement of the profits made by the insider to the corporation may have at least two adverse consequences. First, a constructive trust and disgorgement of profits may prevent the insider from breaching their duty even when such breach would be efficient.[123] Second, even when the insider decides to breach their duty despite the adverse legal consequences, they may decide to underinvest in the exploitation of the corporate opportunity at stake. In fact, they may fear subsequent expropriation.

In the case of the constructive trust, when the remedy allows tracing, such underinvestment could also touch the subsequent investments following the misappropriation of the corporate opportunity. In fact, one may be tempted to disregard the existence of difficulties for an insider in breaching their contract with the corporation efficiently and taking corporate opportunities they are better able to exploit. However, this may have far more meaningful consequences than expected, especially in the long term. It may mean preventing an efficient competitor from operating in the same product market (or subsequently in other ones).[124] At times, it may also prevent or delay the creation of

[121] See text at section III and accompanying notes.

[122] The differences in courts' performance around the word has been highlighted by studies such as M Dakolias, *Court Performance Around the World: A Comparative Perspective* (The World Bank, 1999). The EU is aware of the significant differences existing in courts' performance across different Member States. The European Commission for the Efficiency of Justice (CEPEJ) within the Council of Europe has worked extensively towards the improvement of the situation in those countries which still lag behind. See for instance the SATURN working group on judicial time management: www.coe.int/en/web/cepej/cepej-work/saturn-centre-for-judicial-time-management.

[123] But note that authoritative US doctrine rejects the idea of 'efficient breach' as generally applicable to a bargaining context: M Eisenberg, 'Actual and Virtual Specific Performance, the Theory of Efficient Breach, and the Indifference Principle in Contract Law' (2005) 93 *California Law Review* 975.

[124] Corradi and Nowag, 'Enforcing Corporate Opportunities Rules' (2018).

alternative or completely new product markets until other potential entrants realise the existence of that business opportunity.[125] To understand the extent to which inefficiency may manifest in this context we have to consider industrial variables. Equally, possible corrections the law may try to impose for counteracting inefficiencies should be grounded in industrial economics theory. Clearly, in contexts of open innovation where there is widespread contracting for innovation the negative consequences may be remarkable for the whole industry.[126]

First, the line of business test may represent a kind of correction to the inefficiencies potentially connected to remedies such as the constructive trust. In fact, a possible idea underlying the line of business test is that the company has developed skills that are specific to a given business and has committed itself to specific investments in that line.[127] Protecting corporate opportunities in the line of business of the corporation also means creating incentives for the aforementioned specific investments *ex ante*. This policy prescription has a clear efficiency implication on a general industrial plane; that is, setting incentives for specific investments. Moreover, it may have a more limited but equally important effect on the ex post bargaining plane. In fact, that rule may be viewed as a sort of presumption that those corporate opportunities that fall within the line of business of the corporation are more valuable for the corporation than for the insider. From that point of view, the line of business test may be seen as complementary to strong protection such as that granted by constructive trust.

What has just been advanced may be true on a general basis. In order to verify the validity of this statement, we need to briefly consider a potentially very controversial area; that is, process innovation.[128] An incumbent company may be in a less favourable position than an insider when attempting to introduce innovations in its productive process. For instance, a new technology may require the dismissal of old employees[129] and the sale of old machinery that still generates marginal returns.[130] In the company's analysis, one must take into account a set of factors connected to these changes. A new entrant that has not committed itself to investments that are specific to a certain productive process would not bear such sunk costs. Therefore, the trade-off faced by the corporation and represented by abandoning the old and still marginally profitable

[125] See text at ch 5.IX and accompanying notes.

[126] See text at ch 5.VI and accompanying notes.

[127] Corradi, 'Corporate Opportunities Doctrines Tested' (2016) 771ff.

[128] In the OECD definition, a 'process innovation is the implementation of a new or significantly improved production or delivery method. This includes significant changes in techniques, equipment and/or software': stats.oecd.org/glossary/detail.asp?ID=6870.

[129] In this instance, labour law can be a double-edged sword. On one hand, protective labour law can help employees committing to the acquisition of firm-specific skills that may enhance innovation. See V Acharya, R Baghai and K Subramanian, 'Labor Laws and Innovation (2013) 56 *The Journal of Law and Economics* 997. On the other hand, firm-specific skills that the employees have acquired are not necessarily useful in case of the implementation of new technology, which may in turn require completely different specific investments.

[130] See text at ch 2.V and accompanying notes.

processes may entail that its reservation price is lower than the insider's (given that the company's reservation price is increased by the costs of changes). In other words, there may still be cases in which the line of business formula falls short of representing a perfect complementary match to strong protection of the right to exploit a corporate opportunity – although perhaps such cases are not that frequent.[131] A further problem may be a very wide interpretation of the concept of line of business. A wide interpretation may not match with the idea of specific investment, especially if the test in question includes those business opportunities that are only potentially in the line of business of the corporation. In other words, such a wider interpretation may end up overprotecting business opportunities to the detriment of potential innovations by insiders.

Anglo-American case law does not refer explicitly to the efficiency profiles that I have analysed in this section. However, one may notice certain adjustments to the disgorgement of profits rule. Those adjustments might be connected precisely to the idea that at times a rigid interpretation of the remedy consisting in a disgorgement of profits may create strong counterincentives to efficient takings (or breach of contract, provided that these rules are seen as contractual). For reasons of equity, British[132] and American[133] courts can grant a side compensation (or allowance) to the insider who has been ordered to disgorge their profit to the corporation; that compensation is calculated on the basis of the efforts the insider has put into developing the opportunity. This might be seen *ex ante* as an incentive to accomplish an efficient breach of contract, when the insider values the opportunity more. Nevertheless, it is clear that such an approach might produce some positive effects, but only if the compensation is not merely symbolic and if the rule is applied consistently, which it does not appear to be at present.

Allowances that are too generous may also produce inefficiencies, especially when they are perceived by insiders as an encouragement to breach their duty of loyalty to the company. In any case, the possibility that the courts have to adjust the harshness of the compensation remedy by way of an allowance may grant some degree of flexibility when it is necessary to moderate a very strong version of the constructive trust and account of profits. Nonetheless, ex ante it may not present a sufficient guarantee for an insider with good ideas and who intends to take an opportunity despite their company denying them the authorisation that company law requests for a lawful appropriation. A case law approach to this additional rule concerning a possible allowance may leave uncertainty, especially

[131] See text at ch 5.VII and accompanying notes.

[132] See P Davies and S Worthington (eds), *Gower and Davies' Principles of Modern Company Law* (Sweet & Maxwell, 2012) para 16.184.

[133] A rather mild application of this principle is found, for instance, in *Energy Resources Corporation, Inc v Porter* 14 Mass App Ct 296, 438 NE 2d 391 (1982). This principle was already established in earlier case law. See for instance *Lagarde v Anniston Lime & Stone Co*, 126 Ala 496, 28 So.

as to the quantum that will be granted to the insider in view of their efforts. This might be one of the reasons why, in 2000, Delaware law introduced a provision that allows a company to introduce in their bylaws a waiver of corporate opportunity rules.[134]

The possibility of waiving corporate opportunity rules *ex ante* on a general basis may be particularly important in those industrial sectors in which a director is likely to find important creative opportunities thanks to their personal abilities and connections and therefore would end up turning down an offer to become a director unless that waiver is granted.[135] Such an arrangement is likely to have a very significant impact on the company from a distributional perspective. Nonetheless, in the case of a waiver, the company will ultimately calculate the potential loss that follows the acceptance of the waiver as a trade-off to be taken in exchange for hiring competent directors. Even though in this case the focus is on the distributional profile, it may directly enhance efficiency if the director is the most efficient exploiter of the opportunity at stake. As a matter of fact, empirical research has shown that waivers tend to be largely employed in listed corporations, which seems to confirm the possibility of finding an acceptable trade-off between a company's and a director's interests.[136]

In conclusion, there are several reasons for believing that in cases of failed negotiation, rules such as those devised by Anglo-American jurisdictions may be efficient, especially when a series of conditions occur. Firstly, courts must be swift to apply those remedies. Secondly, there must be complementary rules that contain or counter eventual inefficiencies arising from the obstacles to efficient breach of contract by insiders, such as granting allowances to insiders who have started exploiting business opportunities. Thirdly, there must be the possibility of waiving the application of the corporate opportunity doctrine.

VII. NOTES ON THE TAKING OF CORPORATE OPPORTUNITIES IN A REPEATED GAME CONTEXT

As the focus of this book is mostly on technological innovation, I have focused on one-shot takings of corporate opportunities, ie in a single game context.

[134] Delaware General Corporation Law (DGCL), s 122(17).

[135] See W Allen, R Kraakman and G Subramanian, *Commentaries and Cases on the Law of Business Organization*, 2nd edn (Aspen Publishers, 2009) 350. The authors refer to the fact that the applicability of the corporate opportunity doctrine was waived in the bylaws of DreamWorks Animation SKG, a collaboration among Steven Spielberg, Jeffery Katzenberg and David Geffen. The authors refer to directors who have already acquired a significant bargaining power. Things may work differently in the start-up context. See ch 5.

[136] G Rauterberg and E Talley, 'Contracting Out of the Fiduciary Duty of Loyalty: An Empirical Analysis of Corporate Opportunity Waivers' (2017) 117 *Columbia Law Review* 1075.

I have assumed that a director is interested in setting up a new firm through the exploitation of a corporate opportunity and therefore will no longer be interested in their existing position as a director of a corporation once they have started their new business.

For the sake of completeness, I would like to add that not every corporate opportunity will lead to the establishment of a new entrepreneurial activity. For instance, let's say that the business opportunity at stake consists of a piece of real estate that is sold at a very attractive price, and that an insider wants to buy that property exclusively for the purpose of engaging in price arbitrage, in a one-shot transaction.[137] Such a situation may occur several times without the director being willing to resign. In the case of repeated misappropriations, the eventual dismissal of the director for breach of their fiduciary duty may represent a very effective additional remedy. At times, although this is not the rule, the business opportunities that are appropriated repeatedly may be less valuable than an opportunity that results in the setting up of a new firm (considering that the first are not business opportunities that are supposed to produce a long-term stream of profits).

For all the reasons mentioned above, repeated takings are likely to require a slightly different economic approach and consequently different legal treatment from one-shot takings. The main problem arising in the case of repeated takings is the danger of mutual backscratching; that is, one of the potential manifestations of agency costs in a repeated game context.[138] In other words, those called to provide the authorisation might be prone to being particularly benevolent (ie to authorising the appropriation of corporate opportunities that may be valuable to the company), hoping that the favour will be returned once it is their turn to misappropriate a corporate opportunity. In the case of repeated takings, the best way to contain agency costs would be to assign the power to authorise takings to stakeholders who are not likely to take business opportunities; for example, in the case of a taking by a company's director, the best adjudicators could be considered to be disinterested shareholders.[139]

Nonetheless, mandating authorisation to shareholders may imply a trade-off with technical competence in the subject matter[140] which can be transposed as 'intelligence'[141] and consequent 'predictive accuracy'[142] in negotiation theory terminology; that is, shareholders may not be able to assess the value of the

[137] As, for instance, in *Bhullar* (n 54), but hypothetically excluding that there are further industrial implications, as there might have been in that case.

[138] See Davies and Worthington, *Gower and Davies* (2012) 16.96.

[139] Note that the shareholders' decision on the corporate opportunity at issue is embedded in a voting procedure which is considered as a part of the negotiation process by negotiation theory. See Goldman and Rojot (n 20) 19ff.

[140] A principal's cost in Goshen and Squire's language (n 103).

[141] Trask and Deguire, *Betting the Company* (2013) 245.

[142] Goldman and Rojot (n 20) 69–70.

corporate opportunity (unless they are highly specialised and prone to activism, as in the case of very specific categories of shareholders, such as families or hedge funds).[143] A very strong protection in terms of remedies, such as the Anglo-American one, would not prevent shareholders from concluding bad deals for the corporation.[144] In addition, there are costs involved in calling a shareholders' meeting for every authorisation.[145]

A possible alternative could be the appointment of independent directors who are competent to assess the value of the opportunity.[146] Nonetheless, incentives to backscratching could not be completely eliminated. Independent directors may also be interested in taking corporate opportunities. In the worst-case scenario, they may be unlikely to accept the position unless they are allowed to take corporate opportunities, as they may actually be very well-connected in the industry business network and/or pursuing or looking for business opportunities on behalf of other companies.[147] This may be solved by allowing independent directors to take corporate opportunities that were not presented to them in that specific capacity,[148] as the articles of association of several UK listed companies seem to do.[149] Nonetheless, there would still be an area of potential mutual backscratching for independent directors, ie that of the business opportunities that are presented to them in their capacity as directors and that would need board authorisation. As can be seen, the issue of repeated takings may be quite difficult to solve. Difficulties mostly lie in structuring the bodies that decide on the taking. Nevertheless, when setting the right amount of liability, the reasoning proposed in the previous sections may still apply.

Last but not least, it is unlikely that an efficient norm is one that differentiates between one-shot takings and repeated takings. In fact, this would lead to duplication of rules and it could be difficult to identify *ex ante* one-shot and multiple appropriations.

[143] See Briggs, 'Corporate Governance' (2007); B Black, 'Shareholder Activism and Corporate Governance in the United States' in P Newman (ed), *The New Palgrave Dictionary of Economics and the Law* (Palgrave Macmillan, 1998); S Gillan and L Starks, 'Corporate Governance Proposals and Shareholder Activism: The Role of Institutional Investors' (2000) 57 *Journal of Financial Economics* 275; R Romano, 'Public Pension Fund Activism in Corporate Governance Reconsidered' (1993) 93 *Columbia Law Review* 795.

[144] Whincop (n 9).

[145] For all these considerations, see also Corradi, 'Corporate Agency Costs' (2012) 29ff.

[146] On the role of independent directors in corporate governance, see S Bhojraj et al, 'Effect of Corporate Governance on Bond Ratings and Yields: The Role of Institutional Investors and Outside Directors' (2003) 76 *Journal of Business Law* 455; S Rosenstein and J Wyatt, 'Outside Directors, Board Independence, and Shareholder Wealth' (1990) 26 *Journal of Financial Economics* 175.

[147] S Witney, 'Corporate Opportunities Law and the Non-executive Director' (2016) 16 *Journal of Corporate Law Studies* 145, 163–64.

[148] ibid 147.

[149] ibid 171.

VIII. A NORMATIVE BENCHMARK FOR CONTINENTAL EUROPEAN CORPORATE LAWS

Anglo-American case law and statutory law display a wide array of instruments conceived to provide corporate opportunity rules with some degree of adaptability to the specificities of each case.[150] The combination of the Anglo-American corporate opportunity rules may offer a way out of the difficulties inherent in the need to reconcile efficiency with a non-flexible distributive expectation (ie maximising shareholder value). I am aware that there have been different kinds of proposals to reform corporate opportunity rules. One proposal has taken into consideration a number of very sophisticated variables,[151] including a complex set of affirmative defences.[152] Another has simply focused on the option of total ban, at least for public corporations.[153]

As a simple theoretical hypothesis, I propose simple normative solutions (in the form of alternative options) that may correspond to the arguments developed in this chapter, without even dreaming of a more complex set of rules that includes all the variables identified in the previous sections and the further variables within start-up hubs and in the presence of venture capital (VC) investors that will emerge in chapter five and chapter six. In fact, I believe that such complexity could be managed by a lawmaker only with full consideration of the specificities of the addressees of these rules. The core idea which may be worth proposing is that a very high level of protection of the entitlement to exploit the business opportunity is needed to incentivise disclosure, but a weaker one, ranging from full damages to disgorgement of profits, should characterise the negotiation phase. This idea might lead to a rule of the kind suggested below:

1. Directors must disclose to the board of directors any information they become aware of about any business opportunity in the line of business of the corporation. If they fail to do so, the profits resulting from any unauthorised exploitation of the opportunity are disgorged to the corporation, without any allowance for the activity carried out by the director who misappropriated the opportunity. The court may also award punitive damages in favour of the corporation.
2. When a director appropriates a corporate opportunity after due disclosure and without any authorisation by a majority of disinterested directors, the director's liability is limited to damages to be quantified by the court (*alternatively*, 'the court can declare a constructive trust on the new company. An allowance shall be granted to the director for their efforts in setting up and running the new company').

[150] See text at section VII and accompanying notes.

[151] See for instance M Begert, 'The Corporate Opportunity Doctrine and Outside Business Interests' (1989) 56 *University of Chicago Law Review* 827, 851ff.

[152] ibid 851–52.

[153] Brudney and Clark, 'A New Look' (1981).

3. The above-mentioned provisions can be waived through an article included in the company's articles of association.

The rule outlined above is only one of the many possible examples of a starting point for discussing legal reforms that may facilitate bargaining over business opportunities: it is based on a differential approach. It provides different sanctions against unauthorised takings depending on whether disclosure has been properly effectuated or not. Punitive damages could be replaced with criminal sanctions, even though such a choice would need to address the concerns advanced by Posner[154] and a general ethical disfavour, as already considered.[155]

What really matters is that, given that the probability of detection is likely to be always lower than one, an appropriate sanction has to be higher than mere disgorgement of profits (or full damages) if possible. Once the opportunity has been disclosed, competition (and eventual negotiation) between the company and its insider for the opportunity will follow. Therefore, it is desirable that the party who values the opportunity more is able to exploit it. Damages also assuage distributive concerns inherent in the shareholder value maximisation rule.

IX. THE STATE OF THE ART IN ANGLO-AMERICAN AND IN CONTINENTAL EUROPEAN CORPORATE LAWS

When one tries to assess the state of present corporate laws in the light of the benchmark that was presented in the previous section, some aspects do not seem satisfactory. Firstly, it looks like only Texas courts might provide the level of deterrence that is necessary for the purpose of granting maximum disclosure, but so far such cases seem far too exceptional to be considered meaningful.[156] As to other Anglo-American jurisdictions, disgorgement of profits or damages unfortunately might not be sufficient to force disclosure. It might be that the constructive trust in its proprietary version has disclosure-forcing properties similar to those of punitive damages. Nonetheless, it may be difficult to calculate such properties in the light of neoclassical economics.[157] Secondly, it might be that the much-praised Anglo-American remedial systems create problems in relation to discouraging efficient breaches of duty by insiders, whilst also encouraging flexible solutions. In fact, Anglo-American systems seem to show a certain degree of at least potential flexibility when dealing with efficiency and distributive issues.

154 See text at ch 3.III and accompanying notes.
155 See text at ch 3.I and accompanying notes.
156 See text at ch 7.VI and accompanying notes.
157 See text at section IV and accompanying notes.

An assessment of current continental European corporate law systems may raise more concerns. There are at least three points of concern that it is useful to raise at this stage. Firstly, most of the continental European jurisdictions seem to rely on the general traits of the Anglo-American corporate opportunity doctrine, in the hope that a non-critical integration of the Anglo-American principles will automatically produce efficient results.[158]

Secondly, none of the civil law jurisdictions that have introduced corporate opportunity rules seem to have considered appropriate solutions for maximising disclosure. This may be due to difficulties in introducing punitive damages or criminal sanctions. An exception is presented by Spain, where the possibility of the company asking for a disgorgement of profits (if added to eventual penalties included in the employment contract) might approximate a degree of deterrence comparable to the one obtained by Anglo-American jurisdictions – but this is still probably insufficient.

Thirdly, as a consequence of the lesser flexibility inherent in civil law decision-making, rules necessarily have to be conceived with a higher degree of sophistication *ex ante*. If a rule is not properly designed, once it is introduced it may be more a source of institutional harm than of efficiencies. This is because civil law judges cannot always adjust the law as easily as common law judges.[159]

If we look, for instance, at French, Italian and Spanish law, some points of interest arise. For example, French law mandates sanctions exclusively for failed disclosure.[160] They are extremely low sanctions (a lesser form of liability) and therefore completely inadequate to force disclosure. Nevertheless, on the positive side, such a rule shows that the French system – perhaps an exception in the continental European scene – is well aware of the distinction between disclosure and negotiation and has decided to regulate disclosure exclusively (although inefficiently). From a distributive perspective, French courts seem to show no concern for the expropriation of corporate opportunities. Insiders are free to take corporate opportunities even when these are not authorised. This is a strong distributive choice, which may be read as not in line with the objective of maximising shareholders' value. Moreover, given the fact that French insiders are not incentivised to disclose, there may well be no bargaining at all with the corporation. This may be detrimental, especially in those cases where a company has invested important resources in a given line of business. In such a case, there may well be the problem of increased hold-up costs. Nonetheless, in the future such a choice may end up favouring creative founders,[161] while perhaps stifling the development of a thriving venture capital environment – while depriving

[158] See text at ch 7.I and accompanying notes.
[159] M Graff, 'Law and Finance: Common Law and Civil Law Countries Compared – An Empirical Critique' (2008) 75 *Economica* 60.
[160] See text at ch 3.V and accompanying footnotes.
[161] See text at ch 5.VIII and accompanying notes.

VC investors of adequate protection in cases of non-patented or non-patentable inventions.

As to Italian law, the lack of case law makes the overall framework quite uncertain.[162] Statutory law is the main source of law we have at our disposal so far in relation to remedies. There is no Italian case law on corporate opportunities. Currently, it is extremely difficult to understand how damages will be calculated, given that assessment may be a very uncertain process when complex industrial variables and unpredictable, but nonetheless possible, market changes need to be taken into account. In any case, the current position, at least in Italy, does not lead to the conclusion that disclosure is adequately granted.

X. CONCLUSION

Disclosure necessarily mandates very high sanctions. In the light of the studies by Cooter and Freedman on deterrence, it appears that one should not be particularly concerned with the higher threshold of a given remedy (unless of course the remedy is expensive in administrative terms and it causes harm to the addressee, such as in the case of imprisonment). In fact, securing disclosure can be regarded as the core objective of a corporate opportunity doctrine, because without disclosure there can be no bargaining.

Effective disclosure-forcing remedies might seem harsh at first. Nonetheless, they seem to be justified by the social welfare objectives associated to an efficient allocation of business opportunities obtained through bargaining, ie the pursuance of productive and dynamic efficiency. With reference to the promotion of optimal disclosure, it appears that none of the jurisdictions that are the object of the present analysis offer an optimal solution. Nevertheless, when one considers remedies such as the constructive trust from a behavioural perspective, it may well be that such remedies support disclosure efficiently.

As to bargaining, several potentially efficient solutions may exist. The same rules may have different effects depending on whether, in a specific case, the company or the insider values the opportunity more. In any event, an important point seems to be containing a company's strategic behaviours, especially those strategic behaviours consisting of holding out for an excessively high price. Such behaviour may be contained by full liability or by a traditional disgorgement of profits (assisted by a constructive trust) when such a remedy is appropriately

[162] Italian courts have never dealt with this topic, whereas there are a few Spanish cases; see Audiencia Provincial de Madrid (Sección 28a) Sentencia num 104/2013 of 8 April AC/2013/1431; Audiencia Provincial de Barcelona (Sección 15a) Sentencia num 10/2009 of 13 January AC/2009/1601; Audiencia Provincial de Álava (Sección 1a) Sentencia num 225/2009 of 27 May AC/2009/1580. Of these cases, only one reached the Supreme Court; see Tribunal Supremo (Sala de lo Civil, Sección 1a) Sentencia num 502/2012 of 3 September RJ/2012/9007. None of these cases seem to consider the problem of sanctions in depth.

tempered through allowances in favour of the insider who has efficiently misappropriated the opportunity. Efficient breach of duty, which eventually follows a failure in bargaining around the opportunity, needs to be encouraged.

As a conclusion, and trying to sum up the result of the present analysis, even though we are dealing with the duty of loyalty – that is, a fiduciary duty – from an economics perspective, one should not be concerned about favouring its efficient breach. The true function of the duty appears to be securing the disclosure of business opportunities. In other words, this not only enables the transparency and loyalty of the insider towards their company but also bargaining. Therefore, rules should differentiate between potential breaches of duty by insiders in relation to the presence or absence of preliminary disclosure, and mandate higher sanctions in cases of the absence of disclosure. A breach of the duty of loyalty without disclosure would prevent bargaining and all consequent efficient trades from occurring. Further normative adjustment to achieve optimal allocation may concern the test for identifying a corporate opportunity, the legal treatment of resigning directors, authorisation to take corporate opportunities, and waivers of the corporate opportunity doctrine. All such measures can be better understood in the light of the specific context to which they apply and should be studied carefully, especially in relation to start-ups and venture capital, upon which a large part of our future welfare depends.

5

Corporate Founders and Corporate Opportunities in Highly Innovative Environments

I. INTRODUCTION

STEVE JOBS, JEFF Bezos and Bill Gates have drawn widespread admiration for the extraordinary success of their entrepreneurial careers. During their journeys from cloistered innovators to chief executives of multinational corporations, all three acquired a role in society far surpassing that of a mere entrepreneur. From a sociological perspective, they have been likened to leaders of the masses.[1] Despite their superhero-like auras,[2] these founders of innovative corporations struggled with unique challenges and significant constraints, especially in the early years of their inventive and entrepreneurial activity.[3] The setbacks were manifested in different ways: Gates's first company flopped, while Jobs got thrown out of Apple and started a new company.[4]

When an entrepreneur leaves the corporation they have founded to join a new one, they take a small universe of knowledge with them. Founders who end up sitting on the boards of other corporations retain technical knowledge that is essential to their new employers' survival and expansion. Empirical evidence shows that their presence on a board often correlates to higher board attendance[5] and higher stock returns around announcements of mergers and acquisitions.[6]

[1] M Garita and S Martinez, 'A Sociological Approach Concerning Leadership: How CEO and the Masses Behave' (2016) 2 *Nile Journal of Business and Economics* 15.

[2] S Cherensky, 'A Penny for Their Thoughts: Employee-Inventors, Preinvention Assignment Agreements, Property, and Personhood' (1993) 81 *California Law Review* 595, 605 has named the 18th-century inventors as 'heroes'.

[3] A concise representation of the challenges faced by Bill Gates and Steve Jobs, see J de Mers, '7 Challenges Courageous Leaders Overcome', www.inc.com/jayson-demers/7-challenges-courageous-leaders-overcome.html. For a more detailed representation, see J Wallace and J Erickson, *Hard Drive: Bill Gates and the Making of the Microsoft Empire* (Wiley, 1992). W Isaacson, 'The Real Leadership Lessons of Steve Jobs (2012) 90 *Harvard Business Review* 92.

[4] See text at section II and accompanying notes.

[5] F Li and S Srinivasan, 'Corporate Governance when Founders are Directors (2011) 102 *Journal of Financial Economics* 454, 465.

[6] ibid 464.

The ability of founders to generate technologically innovative business ideas sets them apart from other CEOs and board members. Corporate laws that apply to board members may affect founders in special ways throughout the development of a company, from private start-up to publicly traded corporation. The outstanding inventive capabilities of such founders may represent a variable that requires specific consideration by lawmakers. This may apply not only to world-famous founders such as those cited above, but also to those who have made smaller yet still significant contributions to a corporation's inventions and who end up sitting on that company's board.

Academic literature explores the interplay between innovative founders, corporate law and corporate governance. But it does not address one fundamental question: how can a corporation stimulate a founder to keep on inventing within and for the business?

Literature on founders, for example, deals with the correlation between presence of founders on the board and other variables, such as corporate performance,[7] corporate transparency,[8] the weakness or strength of the board,[9] board-selection mechanisms[10] and market performance.[11] Literature on corporate governance and innovation, by contrast, mostly focuses on general questions, that is, how corporate governance rules can lead to an efficient level of *investment* in innovation. Investment in innovation is usually understood only as *financial investment*.[12]

None of this explains why corporate law and governance rules can end up reducing a founder's incentives and motivation. Consider the corporate opportunity doctrine, which forbids directors and officers from appropriating for themselves any business opportunity that could benefit the corporation. At the very least, this fiduciary duty of loyalty impinges on the mobility of founders by keeping their inventions inside the corporation. It prevents founders from setting up competing companies or exploring new business opportunities – unless they are prepared to pay a prohibitive price to the corporation.

This is more significant than it may sound, especially when we consider the disruptive innovation that drives game-changing tech start-ups. The corporate opportunity doctrine can even chill invention, as it fails to recognise that rich salaries, bonuses and stock options can never supply the 'greatest' reward described by Thomas Edison above – the work itself. The latest literature on innovation argues that high-tech industries rely on network structures and

[7] ibid 462–65.

[8] R Anderson, A Duru and D Reeb, 'Founders, Heirs, and Corporate Opacity in the United States' (2009) 92 *Journal of Financial Economics* 205.

[9] A Ranft and H O'Neill, 'Board Composition and High-Flying Founders: Hints of Trouble to Come?' (2001) 15 *Academy of Management Perspectives* 126.

[10] S Chahine, I Filatotchev and S Zhara, 'Building Perceived Quality of Founder–Involved IPO Firms: Founders' Effects on Board Selection and Stock Market Performance' (2011) 35 *Entrepreneurship Theory and Practice* 319, 321–23.

[11] ibid 327–32.

[12] See text at section II and accompanying notes.

'contracting for innovation'. This contracting often occurs among people who have previously worked in the same corporate context, as happens when former employees or directors decide to start their own company or join another one. Think of the 'traitorous eight' employees who left Shockley Semiconductor Laboratory in 1957 to join Fairchild Semiconductor.[13]

A network structure thrives on a system that encourages corporate mobility. Thus, from a law and economics perspective, it is crucial to understand how directors' mobility dynamics are influenced by directors' duties. By 'mobility dynamics', I mean the possibility for directors to set up competing companies or to exploit new business opportunities without paying a punishingly high price to their former employers. Given the type of corporate governance rules considered in this analysis, we will focus on non-patentable and pre-patentable innovation, with an aside or two on intellectual property (IP) held by employees.

II. THE 'LONE GENIUS' VERSUS THE TEAM, FROM LEONARDO AND EDISON TO THE 'INDUSTRIALISATION OF INVENTION'

Corporate governance literature on innovation has become vast and increasingly comprehensive in recent years as it analyses the different corporate constituencies.[14] A narrower stream of literature seeks to understand the conditions under which corporate directors – who are often trained in finance – will invest in innovation.[15] Some researchers, for instance, analyse the impact of long-termism and short-termism on directors' incentives to promote innovation.[16] Ownership structure seems to influence whether a company focuses on the long term or the short term. Dispersed ownership is likely to correlate with short-termism, growth through acquisition, and lower rates of investment in research and development.[17] Concentrated ownership has been deemed responsible for higher rates of incremental innovation – although it is uncertain whether the

[13] D Assimakopoulos, S Everton and K Tsutsui, 'The Semiconductor Community in the Silicon Valley: A Network Analysis of the SEMI Genealogy Chart (1947–1986)' (2003) 25 *International Journal of Technology Management* 181, 184.

[14] M O'Sullivan, 'The Innovative Enterprise and Corporate Governance' (2000) 24 *Cambridge Journal of Economics* 393; P Aghion, M Dewatripont and P Rey, 'Corporate Governance, Competition Policy and Industrial Policy' (1997) 41 *European Economic Review* 797; M Lehrer, A Tylecote and E Conesa, 'Corporate Governance, Innovation Systems and Industrial Performance' (1999) 6 *Industry and Innovation* 25; B Baysinger, R Kosnik and T Turk, 'Effects of Board and Ownership Structure on Corporate R&D Strategy' (1991) 34 *Academy of Management Journal* 205.

[15] Y Kor, 'Direct and Interaction Effects of Top Management Team and Board Compositions on R&D Investment Strategy' (2006) 27 *Strategic Management Journal* 1081; G Mitchell and W Hamilton, 'Managing R&D as a Strategic Option' (1998) 31 *Research-Technology Management* 15.

[16] B Lundvall et al, 'National Systems of Production, Innovation and Competence Building' (2002) 31 *Research Policy* 213; T Dalziel, R Gentry and M Bowerman, 'An Integrated Agency–Resource Dependence View of the Influence of Directors' Human and Relational Capital on Firms' R&D Spending' (2011) 48 *Journal of Management Studies* 1217.

[17] J Francis and A Smith, 'Agency Costs and Innovation: Some Empirical Evidence' (1995) 19 *Journal of Accounting & Economics* 383, 403–08.

incremental innovation model based on concentrated ownership will survive globalisation.[18]

When corporate ownership structure is dispersed, a longer-term view can become possible in the presence of adequate takeover protections, which eliminate a significant threat to directors' job security. Empirical research shows that, for certain kinds of corporations, takeover legislation and/or takeover contractual protection correlate with significantly higher rates of innovation.[19] On the shareholders' side, literature has focused on how research and development (R&D) is viewed by institutional investors, who may have the power to appoint board members.[20] Scholars have vigorously debated, for example, whether activist investors are 'myopic' – willing to sacrifice the future to make a 'quick buck'.[21]

One stream of research deals with the innovation-enhancing function of independent directors.[22] This kind of study often employs a statistical proxy based on patents, which may capture only part of the innovation that takes place, ie, innovation that is patentable.[23] Another stream examines whether and how executive compensation affects innovation. In highly innovative companies, a significant slice of executive compensation is linked to innovation performance, which is often measured in terms of number of patents secured.[24] The positive correlation between this kind of strategy and innovation outcomes has been confirmed by empirical studies.[25] In fact, in common industrial strategy R&D investments and CEO compensation are often determined simultaneously.[26]

All of the above-mentioned studies focus on the role of directors in *promoting*, *investing in* and *coordinating* innovation processes. What is important to stress is that they describe incentives that emerged during a historical development called 'the industrialisation of invention'.[27] Nonetheless, the history of

[18] C Lane, 'Globalization and the German Model of Capitalism-Erosion or Survival?' (2000) 51 *The British Journal of Sociology* 207.

[19] J Becker-Blease, 'Governance and Innovation' (2011) 17 *Journal of Corporate Finance* 947; M Danielson and J Karpoff, 'On the Uses of Corporate Governance Provisions' (1998) 4 *Journal of Corporate Finance* 347.

[20] D Parthiban, M Hitt and J Gimeno, 'The Influence of Activism by Institutional Investors on R&D' (2001) 44 *Academy of Management Journal* 144; B Bushee, 'The Influence of Institutional Investors on Myopic R&D Investment Behaviour' (1998) 73 *Accounting Review* 305.

[21] L Bebchuk, 'The Myth that Insulating Boards Serves Long-term Value' (2013) 113 *Columbia Law Review* 163.

[22] B Balsmeier, A Buchwald and J Stiebale, 'Outside Directors on the Board and Innovative Firm Performance' (2014) 4 *Research Policy* 1800.

[23] D Balkin, G Markman and L Gomez-Mejia, 'Is CEO Pay in High-technology Firms Related to Innovation?' (2000) 43 *Academy of Management Journal* 1118.

[24] ibid 1122; R Holthausen, D Larcker and R Sloan, 'Business Unit Innovation and the Structure of Executive Compensation' (1995) 19 *Journal of Accounting and Economics* 279.

[25] M Anderson, R Banker and S Ravindran, 'Executive Compensation in the Information Technology Industry' (2000) 46 *Management Science* 4530.

[26] H Ryan Jr and R Wiggins III, 'The Interactions Between R&D Investment Decisions and Compensation Policy' (2002) 31 *Financial Management* 5.

[27] D Noble, *America by Design: Science, Technology and the Rise of Corporate Capitalism* (Oxford University Press, 1977); G Meyer-Thurow, 'The Industrialization of Invention: A Case Study from the German Chemical Industry' (1982) 73 *Isis* 363.

innovation has been far longer than the period described as industrialisation of invention. Inventive environments of a few centuries ago were characterised by different variables.

During the Renaissance, visionary individuals, usually financed by a wealthy prince or king, became 'lone genius' innovators.[28] Italian polymath Leonardo da Vinci is perhaps the most famous example of this kind of inventor. Later on, from the birth of the Industrial Revolution and into the early twentieth century, scientists and engineers were often entrepreneurs. Like television pioneer Philo Farnsworth, they looked for private backers and set up companies to produce what they invented. But Farnsworth was a dying breed.[29] By the time he burst on the scene in the 1920s, industrialisation and mass commercialisation had ushered in a new phenomenon[30] known as corporate-controlled innovation. 'The consulting scientist and the scientific entrepreneur were replaced by the salaried industrial research worker',[31] who worked as part of a team. The contribution of the individual grew less important – although lone inventors continued to exist.[32] Examples after the 1890s included Niels Anton Christensen[33] and Elmer Sperry,[34] inventors, respectively, of the O-ring and of the modern military gyroscope, and more recently Edwin Land, the inventor of the polaroid camera.[35]

Research on corporate laboratories such as AT&T's Bell Labs shows that particularly talented individuals have emerged as creative geniuses on a par with lone inventors, even while working on salary. For instance, DuPont chemist William Hale Charch, the father of moisture-proof cellophane, is still remembered as one of the great twentieth-century inventors.[36] Even so, the industrialisation of invention in most cases separated the roles of entrepreneur and inventor. This made sometimes life frustrating for the inventors, who felt constrained by the entrepreneurs' conservative choices, which often slowed innovation.[37]

[28] T Misa, *Leonardo to the Internet: Technology and Culture from the Renaissance to the Present* (John Hopkins University Press, 2013) XI–XII. Misa reminds us that often we forget that the majority of the inventions in ancient times took place within wealthy courts. Even Johann Guthenberg was a pensioner of a court at the time when he invented the Western system of moveable type printing.

[29] E Schwartz, *The Last Lone Inventor: A Tale of Genius, Deceit, and the Birth of Television* (Harper-Collins, 2002).

[30] A Chandler, 'Evolution of the Large Industrial Corporation: An Evolution of the Transaction-cost Approach' (1982) *Business and Economic History* 116, 122.

[31] Meyer-Thurow, 'The Industrialization of Invention' (1982) 363.

[32] G Wise, 'Inventors and Corporations in the Maturing Electrical Industry, 1890–1940', in R Perkins and D Weber (eds), *Inventive Minds: Creativity in Technology* (Oxford University Press, 1992) 291.

[33] ibid 292.

[34] ibid 293.

[35] R Fierstein, *A Triumph of Genius: Edwin Land, Polaroid, and the Kodak Patent War* (Ankerwycke Publications, 2015).

[36] D Hounshell, 'Invention in the Industrial Research Laboratory: Individual Act or Collective Process?' in Perkins and Weber, *Inventive Minds* (1992) 273, 274ff.

[37] ibid 275, 277.

By the end of the twentieth century, breakthroughs in information technology gave rise to visionary individuals who are now almost as well known as Leonardo da Vinci – if not more so for younger generations. Bill Gates, Steve Jobs, Jeff Bezos, Mark Zuckerberg and many lesser-known leaders of groundbreaking high-tech companies served as both individual inventors and corporate founders. At times, the famous founders teamed up with other bright minds whose names made far fewer headlines. When it is time to turn ideas into products, team innovation becomes crucial again.[38] Nonetheless, the initial spark that ignites technological breakthroughs often comes from one or few individuals.

One may wonder how corporate law and governance treat and incentivise these new charismatic founders. Their emergence offers us a rare opportunity to rethink legal incentives for executives and board members who not only promote, manage and finance innovation but also invent new products and technologies themselves.

The phenomenon of inventors who wear two hats – who both innovate and manage high-tech corporations – has become widespread,[39] as futurist Joanne Pransky has shown in a wide-ranging interview with Dr Cory Kidd, the founder and CEO at Catalia Health. The question-and-answer session demonstrated that some of the most groundbreaking innovators in robotics today are sitting on the boards of companies they have founded.[40] They are the core human assets of the companies they run – not only in managerial terms, but also and especially because of their inventive skills[41] and for their ability to attract new financing.[42]

Founders do not only face incentives to invest in innovation; they also face personal incentives to invent or not for and within a given corporation. Intercorporate mobility – the freedom to hop from one company to another – often influences a founder's creative path and personal struggle. When a founder grows dissatisfied with his or her income or strategic role in a company – or, even worse, comes into conflict with other directors – he or she can leave the company and set up a new one. A founder who wields enough power may even choose to shut down the corporation, take a break to refocus on invention, and

[38] T Hughes, *American Genesis: A Century of Invention and Technological Enthusiasm, 1870–1970* (Penguin Books, 1989).

[39] J Dyer, H Gregersen and C Christensen, 'The Innovator's DNA' (2009) 87 *Harvard Business Review* 60.

[40] 'The Pransky Interview' is a '"Q&A interview" conducted by Joanne Pransky of Industrial Robot Journal as a method to impart the combined technological, business and personal experience of a prominent, robotic industry engineer-turned-entrepreneur regarding the evolution, commercialization and challenges of bringing a technological invention to market'. It is published in *Industrial Robot: An International Journal*.

[41] Y Honjo et al, 'R&D Investment of Start-up Firms: Does Founders' Human Capital Matter?' (2014) 42 *Small Business Economics* 207, 215–19.

[42] E-J Ko and A McKelvie, 'Signaling for More Money: The Roles of Founders' Human Capital and Investor Prominence in Resource Acquisition across Different Stages of Firm Development' (2018) 33 *Journal of Business Venturing* 438.

then set up a new company. This was the case for Dr Cory Kidd when he left Intuitive Automata, which creates interactive robots:

> I basically shut down Intuitive Automata in 2013 … I then moved back to the USA and I spent about a year focused on answering two questions: Where is this technology useful in healthcare? And who is willing to pay for this today? That's where having that network in healthcare and spending a lot of time going back to many of these companies and people that I knew and understanding where and what patient engagement or behaviour-change programs they were paying for was very valuable. That's what really gave us a narrow focus around chronic disease management. [O]nce I had that focus, I launched Catalia Health in 2014 as a patient care management company that delivers everyday care to patients who are managing chronic conditions, through *Mabu*, an interactive robot platform that combines artificial intelligence, psychology and medical best practices.[43]

In other cases, board members turn against founders and squeeze them out of their own corporations, as happened to Steve Jobs:

> As Apple Computer grew, Jobs' vision for the future of computing came into conflict with that of then-CEO John Sculley, and Jobs was removed as head of the Macintosh team. Jobs resigned from Apple Computer in September 1985. After his departure from Apple Computer, Jobs founded the computer company NeXT in 1986. He also purchased Pixar, which was the graphics-arts division of Lucasfilm. A decade later, in 1996, Apple purchased NeXT, and once again took on Jobs as an employee ('Apple co-founder,' 2011). At the time, Apple Computer was in dire fiscal straits, with its market share down to 3.8 percent during the second quarter of 1997 (Kanellos, 1997). Over the next decade, Jobs helped to revive Apple Computer and to re-establish it as a market leader. The newly renamed Apple Inc. eventually challenged ExxonMobil as the most valuable company in 2011.[44]

Such conflicts can arise either because there are differing views among founders, as happened with Jobs and Sculley, or because new investors replacing venture capital (VC) funds begin to dominate the company after its innovation is commercialised. Either way, a founder – a critical resource for the company's innovation strategy – moves to another company.

When inventors serve as executives or directors, their departures raise questions about corporate law rules. One question revolves around the duty not to compete with the company and the corporate opportunity doctrine. That rule is meant to protect the corporation and is highly relevant when a departing board member or officer walks away with an important idea or innovation.

[43] J Pransky, 'The Pransky Interview: Dr Cory Kidd, Founder and CEO at Catalia Health' (2017) 44 *Industrial Robot: An International Journal* 259, 260.

[44] M Steinwart and J Ziegler, 'Remembering Apple CEO Steve Jobs as a "Transformational Leader": Implications for Pedagogy' (2014) 13 *Journal of Leadership Education* 52, 53–54.

III. LIMITED CONVERGENCE IN CORPORATE OPPORTUNITY RULES, DIVERGENCE IN CORPORATE OPPORTUNITY REMEDIES

In the United States of America (US) start-up praxis, in the earlier phases, there is an *ex ante* solution to part of the conflicts arising from how to split profits deriving from an invention. It is called a founders' collaboration agreement or, more simply, an operating agreement.[45] Start-up founders usually sign such an agreement to convey a concept or technology to a newly founded company. The document establishes what each founder's shareholding should be and is designed to ensure that each founder makes a continued effort to realise the concept or technology exclusively for the benefit of the company. The operating agreement often includes a confidentiality clause, through which founders pledge to disclose information about the concept or technology only on an as-needed basis and exclusively with the consent of the other founders.[46] Nonetheless, such clauses are incomplete, as they are unlikely to predict how the business will evolve or which kind of industrial application the ideas connected and/or complementary to those forming the commercial basis of the start-up will have.[47] In many cases, any new business opportunities pursued by the founders will be regulated by corporate opportunity rules and/or the directors' duty not to compete with the corporation, depending on the jurisdiction at issue.

There is a degree of convergence of corporate opportunity rules, to the extent to which the US line of business test and the conflict test applied in several continental European jurisdictions limit the applicability of the corporate opportunity doctrine to the business opportunities pertaining to the industry in which the company is actually (or in the wider interpretation potentially) active.[48] The main exception is still constituted by the UK corporate opportunity doctrine, which seems to stick to a rigid 'no profit' rule.[49]

Despite such a degree of substantial convergence in US and European corporate opportunity tests, a 'genetic' gap continues to divide the Anglo-American and continental European traditions when it comes to remedies.[50] This arises

[45] P Molk, 'How do LLC Owners Contract Around Default Statutory Protections' (2016) 42 *Journal of Corporation Law* 503.

[46] See E Miao and B Helwig, 'Avoiding Common IP Pitfalls: What Every Startup Needs to Know' (2018) 16 *Snippets* 1, 2.

[47] On contract incompleteness, see O Hart and J Moore, 'Foundations of Incomplete Contracts' (1999) 66 *Review of Economic Studies* 115.

[48] M Corradi, 'Corporate Opportunities Doctrines Tested in the Light of the Theory of the Firm – a European (and US) Comparative Perspective (2016) 27 *European Business Law Review* 755, 762. M Corradi and G Helleringer, 'Board Duties: The Duty of Loyalty and Self-Dealing', forthcoming in A Afsharipour and M Gelter (eds) *Comparative Corporate Governance* (Edward Elgar, 2021).

[49] See text at ch 1.IV and accompanying notes.

[50] M Corradi, 'Securing Corporate Opportunities in Europe – Comparative Notes on Monetary Remedies and on their Potential Evolution' (2018) 18 *Journal of Corporate Law Studies* 439.

largely from the availability of a double source of remedies in Anglo-American law – common law and equitable remedies[51] – which is not available in civil law.[52]

Under Anglo-American law, a disgorgement of profits (sometimes called 'accounting of profits' in the UK) does not require a quantification of damages and is usually administered through a constructive trust followed by a transfer order.[53] As already discussed, this grants the corporation access to a proprietary remedy, instead of entitling it to a mere sum of money. It goes without saying that when the product or idea that was misappropriated is economically complementary to the corporation – as is the case with a technological innovation – the possibility of obtaining the good itself and not mere compensation may be efficiency-enhancing from the corporation's point of view.

A disgorgement of profits may also be assisted by tracing; that is, the corporation may be able to ask for a constructive trust on the sale of the corporate opportunity at issue and on any subsequent reinvestment.[54] All the subsequent profits will be traced and disgorged. In a highly innovative environment, Anglo-American corporate opportunity rules seem unfriendly to directors' mobility unless we consider the possibility of a waiver for corporate opportunity rules.[55]

Except in Spain, the core remedy against misappropriations in most continental European jurisdictions is damages, which often prove difficult to quantify.[56] Quantification may be especially difficult for corporate opportunities found in flourishing start-up environments. It is exceedingly hard to predict which of the many new ventures that emerge each year in Silicon Valley – or in Berlin's new innovation district, for that matter – will prove successful.[57] An alternative continental Europe remedy against misappropriations might be the 'unjust enrichment' doctrine, but so far only Spanish law applies such a remedy.[58]

Differences in remedies entail differences in how one protects an investment in an inventive activity. These disparities can be highly relevant to VC funds and entrepreneurs alike. Equally pertinent is how flexibly the rules are applied. In the Anglo-American tradition, corporate opportunity rules are 'genetically' related to the duty of loyalty, which is viewed as a mandatory corporate law rule.[59] This still holds true in the UK. Although it might be argued that some recent interpretations of fiduciary law have rendered the conception less rigid,[60] British courts have endorsed none of these academic ideas. In the US, by contrast,

[51] See text at ch 3.III and V and accompanying notes.

[52] See text at ch 4.III and V and accompanying notes.

[53] For a seminal case see *Holt v Holt* (1670) 1 Chan Cas 190, about a testamentary trust and lease renewal.

[54] *A-G for Hong Kong v Reid* [1994] 1 AC 324 and see text at ch 4.III and accompanying notes.

[55] See text at section XI and accompanying notes.

[56] See ch 4.I and accompanying notes.

[57] B Headd, 'Redefining Business Success: Distinguishing between Closure and Failure' (2003) 21 *Small Business Economics* 51.

[58] See text at ch 3.IV and accompanying notes.

[59] M Eisenberg, 'The Structure of Corporation Law' (1989) 89 *Columbia Law Review* 1461, 1486.

[60] M Conaglen, *Fiduciary Loyalty* (Hart Publishing, 2010).

Delaware and several other states have recently challenged the idea that corporate opportunity rules are mandatory.[61] Corporate opportunity rules are now waivable. This development looks interesting when it comes to innovation incentives for corporate founders who may be interested in the same business opportunity.[62] Given that loyalty must be undivided per se, the easiest way to solve the situation is by allowing a company to waive corporate opportunity rules. Empirical research shows that this solution has been successful in practice.[63]

Even so, no waiver has been adopted in the new continental corporate opportunity rules or in the UK's well-established corporate opportunity doctrine.[64] In most European jurisdictions, fiduciary duties tend to be seen as mandatory and connected to the efficient functioning of the economic system. The inability to waive corporate opportunity rules renders European jurisdictions more rigid than those in the US.

The director's duty not to compete with the corporation is probably the most established continental European counterpart to Anglo-American corporate opportunity rules. It is based on a rationale akin to the corporate opportunity 'line of business test'.[65] Nonetheless, it entails a competing activity and not a single act of appropriation.[66] The German version of this rule (*Wettbewerbsverbot*) may produce some of the effects of corporate opportunity rules. German law applies an *Eintrittsrecht* to the competing activity, a sort of disgorgement of profits. By contrast, legal systems such as those of France[67] and Italy[68] tend to rely upon damages, which may render the remedy inefficient.

Both for corporate opportunities and the duty not to compete, damages may in principle have the effect of dividing an entitlement, creating a degree of Solomonic bargaining.[69] In practice, however, courts may struggle to quantify damages, especially the potential loss of profits. Predicting the market value of a groundbreaking innovation may, after all, be a matter of guessing. Hence damages claims appear to be an inappropriate remedy, even though they are the only relief available in many jurisdictions. Even if directors who misappropriate corporate opportunities are punished with a narrower set of remedies in civil law jurisdictions than in common law jurisdictions,[70] they still will not be granted an *ex ante* waiver. This clearly limits the possible arrangements between corporation and directors.

[61] DGCL, s 122(17).

[62] G Rauterberg and E Talley, 'Contracting Out of the Fiduciary Duty of Loyalty: An Empirical Analysis of Corporate Opportunity Waivers' (2017) 117 *Columbia Law Review* 1075.

[63] ibid.

[64] Or at least there seems to be no UK case law involving waivers under CA 2006 to provide us guidance with this difficult doctrinal question.

[65] Corradi, 'Corporate Opportunities Doctrines' (2016) 762.

[66] ibid.

[67] Cass com 24 February 1998, BJS Juillet 1998 n 266, 813.

[68] Italian Civil Code, Art 2390.

[69] I Ayres and E Talley, 'Solomonic Bargaining: Dividing an Entitlement to Facilitate Coasean Trade' (1995) 104 *Yale Law Journal* 1027.

[70] See ch 3.IV–VI and accompanying notes.

IV. FOUNDERS UNDER THE LENS OF IP THEORY: DO EMPLOYEE INNOVATION INCENTIVES APPLY?

An in-depth discussion about how IP law treats the inventions of founders is beyond the scope of this book. There are two reasons for this. First, IP law is not usually viewed as part of corporate law. Second, the focus of this book is on non-patentable and pre-patentable innovations. When a founder is just thinking about or even working on an invention, IP law is not yet applicable.[71] Yet IP laws covering the rights of employees who innovate and invent on the job have a clear bearing on the corporate law rules analysed here.

This is a complex area of IP law in most jurisdictions, and it is further complicated by significant differences between Anglo-American and European laws.[72] German law strongly protects employees, granting them the right to receive compensation for their inventions through a set of complex provisions.[73] US law, by contrast, does not in principle offer employees any compensation for their inventions, although an invention-reward clause is often inserted in employment contracts.[74] Such rewards can range from a medal or mere recognition to a promotion or a substantial cash bonus that can amount to several million dollars.[75] The German regime involves mandatory law, making it homogenous and relatively easy to assess empirically: several studies explore how satisfied employee-inventors are with their rewards.[76] The US model is contractual, making it highly diversified.[77] Its empirical analysis is more complex, as the level of employee-inventor satisfaction tends to vary from company to company.

US legal and economics scholars have debated whether there should be a proprietary or a non-proprietary approach to the inventions of employees and directors. Should the ownership of inventions be allocated by default to employers – or to employees? This debate is relevant to the analysis of corporate opportunity rules, which have different remedial systems in continental Europe

[71] S Samila and O Sorenson, 'Noncompete Covenants: Incentives to Innovate or Impediments to Growth' (2011) 57 *Management Science* 425, 427.

[72] On US law, see P Van Slyke and M Friedman, 'Employer's Rights to Inventions and Patents of Its Officers, Directors and Employees' (1990) 18 *American Intellectual Property Law Association Quarterly Journal* 127; R Merges, 'The Law and Economics of Employee Inventions' (1999) 13 *Harvard Journal of Law* & Technology 1.

[73] The main point of reference is still the German Employees' Invention Act, dated 25.07.1957, Bundesgesetzblatt I, 756.

[74] Merges, 'Employee Inventions' (1999) 5ff.

[75] ibid 38ff.

[76] J Giummo, 'German Employee Inventors' Compensation Records: A Window into the Returns to Patented Inventions' (2010) 39 *Research Policy* 969; C Leptien, 'Incentives for Employed Inventors: an Empirical Analysis with Special Emphasis on the German Law for Employee's Inventions' (1995) 25 *R&D Management* 213; K Blind et al, 'Motives to Patent: Empirical Evidence from Germany' (2006) 35 *Research Policy* 655.

[77] Merges (n 72) 5ff.

(damages in most cases)[78] than in the US and UK (accounting/disgorgement of profits and a constructive trust, in their proprietary version).[79]

The US debate on default assignments of IP ownership rights has been fierce, partly for historical reasons. For much of the nineteenth century, US law was generous to employees, granting them ownership of their inventions.[80] But the leading case on employees' inventions, *Solomons v United States*, assigned the ownership of such inventions to employers – at least when employees are hired to invent.[81] That case revolved around one Spencer M Clark, head of the US Bureau of Engraving and Printing, who conceived the idea of a self-cancelling stamp and used government employees and property in 1867 to prepare a die or plate therefore. He then took out a patent and demanded compensation for government use of the stamp on whiskey barrels.

Merges has outlined the arguments favouring each side – employer and employee.[82] What interests us most here is the pro-employer argument that inventors are often 'hired to invent', ie their primary job is to solve a specific technical problem through innovation.[83] Seen in this light, common sense says the employer should own the fruit of the employee's work on the job.

It can be debated whether this argument should apply to founders, given that inventing is rarely a director's only task within a corporation. Moreover, founders can to some extent be understood as self-hiring. In certain contexts, such as VC, it is often true that directors sit on the board because of their inventive capabilities, which are critical assets to the new company. These director-founders often leave the board once their intensive inventing activity is no longer indispensable to the corporation.[84] Nonetheless, what grants them a position on the board is their vision combined with their technical skills, rather than their technical skills alone.

But what about employees who are in no way 'hired to invent' yet wind up inventing something meaningful for the company? The same consideration may apply to corporate directors who occasionally become 'inventors for one day'.[85] For employees who are not hired to invent, US law tends to apply a two-step

[78] See text at ch 3.V and accompanying footnotes.

[79] See text at ch 3.III and accompanying footnotes.

[80] C Fisk, 'Removing the "Fuel of Interest" from the "Fire of Genius": Law and the Employee-Inventor, 1830–1930' (1998) 65 *University of Chicago Law Review* 1127.

[81] *Solomons v United States*, 137 US 342 (1890).

[82] Merges (n 72) 2–3.

[83] Merges (n 72) 5.

[84] D Larcker and B Tayan, 'Tesla Motors: The Evolution of Governance from Inception to IPO' Stanford Closer Look Series (May 2011), www.gsb.stanford.edu/faculty-research/publications/tesla-motors-evolution-governance-inception-ipo.

[85] *Johnson Furnace & Engineering Co v Western Furnace Co*, 178 F 819, 823 (8th Cir 1910); *Deane v Hodge*, 35 Minn 146, 27 NW 917, 59 Am R 321. Both cases were on simple innovations. Nowadays it is unlikely that a common director has access to the sophistications of ground-breaking technologies unless they have an engineering background.

test: such inventions belong to the employer when they relate to the employee's duties and are created using company resources. If not, the employer still retains a 'shop right', meaning it can obtain an implied-in-law royalty-free licence on the inventions.[86] This test has some elements in common with the test applied to corporate opportunity misappropriations that occur when a director discovers an opportunity while discharging his or her duties.[87]

One argument supporting the attribution of employee inventions to employers is based on the potential opportunistic behaviour of an employee who owns a crucial 'fragment' or 'parcel' of an invention – a piece needed to obtain a patent.[88] Merges writes that if the law had granted employees ownership of their inventions:

> [A] rational firm would either undertake less R&D or radically redesign the R&D process. The firm might direct employees to design very generic components, similar to other designs available in the market, in order to constrain the bargaining power of employees once they had made an invention. This, of course, has drawbacks. First, it would reduce the distinctiveness of each firm's products. Second, it would encourage each employee to design a component that had maximum sales potential as an individual component, which might well hurt the performance of the firm's specific product.[89]

It is unclear whether this line of reasoning would apply to founders, given that pre-patentable business ideas are often the fruit of one founder's ideas, not of a team's ideas. Even so, the argument seems to ignore the emerging praxis, which shows a high degree of knowledge fragmentation within the innovation process in highly innovative environments.[90]

A further argument in favour of assigning employees' inventions to employers is based on the 'team production' theory of corporate law.[91] According to this theory, it would be difficult and costly to assign each invention to only one employee because inventions often result from a team effort. Rewarding each participant pro rata would also encourage opportunistic behaviour, tempting each employee to free-ride on the efforts of other employees. This argument does not seem to apply to founders, who are easily identifiable as autonomous inventors. Even when there is a team of founders, later joined by a venture capitalist, sociological literature shows that opportunistic behaviour as described

[86] Merges (n 72) 6.

[87] V Brudney and R Clark, 'A New Look at Corporate Opportunities' (1981) 94 *Harvard Law Review* 997.

[88] Merges (n 72) 12ff.

[89] ibid 15–16.

[90] R Gilson, C Sabel and R Scott, 'Contracting for Innovation: Vertical Disintegration and Interfirm Collaboration' (2009) 109 *Columbia Law Review* 431, 434, rejecting the idea that the modularity hypothesis gives a faithful account of the present 'contracting for innovation' praxis in rapidly innovating industries.

[91] Merges (n 72) 20.

above is uncommon in highly creative inventive environments such as Silicon Valley.[92] Great inventors are usually driven by passion for their work and tend to emulate each other – not to lazily free-ride on others' efforts.

Team production theory also argues that employees who own their inventions will focus on their own personal return. Hence 'the marketing and product manufacturing interface tasks required of the newer corporate R&D model will suffer as well. Plans to better integrate the R&D function into overall operations will also suffer'.[93] This argument might hold if innovation tended to revert to vertical integration strategies. Yet, as already said, recent literature shows that in highly innovative environments it is common for groundbreaking innovation to follow patterns of vertical disintegration and collaboration among firms and for most components of a final product to be outsourced.[94]

Now, if we take a closer look at the laws applicable to directors' inventions, we will notice that a director's duty to assign patents to the company may be seen in the US as an extension of the duty to be loyal to the corporation.[95] In Germany, the law covering a director's inventions is even more closely aligned with the duty of loyalty to the corporation. In fact, the German law on employee inventions does not apply to directors at all. Their inventions instead fall under the corporate opportunity doctrine.[96] This approach sounds like a strong additional protection for the corporation. Although it is easily understandable in terms of corporate law and agency costs rationale, it still seems at odds with the approach followed during the age of 'great inventors', when, as Fisk reminds us, employees retained 'significant legal rights to their ideas if they were embodied in patented inventions'.[97] Fisk goes on to note:

> If the judges perceived the inventive employee as a man like Eli Whitney or Thomas Edison, they found it hard to treat him like a servant. However, once employer lawyers disabused judges of the inventor-hero image in favour of the modern vision of inventive employees working in a big, employer-financed laboratory, the law began to change.[98]

[92] A Saxenian, *Regional Advantage. Culture and Competition in Silicon Valley and Route 128* (Harvard University Press, 1994).

[93] Merges (n 72) 30.

[94] Gilson, Sabel and Scott, 'Contracting for Innovation' (2009) 435, 438.

[95] Van Slyke and Friedman, 'Employer's Rights to Inventions' (1990) 129ff.

[96] BGH, Urteil vom 23-09-1985 – II ZR 246/84 (Stuttgart). This is a case of a GmbH resigning director who tried to patent at his name an invention which he had discovered while working for his previous employer – ie the GmbH at issue. The court applied the German corporate opportunity doctrine to the case.

[97] Fisk, 'Removing the "Fuel of Interest" from the "Fire of Genius"' (1998) 1197.

[98] ibid 1198. It is correct to say that the image of these inventors of the past as one genius is only partially true. For instance, Thomas Edison started his revolutionary invention alone – for which he was known as the Wizard of Menlo Park. Nonetheless, later on in his career, he also led what has been considered one of the first R&D laboratories in industrial history. See R Friedel, 'Perspiration in Perspective: Changing Perceptions of Genius and Expertise in American Invention' in Perkins and Weber (n 32) 11, 12 and 18ff.

Now, one may wonder whether some of our modern Silicon Valley heroes are so different from Whitney or Edison in terms of inventive capabilities and reputation. What Fisk describes above seems to open a question on how corporate law should treat the inventions of founders such as Steve Jobs, Marc Tarpenning or Martin Eberhard. Should they be obliged to transfer *all* their inventions to the corporation – and leave them there even after they have stepped down? The literature on employees' inventions does not seem to provide a meaningful reply to this question. In fact, the arguments in favour of assigning inventions to employers do not seem to apply to the relationship between corporation and inventive corporate founders. As already said, the focus here is on inventions that have not yet been patented and on directors' mobility – a sub-question within the cited conundrum, where corporate law rules seem to be particularly important. If a sensible reply to such a vexed question cannot come from literature on employees' inventions, one may need to set the question within a theoretical framework that considers all the variables at play, from the perspective of both innovation theory and corporate theory.

V. OVERVIEW OF AN EVOLVING RESEARCH FIELD – INSTITUTIONAL ECONOMICS, CORPORATE GOVERNANCE AND INNOVATION

When delving into the relationships between corporate governance and innovation,[99] it is common to begin with the framework supplied by David Soskice and Peter Hall in their book *Varieties of Capitalism*.[100] Varieties of capitalism (VOC) literature offered an intriguing perspective on the relationships between legal institutions and innovation. It focused on the divergence between the US and the European corporate models, taking Germany as a central point of reference for its inquiry into European systems of innovation. It presented a

[99] The relationship between corporate governance and innovation has been explored both theoretically and empirically as corporate governance is usually regarded as one of the institutional complementarities that explains trends in innovation. For examples of theoretical versus empirical enquiries, see M Calderini et al, *Corporate Governance, Market Structure and Innovation* (Edward Elgar, 2003); M O'Connor and M Rafferty, 'Corporate Governance and Innovation' (2012) 47 *Journal of Financial and Quantitative Analysis* 397. For the wider picture, see W Lazonick, 'Innovative Enterprise and Historical Transformation' (2002) 3 *Enterprise and Society* 3; W Lazonick, 'The Theory of Market Economy and the Market Foundations of Innovative Enterprise' (2003) 24 *Economic and Industrial Democracy* 9; R Evangelista et al, 'Looking for Regional Systems of Innovation: Evidence from the Italian Innovation Survey' (2002) 36 *Regional Studies* 173; H Wang and J Barney, 'Employees Incentives to Make Firm-Specific Investments: Implications for Resource-based Theories of Corporate Diversification' (2006) 31 *Academy of Management Review* 466. Literature has recently enquired the relationships between takeovers and innovation. See for example J Atanassov, 'Do Hostile Takeovers Stifle Innovation? Evidence from Antitakeover Legislation and Corporate Patenting' (2013) 68 *Journal of Finance* 1097.

[100] D Soskice and P Hall, *Varieties of Capitalism: The Institutional Foundations of Comparative Advantage* (Oxford University Press, 2001). For a critical view, see B Hancké, M Rhodes and M Thatcher (eds), *Beyond Varieties of Capitalism: Conflict, Contradictions, and Complementarities in the European Economy* (Oxford University Press, 2007).

polarised world, with the US leading radical innovation and Europe, generally speaking, engaging in incremental innovation.[101]

Unfortunately, the VOC framework looks somewhat outdated for the purpose of analysing the relationships between corporate governance and innovation. The framework does not sufficiently stress that different systems of innovation coexist within a given country, including Germany. A similar diversity in regional and local innovation systems has long characterised other European countries, notably Italy.[102] This differentiation has increased of late because innovative start-ups have multiplied in many countries and have adopted foreign strategies in the hope of breaking into new markets.[103]

Globalisation has spurred the circulation not only of technology, but also of innovation models, giving start-ups everywhere common methods for seeking finance and exchanging information.[104] The upshot is that different innovation models now coexist in the same country. Germany, for example, now hosts a flourishing start-up scene in Berlin.[105] Yet incremental innovation remains central for the improvement of traditional German high-quality products, such as chemicals and cars.[106] Hence, the polarised 'US-versus-Europe' view may no longer describe how innovation works today. Despite the prevalence of certain path dependences within each country, the situation appears to be increasingly fluid and open to change.

The US start-up and VC-based model has become widespread worldwide.[107] Though several corporate models of innovation still exist, a global entrepreneurship model of innovation seems to have emerged, emphasising mobility and flexibility of resources, as Freeman and Engel argue in 'Models of Innovation'.[108] The present analysis acknowledges the existence of an innovation model based

[101] P Hall and D Gingerich, 'Varieties of Capitalism and Institutional Complementarities in the Political Economy: An Empirical Analysis' (2009) 39 *British Journal of Political Science* 449, 473ff.

[102] Besides large corporations, the Italian economy has been renowned for its industrial districts, which also show rather peculiar innovation patterns. As in Silicon Valley, in Italian districts innovation was strongly influenced by highly specialized employees' mobility. See F Belussi and L Pilotti, 'Knowledge Creation, Learning and Innovation in Italian Industrial Districts' (2002) 84 *Geografiska Annaler* 125, 133.

[103] O Burgel and G Murray, 'The International Market Entry Choices of Start-up Companies in High-Technology Industries' (2000) 8 *Journal of International Marketing* 33.

[104] S Pfotenhauer and S Jasanoff, 'The "Practice Turn" in Innovation Policy and the Global Circulation of Innovation Models' in D Tyfield et al (eds), *The Routledge Handbook of the Political Economy of Science* (Taylor & Francis, 2017) 416. At times, given the openness of R&D models, it may even sound difficult to write about 'innovation models' in the traditional taxonomical way. See G Berkhout et al, 'Innovating the Innovation Process' (2006) 34 *International Journal of Technology Management* 390, 392.

[105] A Kritikos, 'Berlin: A Hub for Startups but not (yet) for Fast-growing Companies' (2016) 6 *DIW Economic Bulletin* 339 (2016); M Andersson and S Koster, 'Sources of Persistence in Regional Start-up Rates – Evidence from Sweden (2010) 11 *Journal of Economic Geography* 179.

[106] Lane, 'Globalization and the German Model' (2000).

[107] See text at ch 6.I and accompanying notes.

[108] J Freeman and J Engel, 'Models of Innovation: Start-ups and Mature Corporations' (2007) 50 *California Management Review* 94.

mostly on companies that develop groundbreaking technology and a potential disappearance of institutional complementarities, endangered by a regulatory race to the bottom.[109] It is precisely in this setting that directors often double as inventors and may encounter corporate governance rules that influence their incentives to innovate.[110] These companies are often created as start-ups and financed through VC. As we have seen, founders can find it difficult to continue their inventive activity within such companies once they have grown to maturity.[111] One can debate whether – and to what extent – a founder's mobility and ability to innovate are helped or hindered by corporate opportunity rules and rules similar in function. But to appreciate how a director's duty of loyalty and compensation influence innovation we must first understand the basic dynamics of innovation – especially the groundbreaking innovation that founders undertake in high-tech clusters.

VI. AT THE CORE OF TECHNOLOGICAL INNOVATION: CREATION, CIRCULATION AND COMBINATION OF KNOWLEDGE BUILDING BLOCKS

One may wonder what qualifies as technological innovation and how the innovation process takes place. The easiest way to understand technological innovation is to start with an explanation of the word 'innovation' and of the word 'technology'. In one sense, what innovation is should not be too controversial: put simply, the term alludes to efforts directed to bringing something new into the world.[112] By contrast, as Brian Arthur explains, 'technology' is a good example of polysemy.[113] Among many possible meanings, Arthur considers three of them: (1) a means to fulfil a human purpose; (2) an assemblage of practices; (3) a collection of devices and engineering practices available to a culture. All such meanings highlight distinctive features pertaining to technology.

At times, innovation is groundbreaking. Other times it may simply consist of slight modifications brought to traditional or well-known and well-tested procedures. In fact, the core value of certain products is represented by the preservation of tradition: for example, for established/conservative luxury brands, the value of their products may depend greatly on design and on the quality of the materials employed. Both variables may go through very limited modifications over time. In other cases, innovation may refine extremely sophisticated

[109] B Amable, 'Institutional Complementarity and Diversity of Social Systems of Innovation and Production' (2000) 7 *Review of International Political Economy* 645, 681.

[110] See text at section VIII and accompanying notes.

[111] Larcker and Tayan, 'Tesla Motors' (2011).

[112] It is true however that the term innovation is not applied exclusively to technology. A Baregheh, J Rowley and S Sambrook, 'Towards a Multidisciplinary Definition of Innovation' (2009) 47 *Management Decision* 1323.

[113] B Arthur, *The Nature of Technology: What it Is and How it Evolves* (The Free Press, 2009) 5.

information technology (IT) processes and/or products. By contrast with all the previous examples, instead of adding something new, at times innovation means 'simplification' rather than 'sophistication' – as research on 'disruptive' innovation has made particularly clear.[114]

The law and economics literature mainly addresses innovation by way of asking how to obtain a greater degree of innovation – but *without* questioning the essence of the innovation process.[115] By contrast, Brian Arthur has explored the nature of innovation. He highlights the 'combinatorial' nature of innovation.[116] In Arthur's view, combinatorial evolution is the main force driving innovation. Combinatorial evolution is using old technologies as 'building blocks' for new ones, so that 'technology creates itself out of itself'.[117] Such an approach has many consequences for the ontological plan. First of all, creation is not just a matter of human will to innovate. Despite the fact that force of will is a precious attribute for the purpose of overcoming obstacles and solving problems, often solutions arise from fortuitous encounters between different building blocks of implicit and explicit knowledge.

According to Arthur, firms tend to *encounter*, rather than choose, a given technology.[118] Therefore, innovation seems to be driven by a series of events, some of which lie beyond the human intentions of an individual or of a team of inventors. These events do not rule out the importance of human intention to innovate, but they definitely highlight its limits. Along with human will, one must consider a series of other factors that contribute to the outcome of an innovative effort. Such variables are, for example, the state of the art in technology,[119] experience and availability of deep crafting knowledge,[120] geographical location,[121] and fortuity (one of the components that affect combinations of building blocks of knowledge) – all of which are factors in conditioning in-depth creative efforts.

The combinatorial nature of innovation shows some limits in the traditional economic analysis of the law as applied to innovation. Economic analyses of the law try either to explain or to orient economic actors' choices as a consequence of economic incentives:[122] incentives (especially economic ones) are introduced for the purpose of driving human actions towards specific goals. Therefore, in a traditional law and economics view, setting incentives for individuals to innovate will create an institutional framework that is conducive to innovation.

[114] See text at next section and accompanying notes.
[115] See text at section V and accompanying notes.
[116] Arthur, *The Nature of Technology* (2009).
[117] ibid 22.
[118] ibid 153.
[119] ibid 22ff.
[120] ibid 159.
[121] ibid 161 for a description of regional clusters.
[122] Merges (n 72). With an angle closer to this analysis, see Samila and Sorenson, 'Noncompete Covenants' (2011).

However, the combinatorial mechanisms explained by Arthur do not necessarily follow the paths designed by incentives to individuals. By contrast, it may well be that what are understood as 'regulatory failures' unexpectedly provide stimuli for innovation. In fact, combinatorial evolution is determined by encounters among building blocks of technology. These encounters can potentially be furthered not only as a consequence of a specific 'combinatory will', but also as a result of regulatory failures. I believe that examples of regulatory failures may be, for instance, human capital migration following lack of proper employment incentives *in loco*, or the need to create networks among firms as a consequence of weak internal governance structures. Another example closer to this analysis may also be represented by the founding of a new successful business on the basis of a non-authorised taking of a corporate opportunity. Evolution by regulatory failures may occur because it is hard to predict which is the best combination for the different blocks of knowledge.

Because of the intrinsic characteristics of innovation, it is necessary to analyse its dynamics within corporations by dividing one's attention: on one hand, one must focus on incentives to innovate as provided to individuals – corporate founders in this analysis – and organisations – here, the business corporation; on the other hand, one must be mindful of the 'objective' dynamics of the innovation phenomenon. Those dynamics are more complex than the ones generated by normative incentives to individuals and/or to firms. They depend upon less visible and interpretable paths (at least on the basis of our present knowledge). While the law may well have a more important role in setting direct incentives to invent for individuals and corporations, the knowledge of potential combinatorial paths – or at least some of them – may also help to channel incentives in a more conscious way. As a matter of fact, one cannot completely exclude the hypothesis that the combinatorial activity described above may better prosper in deregulated corporate environments. This hypothesis puts into question the desirability of corporate opportunity rules in highly innovative environments – or at least it offers an additional argument in favour of the possibility to opt out of corporate opportunity rules.

VII. TECHNOLOGIC INNOVATION TRADITIONAL 'TAXONOMY' VERSUS DISRUPTIVE INNOVATION

From a product market perspective, Abernathy and Clark have identified four different types of innovation:[123] (1) 'architectural innovations', which open new possibilities of linkages to markets and to customers;[124] (2) 'niche

[123] W Abernathy and K Clark, 'Innovation: Mapping the Winds of Creative Destruction' (1985) 14 *Research Policy* 3.

[124] ibid 7.

creations', with the role of conserving and strengthening established designs;[125] (3) 'revolutionary innovations', which disrupt established technical and production competences;[126] and (4) 'incremental innovations', which consist of slow and progressive improvements added to an already existing product.[127] Recent business science literature has introduced a completely new economic perspective of traditional classifications[128] creating a new and alternative category of innovation, known as 'disruptive innovation'. Disruptive innovation is defined by its contrast with 'sustaining innovation', which can be associated with all the types of innovation identified by Clark and reported above. In light of disruptive innovation, older classifications may still prove useful, but they seem embedded in a more complex framework.

Christensen's research started by considering the reasons why very well-managed firms that are characterised by a significant rate of radical and incremental innovation often suffer a sudden economic collapse, without any apparent explanation. According to Christensen, the reason for highly innovative firms' failure in the medium to long run is related to their excessive concerns about consumer demand. In other words, once a product has been brought to the market, well-managed firms tend to (and have to) improve their products in an exhausting run to please consumers' requests for a more sophisticated version of the product in question.[129] However, at a certain point in that process, the offer of increasingly refined and sophisticated products exceeds consumer demand for quality and sophistication.[130]

[125] ibid 10.

[126] ibid 12.

[127] ibid 15. Other classifications of innovations pertain to more specific features and are worth reporting for the purpose of providing a technical language which derives from industrial organisation and which may prove useful as an interface for corporate governance. Research on industrial organisation research has identified the following categories: (1) product innovation: this term is used to depict a creation which is visible outside the firm (see S Bhoovaraghavan et al, 'Resolving the Process vs. Product Innovation Dilemma: A Consumer Choice Theoretic Approach' (1996) 42 *Management Science* 232); (2) process innovation, which is used for describing new production paths which remain internal to the firm (see F Damanpour and S Gopalakrishnan, 'The Dynamics of the Adoption of Product and Process Innovations in Organizations' (2001) 38 *Journal of Management Studies* 45. While both categories may increase competition, they will do so in different ways: product innovation will tend to increase competition on the quality (provided it is not an architectural one, since in that case a new market is created). In contrast, process innovation will tend to increase competition over prices, through cost reduction (provided that the structure of the market allows competition); (3) simple innovation: which relies on a single field of knowledge; (4) complex innovation: which incorporates competences from different fields of knowledge. On the distinction between simple and complex innovation see D Kash and R Rycroft, 'To Manage Complex Innovation You Need to Ask the Right Questions' (2003) 46 *Research-Technology Management* 29.

[128] See for instance J Bower and C Christensen, 'Disruptive Technologies: Catching the Wave' (1995) 73 *Harvard Business Review* 43; C Christensen, *The Innovator's Dilemma* (Harper Business, 2000); C Christensen and M Raynor, *The Innovator's Solution* (Harvard Business School Press, 2003); C Christensen, S Anthony and E Roth, *Seeing What's Next* (Harvard Business School Press, 2004).

[129] Christensen, *The Innovator's Dilemma* (200) 209ff.

[130] ibid 212ff. This phenomenon is described by the author as 'performance oversupply'.

The low-end consumers start looking for a simpler product that can satisfy the same need in a new and more functional way. That new product is characterised by disruptive qualities and is usually conceived to target a niche that pertains to the lower-end segment of a neighbouring product market. From that leverage point, it is readapted to a higher segment of the market, meeting this downwards-shifting demand by consumers who were dissatisfied with a product improved beyond their real needs.[131] Thus, it will eventually enter the sophisticated product market from the bottom end. Once a disruptive product has been launched on the market (and at times has created a new one), incumbent firms may well be unable to adapt their production system to it. In fact, they may have adapted their industrial processes (and complementary assets), values and routines to the old system.[132] Moreover, they may be unable to offer a third alternative and competing disruptive innovation as a consequence of their devoting most, if not all, of their financial resources to sustaining innovation.[133] Christensen exemplifies his disruptive innovation theory through examples taken from different industries – for instance, Black & Decker (B&D) innovations in the 1960s:

> Prior to 1960, handheld electric tools were heavy and rugged, designed for professionals – and very expensive. B&D introduced a line of plastic-encased tools with universal motors that would only last twenty-five to thirty hours of operation – which actually was more than adequate for most do-it-yourselfers who drill a few holes per month. In today's dollars, B&D brought the costs of these tools down from $150 to $20, enabling a whole new population to own and use their own tools.[134]

Canon photocopiers provide an equally interesting example:

> Until the early 1980s, when people needed photocopies, they had to take their originals to the corporate photocopy centre, where a technician ran the job for them. He had to be a technician, because the high-speed Xerox machine there was very complicated and needed service frequently. When Canon and Ricoh introduced their countertop photocopiers, they were slow, produced poor-resolution copies, and didn't enlarge or reduce collate. But they were so inexpensive and simple to use that people could afford to put one right around the corner from their office. At the beginning, people still took their high-volume jobs to the copy centre. But little by little, Canon improved its machines to the point that immediate, convenient access to high-quality, full-featured copying is almost a constitutional right in most workplaces today.[135]

[131] ibid 192–93 and 214–15.

[132] For the significance of routines in firms' development, see O Williamson, 'Strategy Research: Governance and Competence Perspectives' in N Foss and V Mahnke (eds), *Competence, Governance and Entrepreneurship* (Oxford University Press, 2000) 21, 33ff. The concept of 'routines' is commonly employed in the so-called 'competence theory of the firm'. Nevertheless, as may be noticed in this specific case, that theory is not necessarily incompatible with an organisational view (ie one based on a transaction-costs analysis under the Coasean framework). For an overview of the literature on potential integrations between those two theories, see N Foss and V Mahnke, 'Advancing Research on Competence, Governance, and Entrepreneurship' in Foss and Mahnke (ibid) 1–20.

[133] Bower and Christensen (n 128) 47.

[134] Christensen, *The Innovator's Solution* (2003) 56.

[135] ibid 57.

An example in a completely different field is provided by 'credit scoring', described as:

> A formulaic method of determining creditworthiness, substituting for the subjective judgments of bank loan officers. Developed by a Minneapolis firm, Fair Isaac. Used initially to extend Sears and Penney's in-store credit cards. As the technology improved, it was used for general credit cards, and then auto, mortgage, and now small-business loans.[136]

Beside his historical account of disruptive innovations, Christensen has also extended his theory, moving from a 'positive' approach to a 'normative' one (if one can borrow this distinction from legal theory for the purpose of describing business economics and strategy literature).[137]

Christensen is persuaded that a successful business should always take into consideration the eventuality of engaging in disruptive innovation. In order to avoid failure, it would be necessary to limit investment in sustaining innovation, that is, the part of a firm's innovation activity that is directed at improving the original product, either through incremental improvements or through radically new components (such as a new electronic gadget for a car). Financial resources originally invested in sustaining innovation should then be partially diverted to disruptive innovation.[138] The core point of this business strategy would be understanding what is likely to be the 'right' amount of incremental innovation that is needed and what level of innovation is sufficient but not excessive for innovators to survive on the market, without compromising the potential for launching disruptive innovations.

One may wonder what the implications are of disruptive innovation theory for corporate governance. First, most of those innovations that Christensen qualifies as disruptive are not the fruits of massive investments in R&D. Instead, they can be the fruit of a sort of 'diagonal thinking' – which is precisely what many successful corporate founders have engaged in. In the case of disruptive innovation, the traditional way of reasoning about innovation through monetary incentives, investment deployment and massive financing to R&D does not necessarily work. Second, corporate governance has to consider business strategies – such as those suggested by Christensen in the normative part of his research – if they are adopted by managers who are now studying such strategies at top business schools, such as Harvard where Christensen used to teach.

[136] ibid 58.

[137] F Parisi, 'Positive, Normative and Functional Schools in Law and Economics' (2004) 18 *European Journal of Law and Economics* 259.

[138] These are the general ideas contained in Christensen (n 128) 238. As noted by Gilson, Sabel and Scott (n 90) 442, 'In the heyday of vertical integration, incumbency was the goal, allowing firms to see over the horizon of technical development and providing, through economies of scale, the means to realize the possibilities they saw. Now incumbency is seen as a burden, proficiency with current technologies obstructing the view of future directions.Precisely the organizational capabilities that underlie success in the industry as currently understood blind the firm to threats from outside of the dominant conception'.

Agency theory tends to call for the protection of any assets of the firm from misappropriation.[139] However, business opportunities connected to disruptive innovation are often financially non-appealing to a well-established corporation, as they carry lower profit margins when compared to alternative investments.[140] Yet, incumbent corporations should try to become disruptive in order to win their competitive battles in the long term.[141] In other words, the reason that business opportunities deriving from disruptive innovation should be protected from misappropriation is not their present value, and often not even their actualised value. In fact, at times it may be difficult to forecast which innovation will become disruptive and therefore the stream of profits that will arise from it.

To some extent, the allocation of property rights on disruptive innovation may entail a trade-off. If the incumbent corporation retains property rights on all disruptive innovation it may not be able to develop all of it, but it can secure itself against potential competition from insiders.[142] By contrast, if the incumbent corporation does not retain property rights on all disruptive innovation, it may lose intellectual assets, and its competitors will be able to appropriate unprotected innovation. However, it may also be able to contract for innovation around products developed outside its realm.[143] Given that in highly innovative contexts it is hard to state that all innovation should belong uniquely to the corporation, one may ask what would be the most efficient way to treat innovations by corporate founders from a corporate law perspective. Moreover, given the relational nature of contracting for innovation,[144] one may wonder what are the norms that best preserve the relationship between a company and its resigned directors who end up working on a complementary product.

VIII. CORPORATE FOUNDERS AND THEIR INCENTIVES TO INNOVATE WITHIN A CORPORATION: FOUNDERS' AND CORPORATIONS' PERSPECTIVES

Modern literature shows that there is a kind of innovation – disruptive innovation – that does not require massive financial investments, at least in its early

[139] See M Jensen and W Meckling, *Theory of the Firm: Managerial Behaviour, Agency Costs and Ownership Structure* (1976) 3 *Journal of Financial Economics* 305. And see text at ch 2.III and accompanying notes.

[140] Christensen (n 128) XX.

[141] ibid 31ff.

[142] M Corradi and J Nowag, 'Enforcing Corporate Opportunities Rules: Antitrust Risks and Antirust Failures' (2018), www.law.nyu.edu/sites/default/files/upload_documents/Corradi%20AND%20Nowag.pdf.

[143] Gilson, Sabel and Scott (n 90).

[144] A Grandori and M Furlotti, 'Contracting for the Unknown and the Logic of Innovation (2009) 16 *European Management Review* 413, 417. The authors note that in principle a relational contract (intended by them as 'procedural') can also be hierarchical, ie postulate the necessity of the obedience to superiors' orders, but this is not the case of contracts for innovation.

phases, and that this kind of innovation is actually leading the development of technology.[145] It also proposes the idea that innovation occurs as a consequence of the circulation of knowledge building blocks which are often embodied in those individuals who master specific knowledge.[146] What remains to be understood, at an individual level, is what motivates founders to invent. Founders' motivation is often multifaceted, given the complexity of human psychology. It can be juxtaposed to corporate investment strategies, which in contrast are likely to be rationally informed and aimed at improving the cash flow of the corporation.

Understanding corporate founders' motivation is crucial in order to analyse their incentives to innovate.[147] Although corporate founders may be sensitive also to monetary rewards, often their inventive spark is ignited by emotional or intellectual gratification or even by the pursuance of certain higher ideals – and this is what keep on motivating them even once they have achieved their success.[148] As mentioned earlier, Joanne Pransky collected several stories of successful robot inventors who are also founders of corporations.[149] These founders – later often directors of the corporations they had been founders of – show different attitudes toward invention. For many of them, the reward for invention may well go far beyond profit. As director of research for (CNR-IEIIT), Gianmarco Verruggio confesses:

> I remember I went skiing in the Alps and in a hut at the top of the mountain's ski lift, I heard a familiar sound 'bing, bing, bing, bing'. I went inside and I saw a boy putting money into and playing my videogame. It turned out my games were distributed in all the lodges and for me that was an important moment in my life because my moonlighting had turned into a successful achievement being widely used in the real world. This is the same spirit with which I faced the adventure of building Roboethics.[150]

[145] See text at section VI and accompanying notes.

[146] ibid.

[147] An early study on inventors' psychology is the one by J Rossman, *Industrial Creativity; the Psychology of the Inventor* (University Books, 1964). A collection of early studies is in Perkins and Weber (n 32), in particular ch 3. The theory of motivation is extremely complex and literature on this topic is very well developed. For a collection of studies on this subject, see for instance R Ryan (ed), *The Oxford Handbook of Human Motivation* (Oxford University Press, 2012). From a business perspective, see for instance S Scheuer, *Social and Economic Motivation at Work: Theories of Motivation Reassessed* (Copenhagen Business School Press, 2000).

[148] See for instance A Ayres (ed), *Quotable Edison* (Quotable Wisdom Books, 2016), under the voice 'Invention': 'I find out what the world needs. Then I go ahead and try to invent it' (first quotation); 'I never perfected an invention that I did not think about in terms of service it might give others' (fourth quotation). Edison saw money as an instrument to invent more than as a reward for invention. ibid, again under voice 'Invention': 'My main purpose in life is to make enough money to create more inventions' (eleventh quotation).

[149] See n 40.

[150] J Pransky, 'The Pransky Interview: Gianmarco Veruggio, Director of Research, CNR-IEIIT, Genoa Branch; Robotics Pioneer and Inventor' (2017) 44 *Industrial Robot: An International Journal* 6, 10.

To put it in Engel's and Freeman's words, 'Streams of discovery and invention are not simply mean to a commercial end, but are viewed by their creators as interesting and important in their own right'.[151] Nonetheless, for many (if not for all) founders, the monetary aspect matters. Even without greed for monetary profits, at least the financial constraints and their influence on the possibility of implementing creative intuitions may affect the overall motivational process.[152] For instance, Helen Greiner, Founder and CEO of CyPhy Works and CoFounder of iRobot Corporation says:

> One of the most difficult times for me, was when we had raised money in the year 2000 to develop and bring to market an Internet-connected robot. Consumer products were, at this time, much, much harder to raise money for.[153]

At times, the financial side of business can even be harder to deal with than the invention side, as Melonee Wise, CEO of Fetch Robotics, reports from her personal experience:

> I started a company. I got an angel investment. I got an acquisition offer. I failed with an acquisition offer. I got venture capital. I failed at closing it. I spun off of a company. I had a terrible spinoff agreement. I shut down a company. All that definitely impacted how we went forward with Fetch. The mantra in Silicon Valley is "fail fast" and my experience at Unbounded definitely fits that description. And it's true that there is a lot of knowledge that can be gained from failure.[154]

Given the existence of both non-monetary and monetary aspects in the motivational process of founders, the question is how the law – especially corporate law – can set incentives for founders to stimulate their higher inventive capabilities.

As for non-monetary rewards, one should keep in mind that setting up a firm that exploits one's own ideas may well be a gratification in itself. The social acknowledgment of achieving such a result may also constitute a reward.[155] Nonetheless, it is not easy to predict whether a founder will be more likely to obtain this kind of gratification while spending their life working for the same company or while setting up new companies and enriching them with knowledge until they thrive. For sure, there are entrepreneurs whose lives are spent in launching repeatedly successful businesses, with less interest for the maturity

[151] Freeman and Engel, 'Models of Innovation' (2007) 97.

[152] J Armour et al, 'Putting Technology to Good Use for Society: The Role of Corporate, Competition and Tax Law' (2018) European Corporate Governance Institute (ECGI)-Law Working Paper 427, 2ff.

[153] J Pransky, 'The Pransky Interview: Helen Greiner, Serial Robotics Entrepreneur, Founder and CEO of CyPhy Works, CoFounder iRobot Corporation' (2005) 42 *Industrial Robot: An International Journal* 181.

[154] J Pransky, 'The Pransky Interview: Melonee Wise, CEO, Fetch Robotics' (2016) 43 *Industrial Robot: An International Journal* 253, 256.

[155] For a wide overview on several psychological theories on entrepreneurship, see for instance J Baum, M Frese and R Baron (eds), *The Psychology of Entrepreneurship* (Lawrence Erlbaum, 2007).

stage of these corporations.[156] Moreover, a founder may find themselves in a minority on a board while facing obstacles inside the corporation such as personal conflicts with co-founders. It may well be that if a given company no longer expresses their original values and commitment, some of the founders may be willing to leave or may just be squeezed out.[157] Nonetheless, if the inner non-monetary motivation is very strong, the obstacles a founder finds on their path to success may not serve to stop their inventive activity.[158] Still, the law should try to ease the manifestation of such inventive activity. Easing founders' mobility may at times increase the chances that they keep on creating, even if they do not have such strong willpower as Steve Jobs. Therefore, a careful design of rules on resigning directors and the possibility to carve out well-considered corporate opportunity waivers may help smoothing the process.[159]

From the point of view of a corporation, founders' choices and their inventive capabilities acquire a completely different meaning.[160] The corporation needs to provide profits to its investors, and corporate founders and their inventions are seen as profitable industrial assets.[161] From the point of view of the corporation, there is a great difference between a founder/director who resigns by his/her own will and one who is dismissed. The corporation will find it rational to dismiss a director and founder who is no longer useful to the business and eventually replace them with someone able to develop the corporation's potential.[162] Corporate opportunity rules and the duty of directors not to compete with the corporation may become useful as a way of controlling founders' activities once they have resigned.[163] They may allow incumbent companies to keep on extracting some profits from founders' subsequent inventions that are in some way connected to their previous inventive activity within the corporation, especially if a corporation is able to prove that the ideas that are now developed outside its boundaries were actually invented or discovered within its boundaries (ie before a director resigned).[164] When a constructive trust on newly founded corporations is available as a remedy for the misappropriation of corporate opportunities, not even subsequent inventions developed by

[156] Serial entrepreneurs represent an important component of the start-up scene, both in the US and in Europe. J Plehn-Dujowich, 'A Theory of Serial Entrepreneurship' (2010) 35 *Small Business Economics* 377, 379ff.

[157] This is particularly common in the context of VC. See text at ch 6.IV.E and accompanying notes.

[158] See the examples proposed in the text corresponding to n 154.

[159] See text at ch 7.V–VI and accompanying notes.

[160] I am here referring to the general case of a standard corporation. The dynamics of venture capital in this respect are analysed in ch 6.

[161] Whose value is at times difficult to quantify – see L Joia, 'Measuring Intangible Corporate Assets' (2000) 1 *Journal of Intellectual Capital* 68 – but which have become crucial to modern corporations; see B Lev and J Daum, 'The Dominance of Intangible Assets: Consequences for Enterprise Management and Corporate Reporting' (2004) 8 *Measuring Business Excellence* 6.

[162] And this occurs frequently in VC-backed start-ups. See text at ch 6.IV.E and accompanying notes.

[163] And clearly also rules on resigning directors. See text at ch 7.VI and accompanying notes.

[164] ibid.

reinvesting the proceeds from the sale of the misappropriations will be saved from the incumbent corporation's claws.[165] When such rules are applied rigidly to serial start-uppers, they may end up castrating their innovative effort, with detrimental effects on collective welfare. By contrast with the case of a dismissed founder who is no longer perceived as useful, a resigning director who is still useful to the corporation could be convinced to stay through appropriate incentives; especially attractive rewards – although as noted earlier, money may not always matter to inventors.[166]

In all the above situations involving founders and the degree of freedom they enjoy when they leave corporations and set up new businesses, there is an extremely delicate equilibrium between the necessity to protect corporate boundaries and the necessity to preserve founders' creative ability.

As an example, a total ban on the taking of corporate opportunities, together with a strict interpretation of directors' duty not to compete, has the strongest effect in terms of protection of the interests of the incumbent corporation. Nonetheless, it may negatively affect founders/directors. A founder who is willing to resign will be penalised for the sake of protecting corporate investments. A total ban may prevent a founder with high skill levels from setting up a company. On a macro level, a total ban, as described above, might also prevent the occurrence of further potential positive externalities. In fact, a resigning director moving to another corporation or founding a new one may transfer knowledge building blocks, which may be efficiently recombined in another business organisation.[167] The mobility displayed by at least some founders may have helped their innovation skills – thereby contributing to their inventive capabilities – as the experience of Steve Jobs shows us.[168] Therefore, founders' mobility may add new perspectives to the necessity of modulating fiduciary duties, and also the duty of loyalty, which go well beyond the aspects signalled in the recent literature on corporate opportunity rules and VC.[169] This is particularly true in the light of contemporary theory on groundbreaking innovation which takes place to a large extent in the IT sector and which largely relies for innovation upon networks and contracting, of which resigning founders/directors are part.

IX. FOUNDER-LED INNOVATION AND THE CORPORATION IN THE LIGHT OF MODERN HIGH-TECH INNOVATION STRATEGIES

Private innovation can be the outcome of specific R&D budget planning aimed at launching new products or at times can be simply the result of a need to solve

[165] See text at ch 3.III and accompanying notes.
[166] See text corresponding to nn 150–51.
[167] See text at section VI and accompanying notes.
[168] See text corresponding to n 44.
[169] T Woolf, 'The Venture Capitalist's Corporate Opportunity Problem' (2001) *Columbia Business Law Review* 473; Rauterberg and Talley, 'Contracting Out of the Fiduciary Duty of Loyalty' (2017).

practical problems within a corporation's line of business – often for a product that is already on the market and that requires improvements.[170]

Innovation can also produce additional value that is embedded in the organisation's learning process.[171] Innovation may help assimilate and exploit existing information, furthering the firm's so-called absorptive capacity.[172] A firm's absorptive capacity may well in turn improve the long-term performance of the firm.[173] This is especially true nowadays because technology is constantly changing and firms tend to rely upon each other for developing together (often disruptive) components instead of reverting to vertical integration strategies.[174] Employing other producers' components in a firm's existing production requires a high degree of technical learning. Therefore, a company, by learning to innovate, can also improve its chances to integrate externally sourced innovation within its productive process. Such an increase in absorptive capacity is a 'soft' gain which depends on the overall amount of knowledge that is acquired and stored during the learning process undertaken by the firm. Such a soft gain does not derive from the commercial success of a specific product.

One may wonder how both commercial profits deriving from the commercialisation of a specific product and absorptive capacity are connected to corporate governance – and especially to founders' incentives to innovate. The entire agency costs paradigm that inspired Anglo-American corporate governance is fully in line with the idea of capturing the direct profits of R&D – ie those deriving from patenting and commercialisation of new products.[175] Not only rules on directors' inventions, but also corporate opportunity rules and directors' duty not to compete seem to follow the logic of containing agency costs incurred by insiders' misappropriations.

One might also ask whether the objective of increasing a company's 'absorptive capacity' per se might set incentives for a company to engage in innovation. This question would be particularly relevant when founders are free to take their own inventions or when remedies against misappropriations are limited in kind – as is the case in most continental European countries.[176] The idea that a company invests substantially in R&D, with the only objective being to increase its absorptive capacity, while leaving its directors free to take corporate opportunities is not likely to be compatible at least with present corporate theory.

[170] N Rosenberg, 'Why Do Firms Do Basic Research (With Their Own Money)?' (1990) 19 *Research Policy* 165, 169.

[171] W Cohen and D Levinthal, 'Innovation and Learning: The Two Faces of R&D' (1989) 99 *Economic Journal* 569.

[172] W Cohen and D Levinthal, 'Absorptive Capacity: A New Perspective on Learning and Innovation' (1990) 36 *Administrative Science Quarterly* 128.

[173] For an application of this theory along with takeovers see F Vermeulen and H Barkema, 'Learning through Acquisitions' (2001) 44 *Academy of Management Journal* 457.

[174] Gilson, Sabel and Scott (n 90) 438ff.

[175] See text at section II and accompanying notes.

[176] See text at ch 3.IV–V and accompanying notes.

The advantages of absorptive capacity in the long term may be tangible, but its expected return may be extremely difficult to quantify, hence difficult to justify to shareholders. Moreover, such a taking by directors would still be a breach of the duty of loyalty.

From a corporation's perspective, the question is whether there are other ways it can benefit from one of its directors appropriating a corporate opportunity and developing it outside the corporation's boundaries. Such additional benefits can be observed in the phenomenon known as 'high-tech business mafia'. The first to be named 'mafia' was the so-called 'PayPal mafia', although the term 'mafia', which certainly does not evoke the idea of promotion of efficiency, seems inadequate to reflect the positive welfare effect of this phenomenon.[177] The PayPal mafia is composed of former PayPal employees who started extremely innovative companies operating in the same or similar lines of business. This kind of coalition has also arisen in relation to other companies. For instance, Martin Eberhard, former director of Tesla, has set up a new company called 'inEvit', recently sold to 'SF Motors'.

> The company has developed and patented a unique [electric vehicle] EV chassis architecture, battery module design innovations and manufacturing techniques that will allow the EV industry to rapidly scale manufacturing of cost-and-feature-competitive vehicles.[178]

In the US, resigning founders often work in new ventures that are active in the same area of business or innovation as the company they have left. This behaviour could be caught by the European corporate laws directors' duty not to compete, unless the directors had obtained an authorisation by the board or the shareholders' assembly.[179] It is less probable that US corporate laws would enforce such a duty in this type of case. In US law, a director's duty not to compete is usually connected to a separate fiduciary duty or to a misappropriation of a corporate opportunity.[180] Nonetheless, the same behaviours may be caught by corporate opportunity rules, unless the founder is able to demonstrate that they started developing their invention outside the corporation that they later left or that the development started at a later time.[181] This may prove difficult – especially when the new project is even loosely based on previous research.

The danger of being sued on the basis of a misappropriation of a corporate opportunity may be one of the reasons why at times founders do not start

[177] J O'Brien, 'The Paypal Mafia' (2007) 11 *Fortune* 26.

[178] www.prnewswire.com/news-releases/sf-motors-to-acquire-ev-battery-module-startup-inevit-headed-by-industry-pioneer-martin-eberhard-300539637.html.

[179] See for instance Italian Civil Code, Art 2390, para 1, allowing shareholder authorisation.

[180] J Popofsky, 'Corporate Opportunity and Corporate Competition: a Double-Barreled Theory of Fiduciary Liability' (1982) 10 *Hofstra Law Review* 1193, 1209.

[181] See text at ch 7.VI and accompanying notes.

a new venture straight away. For instance, 'Eberhard and Tarpenning went on to do consulting work and mentoring [before starting new companies]'.[182] But in recent times, US companies have increasingly introduced in their articles of association waivers for the corporate opportunity doctrine.[183] It may well be the case that in VC contexts, such waivers are agreed only in favour of the VC firm, and therefore US legal practice still has to discover the full potential of the waiver at stake when properly formulated, ie to stimulate innovation by resigning founders. There is no *ex ante* general waiver in most European corporate opportunity rules at the moment, and therefore such flexibility is not possible.[184]

Legally entitling corporations to promote the disgorgement of profits or the claim of damages deriving from corporate opportunities misappropriations may create path dependencies in the sense of harshly repressing such misappropriations. The idea of repressing such misappropriations may also become part of a culture of exacting 'righteous' conduct from directors. Inevitably, throughout time, it is easy to persuade oneself that such pattern is 'just right'. But words of old may prompt us to look to such patterns from a different perspective. The Tao Te Ching admonishes:

> Thus it was that when Tao was lost, its attributes appeared; when its attributes were lost, benevolence appeared; when benevolence was lost, righteousness appeared; and when righteousness was lost, the proprieties appeared. Now propriety is the attenuated form of leal-heartedness and good faith and is also the commencement of disorders.[185]

It could be said that beyond the partial benefits of rules passed down by tradition, such as the corporate opportunity rule, a corporation is embedded in a far wider, ever-changing and interconnected reality; an embeddedness which is exalted by the nature of groundbreaking technological innovation. And a lawmaker should be careful not to stifle high-tech development for the sake of sticking to old conceptions of right and wrong. A more flexible approach by the lawmaker and by corporations to corporate opportunity rules, valuing resigning directors' freedom, may actually end up benefiting not only the system as a whole but also the incumbent corporation, whose development in a high-tech permeated business environment often depends on its 'value network'.

[182] F Lambert, 'Tesla's Original Team, where are They Now?', electrek.co/2015/05/16/teslas-original-team-where-are-they-now.

[183] DGCL, s 122(17).

[184] See for instance M Gelter and G Helleringer, 'Fiduciary Principles in European Civil Law Systems' in E Criddle, P Miller and R Sitkoff, *The Oxford Handbook of Fiduciary Law* (Oxford University Press, 2019) 600–01 on the German system. For Spain, see *Ley de Sociedades de Capital* (Spanish Stock Company Law) Art 230, para 1, which expressly mentions that the duty of loyalty is mandatory and cannot be waived ('El régimen relativo al deber de lealtad y a la responsabilidad por su infracción es imperativo. No serán válidas las disposiciones estatutarias que lo limiten o sean contrarias al mismo').

[185] Lao Tzu, *Tao Te Ching* (e-artnow, 2013) ch 38.

The concept of a 'value network' is crucial for understanding the technological constraints of a corporation that has grown beyond the start-up phase but that still relies upon cutting-edge technological innovation. 'Value network' is 'the context within which a firm identifies and responds to customers' needs, solves problems, procures input, reacts to competitors and strives for profits'.[186] Clearly, when a new idea has not yet been brought to the market, there is a high degree of freedom from the market. But once an idea is transformed into a marketable product, the situation changes radically. According to Christensen, '[c]ompanies are embedded in value networks because their products generally are embedded, or nested hierarchically, as components within other products and eventually within end system of use'.[187] Therefore, innovation has to follow predetermined paths in order to be valuable within an established value network. If innovation is technology- and consumer-constrained, one has to consider a rather objective, rational and potentially rigid corporate attitude toward it – far from the freedom enjoyed by start-up entrepreneurs.

In corporate strategy terms, innovation will need to be in harmony with the corporate board's time planning in relation to innovation.[188] In other words, especially when the company is striving for a maximisation of short- and medium-run profits, innovation will need to run along the lines of pre-established or not entirely flexible technological paths. Alternative paths, outside firms' value networks, that might prove successful in the long term may well end disastrously in the short or medium term. Literature about disruptive innovation has shown that managers may channel all the financial resources of the company into sustaining innovation (this can be very sophisticated and radical, but still be sustaining innovation) as long as consumers continue demanding an improved product.[189] However, at a certain point the offer of innovation may overcome the demand for it. This is precisely the critical point at which a section of consumers may become interested in switching to a product created through disruptive innovation.[190] If the entrepreneur understands these mechanisms, they will try to reduce the firm's investments in sustaining innovation and switch part of them to research activity that may lead to disruptive innovation.[191] This will not necessarily mean inventing a new product from scratch. However, it will enable a company to absorb disruptive innovation from other innovative companies.

[186] Christensen (n 127) 36ff.

[187] ibid.

[188] On the corporate scope view from a law and economics perspective, see for instance H Hu and JL Westbrook, 'Abolition of the Corporate Duty to Creditors' (2007) 107 *Columbia Law Review* 1321. See also T Hazen, 'The Short-Term/Long-Term Dichotomy and Investment Theory: Implications for Securities Market Regulation and for Corporate Law' (1991) 70 *North Carolina Law Review* 137.

[189] Christensen (n 127) 238ff.

[190] ibid.

[191] ibid.

The fact that contemporary forms of innovation are almost entirely network-based may suggest that a resigning founder developing a new and different product in the same or a similar line of business may not be strictly perceived as a competitor, especially when their product may be complementary to the product already marketed by the incumbent company, entirely or in some of its components. There may be advantages in letting directors develop complementary products, as in future such new products may combine with the incumbent company's products. In fact, cooperation seems to be fundamental in groundbreaking innovation environments. The flexibility granted by corporate opportunity waivers may allow a company to play transparently with its founders: for instance, it may compel them to commit to a given project for the time they are employed by the company and then let them free to use their creative skills in new ventures. If waivers are not a viable option to be pursued through law reforms in Europe, then the lawmaker may want to consider alternative ways to flexibilise corporate opportunity rules.[192]

The introduction of a non-flexible corporate opportunity doctrine in countries which were previously free from it may actually produce more detriment than advantages. Without corporate opportunity rules, technological spillover effects can easily occur, as the Italian experience with industrial districts shows.[193] At the time when industrial districts flourished in Italy, there was no corporate opportunity rule, which was introduced only later with the 2003 Italian corporate law reform. Such a gap in the Italian legislation might have promoted or at least facilitated the diffusion of rather simple innovation in the mechanical field; it is true that the Italian district industry has benefited from the dynamism of new entrants who formerly worked as employees or directors in the same district.[194] The introduction of corporate opportunity rules as presently conceived by several European corporate laws unfortunately might be more detrimental than useful – at least in the context of highly innovative firms. In fact, it does not seem to always protect efficiently the boundaries of the corporation and is not flexible enough to include waivers that can incentivise founders to keep on innovating in new start-ups. Nor does it seem to promote innovation spillovers any longer, as an unreliable remedial system does not mean no remedy at all and can still impose costs on potential efficient takers.

[192] See text at ch 7.II and accompanying notes.

[193] S Iammarino and P McCann, 'The Structure and Evolution of Industrial Clusters: Transactions, Technology and Knowledge Spillovers' (2006) 35 *Research Policy* 1018; C Antonelli, 'Technological Districts Localized Spillovers and Productivity Growth. The Italian Evidence on Technological Externalities in the Core Regions' (1994) 8 *International Review of Applied Economics* 18; R Boschma, and A Ter Wal, 'Knowledge Networks and Innovative Performance in an Industrial District: The Case of a Footwear District in the South of Italy' (2007) 14 *Industry and Innovation* 177.

[194] See text at ch 1.V.B.

X. YOU ARE SMART, YOU HAVE GREAT IDEAS! EUROPEAN OR US FINANCE? IMPLICATIONS FOR THE PRIVATE ORDERING DEBATE

Corporate law may set incentives for corporate founders to take up and maintain positions on the boards of highly innovative corporations – by rewarding them, but also by setting rules that prevent them from leaving and setting up competing businesses. One should not underestimate the love for freedom and independence that many creative individuals manifest throughout their career.[195] Inevitably, corporate founders will need to face corporate opportunity rules and/or the directors' duty not to compete if they decide to leave and set up a new enterprise because they find they no longer fit into the previous corporate framework.[196] A founder has not necessarily already set their mind on leaving when they start a new corporation. Hopefully they have not, as this would not be an auspicious mindset for the foundation of a start-up. Nonetheless, knowing that if they leave because of disagreement with the other members their creative efforts will not be completely depredated may help founders to engage with ease and enthusiasm in a start-up.

When it comes to evaluating a founder's preference to be free from the bounds of corporate opportunity doctrines and functionally similar rules, one may realise that the situation is far more complex than might be expected. A founder may desire freedom but also a system where they have easy access to finance. Perhaps it can be hard to obtain both at the same time. Investors such as angels and VC funds may not enjoy a system where a founder can leave the venture with the (pieces of) the technological knowledge that the company is implementing thanks to the capital the financers have injected into it.[197] For instance, a legal system such as the French one, where courts seem to award only partial damages for non-disclosure of corporate opportunities,[198] may leave a financer perplexed over the degree of protection it receives from the law, even where it is able to obtain some further contractual protection.[199]

A system that promotes strong corporate opportunity rules – but with the option of a waiver – may secure financers' interests yet make founders unhappy. It may lock a founder's inventive efforts within a corporation, although only for a limited time, to secure returns for the financer. This seems in line with a necessary attempt to lock in human capital that otherwise would be totally uncontrolled.[200] Nonetheless, it will not increase founders' mobility, unless a waiver is inserted in favour of the founder. Once again, it appears that Delaware has paved the way to an efficient system of corporate law for highly innovative

[195] See text at section VIII and accompanying notes.
[196] See text ch 7.VI and accompanying notes.
[197] See text at ch 6.IV.D.
[198] See text at ch 3.V.
[199] See text at ch 6.IV.D.
[200] See L Zingales, 'In Search of New Foundations' (2000) 55 *The Journal of Finance* 1623.

corporations, but it still needs to be seen to what extent lawyers will be able to carve out corporate opportunity waivers that can accommodate both the interest of investors to secure corporate opportunities and the interest of the founders to preserve a degree of freedom to move out of the corporation and exploit their knowledge.

These considerations also strongly relate to the everlasting debate about public versus private ordering in corporate law. Private ordering is likely to allow entrepreneurs and their financer to tailor the most appropriate solutions to the ownership of non-patentable innovation.[201] In this respect, it is interesting that US Delaware law may have taken a direction which is almost antithetical to European laws. In fact, most continental European corporate laws regard fiduciary duties and corporate opportunity rules as mandatory. Moreover, in the UK, which is the closest country to the US in terms of legal tradition, one cannot observe an evolution of directors' fiduciary duties toward private ordering. By contrast, recent research shows that in general, UK corporate law has increasingly evolved toward public ordering.[202] This seems at odds with the great efficiencies deriving from private ordering when it comes to reconciling fiduciary duties with corporate founders' incentive to innovate.

Finally, a legal system that is able to accommodate the different aspects of the creative instances present in an innovative start-up does not need to deal with only two categories of constituencies, ie financers and founders.[203] The Winklevoss/Facebook saga shows that the relationships between entrepreneurs, also in pre-founding settings, can be extremely conflictual.[204] Setting up a corporation at an early stage, where all founders are directors, can be a way to protect business opportunities that are developed together. Nonetheless, this is not necessarily the best choice or in any case the choice which teams of founders tend to go for.

Hellmann and Thiele recall the fact that in practice, 'tying the knot too early' can be dangerous. In fact, different entrepreneurs may not know each other that well and therefore they may harbour expectations which end up not being met in practice.[205] For instance, if two partners set up a company 50/50 and only one of them ends up contributing significantly (Hellmann and Thiele cite for instance the Zipcar and Smartix cases),[206] a strict corporate opportunity doctrine can actually enable the abuse of one by the other – by exacting disgorgement of

[201] See text at ch 7.II and accompanying notes.

[202] See M Moore, 'Private Ordering and Public Policy: The Paradoxical Foundations of Corporate Contractarianism' (2014) 34 *Oxford Journal of Legal Studies* 693.

[203] Ch 6 of this book is devoted to the analysis of the relationship between founders and a special kind of financer, ie a venture capitalist.

[204] D Kirkpatrick, *The Facebook Effect: The Inside Story of the Company that is Connecting the World* (Simon and Schuster, 2011).

[205] T Hellmann and V Thiele, 'Contracting Among Founders' (2015) 31 *The Journal of Law, Economics, and Organization* 629, 630.

[206] ibid.

profits that were achieved exclusively thanks to the profit of the active member. The point is that the realisation that one of the two partners is unable to contribute to the venture can become clear ex post and through long-term interaction. A system where entrepreneurs are freer to leave their partners without paying extreme consequences may help in this phase, although one cannot delay tying the knot for ever. In turn, once the knot is tied, when it comes to buying out ineffective partners, by raising outside capital, strong corporate opportunity remedies can make the position of the ineffective partner stronger and therefore raise the cost of the operation.

Again, the complexity of the dynamics between founders suggests that only private ordering can allow modulation of the protection of the boundaries of the corporations in relation to the specificities of the cases.

XI. CONCLUSIONS

The innovative knowledge achieved by corporate founders' creative efforts is normally the fruit of their unbridled activity, stimulated by their vision more than by mere profit. The meta-economics of innovation deems the circulation of such building blocks of knowledge to be responsible for the greatest achievements in innovation. The spreading of information technology has dramatically changed not only the concept of innovation but also the extent to which exceptional progress can be achieved in a very short time.[207] Given the pervasiveness of this phenomenon, one may wonder how the law can ignore the importance of the circulation of building blocks of knowledge and especially the fact that the most important variables propelling such evolutive dynamics are freedom and mobility.

In her comparative sociological study on Silicon Valley and Route 128, Saxenian has identified several features that differentiate the Californian high-tech district from the Massachusetts one – features that led Silicon Valley to long-lasting success, in contrast with Route 128's decline. Her approach is a differential analysis of 'regional systems' of innovation, as characterised by local institutions and culture, industrial structures and corporate organisation.[208] Some of the features that characterise Silicon Valley look particularly relevant to this discussion. First, Saxenian describes loyalty to the network as prevailing over loyalty to the company.[209] Consequently, the boundaries between employers and employees are depicted as 'blurring'.[210] Despite the existence of a form

[207] It would appear that certain dynamics – mobility and spillovers – within this circulation of knowledge could be commonplace in non-IT industrial environments as well, as we just noted regarding Italian industrial districts.

[208] Saxenian, *Regional Advantage* (1994) 7ff.

[209] ibid 36.

[210] ibid 50.

of network loyalty, competitive pressure is particularly strong in Silicon Valley because of the demand for increasing innovation.[211]

Ronald Gilson has provided a complementary explanation of the different innovation dynamics of Silicon Valley and Route 128; an explanation that is based on the differences in legal structure between the two economic environments.[212] According to Gilson, the unlikelihood that an employee's covenant not to compete with the corporation will be enforced under Californian law[213] promotes the intercompany knowledge spillovers that are renowned for being one of the differential reasons for Silicon Valley's economic success compared to Route 128.[214] In Route 128, where such covenants are likely to be enforced, innovation has not peaked in recent times, and the Massachusetts district has instead been declining.[215]

Regardless of their legal origins or their systematic collocation within a given legal system, covenants not to compete and employees' non-compete rules are functionally very close to those imposing negative obligations on directors of a corporation, that is, the prohibition to compete with the company and corporate opportunity rules. In fact, all the named rules are understood as being rules of loyalty, the economic function of which is to protect the immaterial assets of the corporation, represented by the business opportunities embedded in human knowledge. The fact that in highly innovative contexts there is a struggle between inventors and counterparties owning rights on the inventions has already been recognised by literature on IP law in the employment context.[216] Literature has shown that exacerbating the defence of employers' rights can demotivate employees to invent and can become too pervasive, being 'intellectual capital most likely to become commingled or indistinguishable from the skills or knowledge of an employee'.[217] Even though corporate lawyers are less used to delving into innovation problems compared to IP lawyers, this does not mean that the same issues are not applicable to corporate opportunity rules.

Ronald Gilson's analysis of the potential virtues of the Californian approach to non-compete clauses included in employment contracts focuses mainly on incentives to innovate and on 'knowledge spillovers'. In Arthur's terms, knowledge spillovers are precisely one of the potential methods by which the circulation of knowledge building blocks can take place. The duty of loyalty was conceived in order to protect the corporate proprietary boundaries, and this does not help the building blocks of knowledge embedded in human capital

[211] ibid 46.

[212] R Gilson, 'The Legal Infrastructure of High Technology Industrial Districts: Silicon Valley, Route 128, and Covenants Not to Compete' (1999) 74 *NYU Law Review* 575, 586–89.

[213] ibid 607ff.

[214] ibid 620ff.

[215] ibid 603ff.

[216] D Burk and B McDonnell, 'The Goldilocks Hypothesis: Balancing Intellectual Property Rights at the Boundary of the firm (2007) *University of Illinois Law Review* 575.

[217] ibid 609.

to circulate freely. New modulations of the duty of loyalty in highly innovative contexts may contribute to create mobility dynamics with positive externalities in terms of innovation. Each firm active in the same field can have access to such positive externalities through 'contracting for innovation' and efficient network cooperation. In turn, the modulation of the duty of loyalty requires not only the possibility of introducing corporate opportunity waivers but also the acquisition of the legal skills necessary to make good use of such waivers. Waivers that are going to be applied in those environments characterised by complex dynamics both on the founder's and on the financers' side may require great legal sophistication. Nonetheless, the degree of refinement in balancing the interests of the parties that can be achieved by well-crafted waivers is even higher than the one that can be achieved through reforms in IP law, which would apply to the similar problem of employees' inventions. It is well-known that industrial clusters such as Silicon Valley are served by teams of lawyers that have acquired knowledge and skills that go well beyond those of a 'standard' lawyer: 'start-up lawyers' such as these often work as refined 'transaction costs engineers' with industry-specific business knowledge.[218] If the potential for innovation-enhancing corporate opportunity rules exists, especially in US law – because of the introduction of a corporate opportunity waiver under DGCL, s 122(17) – it remains to be seen how the other lawmakers around the world will approach this problem,[219] and whether a large number of specialised start-up lawyers will start engaging in transaction costs engineering in non-US industrial clusters.

[218] J Coyle and J Green, 'Startup Lawyering 2.0' (2016) 95 *North Carolina Law Review* 1403, 1411ff.

[219] See text at ch 7.V and accompanying notes.

6

Corporate Opportunities and Venture Capital

I. INTRODUCTION

MUCH HAS BEEN written about venture capitalism – on its role in nurturing start-ups with cash and know-how; on its reputation for backing superstars and on its centrality to innovation clusters. Less has been written about the laws underpinning this success – laws on contracts, tax and bankruptcy. Still less has been written about how corporate opportunity doctrine improves our understanding of the relationship between venture capitalists and entrepreneurs.

In innovation clusters, characterised by a significantly high start-up density,[1] business opportunities are very frequently encountered, developed (and at times abandoned).[2] It is in such environments that business opportunities can be observed in their full potential: they may start as intuitions and, at times, subsequently transform into extremely successful businesses – possibly even ending up as 'unicorns'.[3] Business ideas develop to their full potential within start-ups, thanks to financial input, technical and managerial support[4] and, more generally, through interaction with a thriving business community.[5] Many of these

[1] P Cooke, 'Regional Innovation Systems, Clusters, and the Knowledge Economy' (2001) 10 *Industrial and Corporate Change* 945.

[2] See A Saxenian, *Regional Advantage* (Harvard University Press, 1994) XI.

[3] A unicorn can be defined as 'newly founded firm that had rapidly grown to a private valuation of a billion or more US dollars'. See M Kenney and J Zysman, 'Unicorns, Cheshire Cats, and the New Dilemmas of Entrepreneurial Finance' (2019) 21 *Venture Capital* 35, 35.

[4] M Gorman and W Sahlman, 'What Do Venture Capitalists Do?' (1989) 4 *Journal of Business Venturing* 231.

[5] This type of community may create itself spontaneously when favourable conditions occur. See E Glaeser and W Kerr, 'Local Industrial Conditions and Entrepreneurship: How Much of the Spatial Distribution Can We Explain?' (2009) 18 *Journal of Economics & Management Strategy* 623. Micro-environments conducive to rapid growth may also be artificially created through so-called incubators and accelerators. Accelerators differ from incubators because they tend to have a limited life span: see S Cohen, 'What do Accelerators Do? Insights from Incubators and Angels' (2013) 8 *Innovations: Technology, Governance, Globalization* 19: 'the most fundamental difference is the limited duration of accelerator programs as compared to the continuous nature of incubators'. There have also been policy attempts to recreate the phenomenon of industrial clusters. See for instance T Altenburg and J Meyer-Stamer, 'How to Promote Clusters: Policy Experiences from Latin America' (1999) 27 *World Development* 1693.

ingredients for growth are provided to start-up founders by independent venture capital funds[6] (IVCFs).[7] IVCFs have acquired a great reputation in the start-up scene, and more widely among the public, thanks to stories of astonishing success, such as Yahoo! and Cisco.[8]

After its invention in the 1940s,[9] venture capital (VC) still attracts the attention of researchers trying to respond to the many unsolved conundrums on the causes of its development.[10] One of the main issues that puzzles researchers is the higher degree of development of the VC industry in the United States of America (US) than in the rest of the world,[11] including Europe – although it has increased in the latter.[12] Studies show that this difference may be also connected, among others,[13] to the legal variable.[14] Literature shows that contract law,[15] tax law[16] and bankruptcy law[17] may be responsible for the success of VC.

[6] Here I adopt the term 'independent venture capital fund' in order to stress its difference from another form of venture capital, ie corporate venture capital, which will also be dealt with in section V.

[7] See S Samila and O Sorenson, 'Venture Capital, Entrepreneurship, and Economic Growth (2011) 93 *The Review of Economics and Statistics* 338. The authors provide statistical evidence that in the US, increases in the supply of VC positively affect firm starts, employment, and aggregate income.

[8] P Gompers and J Lerner, 'The Venture Capital Revolution' (2001) 15 *The Journal of Economic Perspectives* 145.

[9] D Hsu and M Kenney, 'Organizing Venture Capital: The Rise and Demise of American Research & Development Corporation, 1946–1973' (2005) 14 *Industrial and Corporate Change* 579.

[10] See a wide collection of studies on VC, analysed from different angles, in D Cumming (ed), *Venture Capital: Investment Strategies, Structures, and Policies*, Vol 9 (John Wiley & Sons, 2010).

[11] G Bruton, V Fried and S Manigart, 'Institutional Influences on the Worldwide Expansion of Venture Capital' (2005) 29 *Entrepreneurship Theory and Practice* 737.

[12] A recent anthology on this subject is the one by G Gregoriou, M Kooli and R Kraeussl, *Venture Capital in Europe* (Butterworth-Heinemann, 2011).

[13] Non-legal factors may be for instance the institutional and cultural ones. R Nahata, S Hazarika and K Tandon, 'Success in Global Venture Capital Investing: Do Institutional and Cultural Differences Matter?' (2014) 49 *Journal of Financial and Quantitative Analysis* 1039. Government policies may also play a role in the development of VC; see C Keuschnigg and S Nielsen, 'Public Policy for Venture Capital' (2001) 8 *International Tax and Public Finance* 557–72. Another important factor may be the presence of well-developed public markets, which can support successful exit through IPO; see B Black and R Gilson, 'Venture Capital and the Structure of Capital Markets: Banks Versus Stock Markets' (1998) 47 *Journal of Financial Economics* 243. This argument has been expanded by E Rock, 'Greenhorns, Yankees, and Cosmopolitans: Venture Capital, IPOs, Foreign Firms, and US Markets' (2001) 2 *Theoretical Inquiries in Law* 711, explaining that there can be cross-border exit through IPO, as proven by the phenomenon of Israeli high-tech companies going public on the Nasdaq.

[14] Areas of the law which have been investigated for their role influencing the development of VC are bankruptcy laws and capital gain tax laws; see J Armour and D Cumming, 'The Legislative Road to Silicon Valley' (2006) 58 *Oxford Economic Papers* 596. The level of shareholders' protection may also play a vital role; see L Jeng and P Wells, 'The Determinants of Venture Capital Funding: Evidence across Countries (2000) 6 *Journal of Corporate Finance* 241. For a recent empirical study, see T Tykvova, 'Legal Framework Quality and Success of (Different Types of) Venture Capital Investments' (2018) 87 *Journal of Banking & Finance* 333.

[15] J Lerner and A Schoar, 'Does Legal Enforcement Affect Financial Transactions? The Contractual Channel in Private Equity' (2005) 120 *The Quarterly Journal of Economics* 223.

[16] C Keuschnigg and S Nielsen, 'Start-ups, Venture Capitalists, and the Capital Gains Tax' (2004) 88 *Journal of Public Economics* 1011.

[17] Armour and Cumming, 'The Legislative Road' (2006) 630, showing through an empirical and comparative law study that more liberal bankruptcy law increase the demand for VC.

The question on the relationships between the development of VC and the legal variable might find some replies within the wider 'does the law matter?' debate.[18] Nonetheless, several points related to the impact of legal rules on VC remain unexplained. This may be due also to the difficulties inherent in distinguishing the impact of mandatory rules from the impact of default rules and of contractual praxis, the latter two being the prevalent sources of the law in VC praxis.

The peculiarities of VC legal architecture have been the object of both theoretical legal analysis and empirical research.[19] Both kinds of analysis have also focused, to a limited extent, on the role of US corporate opportunity doctrines in IVCFs' investment activity.[20] European researchers have not shown the same degree of interest in this topic so far. Such lack of interest may be explained in part by the fact that corporate opportunity rules have been introduced in several EU Member States only very recently – with the notable exceptions of Germany and the UK.[21] Corporate opportunity rules may turn out to be particularly important for understanding the relationships between venture capitalist and entrepreneur in respect both of the innovation activity pursued by entrepreneurs and of the investment activity carried out by IVCFs. In fact, one of the functions of corporate opportunity rules is preventing misappropriations of new

[18] For a wider framework on the legal-origins theory, see R La Porta, F Lopez-de-Silanes and A Shleifer, 'The Economic Consequences of Legal Origins' (2008) 46 *Journal of Economic Literature* 285; R La Porta et al, 'Law and Finance' (1998) 106 *Journal of Political Economy* 1113. On the importance of the legal framework to VC analysis, see S Kaplan, F Martel and P Strömberg, 'How do Legal Differences and Experience Affect Financial Contracts? (2007) 16 *Journal of Financial Intermediation* 273.

[19] On the legal and financial architecture of VC, see S Kaplan and P Strömberg, 'Venture Capitals as Principals: Contracting, Screening, and Monitoring' (2001) 91 *American Economic Review* 426. For an empirical analysis, see S Kaplan and P Strömberg, 'Financial Contracting Theory Meets the Real World: An Empirical Analysis of Venture Capital Contracts' (2003) 70 *The Review of Economic Studies* 281.

[20] T Woolf, 'The Venture Capitalist's Corporate Opportunity Problem' (2001) *Columbia Business Law Review* 473. For an empirical analysis, see G Rauterberg and E Talley, 'Contracting Out of the Fiduciary Duty of Loyalty: An Empirical Analysis of Corporate Opportunity Waivers' (2017) 117 *Columbia Law Review* 1075.

[21] German legal literature started exploring this issue in the 1950s. See E Mestmäker, *Verwaltung, Konzerngewalt und Recht der Aktionare* (Müller, 1958) 166ff. It was not until the 1970s that the *Bundesgerichtshof* introduced corporate opportunity rules as an extensive interpretation of the principle of loyalty of directors to the company (*die Trueupflicht*) and of their duty to avoid conflicts of interests (*das Gebot der Vermeidung von Interessenkonflikten*). See BGH WM 1977, 361, 362; BGH WM 1983, 498; BGH NJW 1986, 584, 585; BGH WM 1989, 1335, 1339. For later developments in German law and for a comparative perspective, see K Hopt, 'Conflict of Interest, Secrecy and Insider Information of Directors, A Comparative Analysis' (2013) 10 *European Company and Financial Law Review* 167. In relation to the UK, see the seminal case *Regal (Hastings) v Gulliver* [1942] UKHL 1. The UK interpretation of corporate opportunity doctrines has been oscillating between no-profit and no-conflict principles. The no-conflict and no-profit paradigms can be traced back respectively to *Aberdeen Railway Co v Blaikie Brothers* (1854) 1 Macq 461 and *Keech v Sandford* (1726) Sel Cas Ch T King 61. On no-conflict and no-profit paradigms, see D Kershaw, 'Lost in Translation: Corporate Opportunities in Comparative Perspective' (2005) 25 *Oxford Journal of Legal Studies* 603.

business ideas. Given the constant increase of cross-border VC, the question of the role of corporate opportunity rules in the success of VC looks particularly interesting – not only from a European point of view, but also from a global and cross-border perspective.

II. THE CROSS-BORDER DIMENSION OF VENTURE CAPITAL: OLD AND NEW POLICY QUESTIONS

VC emerged in the mid-1940s as a purely US regional phenomenon.[22] From the US,[23] VC rapidly expanded into the whole of Europe[24] as well as the Far East[25] and South-America.[26] Since the beginning of the twenty-first century, it has also been growing in Africa, including in the less economically developed areas of the continent.[27] Nowadays, one can say that VC is truly present worldwide and that it has adapted to the most diversified cultural and

[22] Hsu and Kenney, 'Organizing Venture Capital' (2005). Profit-sharing contracts with certain features in common with venture capital, such as periodic revaluation, have been around since the Middle Ages. See M Brouwer, 'Managing Uncertainty Through Profit Sharing Contracts from Medieval Italy to Silicon Valley' (2005) 9 *Journal of Management and Governance* 237.

[23] P Gompers, 'The Rise and Fall of Venture Capital' (1994) 23 *Business and Economic History* 1.

[24] F Bertoni, M Colombo and A Quas, 'The Patterns of Venture Capital Investment in Europe (2015) 45 *Small Business Economics* 543; L Bottazzi and M Da Rin, 'Venture Capital in Europe and the Financing of Innovative Companies' (2002) 17 *Economic Policy* 229; L Bottazzi, M Da Rin and T Hellmann, 'The Changing Face of the European Venture Capital Industry: Facts and Analysis' (2004) 7 *Journal of Private Equity* 26. VC is not equally successful in every single European country. For studies focused on EU Member States, see S Manigart, 'The Founding Rate of Venture Capital Firms in Three European Countries (1970–1990)' (1994) 9 *Journal of Business Venturing* 525. VC proved rather unsuccessful in France: see M Milosevic and J Fendt, 'Venture Capital and its French Exception: Explaining Performance through Human Capital, Policy and Institutional Failures' (2016) 43 *Science and Public Policy* 660.

[25] For Japan, see C Milhaupt, 'Market for Innovation in the United States and Japan: Venture Capital and the Comparative Corporate Governance Debate' (1996) 91 *Northwestern University Law Review* 865. For China, see D Ahlstrom, G Bruton and K Yeh, 'Venture Capital in China: Past, Present, and Future' (2007) 24 *Asia Pacific Journal of Management* 247. VC models are not homogenous around the world. Sociological variables influence to a very large extent the way VC works in the wider institutional context. See G Bruton and D Ahlstrom, 'An Institutional View of China's Venture Capital Industry: Explaining the Differences between China and the West' (2003) 18 *Journal of Business Venturing* 233. See also P Fu, A Tsui, and G Dess, 'The Dynamics of Guanxi in Chinese Hightech firms: Implications for Knowledge Management and Decision Making (2006) 46 *Management International Review* 277; P Fu, 'Developing Venture Capital Laws in China: Lessons Learned from the United States, Germany, and Japan' (2001) 23 *Loyola of Los Angeles International & Comparative Law Review* 487.

[26] J-L Capelleras et al, 'Venture Creation Speed and Subsequent Growth: Evidence from South America' (2010) 48 *Journal of Small Business Management* 302.

[27] For South Africa, see M Morris, J Watling and M Schindehutte, 'Venture Capitalist Involvement in Portfolio Companies: Insights from South Africa' (2000) 38 *Journal of Small Business Management* 68. African developing regions have also benefited from the introduction of venture capital. See N Biekpe, 'Financing Small Businesses in Sub-Saharan Africa: Review of Some Key Credit Lending Models and Impact of Venture Capital Provision' (2004) 5 *Journal of African Business* 29–44.

economic environments.[28] VC is not only an international phenomenon, but also (and especially) a cross-border financial practice.[29]

The cross-border dimension of VC is extremely complex. First, with reference to mere capital flows, it is well-known that several US IVCFs have been investing abroad for a long time, looking for new profits in less-saturated innovative markets.[30] This occurrence has challenged the original view of VC as a phenomenon strongly characterised by localisation.[31] Second, there has been an increasing flow of capital from foreign countries' IVCFs to the country that nowadays is considered to be the new economic superpower, ie the People's Republic of China – despite the fact that there has also been a traditional presence of local IVCFs in the People's Republic of China.[32] Although IVCFs used to move from the US to third countries in the early days of VC, nowadays providers of cross-border VC are located everywhere. This may seem an extraordinarily positive phenomenon. Nevertheless, there has been a concern that such cross-border activity transfers the profits deriving from innovation to the IVCF's originating country.[33]

For an IVCF, crossing borders means being exposed to a full set of new economic, financial, industrial and legal variables – which may affect positively or negatively the profitability of the investment. The moment of truth regarding the profitability of an IVCF's investments is usually the exit phase.[34]

A. The Legal Variable as a Determinant for Venture Capital Investment

Empirical research has shown that the legal variable – intended in this case as the level of abidance by the rule of law, certainty of the law and investment

[28] Social variables may represent fundamental institutional complementarities in developing countries. See D Hain, S Johan and D Wang, 'Determinants of Cross-Border Venture Capital Investments in Emerging and Developed Economies: The Effects of Relational and Institutional Trust' (2016) 138 *Journal of Business Ethics* 743.

[29] In parallel with the development of the cross-border dimension of VC, research has moved from international to cross-border analysis. See M Wright, S Pruthi and A Lockett, 'International Venture Capital Research: From Cross Country Comparisons to Crossing Borders' (2005) 7 *International Journal of Management Reviews* 135.

[30] I Guler and M Guillén, 'Institutions and the Internationalization of U.S. Venture Capital Firms' (2010) 41 *Journal of International Business Studies* 185.

[31] R Madhavan and A Iriyama, 'Understanding Global Flows of Venture Capital: Human Networks as the "Carrier Wave" of Globalization' (2009) 40 *Journal of International Business Studies* 1241.

[32] H Lu, M Solt and Y Tan, 'Do Foreign and Local Venture Capitalists Behave Alike in Transitional Economies? Evidence from China' (2010) 10 *Journal of International Business and Economics* 68.

[33] W Bradley et al, 'Cross-Border Venture Capital Investments: what is the Role of Public Policy?' (2019) 12 *Journal of Risk and Financial Management* 112.

[34] Exit can take the form either of an IPO or of a sale of an IVCFs' equity stake in a start-up to another corporation or to another IVCF; additionally, it can be full or partial. See D Cumming and J MacIntosh, 'A Cross-country Comparison of Full and Partial Venture Capital Exits' (2003) 27 *Journal of Banking & Finance* 511. For the relationships between exit and corporate opportunity rules, see text at section IV.G and accompanying notes.

protection within a given business environment – is critical for attracting cross-border VC.[35]

The complications related to US IVCFs' investments in countries whose laws and enforcement systems are radically different from those in the US has been highlighted by multiple researchers. Although US IVCFs, especially the largest ones, are successful in imposing US-style contractual terms,[36] local mandatory laws may still influence the profitability of VC cross-border activity. For instance, research on Asian start-ups has shown that the level of 'legality' within the country where the start-up is incorporated is directly proportional to the probability of a successful exit.[37] This may be one of the reasons why many Asian and Pacific start-ups tend to relocate to the US when they are closer to exit – so increasing the probability of yielding higher returns.[38]

A further cross-border element in VC may exist at the level of the start-up. In fact, for a start-up, moving to different geographical areas may also be a core choice pertaining to their marketing strategy.[39] The phenomenon of 'born global firms' – that is, start-ups that select a marketing strategy oriented to foreign countries – has been noted since the 1990s.[40] More generally, start-ups have been known to carry out different cross-border activities along their value chains.[41] One of the most common forms of start-up cross-border activity is the setting-up of sale subsidiaries.[42] Such a decision is often determined by the fact that monitoring an external distributor can be more expensive than selling directly, especially for smaller start-ups.[43] It goes without saying that carrying out commercial or productive activity in a foreign country again entails the interaction with new legal environments.

We can also find several cross-border elements in corporate venture capital (CVC), which is the form of VC financing consisting of an established corporation funding a start-up. It has been noted that CVC has been growing exponentially in the last few decades.[44] In the case of CVC, the reason for

[35] A Schertler and T Tykvova, 'Stay at Home or go Abroad? The Impact of Fiscal and Legal Environments on the Geography of Private Equity Flows' (2008) 21st Australasian Finance and Banking Conference, pdfs.semanticscholar.org/c9ec/830dc21c608edd0f9c622a9fa7577e3f9331.pdf.

[36] Kaplan, Martel and Strömberg, 'Legal Differences' (2007) 275.

[37] D Cumming, G Fleming and A Schwienbacher, 'Legality and Venture Capital Exits' (2006) 12 *Journal of Corporate Finance* 214, 215; by 'legality', the authors mean 'the efficiency of the judicial system, the rule of law, corruption, risk of expropriation, risk of contract repudiation, and shareholder rights'.

[38] D Cumming, G Fleming and A Schwienbacher, 'Corporate Relocation in Venture Capital Finance' (2009) 33 *Entrepreneurship Theory and Practice* 1121.

[39] O Burgel and G Murray, 'The International Market Entry Choices of Start-up Companies in High-Technology Industries' (2000) 8 *Journal of International Marketing* 33.

[40] G Knight and T Cavusgil, 'The Born Global Firm: A Challenge to Traditional Internationalization Theory' (1996) 8 *Advances in International Marketing* 11.

[41] Burgel and Murray, 'International Market Entry Choices' (2000).

[42] ibid 34.

[43] ibid 38.

[44] R Belderbos, J Jacob and B Lokshin, 'Corporate Venture Capital (CVC) Investments and Technological Performance: Geographic Diversity and the Interplay with Technology Alliances' (2018) 33 *Journal of Business Venturing* 20, 21.

investing in a foreign start-up may not consist exclusively of the pursuit of a profitable financial investment. CVC can be seen as source of technological innovation for incumbent corporations.[45] In fact, CVCs may seek to exploit ideas that are conceived by another entrepreneur for the purpose of improving their own business. CVC relies on the commitment and working enthusiasm of a creative team external to the incumbent corporation – a team that is likely to be self-motivated.[46] Cross-border CVC may be a successful strategy for the purpose of sourcing from abroad new blocks of knowledge to be employed in the combinatory process that is the essence of innovation.[47] Nonetheless, cross-border CVC may also come at a price. In fact, collaborating with start-ups that are geographically distant and culturally very different may raise problems of integrating routines and culture – along with a general issue of potential lack of trust.[48]

An introduction to the cross-border dimension of VC is not complete without mentioning that it is not only US IVCFs that have crossed the borders of the US and invested virtually everywhere in the world. It is the VC model of financing that has also been adopted abroad. In fact, foreign countries have promoted their own VC industry. In turn, the existence of local VC, with no proprietary ties to the US VC environment, has often been identified as one of the main variables that determines the willingness of US IVCFs to invest in a foreign country.[49] The reason for this is that the presence of local VC grants the possibility of co-syndication, through which foreign IVCFs can exploit the local expertise and source soft information such as that pertaining to 'indigenous business operations, contacts, culture, and other local factors' acquired by local IVCFs.[50]

B. The Cross-Border Differences in Venture Capital Legal Structure

One can distinguish at least two sets of legal variables which matter for VC: that pertaining to the organisation of IVCFs, ie 'internal rules; and that connected to the relationships between IVCFs and their investees/entrepreneurs, ie to IVCFs' 'external' activity. The first set of rules often follows the law of the country where

[45] G Dushnitsky and M Lenox, 'When Do Incumbents Learn from Entrepreneurial Ventures?: Corporate Venture Capital and Investing Firm Innovation Rates' (2005) 34 *Research Policy* 615.

[46] On founders' motivations to invent see text at ch 5.VIII and accompanying notes.

[47] On innovation as a combination of building-blocks of knowledge, see text at ch 5.VI and accompanying notes.

[48] Y Liu and M Markku, 'Local Partnering in Foreign Ventures: Uncertainty, Experiential Learning, and Syndication in Cross-border Venture Capital Investments (2016) 59 *Academy of Management Journal* 1407.

[49] T Tykvova and A Schertler, 'Does Syndication with Local Venture Capitalists Moderate the Effects of Geographical and Institutional Distance?' (2014) 20 *Journal of International Management* 406.

[50] Liu and Markku, 'Local Partnering in Foreign Ventures' (2016) 1409.

the IVCF is set up or incorporated and where it raises its funds. The second set of rules normally consists of both contract law and corporate law.

The US and Europe differ substantially in terms of law and contractual praxis pertaining to the internal organisation of IVCFs. In fact, unlikely in the US – where the most common organisational form is the limited partnership – in Europe IVCFs are mostly organised in the form of investment companies under different national laws.[51] As to IVCFs' external activity, ie managing the start-ups they invest into, the company that pools together VC and entrepreneur, ie the start-up, is usually set up according to the law of the country where it is incorporated – and the country where the start-up is incorporated may or may not be the country where the company has its real seat. In fact, when corporate mobility is an option, the company at issue may be set up according to the law of a country in which the company or the partnership can exercise its freedom of establishment.[52]

It is worth pointing out that corporate law still differs to a very large extent across the world, despite many rules being similar in function.[53] Moreover, whereas contract law is usually optional law – ie, it is the contracting parties who choose the way to frame their rights and duties – corporate law often includes a core set of mandatory rules.[54] In most European jurisdictions,

[51] Wright, Pruthi and Lockett, 'International Venture Capital Research' (2005) 142–43.

[52] There are two main connection criteria for determining the law applicable to a company: the incorporation theory and the real seat theory. See L Collins et al, *Dicey, Morris & Collins on the Conflict of Laws*, 14th edn (Sweet & Maxwell, 2008) Rules 160–62 (domicile and residence of a company, status and the law of incorporation). US corporate laws adopt the incorporation theory. Hence, corporate mobility is possible and has made it possible to establish a mechanism of regulatory competition. See W Cary, 'Federalism and Corporate Law' (1974) 83 *Yale Law Journal* 663; R Winter, 'State Law, Shareholder Protection and the Theory of the Corporation' (1977) 6 *Journal of Legal Studies* 251, 289–92; L Bebchuk, 'Federalism and the Corporation: The Desirable Limits' (1992) 105 *Harvard Law Review* 1435; R Romano, *The Genius of American Corporate Law* (American Enterprise Institute Press, 1993) 14–31; L Bebchuk and A Ferrell, 'Federalism and Corporate Law, The Race to Protect Managers from Takeovers' (1999) 99 *Columbia Law Review* 1168; L Bebchuk, A Cohen and A Ferrell, 'Does the Evidence Favour State Competition in Corporate Law?' (2002) 90 *California Law Review* 1775; L Bebchuk and A Cohen, 'Firms' Decisions Where to Incorporate' (2003) 46 *Journal of Law and Economics* 383; M Roe, 'Delaware's Competition' (2003) 117 *Harvard Law Review* 588; M Roe, 'Delaware's Politics' (2005) 118 *Harvard Law Review* 2491. Recently, corporate mobility has become an option (with limits) also in the EU, as a consequence of European Court of Justice decisions and European statutory law. See especially Case C-212/97 *Centros Ltd v Erhvervs- og Selskabsstyrelsen* [1999] ECR I-1459; Case C-208/00 *Überseering BV v Nordic Construction Company Baumanagement GmbH* [2002] ECR I-9919; Case C-167/01 *Kamer van Koophandel en Fabrieken voor Amsterdam v Inspire Art Ltd* [2003] ECR I-10155; Case C-9/02 *Hughes de Lasteyrie du Saillant v Ministère de l'Économie, des Finances et de l'Industrie* [2004] ECR I-2409; Case C-411/03 *Sevic Systems AG* [2005] ECR I-10805; Case C-210/06 *Cartesio Oktató és Szolgáltató Betéti Társaság* [2008] ECR I-9641; Case C-378/10 VALE Építési kft. [2012] ECR 00000; Case C-106/16 Polbud EU:C:2017:804. The literature on the legal aspects of VC 'external activity', ie on start-up law, is still scarce, especially in Europe. For a recent comparative study, see A Andhov (ed), *Start-up Law* (Edward Elgar, 2020).

[53] R Kraakman et al, *The Anatomy of Corporate Law: A Comparative and Functional Approach* (Oxford University Press, 2017).

[54] This has been largely recognised also in US corporate law. See J Coffee, 'The Mandatory/Enabling Balance in Corporate Law: An Essay on the Judicial Role' (1989) 89 *Columbia Law Review* 1618.

corporate law rules pertaining to the duty of loyalty used to be strictly mandatory. Nowadays, from a comparative perspective, we are witnessing a progressive erosion of mandatory corporate law rules, in part also in relation to the duty of loyalty. Nonetheless, it is possible to notice a degree of asymmetry in such a transformation of rules from mandatory to default. Whereas this is a worldwide phenomenon for self-dealing rules, the possibility of introducing corporate opportunity waivers remains a singular feature of certain US corporate laws.[55] Such a divergence is not only important from a theoretical perspective; it also bears practical implications because of the cross-border activity carried out by IVCFs.[56] An understanding of the different corporate opportunity doctrines is even more important in this context, as they may be employed to solve, at least in part, a rather intricate set of conflicts of interest.

III. THE MULTI-LAYER DIMENSION OF THE CONFLICT OF INTEREST IN VENTURE CAPITAL

In the typical US IVCF limited partnership,[57] different economic players with conflicting interests interact with each other.[58] Venture capitalists, ie general partners (GPs) may deal with their main financing providers, ie the limited partners.[59] They may also frequently deal with GPs working for different IVCFs, especially when they engage in syndication – that is, a co-financing strategy very commonly employed both in the US and in Europe, although characterised by completely different features in the two economic areas.[60] Moreover, venture capitalists frequently interact with the start-up entrepreneurs and, especially on the verge of each exit, with the prospective acquirers or with the lead underwriter in the case of an initial public offering (IPO).[61] The relationships among the above-mentioned players must be characterised by a high level of trust for VC to work efficiently or – one may even say – for it to simply exist.[62] This has to

[55] See M Corradi and G Helleringer, 'Board Duties: The Duty of Loyalty and Self-Dealing', forthcoming in A Afsharipour and M Gelter (eds) *Comparative Corporate Governance* (Edward Elgar, 2021).

[56] See text at section II.A and accompanying notes.

[57] Partners may in this case subvert substantially the 'ordinary' functioning of the partnership agreement. See L Ribstein, 'Partnership Governance of Large Firms' (2009) 76 *The University of Chicago Law Review* 289, 300ff.

[58] See L Harris, 'A Critical Theory of Private Equity' (2010) 35 *Delaware Journal of Corporate Law* 259, 263ff.

[59] ibid.

[60] See text at section VI and accompanying notes.

[61] W Sahlman, 'The Structure and Governance of Venture-Capital Organizations' (1990) 27 *Journal of Financial Economics* 473, 509.

[62] L Bottazzi, M Da Rin and T Hellmann, 'The Importance of Trust for Investment: Evidence from Venture Capital' (2016) 29 *The Review of Financial Studies* 2283; D Shepherd and A Zacharakis, 'The Venture Capitalist-Entrepreneur Relationship: Control, Trust and Confidence in Co-operative Behaviour' (2001) 3 *Venture Capital: An International Journal of Entrepreneurial Finance* 129.

be constantly kept in mind when analysing the duty of loyalty in the VC context. In fact, loyalty rules, such as the directors' duty of loyalty, can contribute to laying some institutional foundations in terms of building trust. However, when loyalty rules do not exist or are not systematically enforced, trust may be built only through repeated interaction among the same players.

A. Conflict of Interests between General and Limited Partners

Conflicts of interest dynamics 'internal' to IVCFs appear to be simpler than those that exist inside the VC-backed start-up. Limited partners convey financing to the IVCF and expect a return from their investment. GPs invest the fund's liquid assets and also become involved in the management of the corporations in which they invest on behalf of the fund.[63]

From the perspective of the economic agency theory, GPs are agents of their limited partners. Thanks to their position in the start-up, they may engage in behaviours that are profitable for them, but which are not damaging to the limited partners' investment, ie interested but non-conflicted behaviours. For instance, imagine that, after having invested in a given line of business on behalf of the IVCF, GPs seeks to buy for themselves equity in corporations that are active in the same or in a similar line of business. They may do so after having gathered relevant information on the profitability of these corporations, thanks to the privileged observation point they enjoy on the local start-up market. Such information may become available after the IVCF's liquid assets have already been invested entirely and therefore there would be no way to offer such new investment opportunities to the fund.

Nonetheless, GPs may also engage in a series of transactions that can be detrimental to limited partners in various ways.[64] For instance, a completely different situation occurs when a GP seeks to divert to themselves assets belonging to the start-ups they have invested into on behalf of the fund. Such an action may in turn devaluate the IVCF's investment and therefore penalise its limited partners.[65] Asset diversion may well take the form of a misappropriation of a start-up's corporate opportunity by a GP appointed by an IVCF to the board of that start-up.[66] This case, as any other form of general/limited partner conflict

[63] Sahlman, 'Venture-Capital Organizations' (1990).

[64] V Atanasov, V Ivanov and K Litvak, 'Does Reputation Limit Opportunistic Behavior in the VC Industry? Evidence from Litigation Against VCs' (2012) 67 *Journal of Finance* 2215, 2219, according to whom GPs 'use partnership capital to invest in companies controlled by related parties, consume excessive perks, or divert business opportunities from one partnership to another'.

[65] R Bartlett, 'Venture Capital, Agency Costs, and the False Dichotomy of the Corporation' (2006) 54 *UCLA Law Review* 37, 49–51; Harris, 'A Critical Theory' (2019) 263ff.

[66] See for instance *GMS Tech Access Subpartnership v GMG Management* (unpublished), as cited in Atanasov, Ivanov and Litvak, 'Does Reputation Limit Opportunistic Behavior in the VC Industry?' (2012) 2228.

of interest, will eventually be addressed by partnership law and by the further contractual provisions that the general and limited partners may have stipulated for addressing conflicts of interest.[67] An advisory board and investors' committee are present in many IVCFs. The advisory board addresses conflicts of interest and supports the managers. The investors' committee deals with the relationship with the key investors.[68] Both are likely to intervene if they spot a conflict of interest, eventually trying to prevent it.

Apart from the possible legal consequences of a misappropriation of a corporate opportunity, the reputational consequences may be particularly detrimental to the GP who has breached their duty of loyalty as a director, as 'venture funds are organized as limited-term partnerships, which forces VCs to go back to investors to raise capital for new funds every few years'.[69] Raising new capital after engaging in such unethical conduct may be extremely hard to do.

In a different set of cases, a GP appointed by an IVCF to the board of a start-up may act in conflict of interest within the start-up, without being in conflict of interest with the limited partners. This will be the case where a GP moves corporate opportunities from one start-up to another, while having invested on behalf of the IVCF in both, and while both start-ups are operating in the same line of business. A GP may be tempted to do this, for instance, when the IVCF has invested more heavily in one of the start-ups. Therefore, they try to benefit the fund by way of moving the most profitable business opportunities to the start-up in which it is most heavily invested. Such an operation may damage one start-up (and the start-up's entrepreneurs) for the benefit of another, and this clearly cannot be applauded. Nonetheless, the GPs do this with a view to enriching the IVCF, and ultimately its limited partners, who will see their investment better remunerated. It may well be that limited partners would not appreciate this kind of profitable but dishonest detournement of business opportunities from an ethical perspective – at least if they are ethical investors. However, it is also worth noting that – because of their distance from the day-to-day activity of GPs – limited partners are not usually very well equipped to monitor the GPs' activity within the start-ups they invest in.

The examples proposed above may have simultaneous effects both internal and external to the IVCF. Internally, they may affect the financial position of the limited partners either positively or negatively. Internal situations will be regulated by organisational law and by the contract between limited partners and GPs, which would set their legal treatment outside the domain of corporate opportunity rules. External situations, ie on the start-up plans, may involve a breach of the duty of loyalty in the form of a taking of a corporate opportunity, and that pertains more closely to this analysis.

[67] Although the reach of contractual arrangements might have been overstated; see Harris (n 58) 264–65.

[68] S Caselli, *Private Equity and Venture Capital in Europe: Markets, Techniques, and Deals* (Elsevier, 2010) 121.

[69] Atanasov, Ivanov and Litvak (n 64) 2220.

B. Conflict of Interest between GPs and Entrepreneurs

The conflicts of interest within a start-up backed by one or more IVCFs are particularly tangled. A significant corpus of literature deals with the business opportunism of the venture capitalists and of the entrepreneurs. It explains that private contracting is an important tool for containing such opportunism, along with corporate law and corporate governance provisions.[70] A set of studies by Kaplan and Strömberg have collected, systematised and explained the practice of VC contracting, opening a very interesting window on the 'law off the books'.[71]

Some categories of opportunistic behaviour along with their legal remedies have been object of special attention by academics, such as CEO replacements, later-round financing and VC exit, all of which can be highly relevant for understanding corporate opportunity rules from a Law and Economics perspective.[72] Literature also focuses extensively on the way praxis has succeeded in preventing conflict induced by opportunistic behaviour. It analyses the financial structure of VC operations (eg the use of convertible securities versus common stock),[73] as well as exploring in detail VC-backed start-ups' board structures, voting rights, liquidation rights and other allocation rights.[74] In this respect, literature on VC highlights a significant deviation of start-ups from the 'standard' corporation.

When depicting agency costs within a corporation, *The Anatomy of Corporate Law* stresses the importance of the ownership structure variable for determining whether it is the shareholders as a whole or mainly non-controlling shareholders who bear the main agency costs within the corporation.[75]

In corporations with dispersed ownership structures, the shareholders are normally the principals of the directors.[76] In corporations with concentrated ownership structures, the situation is different because the minority shareholders are the principals of the majority shareholders.[77]

Bartlett has shown that start-ups backed by IVCFs provide an example of corporations where the above-mentioned distinction proposed in *The Anatomy*

[70] Lerner and Schoar, 'Does Legal Enforcement Affect Financial Transactions?' (2005).

[71] Kaplan, Martel and Strömberg (n 18); S Kaplan and P Strömberg, 'Characteristics, Contracts, and Actions: Evidence from Venture Capitalist Analyses' (2004) 59 *Journal of Finance* 2177; see also n 19.

[72] B Broughman, 'Investor Opportunism, and Governance in Venture Capital' in Cumming, *Venture Capital* (2010) 347, 347–48;

[73] T Hellmann, 'IPOs, Acquisitions, and the Use of Convertible Securities in Venture Capital' (2006) 81 *Journal of Financial Economics* 649; K Schmidt, 'Convertible Securities and Venture Capital Finance' (2003) 58 *Journal of Finance* 1139.

[74] N Wasserman, 'The Throne vs. the Kingdom: Founder Control and Value Creation in Startups' (2017) 38 *Strategic Management Journal* 255; M Baker and P Gompers, 'The Determinants of Board Structure at the Initial Public Offering' (2003) 46 *The Journal of Law and Economics* 569.

[75] Kraakman et al, *The Anatomy of Corporate Law* (2017) 29ff.

[76] ibid 29.

[77] ibid 46.

and based on the corporate ownership structure does not apply in such a binary way.[78] In start-ups, it is often hard to determine who is the principal and who is the agent, because the situation of each player may radically change throughout time. Therefore, the nature of the conflicts of interest between different constituencies is inherently different in a start-up as compared to a standard corporation.

Fried and Ganor have compared the governance system of standard corporations with that of start-ups. In the standard US business corporation, the main conflicts of interest are between common shareholders and directors, as it is common shareholders whose interest directors are supposed to promote. Moreover, under Delaware corporate law, directors have a fiduciary duty to favour common shareholders, because common shareholders are exposed to potential opportunism by preferred shareholders.[79] By contrast, in a start-up, control is usually held by IVCFs through preferred shares.[80]

The use of preferred shares issued to IVCFs may be aimed at countering the effects of the information asymmetries incurred by the fund *ex ante* when investing in a start-up. In fact, by accepting the issuance of preferred shares to an IVCF,[81] the entrepreneur may signal that they expect to earn profits higher than those awarded by way of the liquidation preferences granted to the IVCF.[82] On top of preferred shares, IVCFs normally also obtain direct control of the board of directors, which is otherwise unusual for preferred shares' bearers.[83] IVCFs can often exercise 'negative control' through so-called 'protective provisions' – that is, veto rights on certain categories of transactions.[84] In start-ups, protective provisions are often conceived as catch-all provisions; they apply to any action 'that materially modifies their rights under their agreement with the company'.[85] As to 'positive control' – that is, the power to take decisions – it has been found that, in the majority of the start-ups, the casting vote in the board is held by a director who is mutually appointed by IVCFs and entrepreneurs.[86] Nonetheless, normally it is only the IVCFs, in the persons of their GPs, that have sufficiently established business relationships to propose suitable candidates for such mutually appointed directorships. Hence a mutually appointed director may be someway more loyal to the IVCF than to the entrepreneur.[87]

[78] Bartlett, 'Venture Capital' (2006) 64ff.

[79] J Fried and M Ganor, 'Agency Costs of Venture Capitalist Control in Start-ups (2006) 81 *NYU Law Review* 967, 977ff.

[80] ibid 972ff.

[81] ibid 983ff.

[82] Note that there is a similar rationale underlying the acceptance of stage financing, as stressed by R Gilson, 'Engineering a Venture Capital Market: Lessons from the American Experience' (2003) 55 *Stanford Law Review* 1067, 1081.

[83] Fried and Ganor, 'Agency Costs' (2006) 986ff.

[84] ibid 987.

[85] ibid.

[86] Kaplan and Strömberg (n 19) 312.

[87] Fried and Ganor (n 79) 988 note that in the standard US corporation independent directors owe their duties only to common shareholders: 976ff.

According to Fried and Ganor, control over the board has the function of containing both entrepreneurial and common shareholders' opportunism.[88] Entrepreneurial opportunism may consist of classic expropriations of private benefits of control (eg exceedingly high salaries). It may also consist of choices contrary to the maximisation of the value of the company, such as in the case of an entrepreneur willing to continue an unprofitable business for the sake of keeping on receiving their salary.[89] This has clearly much to do also with decisions pertaining to the exploitation of corporate opportunities.

While it contains entrepreneurs' and common shareholders' opportunism, preferential shareholders' control may raise new types of agency costs. According to Fried and Ganor,

> preferred-owning VCs in control of the board may, in certain situations, make excessively conservative business decisions, such as choosing immediate 'liquidity events' (major corporate transactions that would end the independent life of the company, such as dissolution or a sale of the business) over higher-value strategies involving more risk.[90]

It goes without saying that such strategic choices often entail taking decisions on whether to pursue certain business opportunities or not. Therefore, they significantly affect the pursuance of corporate opportunities. If a corporate opportunity is sound and deserves to be exploited, but it is not exploited because the IVCF pushes instead for a liquidity event, corporate opportunity doctrines must provide ways to render such an opportunity exploitable outside the boundaries of the corporation.

C. Venture Capital Funds' Conflict of Interests in Syndication

The agency costs structure within VC-backed start-ups may already seem rather complex in the light of what has been explained above. Nonetheless, the situation can be even more complex in the presence of syndication, which takes place when the same start-up is backed by several IVCFs. Syndication may potentially be transformed in an arena hosting extremely harsh conflict among IVCFs. Bartlett has shown that the fear of a partner-IVCF's opportunism may trigger contractual defences that in turn may be employed for engaging in an escalation of opportunistic behaviour. This often occurs in later-round financing.[91]

Normally, start-ups will be initially backed by one or a few IVCFs. The contract between IVCF and start-up is normally based on stage financing. This consists of the provision of an initial amount of capital by the IVCFs in the form of equity, whereas the provision of further funding is normally subject to

[88] Fried and Ganor (n 79) 986.
[89] ibid.
[90] ibid 993–94.
[91] Bartlett (n 65).

the condition that certain milestones are reached by the start-up.[92] New IVCFs, different from those that invested in the start-up initially, may intervene to provide further funding.[93] Nonetheless, new funders will require further protection for their investments, and they will seek to negotiate preferential treatment in respect of those IVCFs that intervened in the first round of financing, especially in terms of enhanced liquidation preferences.[94] The situation can become more complex at every stage, due to the conclusion of more covenants between the start-up and the different IVCFs,[95] which may end up being detrimental to earlier-stage investors and trigger litigation.[96]

IVCFs that have intervened throughout the different stages of the development of a start-up may have diverging opinions about strategic choices, such as whether or not to continue down a given line of investment. For instance, there may be two ways to develop the start-up strategy: one entails continuing along the lines that have already been set in the start-up original pitching; the other entails pivoting by way of abandoning the present line of business and starting a completely new one which requires further investments. The choice between the two means a lot in terms of corporate opportunities, and the different categories of investors may not be inclined to pursue the same strategy, depending on the amount of capital they have invested in the start-up and in the degree of protection awarded to such capital. With limited financial resources, some corporate opportunities will be relinquished and others will be pursued. Corporate opportunities that are relinquished may in turn be exploited in a different start-up, maybe one where the same IVCFs have also invested, so raising further conflicts of interest.[97]

As we have seen, the interests' configuration within a start-up and their complex interaction may affect to a very large extent the pursuance of corporate opportunities and their relinquishment, because the different IVCFs acting in syndication may support diverging decisions. This renders the analysis of corporate opportunity rules in the context of VC even more complex than in an ordinary corporation. This is why, in order to understand the exact role of corporate opportunities in innovative clusters, it is necessary to understand how information about business opportunities circulates in such environments and who is more likely to exploit it in the different phases of a start-up, while the disclosure of information and the likelihood of corporate opportunities' appropriations are also influenced by the legal variables.

[92] D Neher, 'Staged financing: an agency perspective (1999) 66 *The Review of Economic Studies* 255, 256ff; Kaplan and Strömberg (n 19); X Tian, 'The Causes and Consequences of Venture Capital Stage Financing' (2011) 10 *Journal of Financial Economics* 132.

[93] A Lockett and M Wright, 'The Syndication of Venture Capital Investments' (2001) 29 *Omega* 375, 378.

[94] Bartlett (n 65) 88.

[95] ibid 65.

[96] ibid 86.

[97] See text at section IV.E and accompanying notes.

IV. THE RELATIONSHIP BETWEEN VENTURE CAPITALISTS AND ENTREPRENEURS: BUSINESS OPPORTUNISM, UNILATERAL, BILATERAL AND MULTILATERAL RISKS OF MISAPPROPRIATIONS

A. The Circulation of Information in Industrial Clusters

IVCFs normally thrive in technology-intensive industrial clusters. There, ambitious entrepreneurs put their creativity to work for turning their ideas into sources of innovation and delivering them to the market in the form of successful products or services.[98] In industrial clusters, innovation is created and circulates with unusual speed – also as a consequence of the high employment mobility that characterises such economic environments.[99]

IVCFs collect and process in due time sophisticated business information pertaining to the product markets in which they invest and to their potential developments. IVCFs eventually exploit informational economies of scales and scope.[100] Literature shows that, although IVCFs clearly invest in ideas, their focus is mostly oriented towards product markets. They seek to invest in those growing industries that 'are more competitively forgiving than the market as a whole'.[101] IVCFs tend to specialise in one or more specific product markets, and there is empirical evidence that specialised IVCFs usually perform economically much better than the so-called 'generalists', ie those that invest in a number of non-related product markets.[102] This provides us with an important element for discussing the likelihood that a given IVCF GP may be able to transfer relevant business information from one start-up to one of such start-up's direct competitors.

The ability to collect and elaborate sensitive business information does not belong exclusively to IVCFs' GPs. A young entrepreneur who attracts funding may also be able to anticipate what is likely to happen on their product market and to predict the business potential of new ideas.[103] Especially when they

[98] On the sociological and economic variables at play in Silicon Valley, see Saxenian, *Regional Advantage* (1994).

[99] Again, Silicon Valley is emblematic in this respect. See A Saxenian, 'Brain Circulation. How High-Skill Immigration Makes Everyone Better Off' (2002) 20 *Brookings Review* 28; C Benner, 'Learning Communities in a Learning Region: The Soft Infrastructure of Cross-firm Learning Networks in Silicon Valley' (2003) 35 *Environment and Planning* 1809. Nonetheless, these mechanisms are nowadays very common also in non-American business environments, thanks to workers' exchanges with highly developed areas such as the Silicon Valley. See A Saxenian, 'From Brain Drain to Brain Circulation: Transnational Communities and Regional Upgrading in India and China' (2005) 40 *Studies in Comparative International Development* 35; A Saxenian, Y Motoyama and X Quan, *Local and Global Networks of Immigrant Professionals in Silicon Valley* (Public Policy Institute of CA, 2002).

[100] Sahlman (n 61) 500ff. IVCF tend to decide on their investments on the basis of 'chunks' of information that are usually acquired through long-term practice. See A Zacharakis, 'Venture Capital Decision Making' in Cumming (n 10) 9, 10.

[101] B Zider, 'How Venture Capital Works' (1998) 76 *Harvard Business Review* 131, 133.

[102] P Gompers, A Kovner and J Lerner, 'Specialization and Success: Evidence from Venture Capital' (2009) 18 *Journal of Economics & Management Strategy* 817.

[103] This is already noted in the Austrian school of economics. See J Kirzner, *Competition and Entrepreneurship* (University of Chicago Press, 1973).

work in industrial clusters or districts, entrepreneurs have increased chances of acquiring a significant amount of the sensitive business information that circulates among their competitors.[104]

The fact that pieces of sensitive business information may circulate, intentionally or unintentionally, among a wide number of entrepreneurs and GPs may make the boundaries of the 'ownership' of that information[105] blurred, ie difficult to define *ex ante* and ex post.[106] It may be difficult to establish who had a given idea first – because in the words of a Hewlett-Packard executive, 'good ideas come from everywhere'.[107] Therefore, often the original source of information may be unknown. It may also happen that it is a GP appointed as a start-up director who suggests new business ideas to entrepreneurs. Conversely, entrepreneurs may inform GPs appointed on the start-up's board and discuss with them potential business ideas of their own. Investment opportunities may often derive from a combination of information originating from different sources: entrepreneurs, GPs and their competitors. If innovation is an amalgamation of building blocks of knowledge, it may be hard to tell who it belongs to when such blocks have been brought together and combined by different individuals.[108] One may well say that from a meta-legal perspective it belongs to all of them as a team or to the environment itself, rather than a specific individual.

Although the boundaries of the 'ownership' of strategic information may at times be blurred in innovative clusters, the blocks of information that may be employed for behaving opportunistically may be available to different players to different degrees throughout the development stages of a new venture. For instance, generic knowledge of the emergence of a new technology cannot be equated to knowledge of its technical details, which may be necessary in order to appropriate such technology. Currently, when a start-up is founded, the GPs involved in a given VC deal may have a rather blurred knowledge of the technicalities of the start-up's business project compared to the entrepreneur. The entrepreneur may better know the technical specificities of their product and be able to make better judgements on them because they have spent a long time

[104] For Europe, see the pioneering research by P Krugman, *Geography and Trade* (Massachusetts Institute of Technology Press, 1991). See also, M Feldman, 'The New Economics of Innovation, Spillovers and Agglomeration: A Review of Empirical Studies' (1999) 8 *Economics of Innovation and New Technology* 5. For Italian industrial clusters, see for instance M Russo, 'Technical Change and the Industrial District: The Role of Interfirm Relations in the Growth and Transformation of Ceramic Tile Production' (1985) 14 *Italy Research Policy* 329. There is also empirical literature that demonstrates the existence of information networks in clusters. See for instance M Dahl and C Pedersen, 'Knowledge Flows Through Informal Contacts in Industrial Clusters: Myth or Reality?' (2004) 33 *Research Policy* 1673.

[105] Although one may want to keep in mind that this is a very special kind of ownership, originally designed to benefit the public at large. See T Lipinski and J Britz, 'Rethinking the Ownership of Information in the 21st Century: Ethical Implications' (2000) 2 *Ethics and Information Technology* 49.

[106] This is often due also to the blurring of boundaries within a firm. See Saxenian (n 2) 50.

[107] ibid 51.

[108] See text at ch V.F and accompanying notes.

refining their business ideas.[109] Over time, a GP who is appointed as a director of the board of the start-up may also acquire detailed technological knowledge of the specific innovation, although a GP may find it difficult to identify another entrepreneur with the skills necessary for exploiting such ideas.[110]

Start-up directors, regardless of who appointed them, may also encounter – inside or outside their board activity – further business opportunities connected to the business opportunity developed by the start-up. In such cricumstances, GPs may have a competitive advantage vis-à-vis the entrepreneur. They may have a clearer understanding of the value of investment opportunities, given that they may operate also in similar but not identical lines of business. Moreover, they may have much more reliable information on the chances for a given business opportunity to receive financing.[111]

B. The Limits of the Economic Agency Costs Paradigm in Start-up Contexts

The geographical localisation of VC in industrial clusters, the high density of the economic players involved in the industry, the complexity of their networks, the speed at which communication circulates within such contexts and the fluidity of the information proprietary boundaries provide an already intricate starting point for the analysis of the role of corporate opportunity rules in VC-funded start-ups.

One may attempt an extreme simplification, by way of addressing the question of the ownership of business opportunities from a mere agency theory perspective. Nonetheless, things are much more complex in the start-up world than in a standard company. Agency theory may not fully help in this context, as agency theory is built upon binary logics, which presuppose fixed and diametrically opposed roles (the one of agent and the one of principal). In VC-backed start-ups, control is more subject to change: the role of agent and principal are continuously subject to potential reversal. Such a situation may be difficult to tackle from a legal perspective, especially from a civil law one, where codifications tend to rely on easily identifiable and rather static roles.

The size of an IVCF's investment in a start-up, which may range from a small toehold to a large block, may determine the IVCF's financial incentives

[109] In fact, in those who are responsible for the creation and implementation of new ideas, knowledge is often deeply intertwined with action – to the extent that it may be difficult to appropriate by a third party/observer. See T Davenport and L Prusak, *Working Knowledge: How Organizations Manage What They Know* (Harvard Business Press, 1998) 6ff. This may also be one of the causes of the rapid growth of certain very successful start-ups; see B Barringer, J Jones and D Neubaum, 'A Quantitative Content Analysis of the Characteristics of Rapid-growth Firms and Their Founders' (2005) 20 *Journal of Business Venturing* 663.

[110] D Cable and S Shane, 'A Prisoner's Dilemma Approach to Entrepreneur-Venture Capitalist Relationships' (1997) 22 *Academy of Management Review* 142, 144.

[111] ibid 148.

and its capability to influence the start-up's strategic decisions – hence also affecting its propensity to behave opportunistically. Given that both the size of an IVCF's holding in a start-up and the control rights associated with it can vary to a large extent throughout time, it is generally hard to predict the degree of power that a given IVCF has vis-à-vis the entrepreneurs and especially vis- à-vis the other investors in the same start-up. Therefore, it is hard to say who is the agent and who is the principal *ex ante*. To some extent, also IVCFs and entrepreneurs, within their own categories, may be considered as each other's agents, for they may have divergent interests: for instance, an IVCF holding a mere toehold may have interests that are divergent from those of an IVCF holding a big block of shares; or an entrepreneur bringing a limited intellectual contribution to the project may bear interests colliding with another entrepreneur who is entirely involved in the project.[112] Such divergency may become particularly accentuated in the case of syndication and on the verge of potential exit decisions.[113]

Start-up directors may learn of new investment opportunities throughout the whole life of the start-up, until its end. A VC-backed start-up may end in many different ways: it may be wound-up, it may develop into a large corporation, or it may be sold to another corporation or another IVCF.[114] New business opportunities, which represent potential future lines of business development of a corporation, may at a certain point in time become totally irrelevant, such as in the case of a winding-up. In another set of cases, new business opportunities may also acquire a different value in relation to the projects of the new owners of the corporation. This may depend on whether the new owners are interested in the above-mentioned developmental potential or not. In turn, a mere interest in the pursuance of a business opportunity is not a sufficient condition for its appropriation. Its appropriability may depend also on the financial capabilities of the company on the verge of and after exit, which may be significantly higher in the case of an IPO. An IPO may allow the company to pursue very costly corporate opportunities because it is likely to raise more capital than a private sale. Apart from the case of an IPO, what is really interesting is that in the context of VC the financial capability test set by Delaware case law is likely to be highly influenced by the IVCFs that participate in the start-up, far beyond the presence of potential external financers.[115] Hence, internal VC may have a chance to impact the applicability of corporate opportunity rules, at least under Delaware law, which gives a further element of control to IVCFs within the start-up.

Given the complexity inherent in the protection of investment opportunities in VC-backed start-ups, the most convenient analytical framework for untangling

[112] See text at ch 5.X and accompanying notes.
[113] See text at section IV.G and accompanying notes.
[114] ibid.
[115] *Broz v Cellular Info. Systems, Inc*, 673 A.2d 148 (1996) 155.

the diversity of situations that may arise is an evolutionary one, which maps the development of the allocation of business opportunities throughout the different stages of a VC-backed start-up.

C. Business Opportunities in the Company Formation Process

The problem of the protection of investment opportunities in a VC context may arise well before the company is formed. IVCF GPs must be very wary in assessing their prospective investments in start-up projects. The information asymmetry that characterises the pre-investment phases – which is likely to be particularly high in early stage financing[116] – can be reduced by way of auditing and open and honest communication between entrepreneurs and IVCFs.[117] In this phase the vulnerability of the IVCF's financial position can be protected only at the expense of the vulnerability of the entrepreneur's position.

The entrepreneur may fear that once their ideas are disclosed to the IVCF, they may eventually become public – beside the risk that they are directly transferred by GPs to other start-ups in which the IVCF has already invested.[118] This is one of the reasons why IVCF GPs may be asked to sign a confidentiality agreement before engaging in the expected due diligence activity. Such an agreement may protect the entrepreneur for the period they will need for developing their project. Nonetheless, there is also a chance that the agreement at issue is not signed during of the first contact between an entrepreneur and an IVCF.[119]

GPs usually receive applications from thousands of candidates, but will often only be able to provide funding to three or four start-ups at each round. There is a chance that a request to sign a confidentiality agreement at the time the entrepreneurs contact the IVCF may discourage its GPs from entering into further contacts with the start-up, because of the risk that a confidentiality agreement entails for the recipient of confidential information. At this stage, clearly there is no corporate opportunity legal protection, as the IVCF has not invested yet in the start-up, or appointed any of its directors.

[116] Information asymmetry is not the only problem in this stage. In Gilson's words: 'All financial contracts respond to three central problems: uncertainty, information asymmetry, and opportunism in the form of agency costs. The special character of venture capital contracting is shaped by the fact that investing in early stage, high technology companies presents these problems in an extreme form'. See Gilson, 'Engineering a Venture Capital Market' (2003) 1076.

[117] S Glücksman, 'Entrepreneurial Experiences from Venture Capital Funding: Exploring Two-sided Information Asymmetry' (2020) 22 *Venture Capital* 331, 345.

[118] This is the underlying assumption of some of the models that have analysed the welfare implications of this problem from an economics perspective. See S Bhattacharya and J Ritter, 'Innovation and Communication: Signalling with Partial Disclosure' (1983) 50 *Review of Economic Studies* 331. Even from a wide welfare perspective, the effects of disclosure are ambiguous: on one hand the diffusion of information contributes to the advancement of technology; on the other hand, the public appropriability of information contributes to reducing private incentives to R&D.

[119] E Miao and B Helwig, 'Avoiding Common IP Pitfalls: What Every Startup Needs to Know' (2018) 16 *Snippets* 1, 2.

D. Post-Formation Misappropriations of Corporate Opportunities

After the company has been formed and IVCFs have entered with their equity capital into the start-up, the chance of opportunistic behaviours may exponentially grow on both sides. The body of literature on business opportunism and VC is wide, although not particularly focused on corporate opportunities.[120] A distinctive trait of such literature is a progressive change of perspective, from an economic agency (ie unilateral) to a prisoners' dilemma (ie bilateral) approach. When observing the relationship between IVCFs and entrepreneurs from an economic agency perspective, we may be tempted to consider an entrepreneur as an agent of the IVCF, because often the cash comes entirely from the IVCF.[121] Hence, we may base our conflict-of-interest assessment on the idea that the entrepreneur could try to conceal information from the IVCF and to act opportunistically. In turn, following the classic economic agency paradigm, we may suppose that the IVCF, by appointing its GPs on the board of the start-up, may undertake monitoring of the entrepreneur's behaviours. Nonetheless, one may wonder whether such an economic agency paradigm adequately reflects the role of IVCFs within start-ups.

In contrast to the agency perspective, if we consider a dilemma-based framework, we see both the IVCF and the entrepreneur as potential opportunists. They will both face the choice of whether to cooperate or not.[122] For cooperation to take place, there is a need for a high degree of information-sharing. Only through open communication on the technical and business ground can such a venture prosper through mutual cooperation.[123]

Both agency-costs-based models and dilemma-based models tend to assume a limited number of variables. A peculiarity of both models is that they deal with two actors, or better two categories of well-identified players, bearing conflicting interests, ie an IVCF, represented by a GP (who may also act in conflict with the IVCF who has appointed them),[124] and an entrepreneur. Such models might be employed quite successfully for describing only certain kinds of relationships in specific phases of the life of a start-up. When one introduces the dynamic element and a multiplicity of players (eg. more than one IVCF and more than one entrepreneur, with various conflicting interests that constantly change throughout the different phases of the investment), understanding business

[120] See, among many others, B King, 'Strategizing at Leading Venture Capital Firms: Of Planning, Opportunism and Deliberate Emergence' (2008) 41 *Long Range Planning* 345.

[121] R Amit, L Glosten and E Muller, 'Entrepreneurial Ability, Venture Investments, and Risk Sharing' (1990) 36 *Management Science* 1233; J Fiet, 'Reliance upon Informants in the Venture Capital Industry' (1995) 10 *Journal of Business Venturing* 195; M Van Osnabrugge, 'A Comparison of Business Angel and Venture Capitalist Investment Procedures: An Agency Theory-based Analysis' (2000) 2 *Venture Capital: An International Journal of Entrepreneurial Finance* 91.

[122] Cable and Shane, 'A Prisoner's Dilemma Approach' (1997); Shepherd and Zacharakis, 'The Venture Capitalist-Entrepreneur Relationship' (2001) 133ff.

[123] ibid.

[124] See text at section III.A and accompanying notes.

opportunism can become far more challenging. An escalation of opportunistic behaviours, such as the one described by Bartlett,[125] may well manifest itself also in the form of misappropriations of corporate opportunities.

In principle, any of the entrepreneurs and GPs sitting on the board of the start-up may be interested in appropriating corporate opportunities that are discovered inside or outside the start-up. For the start-up to keep working until it is able to market its invention, it is crucial that the different parties are kept together within the organisation and that their conflicts of interests are prevented or solved. Entrepreneurs and IVCFs may be kept together also by extra-legal factors that may contribute to prevent the misappropriation of corporate opportunities, such as information asymmetries and difficult access to financing.

For instance, IVCF-appointed directors on the board of a start-up may need some time to learn about the technical details of the project developed within the start-up in order to be able to appropriate it. However, persuading an alternative financer to take part in the deal may be far more difficult for the entrepreneur than for the IVCF.

Besides extra-legal factors, there are the legal tools that are employed for containing the conflicts of interest arising in the VC context. To provide an accurate picture of the situation, one may distinguish between contractual and non-contractual tools. One may also want to keep in mind the different categories of conflicts arising throughout the life of a start-up, such as conflicts between IVCF and entrepreneur and conflicts between IVCFs.[126] Conflicts between entrepreneurs, ie between founders, have already been analysed in chapter five.[127] When analysing such relationships, a variable which is deeply intertwined with the legal one is the reputational one: in fact, breach of contract or breach of mandatory rules, even when economically efficient, can have reputational consequences in such a clustered environment.

Beside the reputational constraints, a relationship may be simply cemented by reciprocal trust, which may or not be based also on the default protection offered by legal rules.[128] Trust is particularly important in VC cross-border contexts, where one may often observe syndication between foreign and local IVCFs. For instance, Hain, Johan and Wang have found that normally institutional trust is particularly important in developing economies, whereas relational trust is the most relevant form of trust in developed economies.[129] In their words:

> Institutional trust is present ex-ante to the interaction and refers to the trust in the institutional environment, which includes institutional factors related to the legal

[125] See text corresponding to n 91.

[126] Note that the degree of complexity of the conflicts within such a start-up may even increase exponentially when further categories of investors survive from earlier rounds, such as angel investors or corporate venture capitalists. See S Nir, 'One Duty to All: The Fiduciary Duty of Impartiality and Stockholders' Conflict of Interest' (2020) 16 *Hastings Business Law Journal* 1, 26.

[127] See text at ch 5.X.

[128] See text corresponding to n 62.

[129] Hain, Johan and Wang, 'Determinants of Cross-Border Venture Capital Investments' (2016).

framework and its enforceability as well as soft factors, such as a society's attitude to behave fairly and honestly. In contrast, relational trust ex-post unfolds gradually through repeated interactions over time.[130]

Even once mutual trust has built up in the course of a CVF-entrepreneur relationship, it can easily deteriorate in later stages.[131] This is why, trust being a mutable variable, the legal factor is particularly relevant in the course of the whole VC experience, providing stability to the relationships among different constituencies. Legal rules will represent the default regime when trust no longer holds. When intellectual property (IP) protection is not available or suitable to protect inventions,[132] contractual and non-contractual legal tools will be employed for dividing the entitlements to the fruits of the creative activity carried out within the start-up.

E. Contractual and Non-Contractual Legal Instruments for the Allocation of Business Opportunities within a Start-up

One might think that it would be sensible to start an analysis of the legal instruments that are normally employed to contain conflicts over the allocation of business opportunities among the different constituencies of a start-up by focusing first on angel investors (wealthy individuals who provide financial backing in exchange for equity in the start-up). This might help in gaining further insights on the legal technique at the early stages of a new venture, when the information asymmetry is remarkably high. Nonetheless, the nature of the relationships between angel investors and entrepreneurs tends to be rather informal from the outset.[133] Angel investors seem to mitigate their investment risk by way of investing small sums more than by reverting to refined contractual protection.[134] Extra-legal factors, such as trust, are particularly important in the angel–entrepreneur relationship.[135] Of course, one cannot exclude the possibility that, through personal relationships with entrepreneurs, angel

[130] ibid 747.

[131] See S Panda, S Srivastava and S Pandey, 'Nature and Evolution of Trust in Business-to-Business Settings: Insights from VC-Entrepreneur Relationships' (2020) 91 *Industrial Marketing Management* 246. The article documents the mechanisms of transition from trust to distrust in an empirical study on Indian VC.

[132] S Samila and O Sorenson, 'Noncompete Covenants: Incentives to Innovate or Impediments to Growth' (2011) 57 *Management Science* 425, 427.

[133] R Harrison and C Mason, 'Backing the Horse or the Jockey? Due Diligence, Agency Costs, Information and the Evaluation of Risk by Business Angel Investors' (2017) 15 *International Review of Entrepreneurship* 269.

[134] D Ibrahim, 'The (Not So) Puzzling Behavior of Angel Investors' (2008) 61 *Vanderbilt Law Review* 1405, 1419.

[135] Y Bammens and V Collewaert, 'Trust between Entrepreneurs and Angel Investors: Exploring Positive and Negative Implications for Venture Performance Assessments' (2014) 40 *Journal of Management* 1980; Z Ding, K Au and F Chiang, 'Social Trust and Angel Investors' Decisions: A Multilevel Analysis across Nations' (2015) 30 *Journal of Business Venturing* 307.

investors will attempt to extract and exploit business-valuable information from start-ups, or that entrepreneurs will misuse the financing they received from angel investors. Nonetheless, should these occur, they are likely to be solved mostly through informal dispute resolution or simply through exit.[136] Even when an issue reaches the courts, it is likely to fall outside the reach of corporate law. In fact, involvement of angel investors in the boards of directors of start-ups seems to be rare and marginal as compared to the involvement normally enjoyed by IVCFs' GPs.[137] Therefore the application of corporate opportunity rules to such takings is highly unlikely, unless the taker of the opportunity is the entrepreneur.

In contrast to angel investors, IVCFs are renowned for employing very sophisticated and specialised lawyers[138] who can fully grasp the role of the corporate opportunity doctrine in containing conflicts of interest between IVCFs and entrepreneurs, as well as the role of the other contractual and non-contractual legal tools with similar functions. Legal protection achieved through contracting (eg a non-disclosure agreement) is normally characterised by flexibility, and it can be as well-engineered as allowed by the consulting expertise, matured in the field, by the specific legal practitioner involved in drafting the relevant clauses.[139] Non-contractual protection (eg corporate opportunity rules) tends to be less flexible in nature because it normally contains mandatory law elements.

Apart from corporate opportunity rules, another typical area of non-contractual protection is that pertaining to IP rights, which is not the subject of this analysis.[140] When IP rights are set on a given invention, the role of corporate opportunity rules can be only residual. It is also worth remembering that non-contractual protection can consist of both default and mandatory rules and that the lawmaker can turn formerly mandatory rules into default rules, as occurred in Delaware for the corporate opportunity doctrine.[141]

[136] V Collewaert and Y Fassin, 'Conflicts between Entrepreneurs and Investors: The Impact of Perceived Unethical Behavior' (2013) 40 *Small Business Economics* 635, 639ff.

[137] A Wong, 'Angel Finance. The Other Venture Capital' in Cumming (n 10) 71, 83.

[138] M Ueda, 'Banks Versus Venture Capital: Project Evaluation, Screening, and Expropriation' (2004) 59 *Journal of Finance* 601, 602 notices that 'a legal environment that supports through venture capitalists is one that strongly protects rights'. There is a stream of literature that analyses the crucial role of lawyers to VC in highly inventive clusters such as Silicon Valley: M Suchman and M Cahill, 'The Hired Gun as Facilitator: Lawyers and the Suppression of Business Disputes in Silicon Valley' (1996) 21 *Law & Social Inquiry* 679; L Bernstein, 'The Silicon Valley Lawyer as Transaction Cost Engineer' (1995) 74 *Oregon Law Review* 239. For a comparative approach of the effects of the legal variable on other high-tech developed clusters around the world, see A Chander, 'How Law Made Silicon Valley' (2013) 63 *Emory Law Journal* 639.

[139] Although clearly also confidentiality agreements encounter the limit of public policy. See C Bast, 'At What Price Silence: Are Confidentiality Agreements Enforceable?' (1999) 25 *William Mitchell Law Review* 627, 694ff.

[140] And this is of course an entirely different universe with reference to VC-backed start-ups. See M Lemley, 'Reconceiving Patents in the Age of Venture Capital' (2000) 4 *Journal of Small and Emerging Business Law* 137.

[141] See text at ch 7.V and accompanying notes.

VC contractual praxis is not widely accessible to the public.[142] Nonetheless, some relevant empirical research on VC contractual praxis has been carried out by researchers with privileged access to the relevant sources. Such research opens a window into a rather mysterious world.[143]

Firstly, IVCFs usually succeed in including in contracts many clauses that allow them to exercise control over the entrepreneurs, and in general their bargaining power has effects not only on the 'division of the pie', but also on the very contract design.[144] IVCFs can defend their investment from entrepreneurs who do not perform efficiently not only through vesting provisions,[145] but also by dismissing them from a CEO or a director position, which is something to which IVCFs tend to revert to quite easily.[146] When combined with stage financing and negative covenants on major start-up decisions, this sets very strict legal constraints on the entrepreneur, where their only chance is to work hard and succeed.[147] Such harsh bargaining in favour of the IVCF can be read as offering 'the entrepreneur a powerful incentive to perform'.[148] Nonetheless, a strong IVCF decision, such as a CEO's dismissal, could in principle be employed in an abusive way and severely damage the entrepreneur, especially when it occurs before the vesting of their equity.[149]

An expropriation of the start-up by IVCFs to the detriment of the entrepreneur can take place in many ways; for example, through equity tunnelling, ie by way of below-fair-value issuance of new equity aimed at diluting the entrepreneur's equity position.[150] It can also occur directly by way of transfer of assets to other companies in which the IVCF has invested.[151] Misappropriation of corporate opportunities can be understood as a form of direct asset misappropriation.

Gilson shows convincingly that in the US VC context there is a fine balance of interests provided by a set of factors within and outside VC contracts that

[142] Although the US National Venture Capital Association (NVCA) provides a few contract samples at nvca.org/model-legal-documents.

[143] See fn 19 and also P Gompers and J Lerner, 'The Use of Covenants: An Empirical Analysis of Venture Partnership Agreements' (1996) 39 *The Journal of Law and Economics* 463; S Williams, 'Venture Capital Contract Design: An Empirical Analysis of the Connection Between Bargaining Power and Venture Financing Contract Terms' (2017) 23 *Fordham Journal of Corporate & Financial Law* 105.

[144] Williams, 'Venture Capital Contract Design' (2017).

[145] T Hellmann, 'The Allocation of Control Rights in Venture Capital Contracts' (1998) 29 *The Rand Journal of Economics* 57, 58 n 3: '"Vesting" is a legal arrangement in which the entrepreneurs' shares are originally held by the company. Entrepreneurs receive title to these shares according to some contractually specified schedule'.

[146] T Hellmann and M Puri, 'Venture Capital and the Professionalization of Start-up Firms: Empirical Evidence' (2002) 57 *Journal of Finance* 169.

[147] Gilson (n 82) 1083.

[148] ibid.

[149] Broughman, 'Investor Opportunism' (2010) 352.

[150] V Atanasov, B Black and C Ciccotello, 'Unbundling and Measuring Tunneling' (2014) *University of Illinois Law Review* 1697, 1707.

[151] V Atanasov, 'Conflicts of Interest and Litigation in the Venture Capital Industry' in Cumming (n 10) 365, 367.

mitigate the risk of opportunistic behaviours by directors appointed by IVCFs to the boards of start-ups. In fact, GPs' (often almost total) control over start-up activities[152] comes at a price. This price is not immediately evident, because it is hidden in the complex intertwining of the interests of the different types of investors in the IVCF, on the one hand, and of the entrepreneurs, on the other. The compensation of GPs appointed on a start-up's board (mostly coming in the form of carried interests on the VC's ultimate profits)[153] provides an incentive for GPs to commit to the start-up constantly until exit.[154]

Another important point is provided in Atanasov's explanation of Gilson's arguments against the profitability of equity tunnelling. Atanasov notes that:

> [C]ontracts between VCs and their investors help protect entrepreneurs against dilutive down-rounds, because when a VC depresses the price of an investment round, the VC has to use the same price to mark down his entire investment in the start-up. The mark-down will depress the reported value of the VC portfolio, and the VC will have to report poor annual performance to his investors.[155]

It is worth noting that Gilson's fine reconstruction of the counter-incentive for GPs to behave opportunistically is reinforced by what he describes as the 'braiding' of the VC portfolio company contract with the investor–IVCF contract.[156] Nonetheless, Gilson does not delve thoroughly into the hypothesis of asset tunnelling, which may also occur within a start-up. His contribution was written on the verge of the Delaware General Corporation Law (DGCL) reform, introducing the possibility of a waiver for corporate opportunity rules.[157] It goes without saying that such a waiver, when introduced in a start-up in favour of GPs, may at least in principle facilitate asset tunnelling by an IVCF to the detriment of the start-up, in the form of misappropriation of business opportunities.

Asset tunnelling pursued by GPs in their own interest, if discovered, will irremediably compromise the relationship between GP and IVCF and may also bear significant reputational repercussions for the GP who has acted inappopriately.[158] Nonetheless, this will not necessarily be the case if the GP engages in asset tunnelling on behalf of the IVCF.[159] One may also ask whether asset tunnelling would meet the same kind of general constraints described with reference to equity tunnelling. The specific devaluation problem described by Atanasov[160] does not seem to occur in a similar way in the case of asset tunnelling, especially because the repercussions of asset tunnelling on the financial statements of the company may not be immediate, particularly in the case of a misappropriation

152 Gilson (n 82) 1088.
153 ibid 1089.
154 ibid.
155 Atanasov, 'Conflicts of Interest' (2010) 374.
156 Gilson (n 82) 1091.
157 DGCL, s 122(17).
158 See text at section III.A and accompanying notes.
159 ibid.
160 Atanasov (n 151).

of a corporate opportunity which may have never been disclosed to the board and therefore has had no impact on accounting.

Apart from the cited difference, in a start-up context, misappropriations may be hard to prove. There can be cases in which it is difficult to determine where a business idea has first been encountered or has first appeared, because of the nature of the circulation of information in industrial districts.[161] If one cannot clearly localise the business idea at issue within a given start-up then one cannot even propose a claim based on a misappropriation, because the proprietary boundaries of the information at stake are at least unclear. The opportunity may also be considered as being in the public domain. Evidence of a misappropriation of a business opportunity must rely at least upon two prongs: firstly, it must be proven that a well-defined business opportunity object of exploitation within start-up Alpha coincides with the one earlier discovered in start-up Beta; and secondly, it must be proven that the misappropriation occurred through the action of a director of the start-up Alpha.

With the first prong, the more developed, the more technical in nature and the more easily identifiable the business opportunity, the easier it will be to prove that it is the object of a misappropriation. For instance, when identical technical calculations developed within a given start-up appear in another start-up, such a duplication could provide evidence that there was a misappropriation, unless the defendant can prove that such calculations were developed concomitantly and independently. But what about where the business opportunity at issue consists of a contract to be concluded with a third party for developing a joint product? In this case, it may be much more difficult to prove that there was a misappropriation, especially within an industrial cluster.[162] For example, it might be the case that the cited third party first meets the board of start-up Alpha and then the board of start-up Beta. At the start of these interactions, the third party is interested in contracting with Alpha, but ends up contracting with Beta. Alpha might claim that there was a misappropriation of a corporate opportunity if the same GP sits on the board of both Alpha and Beta: it could try to provide evidence that the GP has contributed to convincing the third party to contract with Beta. Nonetheless, such evidence could be hard to provide. The shift of a corporate opportunity from one company to the other may simply be the consequence of the fact that VC tends to encourage start-ups to enter into relationships with each other, forming a so-called 'Keirestu network'.[163] In other words, temporary infatuations, quick marriages and quicker divorces may simply a feature of a highly communitarian environment.

As to the second prong, things are not always crystal-clear there either. Say for instance that two GPs of the same IVCF, Sarah and Rachel, invest in four

[161] See text at section IV.A and accompanying notes.

[162] ibid.

[163] L Lindsey, 'Blurring Firm Boundaries: The Role of Venture Capital in Strategic Alliances' (2008) 63 *Journal of Finance* 1137.

different start-ups, A, B, C and D, all competing for the same (potential) product market. Sarah invests in A and B; Rachel invests in C and D. Imagine also that it is possible to prove that a given business opportunity is first 'found' in A and that, in principle, it can also be profitably pursued by start-ups B, C and D. We now have to consider separately the hypotheses that such a business opportunity is moved to and exploited by start-up B or alternatively by start-up C.

In the case where the business opportunity is exploited by start-up B, the personal connection between A and B is very clear, and one may infer that Sarah has disclosed the start-up A's business information to start-up B, unless she can provide evidence of an alternative path through which the information has reached start-up B. But what about the case where the business opportunity is pursued by start-up C? In this case, there is no personal connection between start-ups A and C, because the IVCF at issue has appointed two different GPs to their boards of A and C, respectively Sarah and Rachel. One may argue that Sarah has no interest in moving start-up A's corporate opportunity to start-up C, managed by Rachel, as Sarah will be interested in A's most profitable exit. Nonetheless, one cannot exclude back-scratching scenarios, where there is a mutual shifting of corporate opportunities (eg Sarah moves a corporate opportunity from start-up A to C and Rachel moves a corporate opportunity from start-up D to B, this time helping Rachel).

One may wonder why a GP would decide to revert to such a cumbersome arrangement and not simply keep corporate opportunities within the start-up where they were found or conceived. There could be several reasons for engaging in mutual back-scratching as described above. For instance, it may happen that Sarah has understood the real value of the corporate opportunity discovered in A too late and has underinvested in A. For instance, she may not have subscribed to the later rounds of financing and therefore she may not be expecting a remarkable profit from A's exit even in the case that such an exit turns out to be very successful. Alternatively, Sarah may have realised that although the business opportunity is valuable, A's team is highly conflictual and therefore is unlikely to pursue such an opportunity efficiently.[164] Therefore, instead of losing the business opportunity to the IVCF, following an IVCF maximisation rationale, Sarah could be prompted to 'save' the business opportunity and have it pursued by C, which has a higher potential for growth.[165]

It should be borne in mind that real-world scenarios may not be as simple as the example that I have just proposed. There may well be cases where different GPs join and leave different start-ups throughout time. In such contexts, their financial interests may change, following their investment choices. This could be the case where the same GP starts as a director in start-up A and then is appointed in start-up B years after a corporate opportunity has been moved from A to B.

[164] For instance, she may have realised that there are disagreements within the company that create delays and at the same time a competitor is coming up with alternative business ideas.

[165] Woolf, 'Venture Capitalist' (2001) 493.

A real case concerning an alleged corporate opportunity misappropriation from a start-up and involving several GPs appointed by the same IVCF was dealt with in Alarm.com, a Delaware Chancery case decided in 2018.[166] In 2009, ABS Inc – a private equity firm specialising in later-stage growth companies – had acquired a controlling equity stake in Alarm Inc and had appointed Mr Terkowitz, an ABS partner, as a director and chairman of the board of Alarm, together with two more directors, also ABS partners, out of the five composing the board.

Before investing in Alarm and while exploring the possibility of such an investment opportunity, ABS had entered into a non-disclosure agreement with Alarm, expiring in December 2011. The non-disclosure agreement left ABS free to pursue investments in competing businesses, as long as it included a clause stating that no confidential information pertaining to Alarm would be disclosed to any competing company without prior written permission by Alarm.

In 2012, as a consequence of a corporate restructuring, Alarm was recapitalised, issuing shares to new investors. The number of its board members was increased to seven, and ABS agreed to appoint only two members. Mr Terkowitz continued to serve in the position of chairman of the board until 2016.

In 2012, Alarm's stockholders entered into a further confidentiality agreement. The 2012 confidentiality agreement still allowed ABS to share Alarm business information to 'permitted disclosees', including partners and former, current or prospective partners. Nonetheless, information-sharing could not take place without previous signing of the non-disclosure agreement also by 'permitted disclosees'. The 2012 Stakeholder Agreement included a corporate opportunity waiver – also to the benefit of ABS – stating that:

> [I]n the event that any Exempted Person acquires knowledge of a potential transaction or matter that may be a corporate opportunity for the Corporation, then such Exempted Person shall have no duty (contractual or otherwise) to communicate or present such corporate opportunity to the Company or any of its subsidiaries, as the case may be, and shall not be liable to the Company or its affiliates or stockholders for breach of any duty (contractual or otherwise) by reason of the fact that such Exempted Person, directly or indirectly, pursues or acquires such opportunity for itself, directs such opportunity to another person, or does not present such opportunity to the Company or any of its subsidiaries.[167]

In 2015, Alarm completed an IPO and was traded in NASDAQ, adopting a Code of Business Conduct addressing conflicts between investment funds and corporation stating that:

> In the interest of clarifying the definition of 'conflict of interest,' if any member of the Board who is also a partner or employee of an entity that is a holder of Alarm Common Stock, or an employee of an entity that manages such an entity

[166] *Alarm.com Holdings, Inc v ABS Capital Partners Inc*, CA No 2017-0583-JTL.
[167] ibid 9.

> (each, a 'Fund'), acquires knowledge of a potential transaction (investment transaction or otherwise) or other matter other than in connection with such individual's service as a member of the Board (including, if applicable, in such individual's capacity as a partner or employee of the Fund or the manager or GP of a Fund) that may be an opportunity of interest for both the Company and such Fund (a 'Corporate Opportunity'), then, provided that such director has acted reasonably and in good faith with respect to the best interests of the corporation, such an event shall be deemed not to be a 'conflict of interest' under this policy.[168]

Mr Terkowitz had regularly attended the board meetings and acquired information on Alarm business strategies. In 2014 and 2016 in particular, he had obtained access to Alarm secret trade information that 'was too sensitive to ever be placed in writing or be included in the board decks'.[169]

In 2017, ABS purchased a significant equity stake in Resolution Inc, a direct competitor of Alarm. It also appointed Phil Clough – an ABS partner without any previous connection to Alarm – to the board of Resolution. Alarm sued ABS, stating that by acquiring Resolution, ABS had used Alarm's trade secrecy. Alarm did not specify how this might have taken place. One may infer from Alarm's claim that it had interpreted the acquisition of Resolution as a per se breach of its non-disclosure agreements. Underlying this claim was an alleged transfer of information pertaining to Alarm from Mr Terkowitz to ABS. While rejecting Alarm's claims, the Delaware Chancery Court stated that:

> When a corporation has waived that claim, it gives up the most powerful remedial tool that a court of equity possesses. Once a corporation has given up its most effective check on fiduciary misbehaviour, it would be counterintuitive to permit the same corporation to pursue the lesser theories that could be asserted against a non-fiduciary. Respecting the waiver contemplated by Section 122(17) requires that courts not attempt to forge a fiduciary substitute.[170]

The Alarm.com decision sheds light on several legal issues that may surround misappropriations of business opportunities in VC-backed start-ups contexts. Firstly, it may be difficult to prove that there is an actual misappropriation (in this case, there was a sort of intuition concerning a potential misappropriation, backed only by a rather loose allegation of a breach of a trade secret). Secondly, when the same IVCF appoints two different GPs in two competing start-ups, the transfer of sensible information from one partner to the other cannot be automatically inferred.

The Alarm.com decision is also particularly important because it states an important principle with reference to the relationship between a corporate opportunity waiver and the possibility to employ legal tools for the protection of business ideas that are alternative to the corporate opportunity doctrine, such as for instance non-disclosure agreements. The Delaware Chancery makes

[168] ibid 10.
[169] ibid 11.
[170] ibid 18–19.

it clear that a waiver for the strictest rules (corporate opportunity rules) also implies a waiver for the looser ones (non-disclosure agreements).

The Alarm.com decision also provides a practical example of the coexistence of multiple layers of rules with similar functions. Apart from non-disclosure rules, empirical research has shown that also non-compete agreements are extremely common in VC legal practice. For instance, Kaplan and Strömberg have found empirical evidence of widespread use of non-compete clauses in their sample.[171]

Nonetheless, it has to be made clear that non-compete clauses are usually established for the benefit of the IVCF.[172] Alarm.com makes it clear that, even in the unlikely case that such clauses are introduced in favour of the entrepreneur, a waiver of the corporate opportunity doctrine may have the effect of nullifying such additional protection. If that is the case, one may wonder what protections are enjoyed by the entrepreneur against potential abusive conduct by IVCFs consisting of asset tunnelling. It may look like there is no legal protection at all once a waiver for corporate opportunities has been introduced.[173]

Without corporate opportunity rules, the main source of constraints for an IVCF intending to move business opportunities from one start-up to another may be of a reputational nature.[174] Waivers for corporate opportunity rules awarded to IVCFs are usually intended to solve problems deriving from 'divided loyalty'.[175] Normally, 'divided loyalty' does not describe situations where a GP moves corporate opportunities to one start-up to another to the detriment of the first. Instead, it usually depicts a situation where a GP becomes aware of a business opportunity and can offer it only to one of the start-ups on whose boards they sit.[176] It can also describe cases where, by pure chance, the same business opportunity emerges in different start-ups (eg two start-ups are contacted by the same third party to develop a joint project) and only one of them will be able to pursue it (eg the third party will be able to contract with only one of the two start-ups). In this case, a GP also serving as a director in several start-ups will only be able to 'serve one of the two masters'.

By contrast with the previous examples, situations of divided loyalty can be induced by a GP in pursuance of self-interest. This can be done in ways that are not detectable at first sight. Dessi discusses the case where an IVCF, in pursuance of the most efficient strategy possible, can constrain an entrepreneur to abandon a project 'that he finds particularly interesting (e.g. it was "his idea"), or one that could give him considerable personal prestige, even though their expected

[171] Kaplan and Strömberg (n 19) 292 and 289, Table 2(E).
[172] Woolf (n 20) 495.
[173] Atanasov (n 151) 374.
[174] D Hsu, 'What Do Entrepreneurs Pay for Venture Capital Affiliation?' (2004) 59 *Journal of Finance* 1805, 1807, shows that 'entrepreneurs are willing to forego offers with higher valuations in order to affiliate with more reputable VCs'.
[175] Woolf (n 20) 473–74.
[176] ibid 490.

profitability is much lower than for an alternative project'.[177] The point is that unfortunately the same control powers can be employed for forcing the entrepreneur to relinquish a project which has a very high profitability, with the excuse that it seems too risky. Given the uncertainty that surrounds the majority of start-up projects, an IVCF could justify this quite easily. Later, the same project may be pursued in another start-up where the same IVCF has also invested. If this occurs after some time, it may be difficult to provide evidence of a misappropriation. In situations where there is no clear evidence of a misappropriation, reputational sanctions may not be effective.

Gilson has described the conditions under which reputational sanctions may work effectively:

> For a reputation market to operate, three attributes must be present. First, the party whose discretion will be policed by the market must anticipate repeated future transactions. Second, participants must have shared expectations of what constitutes appropriate behaviour by the party to whom discretion has been transferred. Finally, those who will deal with the advantaged party in the future must be able to observe whether that party's behaviour in past dealings conforms to shared expectations.[178]

Gilson concludes that 'All three of these attributes appear present in the venture capital market'.[179] The idea underlying reputational sanctions in this context is that even if the entrepreneur is normally not a repeat player, they may be able to communicate their disappointment for an IVCF's misconduct to their peers.[180] IT has rendered such communication easier, in particular through dedicated platforms.[181] Nonetheless, as already noted, observability may not be immediate in certain cases, such as the one proposed above.[182] Moreover, observability seems to be predictable in geographically clustered environments such as the one analysed by Gilson, ie Sand Hill Road in Silicon Valley.[183] Not all IVCFs operate in such a clustered environment. Hence observability cannot be intended as a generalised occurrence.

Reputational constraints can be raised to a more significant level when an IVCF is involved in litigation. According to empirical research, about half of the allegations in disputes involving VC have to do with tunnelling, and a significant proportion of this half involve misappropriations of corporate opportunities.[184] Empirical research shows that IVCFs involved in litigation tend to raise significant less capital than their peers and also to lose their access to the best investment opportunities.[185] This may depend on the fact that information on

[177] R Dessi, 'Venture Capitalists, Monitoring and Advising' in Cumming (n 10) 169, 170.
[178] Gilson (n 82) 1086.
[179] ibid.
[180] Broughman (n 72) 352.
[181] ibid.
[182] See text corresponding to n 177.
[183] Gilson (n 82) 1087.
[184] Atanasov (n 151) 381.
[185] Atanasov, Ivanov and Litvak (n 64) 2244.

their conduct can become publicly available when a lawsuit is brought against a VC.[186] Nonetheless, it is also true that involvement in litigation may not necessarily mean that a IVCF is guilty of a misappropriation. It may also be victim of a hazardous litigation attempt. As to economic incentives to litigate, given that most claims against IVCFs tend to be unsuccessful, and also given the stage financing constraints,[187] entrepreneurs may decide not to revert to such dispute resolution methods.[188]

There also seem to be virtuous and non-virtuous path-dependencies in VC litigation. Atanasov, Ivanov and Litvak have demonstrated that on a per-deal basis, IVCFs that have engaged in litigation in the past are more likely to engage in litigation again.[189] This may provide evidence of the fact that at least when dealing with less-reputable IVCFs, or when operating in environments where reputational sanctions are less likely to work, the legal protection granted by the corporate opportunity doctrine may be of the utmost importance. Therefore, it may well be that those environments where VC has not developed to a full extent may not be ready to welcome corporate opportunity waivers without their potential drawbacks.

F. The Legal Aspects of the Conflicts of Interests Among Venture Capital Funds Acting in Syndication

Apart from the protection deriving from an IVCF's reputational constraints vis-à-vis prospective start-ups, an entrepreneur may seem to be rather unprotected from asset tunnelling by an IVCF via misappropriations of corporate opportunities, especially when corporate opportunity doctrines have been waived. Nonetheless, protection from an IVCF's opportunistic conduct may derive from further non-legal factors, such as those depending on the relationships between IVCFs.

While conflicts between IVCFs which are in syndication are not infrequent,[190] there are valid reasons why IVCFs may want to avoid such conflicts at any cost, especially those which are based on a clearly disreputable activity, such as asset tunnelling. In fact, whereas equity dilution may be justified by a 'pay-for-play' rationale, one may argue that asset diversion is an outright 'theft' which is rather difficult to justify from an efficiency perspective. Therefore, one may expect a degree of monitoring activity by IVCFs of each other, in order to detect potential misappropriations.[191]

[186] ibid.
[187] Woolf (n 20) 475 and 490.
[188] ibid.
[189] Atanasov, Ivanov and Litvak (n 64) 2236.
[190] See text at section III.C and accompanying notes.
[191] Woolf (n 20) 504.

One may wonder what an IVCF would lose if it had to be excluded from syndication. Quasi-rents deriving from syndication are considerable. Firstly, losing one's reputation of being trustworthy and reliable may mean losing excellent future investment opportunities. In fact, often some of the best investment opportunities are made available to an IVCF through so-called warm referrals, which come from other trusted IVCFs.[192] Syndication also increases the chances of gaining access to a larger number of investment targets.[193] Taking part in several successful financing rounds does not only allow an IVCF to diversify its investments.[194] It also facilitates 'window dressing', so improving the image of an IVCF within the start-up community.[195] Apart from such a potential adverse effect on future investment opportunities, there is also a series of 'softer' benefits deriving from syndication which would be lost, such as, for instance, the fact that syndication allows IVCFs to supplement each other's management experience.[196] Moreover, in general syndication tends to reduce the cost of due diligence, because several IVCFs can cooperate to source and process relevant information pertaining to prospective investments.[197] All the described features of syndication are particularly remarkable in the US VC environment.[198]

Given that the quasi-rents deriving from syndication with other reputable IVCFs can be considerable, opportunism (or at least certain forms of opportunism) to the detriment of other IVCFs may end up being rare.[199] Atanasov explains with a practical example what reputational constraints deriving from syndication would look like in the case of several IVCFs holding equity in the same start-up. He focuses on the case of equity dilution. In fact, say Alpha, Beta and Gamma, all reputable IVCFs, participate in round 1 financing, but Gamma does not participate in round 2. If Alpha and Beta try to dilute common shareholders (ie entrepreneurs, in most cases) by setting a low price in round 2, Gamma's investment will also be diluted. Thanks to Alpha's and Beta's interest in preserving their relationship with Gamma, the entrepreneurs' financial interests will also be spared from dilution.[200]

One can imagine that a non-legal protection deriving from reputational constraint among IVCF works in the same way in the case of misappropriation of corporate opportunities. Nonetheless, for corporate opportunities, one may

[192] Zacharakis, 'Venture Capital' (2010) 12ff.

[193] D Cumming, 'The Determinants of Venture Capital Portfolio Size: Empirical Evidence' (2006) 79 *Journal of Business* 1083.

[194] R Wilson, 'The Theory of Syndicates' (1968) 36 *Econometrica* 119; W Bygrave, 'Syndicated Investments by Venture Capital Firms: A Networking Perspective' (1987) 2 *Journal of Business Venturing* 139.

[195] J Lerner, 'The Syndication of Venture Capital Investments' (1994) 23 *Financial Management* 16.

[196] J Brander, R Amit and W Antweiler, 'Venture Capital Syndication: Improved Venture Selection versus the Value-Added Hypothesis' (2002) 11 *Journal of Economics and Management Strategy* 423.

[197] Zacharakis (n 100) 21.

[198] Compare this to the main features of the EU syndication among IVCFs as described in the text at section VI and accompanying notes.

[199] Atanasov, Ivanov and Litvak (n 64) 2020.

[200] Atanasov (n 151) 377.

also imagine alternative scenarios, and not all of them are equally favourable to the entrepreneur. Firstly, there might be cases of mutual back-scratching among IVCFs willing to appropriate corporate opportunities. Secondly, in a different scenario, conflicts with entrepreneurs arise with reference to the timing and/or modality of pursuance of business opportunities. IVCFs' interest may well be aligned in terms of attempting to transfer opportunities to other start-ups where they also syndicate. In fact, reciprocity is common in syndication.[201] In this case, only the reputational constraints vis-à-vis the entrepreneur will be in place, which in turn, as already stated, may not always be effective.[202] Therefore, the entrepreneur may feel protected from misappropriation only if the corporate opportunity doctrine has not been waived in favour of IVCFs.

It has to be noted that protection mechanisms similar to those that exist in cases of VC syndication may occur also when a start-up is backed by outside debt. In fact, especially when it is particularly intense, asset tunnelling can lead the company to bankruptcy. In case of bankruptcy, a bank can claim the assets back by alleging fraudulent conveyance.[203] This can act as a deterrent against the VC.[204]

G. Corporate Opportunity Doctrine on the Verge of Exit

A final note concerns the corporate opportunity doctrine and the specific conflicts of interests that surround exit. Firstly, one is accustomed to considering exit as a strategy that pertains to IVCFs, but entrepreneurs may also want to exit their investment at some point. At times, they will be forced to leave.[205] In the VC capital context, entrepreneurs' exits may be surrounded by legal hindrances and many uncertainties. Utset reminds us that there are

> various contractual provisions that, as a whole, make voluntary or involuntary entrepreneurial exits very costly: (1) vesting schedules for stock awards, (2) requirements to sell back stock at book value, (3) non-compete agreements, (4) non-disclosure agreements, and (5) the corporate opportunity doctrine.[206]

Entrepreneurs' exits create perverse informational counterincentives for the entrepreneur to withhold part of their technological knowledge, hoping to be able to exploit it in their new activity.[207] As Utset states:

> While venture capitalists usually expect that the venture will be restricted to the one original innovation, the corporate opportunity, non-disclosure, non-compete, and

[201] Zacharakis (n 100) 12.
[202] See text corresponding to nn 182–85.
[203] Broughman (n 72) 352.
[204] ibid.
[205] See text at ch 5.II and accompanying notes.
[206] M Utset, 'Reciprocal Fairness, Strategic Behavior and Venture Survival: A Theory of Venture Capital-Financed Firms' (2002) *Wisconsin Law Review* 45, 154.
[207] ibid 137–38.

> trade secret constraints increase the probability that a second innovation will be deemed the property of the venture. This informational problem is exacerbated by the general difficulty of establishing clear-cut property rights over the information.[208]

This is why I believe that the potentiality of the waiver first experienced in DGCL has not been explored yet and could be employed also for tackling this kind of problem, by way of distributing equitably the fruits of the innovation between VC and entrepreneur.

Also, given the set of anti-exit provisions depicted above, entrepreneurs may find it difficult to exit without the agreement of the IVCF. By contrast, for IVCFs, exit is physiological and is ultimately the reason why an IVCF agrees to invest in a start-up. According to Cumming and Macintosh, there are five principal ways for an IVCF to exit its investment.[209] First, it can revert to an IPO. Second, the company can be sold to a third acquirer – this operation being known as an acquisition exit. Third, an IVCF can simply sell its own shares in the company. Fourth, the entrepreneurs can operate a buyback, purchasing the IVCF's shares. Fifth, an IVCF can write off its investment, and this usually occurs when the company fails.

As a general observation, one may notice that a valuable corporate opportunity, when pursued, increases the value of the company. The announcement of the future exploitation of a corporate opportunity may also increase the company's value. For an investor intending to exit, without considering reputational constraints, the best bargain would consist of selling its shares at the value that incorporates also actualised prospective corporate opportunities, while trading them in secret with third parties. In fact, pursuing a corporate opportunity requires time, and by the time it is implemented, the IVCF at issue would have already exited the investment.

If we analyse the incentives for am IVCF to move corporate opportunities to other investees, we can imagine that whenever the IVCF reverts to a partial exit, trying to shift business opportunities to other start-ups may entail a trade-off (loss in the value of the investment where the business opportunity originates). There are several reasons for partial exit. In the case of an IPO, the very high information asymmetry between retail investors and insiders may prompt prospective investors to free-ride on a reliable, informed third party. Athough expert investment bankers can usually be considered as reliable, in the case of high-tech firms, they may not be. In fact, as investment bankers are usually 'generalists', they are not likely to be knowledgeable in the area in which the VC-backed corporation operates. A VC still preserving a partial post-IPO investment in a corporation may provide a reliable signal to a prospective investor.[210]

[208] ibid.
[209] Cumming and Macintosh, 'A Cross-country Comparison' (2003) 512.
[210] ibid 517ff.

When an IVCF's exit is not partial, a misappropriation which is well-hidden or difficult to prove may not encounter any reputational sanctions, and in the presence of a waiver for the corporate opportunity doctrine, it may well go unpunished. This may prompt lawyers to design waivers ad hoc for this situation, by limiting the waiver to the investment phases occurring before exit, while preserving the applicability of the doctrine for resigning directors.

V. COMPLICATING THE TAXONOMY: CORPORATE VENTURE CAPITAL AND THE CORPORATE OPPORTUNITY PARADIGM

CVC consists of a well-established corporation investing in one or more start-ups and providing entrepreneurs with the technical expertise they need for the purpose of developing their business.[211] This investment technique may be less well known to the public than independent VC. Nowadays, most of the leading world corporations revert to this investment technique. Among them, one can recall for instance Google with GV (formerly Google Ventures),[212] Intel with Intel Capital,[213] Baidu with Baidu Ventures,[214] Legend with Legend Capital,[215] Salesforce with Salesforce Ventures,[216] and Samsung with Samsung Ventures.[217]

One may wonder why an established corporation would be willing to invest in start-ups. There are several potential reasons. Firstly, a company may simply bet on the profitability of the start-up. In this case, an established corporation can enter the capital of a start-up, often with a minority holding, and wait until exit.[218] An established corporation may well be able to estimate the chances of success of newcomers because it has knowledge of its own product market and also of those product markets that are on the same supply chain or are just slightly differentiated. This investment technique can correspond to what is known in economic literature as passive investment – that is, an investment which does not involve the active participation of the investor in the investee's industrial strategies.[219]

The interest of an established corporation for start-ups can go well beyond pursuing passive investment. Literature on CVC focuses especially on explorative and exploitative strategies. Exploration is usually directed towards generating

[211] M Maula, E Autio and G Murray, 'Corporate Venture Capitalists and Independent Venture Capitalists: What Do They Know, Who Do They Know and Should Entrepreneurs Care?' (2005) 7 *Venture Capital: An International Journal of Entrepreneurial Finance* 3, 6.

[212] www.gv.com.

[213] www.intel.com/content/www/us/en/intel-capital/overview.html.

[214] bv.ai/en.

[215] www.legendcapital.com.cn/en.

[216] www.salesforce.com/company/ventures.

[217] www.samsungventure.co.kr/english/jsp/investment/sector.jsp.

[218] H Chesbrough, 'Making Sense of Corporate Venture Capital' (2002) 80 *Harvard Business Review* 9, 9–10.

[219] ibid.

variation by way of investigating unknown technologies.[220] It 'is characterized by both high uncertainty and slow performance in learning outcomes',[221] but in the long run it may help an established corporation to embrace radical innovation.[222] By contrast, exploitation implies a direct use of the knowledge already held by another firm. Hence it is directed at improving the productive efficiency of the incumbent corporation in the present.[223] Exploitation is far more short-term-oriented than exploration, and it seems to be aimed at lesser radical innovations that can be easily integrated within the ongoing concern of the corporation.[224] Clearly, exploration does not exclude exploitation or vice versa. As a matter of fact, companies such as Samsung and Intel are renowned for engaging in both at the same time.[225] Moreover, literature shows that normally the most efficient CVC investment strategy, from the perspective of maximising innovation, consists of diversifying the portfolio of start-ups.[226]

A fourth potential strategy consists of what has been called an enabling investment.[227] In this case, the incumbent corporation aims to develop its ecosystem with a view to boosting demand for its products.[228] An example of enabling investment is provided by Intel, which in the 1990s invested heavily in companies that could spur demand for Intel's microprocessors.[229] Finally, another potential reason for investing in start-ups may have to do with an incumbent's concern for the emergence of potential competitors, whose dynamics may endanger the very existence of an incumbent corporation.[230] This strategy could be considered as a version of the exploration one, but with a negative connotation. An incumbent corporation may be willing to hold knowledge of potential competitors and control them in order to delay innovation, following a rationale similar to the one underlying the so-called killer mergers.[231] The ideas developed in an innovative start-up may be threatening for the incumbent corporation, especially when it has invested in an older technology with very high sunk costs. In fact, in the case where the technology developed by the start-up becomes the new standard, the incumbent may need to face those sunk costs while trying to adapt to disruption.[232]

[220] S Lee, G Park and J Kang, 'The Double-Edged Effects of the Corporate Venture Capital Unit's Structural Autonomy on Corporate Investors' Explorative and Exploitative Innovation' (2018) 88 *Journal of Business Research* 141.
[221] ibid 142.
[222] ibid.
[223] ibid.
[224] ibid.
[225] ibid 143.
[226] A Wadhwa, C Phelps and S Kotha, 'Corporate Venture Capital Portfolios and Firm Innovation' (2016) 31 *Journal of Business Venturing* 95, 96.
[227] Chesbrough, 'Corporate Venture Capital' (2002) 6–7.
[228] ibid.
[229] ibid.
[230] M Maula, T Keil and S Zahra, 'Top Management's Attention to Discontinuous Technological Change: Corporate Venture Capital as an Alert Mechanism' (2013) 24 *Organization Science* 926.
[231] See ch 5.
[232] Chs 2, 4 and 5.

On the entrepreneurial side, the reasons for entering into a CVC arrangement may be similar to the ones that occur in the case of pure VC financing.[233] An established corporation may be capable of providing a start-up with its expertise, thus helping it to overcome the main obstacles that arise while transforming a series of ideas into a marketable product.[234] There is statistical evidence of efficiencies resulting from CVC practice. According to empirical studies, a start-up's connection to CVC increases the start-up's likelihood of attracting prestigious underwriters when it goes public.[235] Therefore, CVC is often value-creating.

CVC can be structured in different ways. Such differences occur both in the organisational structure adopted by the investor and in the typologies of the investees. On the investor's side, there are cases where the corporation invests directly in start-ups, as well as cases where the corporation sets up a subsidiary which carries out the investment activity independently from the parent company.[236] On the investee's side, CVC can be either internal or external. In the case of internal CVC, the start-up is a subsidiary or a branch of the corporation.[237] If the business ideas developed in internal CVC prove interesting, the incumbent corporation may decide to spin-off the newly established line of business, and those ideas may be exploited within a start-up financed but not necessarily fully controlled by the incumbent corporation.[238] By contrast, external CVC is invested in business opportunities that are being implemented within a separate start-up company, which originally bears no financial or organisational connection to the corporation that provides CVC financing.[239] In the international praxis, external CVC tends to take the form of acquisition of minority shareholdings.[240]

While CVC can be value-creating and can accommodate the interests of both incumbent companies and novel entrepreneurs, such an investing technique can also be dense in terms of conflicts of interest. Of course, there can be cases where such conflicts of interest do not occur because the corporate venture capitalist[241] and the entrepreneur's interest are fully aligned, as it can be in the case of an enabling CVC: in this case the corporate venture capitalist has

[233] M Colombo and K Shafi, 'Swimming with Sharks in Europe: When Are They Dangerous and What Can New Ventures Do to Defend Themselves?' (2016) 37 *Strategic Management Journal* 2307.

[234] ibid.

[235] A Ginsberg, I Hasan and C Tucci, 'The Influence of Corporate Venture Capital Investment on the Likelihood of Attracting a Prestigious Underwriter' (2011) 14 *Advances in Financial Economics* 165.

[236] Lee, Park and Kang Kang, 'The Double-Edged Effects' (2018) 142–43.

[237] M Rice et al, 'Corporate Venture Capital Models for Promoting Radical Innovation' (2000) 8 *Journal of Marketing Theory and Practice* 1.

[238] A Parhankangas and P Arenius, 'From a Corporate Venture to an Independent Company: A Base for a Taxonomy for Corporate Spin-off Firms' (2003) 32 *Research Policy* 463.

[239] T Winters and D Murfin, 'Venture Capital Investing for Corporate Development Objectives (1998) 3 *Journal of Business Venturing* 207.

[240] Wadhwa, Phelps and Kotha, 'Corporate Venture Capital Portfolios' (2016).

[241] ie the organisation managing CVC, a company or one of its subsidiaries.

an interest in the full success of the independent start-up, as it aims to increase its sales to the start-up. Nonetheless, it is well known that the likelihood that CVC is value creating may depend in most cases on the existence of a strategical overlap between the CVC corporation and the start-up.[242] When such an overlap exists, the efficiencies connected to CVC may be surrounded by an inherent conflict of interest deriving from the existence of competing industrial interests.[243] While the entrepreneur will aim to materialise their creativity and eventually make a profit out of their inventions,[244] the corporate venture capitalist may be interested in those inventions because they may help develop or protect their own business in the various ways outlined above.[245] As noted by Colombo and Shafi, 'CVCs whose parent company operates in the same industry as the focal new venture … are simultaneously the most dangerous and (potentially) the most valuable partners'.[246] In these cases in particular, the protection of the start-up's efforts from asset tunnelling is a crucial element of the success of CVC. It goes without saying that in the case of a start-up, often the main assets are the entrepreneurs' ideas. Such ideas may look particularly attractive for an incumbent company whose resources are mostly employed for sustaining their current going concern which is still producing marginal profits.[247] The intense self-interested targeting activity carried out by the corporate venture capitalist in this context has prompted literature to depict the situation where a corporate investor seeks a partnership with a competing start-up as 'swimming with sharks'.[248]

The fact that the core economic activity of the corporate venture capitalist is industrial in nature and the potential connection of such activity to the one carried out by the start-up is one of the reasons why – despite the similarities highlighted above – CVC and IVC cannot be approached in the same way. Firstly, the time pressure intended as a fixed term for exit may be far more relevant in the case of IVC than in the case of CVC. In fact, a corporate venture capitalist can afford to wait for the start-up to produce results without the same degree of urgency as with IVC, especially when the investment is repaying in terms of learning about or acquiring (or eventually delaying) new technologies. For this reason, the degree of tension around exit is likely to be different in the case of CVC. This may also depend on whether the CVC is exploitative

[242] V Ivanov and F Xie, 'Do Corporate Venture Capitalists Add Value to Start-up Firms? Evidence from IPOs and Acquisitions of VC-backed Companies' (2010) 39 *Financial Management* 129.

[243] The dilemma between cooperation and competition has been known for a long time in relation to horizontal alliances. See for instance R Gulati and H Singh, 'The Architecture of Cooperation: Managing Coordination Costs and Appropriation Concerns in Strategic Alliances' (1998) 43 *Administrative Science Quarterly* 781.

[244] See text at ch 5.VIII and accompanying notes.

[245] See text corresponding to nn 225–34.

[246] Colombo and Shafi, 'Swimming with Sharks in Europe' (2016).

[247] See text at ch 5.VII and accompanying notes.

[248] R Katila, J Rosenberger and K Eisenhardt, 'Swimming with Sharks: Technology Ventures, Defense Mechanisms and Corporate Relationships' (2008) 53 *Administrative Science Quarterly* 295.

or explorative: explorative investment may require a high degree of patience while potential new inventions are monitored.

Secondly, whereas an IVCF may face incentives to move corporate opportunities from one start-up to another, a corporate venture capitalist may be directly interested in the investment opportunity at stake or may also want to prevent such an investment opportunity from being disclosed to a competitor. Therefore, the chances that a business opportunity is moved outside the start-up and to other start-ups or other competitors are likely to be lower in the CVC context.

Thirdly, whereas IVCFs face reputational concerns, corporate venture capitalists may be less exposed to (although not immune from) reputational sanctions, because their revenues do not depend exclusively on their CVC investments.

Fourthly, most of the directors appointed by corporate venture capitalists on start-ups' boards tend to be compensated with a salary and bonuses.[249] Therefore, their economic interests do not seem to be aligned to the one of the entrepreneurs as in the case of the complex system described by Gilson with reference to IVC.[250]

Incentives for a corporate venture capitalist to misappropriate corporate opportunities belonging to the start-up may change throughout time and may be tempered through legal and non-legal strategies. As with IVC, with CVC there is a potential threat that a misappropriation of corporate opportunities occurs after the first contacts. It is a well-known phenomenon that many CVC financings are not likely to take place because of a real or perceived threat of misappropriation in the due diligence process.[251] Arrows is noted as having described such a situation as 'the paradox of disclosure':[252]

> Because of information asymmetry, investors face adverse selection problems that might deter them from investing in new ventures … Entrepreneurs can reveal technical details to mitigate these problems … They, however, often opt not to disclose technical details to avoid the ensuing moral hazard problem; an investor may exploit the information and copy the invention.[253]

As in the case of IVC,[254] in this phase, corporate law protection is not available. In fact, the corporate venture capitalist is not a shareholder of the start-up at this point, nor is it involved in its board of directors. The only potential protection available to the entrepreneur in this phase is a confidentiality or 'non-disclosure' agreement, as the chances of successful patenting in this very early phase seem to be extremely low. Nonetheless, as in the case of IVC, the entrepreneur may

[249] V Ivanov and F Xie, 'Corporate Venture Capital' in Cumming (n 10) 51.

[250] Gilson (n 82).

[251] G Dushnitsky and J Shaver, 'Limitations to Interorganizational Knowledge Acquisition: The Paradox of Corporate Venture Capital' (2009) 30 *Strategic Management Journal* 1045.

[252] ibid 1046.

[253] ibid 1048. I am quoting as reported in Dushnitsky and Shaver (n 251) as I am unable to retrieve the original source due to Covid-19 related library access restrictions.

[254] See text at section IV.C and accompanying notes.

encounter difficulties in monitoring the dispersion of confidential information. Even when the entrepreneur persuades the corporate venture capitalist to sign a confidentiality agreement, such agreements[255] tend to exclude remedies such as damages. Therefore, this is not usually considered as a sound legal protection.

The two main non-legal instruments that entrepreneurs can adopt in order to defend themselves from potential threats of misappropriations in the founding phase are timing and social defences.[256] Timing simply means that they will tend to delay their contacts with corporate venture capitalists until their business is better protected from misappropriation.[257] Such protection may correspond to the possibility of the start-up having access to patenting and/or a better-developed product portfolio and strategic agenda.[258]

Social defences pertain to the affiliation with what Hallen, Katila and Rosenberg call 'third-party chaperones' or 'central venture capital investors'; that is, an IVCF that will monitor the conflict of interest between corporate venture capitalist and entrepreneur.[259] In this case, young start-ups borrow from a third party the power they do not yet enjoy. Such a third party is supposed to align their interests with the entrepreneurs, or at least is less likely to behave as a shark compared to a corporate venture capitalist.[260] According to Hallen, Katila and Rosenberger, the role of this third party consists of disciplining the other investors through reputational constraints, thanks to their authoritative 'voice'.[261] An IVCF would be able to impose reputational constraints on corporate venture capitalists because corporate venture capitalists would be interested in preserving their chance to be involved in syndication with IVCFs that are highly reputable and that therefore have access to the higher-quality ventures.[262] Authoritative third parties could also help the start-up to find other financers whose interests are better-aligned with those of the start-up and who are less likely to prey on it.[263] The most effective predators are normally larger corporations with high R&D investments, because they can easily absorb new technology thanks to their acquired knowledge (ie absorptive capacity).[264] An incumbent corporation with such features and which is also in the same line of business as the start-up/investee is likely to be the perfect 'white pointer'. Start-ups tend to trust such a dangerous predator more easily if they have previously associated with an important IVCF.[265]

[255] And this is often unsuccessful; see Woolf (n 20).
[256] Colombo and Shafi (n 233) 2308.
[257] Katila, Rosenberger and Eisenhardt, 'Swimming with Sharks' (2008) 304ff.
[258] ibid.
[259] B Hallen, R Katila and J Rosenberg, 'How Do Social Defenses Work? A Resource-Dependence Lens on Technology Ventures, Venture Capital Investors, and Corporate Relationships' (2014) 57 *Academy of Management Journal* 1078.
[260] ibid 1080.
[261] ibid 1081–82.
[262] ibid 1082.
[263] ibid 1083.
[264] ibid 1093.
[265] ibid.

Several studies have focused on the likelihood that a strong IP rights and trade secrets regime will increase the chances of a start-up eventually reverting to a corporate venture capitalist belonging to the same industry. It has been found that in those industries where IP rights are strong, such as for instance biotechnology and pharmaceuticals, the chances of this occurring are higher.[266] One may notice that corporate opportunity doctrines can have a protective potential which is close to the one of IP rights, when assisted by a full range of proprietary and non-proprietary remedies as in the Anglo-American jurisdictions.[267] Therefore, it may well be that although corporate opportunity waivers have recently proliferated in the US, for CVC the corporate opportunity doctrine may still have a significant role to play, ie in securing those brave entrepreneurs that are willing to 'swim with the sharks'. By contrast, corporate opportunity rules may have less to say in those cases where the corporate venture capitalist invests following non-aggressive strategies, such as in the case of passive investment or of enabling investment. Still, also in these cases, they may serve their traditional objective of securing the corporate boundaries in the interest of the investors.[268]

VI. WELCOMING CROSS-BORDER VENTURE CAPITAL IN EUROPE: WHY DO CORPORATE OPPORTUNITIES MATTER?

The EU Commission's efforts in promoting VC in Europe have been remarkable throughout the first two decades of the twenty-first century. VC today is a prominent segment of the European financial industry. EU IVCFs have their own private regulatory body, Invest Europe (IE), known before 2015 as the European Private Equity and Venture Capital Association (EVCA) and established within the European Economic and Social Committee (EESC).[269] IE is active not only in standard-setting and research, but also in policy-making. Despite such remarkable progress, in the EU reports analysing the potential policy approaches to promote VC there is a surprising lack of focus on the legal variable, which is cited among the other relevant variables but not analysed in detail as it deserves to be.

In its report, 'Science, Research and Innovation Performance of the EU',[270] the EU Commission acknowledges the centrality of research innovation to achieving the objective of a green Europe.[271] Despite the EU accounting for

[266] R Levin et al, 'Appropriating the Returns from Industrial Research and Development' (1987) *Brookings Papers on Economic Activity* 783, 818.
[267] See text at ch 3.III and accompanying notes.
[268] See text at ch 2.III and accompanying notes.
[269] investeurope.eu.
[270] Science, Research and Innovation Performance of the EU 2020 A Fair, Green and Digital Europe, ec.europa.eu/research/srip/interactive.
[271] ibid 1.

seven ecosystems in the world's 'top 30' start-up ecosystems (compared to 12 in the United States and three in China),[272] as of 2020, only seven per cent of the world's unicorns are located in the EU (compared to around 49 per cent in the US and 29 per cent in China).[273] These figures might seem rather discouraging given not only the immense human potential existing within the EU but also the availability of a wide and prosperous EU internal market endowed with very advanced free-market policies.

Among the potential reasons for the limited development of the European start-up scene, the 2020 report cited above stresses the substantial differences in the development of the US and EU VC.[274] Eight times more VC was raised in the US compared to the EU in 2018.[275] The gap is particularly remarkable in late-stage financing, which may constrain scaling-up in the EU.[276]

The problem of the limited development of VC in Europe has been tackled by the EU institutions at least since 2007, notably with a communication by the EU Commission titled 'Removing Obstacles to Cross-border Investments by Venture Capital Funds' in that year.[277] The communication stressed the importance of VC for job creation and for achieving sustainability. Nonetheless, it also made clear that VC was not developing rapidly enough because of 'lack of an equity investment culture, informational problems, fragmented market and high costs'.[278] The communication stressed the cruciality of its strong policy of public support to start-ups.[279] As next steps forward, the EU Commission took steps to tackle the obstacles faced by IVCFs when committing to cross-border investments. Among those obstacles, the Commission identified the double taxation regime in certain countries. It also stressed the importance of developing a cross-border private-placement regime.[280] Nonetheless, the legal issues inherent in the start-up, ie in the investee, are still lacking in EU policy considerations.

Although things seem to have improved since 2007, The EU Commission 2016 report, 'Assessing the Potential for EU Investment in Venture Capital and Other Risk Capital Fund of Funds',[281] still stresses the existence of several obstacles to intra-EU cross-border investments. Some may derive from differences in taxation regimes; US taxation is often more favourable to VC.[282] As a

[272] ibid 26.
[273] ibid 158.
[274] ibid 530.
[275] ibid.
[276] ibid 532.
[277] Brussels, 21.12.2007 COM (2007) 853 final.
[278] para 3.
[279] para 4.
[280] para 6.1.
[281] European Commission, 'Assessing the Potential for EU Investment in Venture Capital and Other Risk Capital Fund of Funds' (2016), ec.europa.eu/programmes/horizon2020/en/news/assessing-potential-eu-investment-venture-capital-and-other-risk-capital-fund-funds.
[282] ibid 37.

clear taxation policy is fundamental to business, these issues are also tackled in a separate report[283] and in further policy research on a consolidated tax basis.[284]

The 2016 Commission report mentions very few legal issues pertaining to VC activity. For instance, it cites problems of mutual recognition principles when money is repatriated following exit in cross-border VC operations.[285] Moreover it mentions the fact that a few EU Member States (such as for instance the Netherlands) have adopted a special VC regime, whereas the majority of the EU countries apply ordinary company law rules to IVCFs.[286] Again, there is no reference to the legal problems inherent to the start-ups.

The EU policies for the promotion of VC have encompassed not only indirect injections of capital through the Venture EU Funds-of-Funds project, but also dedicated legislation for European Venture Capital Funds, ie for those IVCFs that wish to employ the European Venture Capital Fund (EuVECA) designation,[287] and the offer of 'a voluntary EU-wide marketing passport to qualifying fund managers, while sparing them the costs associated with authorisation and compliance with the AIFMD (Alternative Investment Fund Managers Directive)'.[288] Article 9(1) of the Regulation provides rules on conflict of interest:

> Managers of qualifying venture capital funds shall identify and avoid conflicts of interest and, where they cannot be avoided, manage and monitor and, in accordance with paragraph 4, disclose promptly, those conflicts of interest in order to prevent them from adversely affecting the interests of the qualifying venture capital funds and the investors therein and to ensure that the qualifying venture capital funds they manage are fairly treated.

Although a European IVCF will not necessarily opt for an 'EuVECA' designation, the Regulation acknowledges the importance of constraining conflicts of interest within IVCFs. Such an awareness has surrounded the conflict-of-interest issues arising in the internal operation of the IVCF. The EU lawmaker might have underestimated the fact that the game for establishing a successful VC environment is also played at the level of the investee, ie the start-up. Bottazzi and Da Rin depict the attitude of a European engineer willing to develop a start-up in a rather crude way:

> Our engineer ponders these possibilities. He discards business angels since they are a good source of funds only for smaller start-ups. A corporate venture capitalist is

[283] European Commission, 'Report of Expert Group on Removing Tax Obstacles to Cross-border Venture Capital Investments' (2009), ec.europa.eu/taxation_customs/sites/taxation/files/resources/documents/taxation/company_tax/initiatives_small_business/venture_capital/tax_obstacles_venture_capital_en.pdf.

[284] Proposal for a Council Directive on a Common Corporate Tax Base, 25.10.2016 COM(2016) 685 final.

[285] 'Assessing the Potential for EU Investment' (2006) 30.

[286] ibid 31.

[287] EU Reg No 345/2013 of 17 April 2013 on European Venture Capital Funds, OJ L 115/1.

[288] www.investeurope.eu/policy/key-policy-areas/euveca.

> also unattractive since, especially in Europe, they tend to be slow and a start-up that threatens to 'cannibalize' a revenue of the parent company may end up being delayed or even stopped. Our engineer decides to seek support from a venture capitalist. What should he expect?[289]

Such a depiction may unfortunately reflect the European context. Therefore, we should ask ourselves what the law could do to improve our entrepreneurs' financial perspectives when approaching different kinds of VC. We may also wonder how corporate opportunity rules could play a role in such a general improvement.

To begin with, there may be complementarities between the present state of VC in Europe and a very complex set of institutional variables, only some of which are legal in nature.[290] I also believe that marginal changes to such institutional variables, such as changes to certain aspects of the law, may trigger a beneficial cascade of improvements. I start by considering Europe at large, on the basis of the theoretical and empirical research that has been carried out on European VC, while being aware that the EU is an extremely fragmented territory from an entrepreneurial perspective and even more so from a VC perspective.[291]

First, whereas US IVCFs are mainly funded by other institutional investors, EU IVCFs are in most cases so-called 'captive funds'; that is, funds not only funded by but also controlled by other financial institutions, namely banks.[292] Also 'public VC' funding (ie financing provided by the state or by a state entity) is frequent in the EU,[293] whereas it is virtually non-existent in the US.[294] Another meaningful feature of EU IVCFs is that they tend to provide smaller financing and to a wider number of start-ups compared to US IVCFs.[295] Moreover, EU IVCFs are less active in funding early-stage start-ups than their US counterparts.[296] Finally, EU IVCFs seem to invest in sectors that are not particularly renowned for their high innovation rate, such as the agricultural sector.[297]

Particularly interesting differences are noted with reference to syndication. Syndication is especially important for IVCFs when investing on a

[289] Bottazzi and Da Rin, 'Venture Capital in Europe' (2002) 233.

[290] On the concept of institutional complementarity, see ch 1.II and accompanying notes.

[291] European Commission, 'Report of Expert Group' (2009) 1.

[292] Bottazzi and Da Rin (n 24) 241. This normally entails deviations in their behaviour. See T Tykvova, 'German Banks as Venture Capitalists' in G Gregoriou (ed), *Venture Capital in Europe* (Butterworth-Heinemann, 2007) 331.

[293] B Leleux and B Surlemont, 'Public Versus Private Venture Capital: Seeding or Crowding Out? A Pan-European Analysis' (2003) 18 *Journal of Business Venturing* 81, 83; 100: the authors demystify the idea according to which public VC would intervene to create a virtuous private VC where it had not existed earlier. As a matter of fact, public VC funds tend to be latecomers in an already existing VC industry.

[294] Bottazzi and Da Rin (n 24) 241.

[295] ibid 243.

[296] ibid 241.

[297] ibid 243.

cross-border basis.[298] In fact, a local IVCF can provide very important information as to the main features of the local market, and it may also have a grasp of the local laws that apply to the start-up.[299] When we focus on corporate opportunity rules, it might be the case that the rules that are beneficial for local VC investments are not equally advantageous for cross-border VC investments – and not to mention the fact that a foreign investor may prefer to keep on operating under their national rules.[300]

For instance, in Europe, syndication is radically different.[301] It tends to be justified more often by monetary reasons (lesser availability of capital) than in the US.[302] In Europe, IVCFs tend to be less collaborative with each other and tend not to share widely their investment opportunities.[303] By contrast, in the US, syndication seems to reflect a complex *modus operandi* which involves many more industrial variables (eg economies of scale and scope in assessing the profitability of certain investments).[304] On top of that, as US IVCFs tend to be more involved in the management of start-ups,[305] they are also more likely to come across corporate opportunities and find themselves in a position of divided loyalty. US IVCFs are also very active in foreign start-up management once they have invested abroad.[306] Therefore, a waiver of corporate opportunity rules seems to be far more important to US IVCFs, also when they are operating outside the US.[307]

Because of the more individualistic approach adopted by European IVCFs, those reputational constraints among IVCFs that also protect the entrepreneur from misappropriation of corporate opportunities seem to be less relevant in the European context. In order to favour the local VC market, the lawmaker should provide entrepreneurs with alternative protection from asset tunnelling. A good substitute for reputational constraints deriving from syndication can be a strong corporate opportunity rule which cannot be waived; this will mean the entrepreneur cannot be put in a difficult bargaining position vis-à-vis the IVCF.[308] This is

[298] Tykvova and Schertler, 'Syndication with Local Venture Capitalists' (2014).

[299] J Luo et al, 'Syndication Through Social Embeddedness: A Comparison of Foreign, Private and State-owned Venture Capital (VC) Firms' (2019) 36 *Asia Pacific Journal of Management* 499, 512.

[300] This is proven by the fact that when it comes to the contractual praxis, the US tend to impose their own model. See above text corresponding to n 36.

[301] K Arundale, 'Syndication and Cross-border Collaboration by Venture Capital Firms in Europe and the USA: A Comparative Study' (2020) 22 *Venture Capital* 355.

[302] ibid 363. Although this is not always the prevalent reason according to the author. But it must be noted that the study mostly focuses on UK companies on the European side. Therefore, this specific argument may not hold for the rest of the European IVCF, because the UK has the largest IVC industry in Europe.

[303] ibid 369.

[304] See section 4.VI and accompanying notes.

[305] Bottazzi, Da Rin and Hellman, 'The Changing Face' (2004) 27; note that this is the traditional view, although things are improving for EU IVCFs.

[306] Arundale, 'Syndication and Cross-border Collaboration' (2020) 4.5.1.

[307] Woolf (n 20).

[308] Woolf (n 20).

the kind of rule that protects UK entrepreneurs, as it is questionable whether the UK corporate opportunity might be waivable and there is no case law affirming such a possibility.

By contrast, if the lawmaker intends to attract IVCFs that follow an investment style similar to that in the US, it should introduce the possibility of a waiver for corporate opportunity rules.[309] But this in turn might be received with disfavour by local entrepreneurs, who might already need to overcome the uncertainty of dealing with a foreign investor who is alien to the local entrepreneurial scene and therefore perhaps not that trustworthy.

If a US VC investor would probably be unhappy without the possibility of a waiver, it would be equally disappointed with the weakness of many EU Member States' corporate opportunity rules when it comes to preventing the entrepreneur from misappropriating start-ups' inventions.[310] The absence or weakness of such a legal protection in many EU countries might also explain why US IVCFs do not tend to engage in seed funding in Europe:[311] they might prefer to wait for a start-up to patent its invention and therefore obtain tighter corporate control on the invention, backed by IP rights.

A further problem for foreign IVCFs may well be the fact that EU Member States' corporate rules are rather diversified, and therefore there will be no straightforward and homogeneous corporate opportunity rule for defending a misappropriation of technological innovation which is not patentable.[312] EU corporate mobility has prompted many start-ups to incorporate in the UK under the aegis of the freedom of establishment. The UK has a rather well-developed and moderately clear corporate opportunity doctrine, assisted by a corpus of precedents.[313] Another advantage is that from a linguistic perspective, UK law is far more easily accessible than other EU Member States' laws by US IVCFs. The cited incorporation trend might have provided a solution to the lack of homogeneity in EU Member States' legislations. Nonetheless, Brexit has endangered corporate mobility, and it is unknown where the foreign start-ups that have incorporated in the UK might relocate to.[314] A potential candidate for new EU cross-border incorporations might be Ireland, but recent empirical research does not show a significant trend of new EU cross-border incorporations in Ireland.[315]

[309] Tykvova and Schertler (n 49) 418, showing the difficulties for a foreign IVCF in adapting to local corporate governance.

[310] See text at ch 3.IV–V and accompanying notes.

[311] Arundale (n 301) 359.

[312] M Corradi, 'Corporate Opportunities Doctrines Tested in the Light of the Theory of the Firm – a European (and US) Comparative Perspective' (2016) 27 *European Business Law Review* 755.

[313] J Lowry, 'Codifying the Corporate Opportunity Doctrine: The (UK) Companies Act' (2012) 1 *International Review of Law* 5.

[314] A Johnston, 'Company Law and Corporate Governance After Brexit: From Short-term Disruption to Long-term Sustainability?' (2020) 8 *ETUI Research Paper-Policy Brief*.

[315] T Biermeyer and M Meyer, 'Cross-border Corporate Mobility in the EU: Empirical Findings 2020 (Edition 1)', papers.ssrn.com/sol3/papers.cfm?abstract_id=3674089, 2.

Empirical research has shown that US IVCFs underperform when they invest in Europe and European IVCFs overperform when they invest in the US.[316] As Arundel reports in her article, an opinion circulating in the VC circles is that 'Europeans with US syndicates will get a lift and the US with European syndicates will get a drag'.[317] Corporate opportunity rules may not be the central factor in determining this difference, but the US corporate opportunity rules, as already noted, may contribute to create an environment far more conducive to profitable investment strategies and may make US IVCFs' GPs more at ease when making deals.

Because the European VC scene is not always that attractive, many European entrepreneurs tend to revert to CVC. One may wonder how they protect themselves from sharks. Colombo and Shafi have found that European entrepreneurs tend to accept financing from companies that operate in the same line of business when the IP protection is not strong, ie when the inventions are not easily patentable.[318] The authors suggest that this may simply be due to the lack of alternatives.[319] This is due to the fact that IVCFs are less prone to early-stage investments in Europe than in the US.[320] Moreover, governmental VC, which in turn is often available in early-stage financing in Europe, may tend to exclude start-ups with low added value.[321]

As a matter of fact, the situation of relative lack of legal or social protection for the entrepreneur depicted above is precisely the one where strict corporate opportunity rules may be particularly beneficial. By providing the entrepreneur with minimum protection against knowledge misappropriation, corporate opportunity rules may contribute to boosting entrepreneurs' confidence in CVC. Moreover, they may help prevent the most talented and ambitious entrepreneurs from leaving their countries in search of a more effective and just financing system. Again, the set of problematics identified with reference to local and cross-border IVC and CVC suggests that there is no unique solution to the series of rather tangled situations that can surround the entrepreneur sharing knowledge with their financers. The availability of a vast array of effective sanctions and the possibility to opt out of corporate opportunity rules suggest that the policies first introduced by Delaware law are the ones that are most likely to adapt to differentiated circumstances.

[316] U Hege, F Palomino and A Schwienbacher, 'Venture Capital Performance: The Disparity between Europe and the United States' (2009) 30 *Finance* 7.

[317] Arundel (n 302).

[318] Colombo and Shafi (n 233) 2309.

[319] ibid.

[320] F Bertoni, M Colombo and Anita Quas, 'The Patterns of Venture Capital Investment in Europe' (2015) 45 *Small Business Economics* 543, 549.

[321] Colombo and Shafi (n 233) 2319.

VII. CONCLUSION

The kind of start-up IVCFs and corporate venture capitalists normally deal with is naturally rich in inventive business opportunities. Therefore, it is inevitable that, along with other functionally similar legal tools (non-compete and non-disclosure agreements), corporate opportunity rules provide a basis for the protection of a VC investment – defending the start-up from misappropriations by entrepreneurs. Nonetheless, the chances of bilateral opportunism are very high in both contexts. Whereas IVCFs' GPs investing in competing start-ups are often in a position of divided loyalty, corporate venture capitalists may simply attempt to prey on entrepreneurs' inventions. While corporate opportunity waivers seem to facilitate IVCFs' investments, relieving them from the legal issues deriving from divided loyalty, the same waivers may not necessarily be beneficial in a corporate venture capital context. In fact, especially where IVCF funding is not available, it is crucial that an entrepreneur can trust corporate venture capitalists. Many factors contribute to complicating the nature of the conflict of interest within the VC context: the presence of syndication, ie IVCFs and corporate venture capitalists with potentially diverging interests; entrepreneurs with potentially diverging interests among themselves and in relation to their funder; and the dynamics of such conflicts, which are ever-changing, depending on the entry of new investors.

As if such a complexity was not enough, the picture is also complicated by the intensity of cross-border investments. In the face of the multiplicity of situations that can occur in VC contexts, the possibility of modulating corporate opportunity rules through private ordering is particularly important. And in those phases of the development of a start-up where the protection of the boundaries of the corporation is crucial, a sound remedial system is equally important. In a world where innovation is at the core of welfare creation, an attentive consideration of the legal factors – and especially of corporate opportunity rules – along with all the other institutional factors, is fundamental and cannot be further delayed.

7

Corporate Opportunity Doctrines: One Size Fits All or Multiple Efficient Solutions?

I. AN OVERVIEW OF THE DEBATE ON PRIVATE ORDERING IN CORPORATE LAW

THE DEBATE ON the economic efficiency of corporate opportunity rules can be understood in all its fullness if we consider such rules in the light of the functions carried out by the corporation within a social and economic system as a whole.[1] Corporate opportunity rules affect entrepreneurial freedom and technological innovation,[2] the development of the financial system[3] and the potential for corporate growth[4] – all variables that significantly affect collective welfare. Therefore, questions such as whether corporate opportunity rules should be conceived as either mandatory or default, and on whether they should be formulated as a broad standard or as a set of stringent provisions, can be framed within the debate on the role of the corporation within society.[5,6]

[1] An example of competing views is the following: while applying the 'maximizing shareholders' profits' paradigm, at the core of the law and finance theory, M Jensen, 'Eclipse of the Public Corporation' (1989) 67 *Harvard Business Review* 61, 64 predicted the absence of a future for corporations active in industries with slow-term growth, such as tobacco, brewing, and newspapers, because of the rise in agency costs. In reply to Jensen, see C Doidge et al, 'Eclipse of the Public Corporation or Eclipse of the Public Markets?' (2018) 30 *Journal of Applied Corporate Finance* 8, who instead identified the main problem faced by young and innovative US entrepreneurs in accessing listings on stock exchanges.

[2] See text at ch 5.VIII and accompanying footnotes.

[3] Both in terms of VC, for which see ch 6, and in general, by protecting corporate proprietary boundaries.

[4] M Corradi, 'Corporate Opportunities Doctrines Tested in the Light of the Theory of the Firm – a European (and US) Comparative Perspective' (2016) 27 *European Business Law Review* 755, 758, 770.

[5] L Davoudi, C McKenna and R Olegario, 'The Historical Role of the Corporation in Society' (2018) 6 *Journal of the British Academy* 17, who claim social purpose has been one of the defining traits of corporations until the introduction of general incorporation laws at the end of the nineteenth century, in the US and in the UK. Nowadays, after several decades of primacy of the 'maximizing shareholders' profits' rule, there is rehearsal of the social role of corporations, in the form of corporate social responsibility (CSR). Actually, the adoption of CSR standards seems to reflect the preferences not only of stakeholders at large, but also of shareholders. See K Lins, H Servaes and A Tamayo, 'Social Capital, Trust, and Firm Performance: The Value of Corporate

Historical, economic, and political perspectives may all together contribute to the understanding of what a corporation should do for a social and economic system and of what rules should be functional to such activity – including the rules on directors' duties.[7]

Nowadays, the quest for the corporation's raison d'être and to understand the nature of the corporate interest is surrounded by many more question marks than a few decades ago, especially in the light of the evolution of artificial intelligence and information technology. Academic literature laments the fact that modern corporate theory continues to apply the 'maximising shareholders' value' rule and the economic agency theory – ie the most common perspective still adopted in the law and finance theory – without considering the significant impact of technological innovation on corporations.[8]

> In a networked age, all businesses need to 'go digital.' Companies need to become innovation machines, and this means that every firm needs to become a 'tech' company and a 'media' company. If they do not, younger and more agile competitors better attuned to the realities of the new digital world will replace them.[9]

Certainly, digitalisation has brought forward new organisational forms which tend to erode the boundaries of the corporation,[10] and the corporation itself is, more than ever, also a source of technological innovation: these are remarkable

Social Responsibility During the Financial Crisis' (2017) 72 *Journal of Finance* 1785, showing that firms with high social capital, as measured by CSR intensity, had stock returns that were four to seven percentage points higher than firms with low social capital. The level of CSR is not homogeneous across different legal families. See H Liang and L Renneboog, 'On the Foundations of Corporate Social Responsibility' (2017) 72 *Journal of Finance* 853, showing that firms from common law countries have lower CSR than companies from civil law countries, with Scandinavian civil law firms having the highest CSR rating.

[6] The impact of rules aimed at containing agency costs is so profound that in a moment of crisis, such as the one triggered by the present Covid-19 pandemic, they can be employed as policy tools. See, with reference to the relaxation of related party transactions, L Enriques, 'Pandemic-Resistant Corporate Law: How to Help Companies Cope with Existential Threats and Extreme Uncertainty During the Covid-19 Crisis' (2020) 17 *European Company and Financial Law Review* 257, 266.

[7] For instance, for alternative views on short-termism v long-termism, see T Belinfanti and L Stout, 'Contested Visions: The value of Systems Theory for Corporate Law' (2017) 166 *University of Pennsylvania Law Review* 579.

[8] M Fenwick and E Vermeulen, 'The End of the Corporation: Transformation in Corporate Governance' (2020) *Challenges and Opportunities of Corporate Governance Transformation in the Digital Era* IGI Global, 1. A few renowned scholars are starting to tackle the impact of artificial intelligence on traditional corporate theory cost analysis. See for instance J Armour and H Eidenmuller, 'Self-Driving Corporations?' (2020) 10 *Harvard Business Law Review* 87; J Armour et al, 'Putting Technology to Good Use for Society: The Role of Corporate, Competition and Tax Law' (2018) European Corporate Governance Institute (ECGI)-Law Working Paper, 427. For the impact of artificial intelligence on directors' duties, see F Möslein, 'Robots in the Boardroom: Artificial Intelligence and Corporate Law' in W Barfield and U Pagallo (eds), *Research Handbook on the Law of Artificial Intelligence* (Edward Elgar, 2018).

[9] Fenwick and Vermeulen, 'The End of the Corporation' (2020) 1.

[10] ibid 10. See also M Fenwick and J McCahery, and Erik PM Vermeulen, 'The End of "Corporate" Governance: Hello "Platform" Governance' (2019) 20 *European Business Organization Law Review* 171.

signs of change. But these changes are occurring within an organisational form – the corporation – that by itself has had an elusive identity since its creation. Janus Bifrons and the symbolic messages represented by this ancient Roman mythical figure – its dual identity and also its function as a bridge between past and future – are a good metaphor for the corporation. From the start, corporations have been set up for the purpose of carrying out private business activity; nonetheless, from their early days, they have been creations of a public authority, through the granting of a privilege.[11] In addition, past and future seem to be engaged in a continuous dance within the essence of a corporation. The private nature of the corporation has emerged over time, leading us to believe from time to time that any manifestation of the autonomy of the will was allowed in corporate finance engineering. Nonetheless, the abuse of the corporate form by unscrupulous private actors has repeatedly provoked lawmakers to respond by bringing some aspects of the corporation back under strict public control.[12] Hence, there seems not to be an endpoint for these 'run towards the future' and 'return to the past' dynamics, despite academic predictions of the end of history for corporate law.[13]

The legal concept of the modern 'public company' emerged in a historical era when mercantilism was the propulsive ideology for economic cross-border expansion and for colonisations. The mercantilist ideology aimed at empowering the state through empowering its merchants.[14] Hence, the first corporations

[11] H Butler, 'Nineteenth-century Jurisdictional Competition in the Granting of Corporate Privileges' (1985) 14 *Journal of Legal Studies* 129. Even in the US, the corporation has never had a purely private genome. US corporations were originally founded by privilege granted on the basis of an individual legislative act. It was not until the end of the nineteenth century that states started moving to a general incorporation system, exclusively based on compliance with general corporate law rules. This occurred under the pressure of an increasingly significant interstate commerce and under the aegis of the Supreme Court, with the case of *Paul v Virgina* 75 US (8 Wall) 168 (1869). In that case, the Supreme Court decided that US states could not prevent a corporation from engaging in interstate business but could grant permission to trade under reasonable conditions. The impact of such a decision was major, because it started the regulatory competition among states for attracting other states' corporations to do business in their territory.

[12] The consequences of a public company's 'mala gestio' for a country as a whole revealed themselves in the early ages of the companies based on public charters, with the Dutch tulip mania of 1634–37 and the Mississippi and South Sea bubbles of 1719–20. See P Garber, *Famous First Bubbles: The Fundamentals of Early Manias* (Massachusetts Institute of Technology Press, 2001). A later intervention was for instance the 1890 Sherman Act, following the emergence of Standard Oil as a quasi-monopolistic player. A very recent and pervasive forms of federal intervention is the Sarban-Oxley Act, following the ENRON scandal. For a compilation of research on the legislation following the ENRON scandal, see J Armour and J McCahery (eds), *After Enron: Improving Corporate Law and Modernising Securities Regulation in Europe and the US* (Hart Publishing, 2006).

[13] H Hansmann and R Kraakman, 'The End of History for Corporate Law' (2000) 89 *Georgia Law Review* 439.

[14] E Heckscher, *Mercantilism* (Routledge, 2013) 22–24 explains that, in order to empower trading companies and obtain external political influence, the state had to exercise internal tight political power, directed to break infra-state institutions. Hence, the internal and cross-border dimensions were two indivisible variables that characterised the environment in which the first trading companies were conceived.

were the product of political choices expressly designed for the purpose of empowering the international influence of the state through cross-border private business.[15] Nowadays, the emergence of GAFA (Google, Apple, Facebook, Amazon) on the global scene seems to go well beyond such an indirect acquisition of cross-border influence. GAFA might be seen by some as neo-mercantilist (ie cross-border) instruments in the hands of their host state, the United States of America (US).[16] But beyond the mercantilist perspective, great concern has been expressed over GAFA's ability to dominate the citizen's private life, which goes way beyond the power traditionally covered by the state's public action[17] and thus goes way beyond their function of 'new public utilities'.[18]

In forms other than GAFA, the intersection between services of public utility and corporations was already well-known before the development of high-tech and beyond mercantilist rationales: in the US, this intersection has been present at least since the second half of the nineteenth century.[19] In several developed economies, the corporate form is still largely employed for providing services of public utility, often in the form of public–private partnership.[20] Moreover, in several EU Member States, fully state-owned companies were the primary source of gross domestic product until the age of privatisation.[21] In this sector,

[15] D Irwin, 'Mercantilism as Strategic Trade Policy: the Anglo-Dutch Rivalry for the East India Trade' (1991) 99 *Journal of Political Economy* 1296. The Dutch and English Companies of Indies provided an early example of a Cournot oligopoly. See D Irwin, 'Strategic Trade Policy and Mercantilist Trade Rivalries' (1992) 82 *The American Economic Review* 134, 136.

[16] Proposals for a series of regulations to be enacted in order to monitor and direct the public power acquired by GAFA are not missing from the present debate. See for instance S Rahman, 'The New Utilities: Private Power, Social Infrastructure, and the Revival of the Public Utility Concept' (2017) 39 *Cardozo Law Review* 1621. Nonetheless, there is scepticism around the capability of the US administration to interfere heavily with such important economic players. The passivity of the US antitrust enforcers vis-à-vis GAFA has been highlighted by multiple authors. See for instance Z Foge, 'American Oligarchy: How the Enfeebling of Antitrust Law Corrodes the Republic' (2019) 12 *Journal of Business Entrepreneurship & Law* 119. This might be a rather simplistic way to read the US administration's alleged soft approach to GAFA's anticompetitive practices. The US may well derive a high degree of control of the world's sensitive data through GAFA. Nonetheless, it may also be that the political influence deriving from data control is overestimated. Research has shown that the ownership of some core elements of the internet infrastructure has shifted towards Europe and the BRICS. See D Winseck, 'The Geopolitical Economy of the Global Internet Infrastructure' (2017) 7 *Journal of Information Policy* 228. The situation in relation to the public–private power relationship in this area is yet to be fully understood.

[17] The most pessimistic views predict a remarkable antidemocratic influence of the big-tech companies on citizens. See S Vaidhyanathan, *Antisocial Media: How Facebook Disconnects Us and Undermines Democracy* (Oxford University Press, 2018); F Fukuyama, B Richman and A Goel, 'How to Save Democracy from Technology: Ending Big Tech's Information Monopoly' (2021) 100 *Foreign Affairs* 98.

[18] Rahman, 'The New Utilities' (2017) 1626ff.

[19] F Hanft, 'Control of Public Utilities in Minnesota' (1931) 16 *Minnesota Law Review* 457, 473–74, reporting on corporations active in the provision of railroad services and in the supply of gas and water.

[20] G Grossi and C Richard, 'Municipal Corporatization in Germany and Italy' (2008) 10 *Public Management Review* 597.

[21] See text at ch 1.V.C and VII and accompanying notes.

corporate opportunity rules may well have a completely different effect than in the fully private sector.[22]

For all types of corporation, rules directed towards containing agency costs may have been seen as promoting investments, in the interest of collective welfare. Nonetheless, it is questionable whether problems which may have public interest repercussions can be tackled by way of private contractual autonomy.[23] In the early days of the corporation, the Hudson's Bay Company provides us with an example of a corporation facing extremely high agency costs – this was due to the fact that it was active in a cross-border business at a time where there was no technology that could enable efficient monitoring.[24] But the company's founders introduced efficient solutions to such problems. 'A range of payoffs, bonds, and performance incentives encouraged honesty and a high level of effort, making it expensive for managers to cheat.'[25] Internal monitoring ('spies', ie whistleblowers) was also extensively employed to contain opportunistic behaviour.[26]

If, on the one hand, 'Corporations often lie at the intersection of public and private law',[27] on the other hand, the private and the public variables are not monoliths. For instance, after having considered many economic aspects surrounding corporate opportunity rules, one may wonder whether it is possible to come up with an unequivocal policy indication on whether such rules should be mandatory or not. Whereas US corporate laws have implemented the idea of a waiver for corporate opportunity rules since 2001,[28] in several European jurisdictions, corporate opportunity rules seem to be mandatory.[29]

[22] See text at ch 1.V.C and accompanying notes.

[23] But note also that the regulatory framework around which private ordering is organized may be understood as a form of protection of the public interest. See M Moore, *Corporate Governance in the Shadow of the State* (Hart Publishing, 2013) 236: 'the fact that the state creates the structural preconditions for private ordering arguably entitles it – quid pro quo – to set regulatory boundaries to the appropriate scope of such where this is seemingly justified by public interest considerations, and irrespective of whether the resulting constraints align with the collective private preferences of contractors'.

[24] A Carlos and S Nicholas, 'Managing the Manager: An Application of the Principal Agent Model to the Hudson's Bay Company' (1993) *Oxford Economic Papers* 243, 244.

[25] ibid 245.

[26] ibid 246. Both methods were commonly used in most chartered corporations from the seventeenth century onwards. See S Jones and S Ville, 'Efficient Transactors or Rent-seeking Monopolists? The Rationale for Early Chartered Trading Companies' (1996) 56 *Journal of Economic History* 898, 904–05.

[27] R Epstein, 'Contract and Trust in Corporate Law: The Case of Corporate Opportunity' (1996) 21 *Delaware Journal of Corporate Law* 1, 7.

[28] The first mover was Delaware, with an amendment of DGCL in the year 2000 whereby it introduced DGCL, s 122(17).

[29] See for instance M Gelter and G Helleringer, 'Fiduciary Principles in European Civil Law Systems' in E Criddle, P Miller and R Sitkoff (eds), *The Oxford Handbook of Fiduciary Law* (Oxford University Press, 2019) 600–01 on the German system. Nonetheless, also note that recently German jurisprudence has shown interest in the possibility to waive the duty of loyalty. See A Hellgardt, 'Abdingbarkeit der Gesellschaftsrechtlichen Treuepflicht' in S Grundmann et al (eds), *Unternehmen, Markt und Verantwortung: Festschrift für Klaus J. Hopt zum 70. Geburtstag am 24. August 2010* (DeGruyter, 2010) 765, 778, 781ff, with reference to waivers for the corporate opportunity doctrine

It is not clear whether corporate directors' fiduciary duties were developed independently in civil law systems or were later consciously imported from common law systems.[30] By contrast, corporate opportunity doctrines are a rather clear act of transplant, which took place either before or on the verge of the introduction into Delaware law of the possibility of a corporate opportunity waiver.[31] If a general reliance on foreign law clauses may at times have unpredictable effects,[32] analysing specific solutions, such as those pertaining to corporate opportunity rules within Anglo-American jurisdictions, may be extremely useful for lawmakers in other jurisdictions.[33] But even once lawmakers have understood foreign approaches to corporate opportunity rules, their experiences will not necessarily help to simplify the substantive reality to which these rules apply. The multiplicity of manifestations of this legal paradigm – the public versus private dimension of the corporation, the fact that a corporation may display a prevalence of either of these two dimensions through its development from start-up to unicorn, and the existence of diversified economic, industrial and financial environments in which corporations operate – mean that an extremely refined legal adaptation is required. Such a refined adaptation can be better obtained by calibrating the different aspects of the doctrine on a casuistic base.

II. DOES ONE SIZE FIT ALL? A CONTRACT-BASED APPROACH

What is remarkable about the Delaware approach to corporate opportunity rules is that the long-term experience of the rules, matured by Delaware's courts while dealing with the major US public corporations,[34] has prompted the Delaware

in closed corporations. For Spain, see *Ley de Sociedades de Capital* (Spanish Stock Company Law) Art 230, para 1, which expressly mentions that the duty of loyalty is mandatory and cannot be waived ('El régimen relativo al deber de lealtad y a la responsabilidad por su infracción es imperativo. No serán válidas las disposiciones estatutarias que lo limiten o sean contrarias al mismo').

[30] C Gerner-Beuerle and M Schillig, *Comparative Company Law* (Oxford University Press, 2019) 467ff.

[31] See ch 1, n 13.

[32] Anglo-American fiduciary duties are expressly referred to in, for instance, Italian case law. See Cass n 16707, 24 August 2004 [2005] *Foro Italiano*, I, 1844ff. General consideration of transplant of directors' fiduciary duties can be found in H Fleischer, 'Legal Transplant in European Company Law – The Case of Fiduciary Duties' (2005) 2 *European Company Financial Law Review* 378.

[33] See H Fleischer, 'Gegenwartsfragen der Geschäftschancenlehre im Englischen und Deutschen Gesellschaftsrecht' in J Taeger and A Wiebe (eds), *Informatik – Wirtschaft – Recht. Regulierung in der Wissensgesellschaft: Festschrift für Wolfgang Kilian* (Nomos, 2004); H Fleischer, 'Gelöste und Ungelöste Probleme der Gesellschaftsrechtlichen Geschäftschancenlehre' (2003) *Neue Zeitschrift für Gesellschaftsrecht* 985.

[34] S Arsht, 'A History of Delaware Corporation Law' (1976) 1 *Delaware Journal of Corporate Law* 1, 9: as early as 1901, Delaware corporate law had already gone through several reforms and permitted the certificate of incorporation to 'contain any provision which the incorporators may choose to insert for the regulation of the business and for the conduct of the affairs of the corporation, and any provisions creating, defining, limiting and regulating the powers of the corporation, the directors and the stockholders, or any classes of the stockholders, provided, such provisions are

lawmaker to reconcile the possibility of a waiver with an articulated set of corporate opportunity rules, assisted by an efficient set of remedies.[35] By introducing the possibility of a waiver, the Delaware lawmaker has not relinquished its corporate opportunity doctrine in any way whatsoever. The application of corporate opportunity rules has simply been rendered adaptable to different economic environments. One may wonder whether the Delaware solution would work for economic environments different from that of the US. Anderson and Gupta's statement on simplistic copy-and-paste law-making should sound as a warning:

> [A] host country must take into account its own level of financial development and the strength of its legal system before blindly adopting or emulating any corporate governance practices mandated or promoted by other countries or international organizations. Similarly, a company must consider the depth of the host countries' financial markets and the extent to which investor protection really matters before importing the so-called good governance practices from other countries.[36]

These words sound true with reference to the introduction of corporate opportunity rules in several continental European countries, where they were previously unknown, and where the absence of such rules may have actually permitted the development of efficient dynamics based on innovation spilllover.[37] Apart from free-taking, possible alternatives to the Delaware solution may include a total ban, or a set of non-waivable rules assisted by various kinds of remedies, usually classified by jurisprudence as 'property' or 'liability' rules.[38]

The analysis conducted on the UK, Italian and Spanish economies has opened a window on the effect of two extreme rules: a (seemingly) non-waivable no-profit rule – the UK one – which approximates a ban to the extent that the insider may have a hard time obtaining authorisation to appropriate the business opportunity ex post;[39] and free-taking – the former Italian rule – within the limits of a waivable directors' duty not to compete with the corporation.[40] Neither of these solutions may be ideal, especially in those economies that are highly diversified.[41] For instance, on the one hand, free-taking may favour

not contrary to the laws of this State'. Since then, the dialectic between legislature and court has allowed a fine tuning of directors' duties to the best business practice. See R Romano, *The Genius of American Corporate Law* (American Enterprise Institute, 1993). Whether such fine tuning has characterized also the last two decades is questionable. See W Carney and G Shepherd, 'The Mystery of Delaware Law's Continuing Success' (2009) *University of Illinois Law Review* 1.

[35] G Rauterberg and E Talley, 'Contracting Out of the Fiduciary Duty of Loyalty: An Empirical Analysis of Corporate Opportunity Waivers' (2017) 117 *Columbia Law Review* 1075.

[36] A Anderson and P Gupta, 'Corporate Governance: Does One Size Fit All?' (2013) 24 *Journal of Corporate Accounting & Finance* 51, 52.

[37] See ch 1.

[38] Z Goshen, 'The Efficiency of Controlling Corporate Self-Dealing: Theory Meets Reality' (2003) 91 *California Law Review* 393, 401ff.

[39] See text at ch 1.V.A and accompanying notes.

[40] See text at ch 1.V.B–C and accompanying footnotes. In the Italian system, the directors' duty not to compete has been considered as waivable ex ante. See Cass n 3091, 31 October 1975.

[41] See text at ch 1.V.B–C, VI and VII and accompanying notes.

technologic spillovers[42] and a degree of recombination of building blocks of knowledge embedded in the persons of founders/directors.[43] On the other hand, it may also fail to protect investments in start-ups and therefore render them less appealing for venture capital (VC) investors. In fact, especially in the seed phase, patent protection is rarely available, and therefore a corporate opportunity doctrine is a valuable legal tool for protecting intellectual capital.[44]

There may be many other reasons for which free-taking could be undesirable: one may say that whenever the objective to protect the proprietary boundaries of the corporation prevails on other competing objectives, a free-taking regime is undesirable. This may well be the case not only when there is a necessity to attract new investors, but also for instance when a company is trying to achieve vertical integration or has a need to protect its economies of scale or scope.[45] It may also be that an inflexible corporate opportunity doctrine is complementary to other institutional variables, as in the case of certain sectors of a state's economy – for instance, the financial services sector in the UK.[46] Nonetheless, economic systems are also subject to evolution and therefore flexibility, and a vast array of legal choices may enable economic operators to find the most efficient legal arrangement for an ever-changing set of variables.

For instance, the UK is losing its primacy in the European financial services market after Brexit.[47] Nonetheless, the country is also successfully attempting to develop several prominent high-tech districts, an operation which may well end up with the UK improving its position as a primary European tech hub, thanks to reliable institutions and excellent education offerings.[48] Such changes may require rethinking of certain corporate law rules, including corporate opportunity rules, to bring them more in line with tech-hub dynamics – such as the quick circulation of building blocks of knowledge embedded in highly skilled employees and founders/directors.[49] The UK's Department for Business Innovation and Skills, has already started to move in this direction with its Consultation on Measures to Reform Post-Termination Non-Compete Clauses in Contracts of Employment, which closes on 26 February 2021.[50] We cannot exclude the

[42] See text at ch 1.V.B and VII and accompanying notes.

[43] See text at ch 5.VI and accompanying notes.

[44] See text at ch 2.V and accompanying notes.

[45] Corradi, 'Corporate Opportunities Doctrines' (2016) 771, 793.

[46] See text at ch 1.IV and accompanying notes.

[47] While apparently Amsterdam is overtaking London in the financial services sector. See H Jones, 'Amsterdam Displaces London as Europe's Top Stocks Centre after Brexit', www.reuters.com/article/us-britain-eu-markets/amsterdam-displaces-london-as-europes-top-stocks-centre-after-brexit-idUSKBN2AB0I8.

[48] www.techrepublic.com/article/why-britain-has-become-the-top-tech-hub-in-europe.

[49] See text at chapter 5.VI and 8 and accompanying notes.

[50] assets.publishing.service.gov.uk/government/uploads/system/uploads/attachment_data/file/941110/non-compete-consultation-document.pdf. A policy recommendation, authored by B Bjørst, 'Restrictive Covenants in Employment Contracts – an Unnoticed Hindrance to Growth in Europe' (on file with the author), was brought to the attention of the EU Parliament in 2015. Unfortunately, EU institutions have not undertaken any action yet to implement the recommendation.

possibility that UK courts will start interpreting the corporate opportunity doctrine in a more flexible way if that proves necessary for the success of start-up hubs.

A further call for flexibility, which is theoretical in nature and not restricted to the analysis of a specific business environment, is the one emerging through the new reading of the Law and Economics of corporate governance, introduced by Goshen and Squire.[51] What emerges from Goshen and Squire's analysis is a reading that is far more articulate than the traditional one provided by the economic agency theory alone. If the costs to be considered when engineering an efficient corporate governance system are not only agency costs (referred to as 'conflict costs' by the authors) but also competence costs, and both types of costs are raised by both agents' and principals' qualities and behaviours, it is inevitable that even in a rather homogenous economic environment there will also be several potential recombinations of the said sets of costs.[52] Therefore, corporate opportunity rules may also need to be adapted to the specific cost variables found in different corporations and in different economic environments.

If an inflexible set of rules corresponds to a one-size-fits-all solution, the possibility of a waiver corresponds to the idea of tailoring one's duty of loyalty while being able to rely upon a certain default legal framework, assisted by remedies that are not typical contractual remedies but instead remedies normally imposed on fiduciaries (ie constructive trust and disgorgement of profits). Ayres and Gertner have shown that setting default rules is an extremely difficult task, entailing a choice between 'untailored default rules' (what the parties would have contracted for) and 'tailored default rules' (a 'single, off-the rack standard that in some sense represents what the majority of contracting parties would want').[53] Untailored default rules may force bargaining and help achieve allocative efficiency.[54]

Nonetheless, struggling to engineer the best default rules possible may represent the main efficient way forward. One may be tempted to say that a possible alternative solution is to leave parties free to contract over corporate opportunities in a free-taking environment and to hope that they will come up with brilliant ideas to protect the corporation's proprietary boundaries when

By contrast, the recommendation was implemented by the Danish Government, with the adoption of the 'Act on Restrictive Employment Clauses', Act No 1565 of 15 December 2015, whose Art 3 introduces strict limits on the validity of non-compete clauses. In an email exchange, Dr Bjørst reported that, following the adoption of Act No 1565/2015 of 15 December 2015, Danish employers reacted to the limits imposed on the validity of non-compete clauses by including very high liquidated damages in the employment contracts, as a way to prevent the disclosure of trade secrets.

[51] Z Goshen and R Squire, 'Principal Costs: A New Theory for Corporate Law and Governance' (2017) 117 *Columbia Law Review* 767.

[52] ibid 801ff.

[53] I Ayres and R Gertner, 'Filling Gaps in Incomplete Contracts: An Economic Theory of Default Rules' (1989) 99 *Yale Law Journal* 87, 91.

[54] See text at ch 4.II.

needed. Such an approach may mean throwing the baby out with bathwater. In fact,

> corporate opportunity and corporate competition claims are actually far more powerful than their restrictive covenant and trade secret counterparts, as these fiduciary duty theories do not require proof of an agreement, evidence of secrecy measures, or other factual and legal clutter that tends to derail contract and trade secret charges. Moreover, under the deterrence rationale of these doctrines, fiduciaries bear the heavy burden of proving their full disclosure, complete loyalty, and utmost good faith during their agency relationships.[55]

In other words, if a powerful claim, such as a corporate opportunity one, is unavailable to the corporation even by default, there is little chance that the parties will be able to arrange a well-suited corporate boundaries protection mechanism. Moreover, what is unique to Anglo-American corporate opportunity rules is their remedial system, which would risk being lost within a free-taking regime. As a conclusion, granting the possibility to the company and insiders of contracting around corporate opportunity rules seems to be crucial to the adaptation of such rules to different kinds of companies and different kinds of economic environments. Nonetheless, a default regime based on a solid defence of the corporate proprietary boundaries may still be considered as essential for the correct functioning of many ventures, as it will build up investors' confidence.

III. THE ABSENCE OF A CLEAR DEFINITION OF 'CORPORATE OPPORTUNITY': WEAKNESS OR STRENGTH?

Although US courts have dealt with corporate opportunity cases since the second half of the nineteenth century,[56] they have refrained from providing an exact definition of 'corporate opportunity'. Similarly, a definition is not retrievable in UK case law. At times, jurisprudence has tried to define what a 'taking' of a corporate opportunity is[57] or has attempted to identify common patterns that occur in corporate opportunity cases.[58] Nonetheless, the object of such takings – or the objective element that appears within such patterns – remains difficult to classify under one single definition. This may be one of the many reasons why corporate opportunity doctrines have been seen as a set

[55] W Schaller, 'Corporate Opportunities and Corporate Competition in Illinois: A Comparative Discussion of Fiduciary Duties' (2012) 46 *John Marshall Law Review* 1, 2.

[56] D Kershaw, *The Foundations of Anglo-American Corporate Fiduciary Law* (Cambridge University Press, 2018) 430ff.

[57] R Carter, 'Corporate Opportunity' (1977–78) 3 *Journal of Corporation Law* 422, 424. Carter then acknowledges that in practice 'The situation has become so confused that it is virtually impossible in many jurisdictions to predict what rule will be applied'.

[58] Schaller, 'Corporate Opportunities' (2012) 18.

of tangled and often contradictory precedents in need of systematisation and clarification.[59]

Despite the unavailability of a definition of corporate opportunity, case law may help to predict whether, from an empirical perspective, a corporate opportunity claim is likely to be successful or not. A corporate opportunity usually occurs when an insider exploits information – that normally is not available to the corporation without the insider's disclosure – to conclude a deal to their own benefit. The object of such a deal can be of almost any kind. It can be something very tangible, such as a piece of land,[60] technical equipment,[61] or even a business (eg a cinema).[62] Or it can be something valuable but intangible, such as a trade secret (eg Pepsi-Cola's secret formula),[63] a cellular telephone service,[64] a mining licence,[65] stock of a corporation,[66] or again, stock of a corporation, even within an IPO.[67] A corporate opportunity could also be the offer of a contract to be the developer of a given line of business on behalf of a third party.[68]

I have already mentioned that a lawmaker can pursue extremely diversified policy objectives through a corporate opportunity doctrine – and this can be understood further in the light of the diversity of the claims reported above.[69] If the policy objective at the core of corporate opportunity rules is strengthening the corporate boundaries, the lawmaker should attempt to apply the corporate opportunity doctrine to a much greater number of cases – in order to contain any possible leak of valuable business information. This seems to correspond to the UK approach, with its highly criticised[70] no-profit rule[71] and with its refusal to limit the application of the corporate opportunity doctrine to the business opportunities found by a director while acting in their capacity as a director.[72]

[59] In the US, see E Orlinsky, 'Corporate Opportunity Doctrine and Interested Director Transactions: A Framework for Analysis in an Attempt to Restore Predictability' (1999) 24 *Delaware Journal of Corporate Law* 451. In the UK, see D Kershaw, 'Does It Matter How the Law Thinks about Corporate Opportunities?' (2005) 25 *Oxford Journal of Legal Studies* 533.

[60] *Bhullar v Bhullar* [2003] EWCA Civ 424.

[61] US: *American Metal Forming Corporation v W Pittman* 52 F3d 504; *Knox Glass Bottle Co v Underwood* 89 So 2d 799 (Miss 1956).

[62] *Regal (Hastings) Ltd v Gulliver* (1942) 1 All ER 378 (HL).

[63] US: *Guth v Loft* 5 A 2d 503 (Del 1939).

[64] *Broz v Cellular Information Systems, Inc* 673 A 2d.

[65] *Queensland Mines Ltd v Hudson* (1978) AJLR 399 and *Peso Silver Mines (NPL)* v *Cropper* (1976) SCR 673 (Supreme Court of Canada).

[66] US: *Faraclas v City Vending Co* 194 A 2d 298 (Md 1963). But see an opposite view in *Weigel* v *Shapiro J W* 608 F2d 268. The question has been debated for a long time. On this point, see V Brudney, 'Insider Securities Dealing during Corporate Crisis' (1962) 61 *Michigan Law Review* 1.

[67] *In re eBay Inc Shareholders Litigation* 2004 WL 253521 (Del Ch 2004).

[68] *Industrial Development Consultants Ltd v Cooley* [1972] 1 WLR 443.

[69] See text corresponding to nn 60–68.

[70] D Kershaw, 'Lost in Translation: Corporate Opportunities in Comparative Perspective' (2005) 25 *Oxford Journal of Legal Studies* 603.

[71] *Regal (Hastings) Ltd v Gulliver* (n 62).

[72] *Bhullar v Bhullar* (n 60).

By contrast, if the lawmaker also wants to grant a degree of mobility to directors in order to set incentives for innovation, then the lawmaker should try to achieve a degree of flexibility in the application of the doctrine to cases involving innovative business opportunities.[73] One of the possible ways to do so is to refuse to identify a given inventive business opportunity as corporate. Clearly, the pursuance of the flexibilisation of such rules does not need to rely entirely on the manipulation of the test employed for identifying corporate opportunities. The narrowing or the stretching of interpretative activity of the business areas covered by the corporate opportunity rules can be achieved by reverting to other legal tools, such as for instance waivers,[74] *ex ante* ad hoc authorisations,[75] ex post ratifications and also the express regulation of 'strategic takings' by resigning directors.[76]

A detailed but non-exhaustive enumeration of the variables that can be considered when assessing a corporate opportunity case is provided by Laskin J in the Canadian case of *Canadian Aero Service Ltd v O'Malley*:

> The general standards of loyalty, good faith and avoidance of a conflict of duty and self-interest to which the conduct of a director or senior officer must conform, must be tested in each case by many factors which it would be reckless to attempt to enumerate exhaustively. Among them are the factor of position or office held, the nature of the corporate opportunity, its ripeness, its specificness and the director's or managerial officer's relation to it, the amount of knowledge possessed, the circumstances in which it was obtained and whether it was special or, indeed, even private, the factor of time in the continuation of fiduciary duty where the alleged breach occurs after termination of the relationship with the company, and the circumstances under which the relationship was terminated, that is whether by retirement or resignation or discharge.[77]

Apparently, in US law, even before the introduction of the possibility of a corporate opportunity waiver, there was 'reason to believe that parties' already enjoyed 'some limited ability to modify the corporate opportunity doctrine contractually, not by limiting damages, but instead by crafting an express definition of a "corporate opportunity"'.[78] But the most interesting examples of how the corporate opportunity doctrine can be stretched or narrowed for pursuing specific policy objectives are provided by two recent decisions of the Delaware Chancery.

[73] See text at ch 5.VIII and XI and accompanying notes.

[74] See text at section V and accompanying notes.

[75] See text at section IV and accompanying notes.

[76] See text at section VI and accompanying notes.

[77] *Canadian Aero Service Ltd v O'Malley* (1973) 40 DLR (3d) 371, 391.

[78] E Talley, 'Turning Servile Opportunities to Gold: A Strategic Analysis of the Corporate Opportunities Doctrine' (1998) 108 *Yale Law Journal* 277, 287, fn 20, last sentence. See also J Macey, 'Fiduciary Duties as Residual Claims: Obligations to Nonshareholder Constituencies from a Theory of the Firm Perspective' (1998) 84 *Cornell Law Review* 1266, 1278.

In the *Personal Touch Holding Corp v Glaubach* case,[79] the plaintiff was a company operating a home healthcare service. The opportunity contended in the case was the acquisition of the AAA Building, which hosted offices that the company was interested in acquiring. The company chairman, Mr Glaubach, had used information gathered in the course of the company's property search and secretly purchased the AAA Building. He had then offered the AAA Building to the company under lease.

The Delaware Chancery decided that the business opportunity consisting in the purchase of that building was corporate. In coming to such a decision, the court had to climb over what is perhaps the most iconic of the four prongs contained in the Broz test,[80] ie the line of business test. As the purchase of buildings was not in the line of business of the corporation, the Delaware Chancery recalled a previous decision, *Equity Corp v Milton*,[81] in which the Delaware Supreme Court had made it clear that a corporate opportunity case can be founded either on the line of business test or on the expectancy test. The Delaware Chancery in *Personal Touch* stressed the fact that the Delaware Supreme Court in *Equity Corp v Milton* presented the two tests as alternatives.[82] The Delaware Chancery subsequently noted that the relevance of the line of business test was overshadowed in this situation by the fact that

> (i) the Company had a clear interest and expectancy in acquiring the AAA Building …, and (ii) the opportunity presented concerns an operational decision about how to manage or expand an existing business – ie, whether it is better to buy or lease office space – as opposed to the opportunity to acquire a new business.[83]

In the *Personal Touch* case, there was no innovation or creative effort by the director of a corporation; only a pure financial speculation in breach of the duty of loyalty. Hence the Delaware Chancery reverted to old precedents in order to stretch the reach of the corporate opportunity doctrine. This is consistent with the idea of strengthening the corporate proprietary boundaries, following the agency costs paradigm.

Again in 2019, the Delaware Chancery also made it clear that stretching the reach of the corporate opportunity doctrine is not a general Delaware policy objective. In *Outlaw Beverage, Inc v Collins*,[84] the Delaware Chancery decided a case where Mr Lance Collins, a former director of Outlaw Beverage, Inc, had developed a business with 7-Eleven for the production of a private-label energy drink to compete with another manufacturer known as Bang. It has to be noted that in this case, Mr Collins could avail himself of a corporate opportunity

[79] *Personal Touch Holding Corp v Glaubach* 2019 WL 937180 (Del Ch Feb 25, 2019).
[80] *Broz v Cellular Information Systems, Inc* 673 A 2d 148, 154–55 (Del 1996).
[81] *Equity Corp v Milton* 221 A 2d 494 (Del 1966).
[82] *Equity Corp v Milton* 221 A 2d 494, 497.
[83] *Personal Touch*, citing *Kohls v Duthie* 791 A 2d 772 (Del Ch 2000) 46, text corresponding to fn 221 of the decision.
[84] *Outlaw Beverage, Inc v Collins* CA No 2019-0342-AGB (Del Ch June 18, 2019) (transcript).

waiver which did not apply to those corporate opportunities developed solely and exclusively in his capacity as a director of Outlaw. The Delaware Chancery analysed the activity undertaken by Mr Collins to develop the new beverage (branding, labelling and invention of the drink formula) and it concluded that such activity had no connection with the activity of Outlaw Beverage. But what is even more interesting is the Court's analysis of the essence of the contested opportunity. The business idea was disclosed to Mr Collins at a reunion with several representatives of 7-Eleven while Mr Collins was still a director of Outlaw Beverage. The Court noted that

> the opportunity that arose as a result of that meeting did not concern a tangible product, an actual business, or anything concrete in form. Rather, the opportunity that was presented was little more than a general idea or concept – that is, the idea of creating a Bang-like product for 7-Eleven's use as a private-label product.[85]

I believe that this decision is particularly emblematic of the degree of flexibility that can be achieved through a careful and experienced analysis of all the different variables of the case. I am not sure whether the Delaware Chancery followed a precise policy objective while drafting this judgment. Nonetheless, I believe that the clarifications pertaining to the differences between a mere idea and a tangible corporate opportunity may definitely help in addressing situations where a corporate director of a start-up matures mere ideas that they will eventually exploit once they have resigned or been dismissed. Subtracting mere ideas from the reach of the corporate opportunity doctrine may enhance the circulation of such building blocks of knowledge that are embedded in inventors/founders/directors' experience and therefore provide a great support to innovation dynamics.[86]

The reasoning adopted by the Delaware Chancery in *Outlaw Beverage* bears some resemblance to the rationale underlying the 'maturing business opportunity' rule. Nonetheless, such a test was applied to resigning directors.[87] I believe that re-adapting such a test to the cases of incumbent directors, while also revising the no-profit rule and adopting the director's capacity test, may help to flexibilise UK law, even without the possibility of corporate opportunity waivers.

As to the civil law jurisdictions, there has been an interesting convergence in form, with the French, German, Italian and Spanish jurisdictions adopting terminologies that are not direct translations of the term 'corporate opportunity' but are closer in meaning to the term 'business opportunity' ('*opportunité d'affaires*', '*Geschäftschance*', '*opportunità d'affari*', '*oportunidad de negocio*'). Whatever the interpretation of these terms is and will be, what really matters for civil law courts is that they commit to an attentive scrutiny of the underlying policy objectives pursued by the corporate opportunity doctrine, so that they do

[85] ibid 15.
[86] See text at ch 5.VI, VIII and XI and accompanying notes.
[87] *Canadian Aero Service Ltd v O'Malley* (1973) 40 DLR (3d) 371, 382.

not give more importance to form than to substance. Non-lawyers often tend to ignore the extent to which legal traditions are essentially conservative and highly defensive in relation to their legal categories and terminology.[88] Especially in civil law systems, a rigid interpretation of these terms in the earlier phases of the application of such new rules may prove fatal to an efficient law-making that preserves the possibility of adapting such rules to diversified economic environments. It might be that allowing the parties to contribute to the definition of 'corporate opportunity' by way of specific clauses in the corporate bylaw may constitute a potential way to prevent excessive rigidity in the application of such rules.[89]

A final note concerns the law of evidence. The allocation of the burden of proof of the corporate ownership of a given business opportunity can be another effective policy tool to be employed for modulating the effects of the doctrine.[90] To give an example, let us consider a business opportunity consisting of technological innovation.[91] In this case, courts could allocate to the incumbent company the burden of proving that the business opportunity is a corporate one, for instance by providing evidence that the corporation has invested its resources and/or has taken steps to integrate the business opportunity into its productive process. This kind of adjustment – whereby the courts would, for instance, require the company to show the importance to its going concern of a given innovative corporate opportunity, when it is unwilling to let its founder/director leave – may help to diversify the judicial response to different kinds of corporate opportunities.

IV. THE LIMITED EFFECTIVENESS OF AN *EX ANTE* AUTHORISATION TO TAKE CORPORATE OPPORTUNITIES

An *ex ante* authorisation by a company to its director to appropriate a corporate opportunity is possible under most corporate law systems that have a corporate opportunity doctrine, either in the form of a decision by a majority

[88] See M Krygier, 'Law as Tradition' (1986) 5 *Law and Philosophy* 237. The author claims that adherence to tradition is a central feature of any legal system. In reality, European legislation has stirred up the resistance that still exists within European legal traditions as to the style of legislation. See on this point W Wiegand, 'Americanization of Law: Reception or Convergence?' in L Friedman and H Scheiber (eds), *Legal Culture and the Legal Profession* (Westview Press, 1996) 146: 'When the members of the EC fulfill their obligation to create national rules within the framework of EC directives, they start … with definitions of subjects and terms. This technique, well known to American lawyers, has no basis in European legal history'.

[89] See the equivalent power under US Delaware law, as explained by Talley and by Macey (see n 78).

[90] See M Salzwedel, 'A Contractual Theory of Corporate Opportunity and a Proposed Statute' (2002) 23 *Pace Law Review* 83, 124.

[91] See text at ch 5.V ff and accompanying notes.

of non-conflicted directors or in the form of a decision by the shareholders' meeting.[92] The general costs surrounding such an authorisation have already been outlined with reference to the bargaining context.[93] This is the area of corporate opportunity doctrines that most clearly exemplifies the necessity to adopt a paradigm that includes not only agency costs (which, following Goshen and Squire, we can call 'conflict costs'),[94] but also competence costs and that analyses both agents' and principals' costs. Such a complex analysis is especially important in a context where the corporate opportunity whose taking is supposed to be authorised consists of a technological innovation – due to the fact that assessing the value of technological innovation requires well-developed technical competence.

A good example to consider is a technological innovation within a start-up – perhaps an idea that has not yet been patented or that cannot be patented, but that may become marketable within a short period of time. In a VC context, both a general partner (GP) – of an independent venture capital fund (IVCF) – and a corporate venture capitalist may well be able to appreciate the technical aspects of a given innovation. A corporate venture capitalist is likely to be active in a similar industry and therefore to possess all the knowledge they need to assess the technical soundness of a technological innovation.[95] A GP of an IVCF may also be entirely capable of such an assessment, especially in the US VC context, where GPs are likely to be deeply involved in a start-up's management.[96] Unsurprisingly, the least objective evaluation might come from the founder/inventor. Although they know their invention well from a technical

[92] For example, in civil law, see the Spanish *Ley de Sociedades de Capital* (Spanish Stock Company Law) Art 230, para 2, mandating the approval of the shareholders' assembly for operations that exceed the value of 10% of the company's assets. For smaller operations, an authorisation of a majority of non-conflicted directors is sufficient. In common law, see for instance the UK situation, as explained by A Keay, 'The Authorising of Directors' Conflicts of Interest: Getting a Balance?' (2012) 12 *Journal of Corporate Law Studies* 129, 132, 136ff. Once disclosure has been effectuated, UK law requires either the traditional common law solution (within the limits set by *Cook v Deeks* [1916] AC 554 – ie an authorisation by the shareholders' meeting), or now, under CA 2006, s 175(4)(b), an authorisation by a majority of non-conflicted directors – potentially outside the limits set by *Cook v Deeks*. In Italian law, there seems to be a possibility of obtaining an authorisation by the shareholders' assembly or by the board. See F Barachini, 'L'Appropriazione delle *Corporate Opportunities*' in P Abbadessa and G Portale (eds), *Il Nuovo Diritto delle Società, Liber Amicorum Gian Franco Campobasso* (UTET, 2006) 608, 644ff. According to Talley, 'Turning Servile Opportunities to Gold' (1998) 297, in US Delaware law 'A number of routes are available, but the most common consists of approval or ratification by either an affirmative vote of the disinterested directors, and, in the case of a senior executive, approval by a disinterested superior (both subject to review under the relatively lax business judgment rule), or alternatively, approval or ratification by the disinterested shareholders (subject to a "waste" standard of review). Even in the absence of either of the above two forms of rejection, a disclosing fiduciary may still be able to demonstrate proper rejection by demonstrating that appropriating the opportunity was "fair" to the corporation'.

[93] See text at ch 4.V and accompanying notes.

[94] Goshen and Squire, 'Principal Costs' (2017).

[95] See text at ch 6.V and accompanying notes.

[96] See ch 6.VI and accompanying notes.

perspective, it is well-known that having to evaluate one's own creations often triggers endowment effects.[97] But in this case, the more objective assessment carried out by the VC investors would prevail, because they would be in charge of authorising the taking.

The point is that technical competence is not necessarily enough to come to the right conclusions about the success prospects of a given innovation. For instance, consider three recent innovation flops: Smart Glasses, Blackberry and the Samsung Galaxy Fold. All these inventions were technically extremely advanced;[98] the problem was the limited appeal they had for consumers. But there is still the question of whether such marketing competences are enough to supplement the technical evaluation of an invention. Apart from employing consumer polls in order to try to understand the potentiality of a new product, intuition on the personality and charisma of the founder (ie of the insider willing to leave) may be crucial – and it is well known that investors can make huge mistakes in evaluating founders' personality.[99] In the case of Apple, for instance, Steve Jobs, even after his death, is still a determining element of Apple's marketing strategy.[100] At times, only the insider willing to appropriate a corporate opportunity that they have contributed to the invention of may know how much passion, capability and dedication they are ready to put into their endeavour and how effectively they will be able to communicate their mission to the consumers. Such intensive insistence on their mission may manifest only when founders have actually left the corporation they have worked for to open their own venture.[101] Moreover, contemporary successful innovators and founders often display the psychological traits of facilitators more than those of tyrannical characters:[102] and an investor who is used to tough bargaining might underestimate the soft skills of such a founder and assign a lower value to their project.

In summary, the competence needed to price the future of a given innovation may also require a deep understanding of the psychological dynamics of the insider who is willing to leave, and an understanding that such an insider, if asked to develop the same innovation within the incumbent company, will probably not be able to manifest the positive sides of their personality as well as they would do within their own newly created organisation. Inevitably, such an

[97] See ch 4.III and accompanying notes.

[98] aayushjain.com/top-failed-products-failure-examples-and-best-management-lessons.

[99] A Mosteller, 'How Steve Jobs and Jeff Bezos Handled Rejection', www.lendio.com/blog/small-business-tools/jobs-bezos-rejection.

[100] E Bell and T Scott, 'Vernacular Mourning and Corporate Memorialization in Framing the Death of Steve Jobs' (2016) 23 *Organization* 114.

[101] S Eisner, 'The "In-Factor": Signature Traits of Innovation's Leaders' (2016) 32 *Journal of Applied Business Research* 185, 196ff. Eisner describes the personality traits common to modern founders with a series of IN-factors, such as 'invested; integrated; in touch; intelligent; in place'.

[102] I Nonala and M Kenney, 'Towards a New Theory of Innovation Management: A Case Study Comparing Canon, Inc. and Apple Computer, Inc.' (1991) 8 *Journal of Engineering and Technology Management* 67.

estimation requires many more skills than merely technical ones and therefore the most competent constituency (in this case the non-conflicted components of the board) may not necessarily be the best judge.

One may wonder whether in such a context 'principals' conflict costs'[103] might also play a role. For instance, in a VC-backed start-up, the presence of different kinds of founders may raise significant principals' conflict costs. An example is a start-up that is backed by both an IVCF and a CVC, where the question of whether a given corporate opportunity will be relinquished by the company has to be deliberated. Although it may be sensible to let the insider appropriate and develop the opportunity, the CVC may be interested in preventing the director from doing so where this would create competition for its other industrial activities.[104] Another example is where there are personal conflicts between a founder who decides to stay with the incumbent corporation and one who decides to leave (as with the example of Steve Jobs).[105] While VC investors may want to help the insider who is seeking an authorisation to appropriate a corporate opportunity, the insider's co-founder, for reasons of personal acrimony, may decide to deny such an authorisation, thus creating an approach that conflicts with the one of the VC investors.

It is clear that authorisations may not necessarily involve innovative business opportunities. At times, the value of a given business opportunity can be easy to assess and the procedure can roll smoothly. Nonetheless, the potential complexity surrounding such an authorisation within a start-up context suggests that the possibility of introducing a waiver is to be regarded as particularly important. For instance, an ad hoc waiver may exclude the application of the corporate opportunity doctrine to those corporate opportunities that a start-up decides not to pursue – hence liberating the insider from a potentially difficult authorisation procedure.

V. THE BENEFITS OF A WAIVER FOR CORPORATE OPPORTUNITIES

In some jurisdictions, legal doctrine has created an aura of sacredness around the directors' duty of loyalty.[106] Conflicted transactions have been regarded for a long time as the columns of Hercules of the permitted activity – but increasingly several aspects of the directors' duty of loyalty have been relaxed

[103] Goshen and Squire (n 51) 791.

[104] See text at ch 6.V and accompanying notes.

[105] See text at ch 5.II and accompanying notes.

[106] This was also the situation in the Delaware jurisdiction with reference to corporate opportunity rules, at least in its seminal case *Guth v Loft* (n 63) 510: 'The rule, inveterate and uncompromising in its rigidity, does not rest upon the narrow ground of injury or damage to the corporation resulting from a betrayal of confidence, but upon a broader foundation of a wise public policy that, for the purpose of removing all temptation, extinguishes all possibility of profit flowing from a breach of the confidence imposed by the fiduciary relation'.

in most jurisdictions.[107] In the 1990s, legal doctrine was already foreseeing corporate opportunities as a column ready to fall under the pressure of legal innovation.[108]

It is worth remembering that corporate opportunities were not always subject to the same stringent regime in the country where they were first introduced – that is, the US. In fact, in an early case, *Anniston Lime*, not all of the business opportunities in the line of business of the corporation were assigned to the corporation. In that decision, the court made clear that there had to be an expectation based on contractual rights in order to create a corporate proprietary right to a given business opportunity.[109] Therefore, the transformation of a mere business opportunity into a corporate opportunity required a consensual activity by the representatives of the corporation. To some extent, the idea of a waiver, ie a contractual exemption for directors from the doctrine, has shared some gene with the primordial logic of corporate opportunity doctrines. Although in the case of a waiver the contract is between corporation and director (whereas in *Anniston Lime* it was between the corporation and a third party), it is still an element deriving from contractual will that allows for the disapplication of the doctrine.

In the case of Delaware law, the introduction of the possibility of waiving the corporate opportunity doctrine was probably motivated by the need to allow IVCFs to operate in a position of psychologically divided loyalty[110] but also by the need to avoid the lengthy process required for an authorisation.[111] The limits of a mandatory corporate opportunity doctrine emerged clearly in the *Tri-star* case.[112] Tri-star's charter provisions identified a set of business opportunities that Tri-star was not interested in pursuing and exculpated its directors from breach of the duty of loyalty. The Delaware Chancery considered such an exculpation attempt introduced in the charter as being in contrast with the mandatory nature of corporate opportunity rules.

In the post-*Tri-star* Delaware legal regime, Delaware General Corporation Law (DGCL), s 122(17) states that a corporation has power to

> [r]enounce, in its certificate of incorporation or by action of its board of directors, any interest or expectancy of the corporation in specified business opportunities or

[107] J Velasco, 'The Diminishing Duty of Loyalty' (2018) 75 *Washington & Lee Law Review* 1035. See also C Bruner, 'Opting Out of Fiduciary Duties and Liabilities in US and UK Business Entities' in G Smith and A Gold, *Research Handbook on Fiduciary Law* (Edward Elgar, 2018), highlighting several persisting differences between the US and the UK system.

[108] Epstein, 'Contract and Trust in Corporate Law' (1996) 13–17, also recalling, at 17, that in the 1960s it was already common practice to introduce a waiver for corporate opportunities in standard agreements for limited partnerships.

[109] *Lagarde v Anniston Lime & Stone Co* 126 Ala 496, 28 So 199 (1900).

[110] T Woolf, 'The Venture Capitalist's Corporate Opportunity Problem' (2001) *Columbia Business Law Review* 473.

[111] C Austin and D Gottlieb, 'Renouncing Corporate Opportunities in Spin-Offs, Carve-Out IPOs, and Private Equity Investments' (2003) 17 *Corporate & Securities Law Advisor* 2, 4.

[112] *Siegman v Tri-Star Pictures, Inc*, CA No 9477 (Del Ch 5 May 1989, revised 30 May 1989).

> specified classes or categories of business opportunities that are presented to the corporation or 1 or more of its officers, directors or stockholders.[113]

Empirical research has shown that the option introduced by DGCL, s 122(17) has met with great success in practice, and in contexts way beyond the VC industry.[114] Nonetheless, a full appreciation of the operational significance of a waiver comes only with an exact perception of its limits. The exact limits within which the freedom to waive corporate opportunity doctrines can be exercised seems still undefined, because DGCL refers to 'specified business opportunities or specified classes or categories' and does not seem to contemplate any reference to a general waiver.

The Delaware legislative synopsis – s 3 – states that:

> By way of example, the classes or categories of business opportunities may be specified by any manner of defining or delineating business opportunities or the corporation's or any other party's entitlement thereto or interest therein, including, without limitation, by line or type of business, identity of the originator of the business opportunity, identity of the party or parties to or having an interest in the business opportunity, identity of the recipient of the business opportunity, periods of time or geographical location.[115]

The indications provided by the Delaware legislative synopsis are not quite exhaustive. From its wording, it appears that a waiver requires several specifications, although there is no mention of the consequences of the absence of such specifications. The Delaware Chancery, in footnote 46 of its recent *Alarm.com* decision, states that:

> No one has challenged the scope of the waiver, and this decision provides no opportunity to opine on the validity of a broad and general renunciation of corporate opportunities, as contrasted with a more tailored provision addressing a specified business opportunity or a well-defined class or category of business opportunities.[116]

This seems to indicate the possibility that the Court of Chancery may decide for the invalidity of a general waiver in the future. As a matter of fact, the Delaware Chancery seems to attach remarkable legal effects to corporate opportunity waivers, and it is therefore not surprising that a way is needed for a waiver to be limited in its reach. A valid corporate opportunity waiver is so far-reaching that it applies also to other contracts or clauses that are similar in function

[113] DGCL, s 122(17).

[114] Rauterberg and Talley, 'Contracting Out of the Fiduciary Duty of Loyalty' (2017). It is interesting to note that US jurisprudence has identified a recent increase in the introduction of rules that are functionally similar to corporate opportunity rules, ie non-compete covenants in CEOs' employment contracts. See N Bishara, K Martin and R Thomas, 'When Do CEOs Have Covenants not to Compete in their Employment Contracts?' (2015) 68 *Vanderbilt Law Review* 12. The study shows that such contracts are rarer in states such as California where normally non-compete clauses are not enforced.

[115] Delaware Bill Summary, s 363, 140th Gen Assembly (Del 2000); 72 Del Laws, c 343, § 3 (2000).

[116] *Alarm.com Holdings, Inc v ABS Capital Partners Inc* CA No 2017-0583-JTL.

(such as non-compete or non-disclosure) but that are assisted by weaker remedies as compared to corporate opportunity rules.[117] For the time being, not even further cases, such as *Outlaw Beverage* and *Armored Combat League, LLC v Brooks*[118] seem to offer a clear indication of what is permitted and what is not when drafting a corporate opportunity waiver.

In *Outlaw Beverage*, it was reported that Article XII of Outlaw's certificate of incorporation renounced any 'interest or expectancy … in, or in being offered an opportunity to participate in, an Excluded Opportunity'.[119] An 'Excluded Opportunity' was defined as

> any matter, transaction, or interest that is presented to, or acquired, created or developed by, or which otherwise comes into the possession of (i) any director of this corporation who is not an employee of this corporation … unless such matter, transaction or interest is presented to, or acquired, created or developed by, or otherwise comes into the possession of [the director] expressly and solely in such [person's] capacity as a director of this corporation.[120]

The wording 'Excluded Opportunity' is based on the 'expressly and solely in their capacity' test. The validity of such a clause was not contested, and the court concluded that the director had acquired the opportunity outside his capacity as a director. Hence, it looks like such a degree of (rather undetailed) specification was accepted by the court. As noted by Nate Emeritz and Brian Currie,

> the Court of Chancery's approach to construing corporate opportunity waivers is also quite valuable to effective corporate planning and drafting, particularly because we would generally expect the language of those waivers to be closely examined in any litigation.[121]

Therefore, future case law will certainly assist in clarifying the limits within which corporate opportunity waivers can be validly drafted. At the present time, an important mistake to avoid is the use of language that exculpates directors instead of language that refers directly to the will to renounce/waive the doctrine. Words exculpating directors would clearly recall the (unfavourable) *Tri-star* decision.[122]

Of course, when devising a waiver, much attention should be given to the exact objective that is being pursued through such a provision. One of the reasons why DGCL requires some limits to the scope of the waiver may be that the power to waive corporate opportunity rules may be used also for purposes that have no welfare benefits worthy of protection. For instance, it is true that

[117] ibid 18–19.

[118] *Armored Combat League, LLC v Brooks*, CA No 2019-0463-MTZ (Del Ch 2 July 2019) (transcript).

[119] *Outlaw Beverage, Inc v Collins* (n 84).

[120] ibid 12.

[121] N Emeritz and B Currie, 'Corporate Opportunity Doctrine: Litigation Continues into 2020', corpgov.law.harvard.edu/2020/02/27/corporate-opportunity-doctrine-litigation-continues-into-2020.

[122] Austin and Gottlieb, 'Renouncing Corporate Opportunities' (2003) 6.

directors appointed by IVCFs are often in a position of divided loyalty towards their different investees, and that this is intrinsic to their activity. But a waiver in their favour should be written in a way that does not enable them to take corporate opportunities for their personal benefit. Instead, it should refer to their potential situation of divided loyalty and in that case exonerate them from abiding by the corporate opportunity doctrine. Otherwise, a general waiver may actually promote GP misconduct.

Finally, a problem that a corporate opportunity waiver cannot solve relates to the potential asymmetries of the different parties who bargain around such waiver. Imagine a penniless continental European entrepreneur who can only revert to CVC for a seed investment.[123] If European corporate laws allowed waivers of corporate opportunity doctrines,[124] such an entrepreneur may be compelled to accept such a waiver in favour of the corporate venture capitalist, in order to have access to financing. Moreover, mechanisms such as the approval of the waiver by the board of directors or by the shareholder assembly may not help in this context – not only for the reasons outlined above[125] – but also because the problem resides not in the law but in the differences in the bargaining power of the parties. This is why waivers may be more beneficial in financial systems where the competition among providers of VC is fiercer and there are therefore mechanisms of reputational checks-and-balances among investors.[126]

VI. RULES ON RESIGNING DIRECTORS AND THEIR VITAL IMPORTANCE FOR VENTURE CAPITAL

One may argue that the legal treatment of misappropriations of corporate opportunities by resigning directors is no longer as relevant in those jurisdictions where it is possible to waive corporate opportunity rules. I have already cited the Delaware corporate law reforms, which were subsequently emulated in the laws of many US states.[127] Nonetheless, it is worth remembering once again that at least some of the examples of European corporate legislation cited in this book do not contemplate the possibility of a waiver.[128] Moreover, even in those jurisdictions (such as Delaware) which allow for the introduction of waivers for corporate opportunity rules, there will not necessarily be a demand for such a waiver within every single corporation. Even when such a waiver is required by certain directors, it is not certain that it will be granted. Furthermore, the waiver may be favoured by only some of the directors and/or may be limited to certain

[123] See text at ch 6.VI and accompanying notes.

[124] At the time such a general waiver does not seem to be possible at least under German and Spanish law. See n 29.

[125] See section IV and accompanying notes.

[126] See text at ch 6.IV.F and accompanying notes.

[127] Rauterberg and Talley (n 35) 1078, fn 11.

[128] See section V and accompanying notes.

types of corporate opportunities.[129] In particular, I have already mentioned that in VC practice, because of the imbalance in bargaining power between IVCF and entrepreneur, a waiver is more likely to be asymmetric, ie just in favour of the IVCF.[130] As a consequence of the lack of pervasiveness of waivers for corporate opportunity rules, one may say that rules on resigning directors still have a significant impact in all the jurisdictions cited here.

The debate on the applicability of corporate opportunity rules to resigning corporate directors is illustrative of the divergent paths of two policy objectives underlying this legal doctrine. On one hand is the most well-known and original policy objective, ie the protection of corporate proprietary boundaries, often understood through the lens of economic agency theory.[131] On the other hand is the demand for a degree of openness in corporate boundaries, mandated by a smooth functioning of the VC industry in cases of divided loyalty,[132] but also required by certain legal aspects surrounding technological innovation, such as 'contracting for innovation' within an open innovation context.[133]

A director who is subject to corporate opportunity rules may strategically decide to resign from their position precisely because they intend to exploit a corporate opportunity which they may be prevented from appropriating while still serving on the board of the corporation.[134] At first glance, one may recognise in such a strategy a possible intent to circumvent the law.[135] From an agency theory perspective, such a scheme belongs to the category of an agent's actions contrary to the interests of the principal. It may also be considered as particularly pernicious for a corporation, precisely because it is somewhat less easy to detect than an outright misappropriation.

Nonetheless, if we consider a wider set of policy objectives than the protection of corporate proprietary boundaries suggested by economic agency theory, we soon realise that a too-strict application of corporate opportunity rules to resigning directors may set obstacles to several of the efficient dynamics upon which the technological innovation industry is based. This is true particularly from the point of view of the functioning of technological innovation dynamics.[136]

Despite the increasing general awareness of efficiency dynamics that goes well beyond the agency theory paradigm, the law may not immediately adapt to the new academic findings. For instance, UK law shows a high degree of refinement in its analysis of directors' resignations, although it sticks to a rather

[129] See n 29.
[130] See text at ch 6.IV.E and accompanying notes.
[131] See text at ch 2.III and accompanying notes.
[132] See text at ch 6.IV.E and accompanying notes.
[133] See text at ch 5.VI and accompanying notes.
[134] *Export Finance Ltd* v *Umunna* ([1989] BCLC 460, 480f–g.
[135] R Cassim, 'Post-resignation Duties of Directors: The Application of the Fiduciary Duty not to Misappropriate Corporate Opportunities' (2008) 125 *South African Law Journal* 731, 736.
[136] See text at ch 5.VI and VIII and accompanying notes.

conservative approach. UK law imposes a set of rather articulate restrictions on resigning directors. CA 2006, s 170(2)(a) states that:

> A person who ceases to be a director continues to be subject – (a) to the duty in section 175 [duty to avoid conflicts of interest] as regards the exploitation of any property, information or opportunity of which he became aware at a time when he was a director.

This formulation seems to derive from the fact that, in UK law, directors may also have had space for manoeuvre through strategic resignation, because Lord Russell's dictum in *Regal (Hastings) Ltd v Gulliver* requires that the profit originates 'by reason and in course of their office of directors'.[137]

To avoid any possibility of evading the general ban on appropriation of corporate opportunities, case law tends to apply a rigid 'no-conflict' rule to directors who have resigned. For example, in *IDC* v *Cooley*,[138] the exploitation – at a point subsequent to his resignation – of a conflicted situation which arose when Cooley was a director of Industrial Development Consultants ltd (IDC) was understood as a violation of directors' duties, despite evidence that IDC would hardly have been able to appropriate that business opportunity. It seems that this position was adopted by CA 2006, s 170(2), which states that a person who ceases to be a director continues to be subject to the duty to avoid conflicts of interests as regards the exploitation of any opportunity of which he became aware at a time when he was a director. For that reason, *IDC* v *Cooley* may well be considered a leading case for interpreting s 170(2), whilst stressing

> three factors that are particularly important to its application: first, taking steps whilst a director to position oneself to obtain the opportunity; secondly, not disclosing to the company what you know about the opportunity; and, thirdly, resigning with the intention of exploiting the opportunity.[139]

Nonetheless, one cannot forget that additional specifications exist in English common law, which mainly pertain to the argument in the 'maturing business opportunity rule' as stated in *Island Export Finance Ltd v Umunna*.[140] That rule was originally developed by the Supreme Court of Canada in *Canadian Aero Service Ltd v O'Malley*,[141] and considers the appropriation of a corporate opportunity by a director who has resigned to be a violation of fiduciary duties when the opportunity is one the company is actively pursuing and the director either exploited it because of their former position and/or they resigned to do so.

The cited rule is not so distant from that formulated in *IDC*, at least from a substantive point of view: in fact, the main differences seem to be on the one hand, the relevance of the opportunity's disclosure, which is cited only in

[137] *Regal (Hastings) Ltd v Gulliver* (n 62) 385D.
[138] *IDC* v *Cooley* [1972] 1 WLR 443.
[139] D Kershaw, *Company Law in Context* (Oxford University Press, 2012) 562.
[140] *Export Finance Ltd* v *Umunna* (n 134).
[141] *Canadian Aero Service Ltd v O'Malley* (1973) 40 DLR (3d) 371.

IDC, and perhaps on the other hand, the degree of ripeness of the opportunity. Nonetheless, in *IDC* the opportunity was also quite mature; therefore, the judge may just have implicitly considered this variable without explicitly stating it.

The real difference may be what Paul Morgan QC indicated in *Quarter Master UK Ltd v Pyke*[142] as the existence of two additional defences to be considered beyond the degree of ripeness of the opportunity, ie that before resignation, the director did not act in breach of duty (conflict of interest) and that after resignation, they did not use pre-existing property of the company. Still, the real extent of the rule remains unclear even after those additional defences, because according to the reasoning in *Pyke*, the degree of strictness of the rule depends on the extent to which a conflict of interest is envisaged and on the meaning of 'property' of the company. A decision subsequent to the entry into force of CA 2006 seems to confirm the importance of the first cited *Pyke* point, concerning loyalty. In fact, in *Foster Bryant Surveying Ltd v Bryant*,[143] Rix LJ, while admitting the availability of the maturing opportunity test, still maintained the possibility of the resigning director being responsible for the appropriation of a non-maturing business opportunity when a breach of fiduciary duty has occurred. The standards that have been set with reference to resigned directors do not appear to be substantively different from those of existing directors. Moreover, the same subtleties concerning the concept of 'conflict' seem to reappear in this context.

Cassim has shown that further issues may arise from a reading of the explicit interpretation of 'strategic resignation' provided in *Canadian Aero Service Ltd v O'Malley*. In this decision, the court provided a further specification. It stated that a resigning director is prevented from appropriating a corporate opportunity

> where the resignation may fairly be said to have been prompted or influenced by a wish to acquire for himself the opportunity sought by the company, or where it was his position with the company rather than a fresh initiative that led him to the opportunity which he later acquired.[144]

Cassim notices that this dictum includes two separate principles. The first principle applies when resignation arises out of the desire to pursue a business opportunity sought by the company, ie a maturing business opportunity. This means that when a director is 'prompted or influenced' to resign for reasons that have nothing to do with the pursuance of corporate opportunities, they will not be considered as misappropriating.[145] The second rule applies to a director who was led to the opportunity thanks to their position with the company.[146] This rule is rather ambiguous, because, if interpreted very widely, it may prevent

[142] [2004] EWHC 1815 (Ch).
[143] [2007] EWCA Civ 200.
[144] *Canadian Aero Service Ltd v O'Malley* (n 141).
[145] *Export Finance Ltd* v *Umunna* (n 134).
[146] Cassim, 'Post-resignation Duties of Directors' (2008) 747.

directors from exploiting the knowledge and the connections they matured while being directors.[147]

This is probably why in *Umunna*, Hutchison J ruled that it is not a breach of corporate opportunity rules for a director keeping on exploiting the knowledge acquired in the previous corporation within their new business activity.[148] Such a narrowing of the potential reach of *Canadian Aero Service Ltd v O'Malley* can certainly be welcomed, especially in a view of flexibilising the law and tuning it to the circulation freedom that promotes the development of high-tech hubs. In fact, a wider interpretation of the Canadian precedent would have had the effect of completely stifling the directors' mobility, which is one of the sources of innovation in such innovative industrial clusters.[149]

UK and Commonwealth courts have been able to develop their theories on resigning directors through several decades of experience. By contrast, such rules are very new to civil law systems, with the exception of Germany.

In Spain, the Supreme Court has dealt with this problem in a case involving the Cluster Competitiveness Group SA. This was the case of a company whose main object was providing business consultancy for improving the competitiveness of privately and publicly owned businesses.[150] Mr Rafael, a former director of Cluster Competitiveness, resigned from his position as director in June 2005 and took up two important consultancies – one on his own (in July 2005) and one through a newly founded company (in December 2005). Mr Rafael had already discussed these two consultancy projects with his clients when he was a director of the Cluster Competitiveness Group SA. The Tribunal of Barcelona awarded damages to Cluster Competitiveness; damages which were in turn denied by the Court of Appeal.

The Spanish Supreme Court quashed the decision of the Court of Appeal. It did so by affirming the existence of a post-resignation duty of loyalty to the corporation, based on the principle of good faith – also referring to the legal doctrine of 'preparatory acts' – that is, pre-resignation negotiations of the resigning director functional to post-resignation appropriation of the corporate opportunity.[151] In particular, it attributed the first opportunity (July 2005) to Cluster Competitiveness, but not the second (December 2005).[152] As to the first opportunity, it considered, among other factors, an express manifestation (in a fax, ie in writing) of interest by Cluster Competitiveness in the opportunity at issue.[153] With reference to the second opportunity, it considered, among other factors, the more significant delay between Mr Rafael's resignation and the conclusion of the second contract.[154]

[147] ibid 748ff.
[148] *Export Finance Ltd* v *Umunna* (n 134) 482 c–d.
[149] See text at ch 5.VIII and accompanying notes.
[150] STS (Sala de lo Civil, Sección 1a), de 3 de septiembre de 2012 (RJ 2012/9007).
[151] ibid under 'Tercero'.
[152] ibid under 'Cuarto'.
[153] ibid.
[154] ibid.

There are a few points worth making with reference to this decision. Although such cases were not cited in the decision, the 'intencionada preparación del aprovechamiento de la oportunidad de negocio por parte del administrador' (intentional preparation of the exploitation of the corporate opportunity by the director) seems to refer to a precise strategy adopted by the director. Once again, it looks like the British corporate opportunity doctrine has had a remarkable impact on the Spanish one.[155]

Secondly, it was not made clear whether Mr Rafael represented the main human capital asset of Cluster Competitiveness – ie whether Cluster Competitiveness would have been able to appropriate the business opportunity at issue without the contribution of Mr Rafael. If that was the case, from an industrial organisation perspective, the situation presents some parallels with cases such as that of Saatchi and Saatchi, whereby the key employees of an important London consultancy resigned collectively after a refusal by the main blockholder to approve a generous option package – depleting the company of its major asset.[156] Such cases prompted industrial organisation literature to rethink the concept of control in view of the relevance of human assets in a service-oriented economy.[157] The main difference here is that Mr Rafael was a director of the company. If Mr Rafael represented the main human capital asset of Cluster Competitiveness, the decision may provide a legal tool to the company to (temporarily) lock in human assets. By contrast, such an operation was unsuccessful in Saatchi and Saatchi on the basis of mere employment contracts.[158]

Such an achievement could be beneficial for investors in companies such as Cluster Competitiveness, but detrimental to the innovation dynamics we have discussed above.[159] Nonetheless, we can notice that the Spanish decision is rather balanced and it allocates to the resigning director only one of the business opportunities (ie the ripest one).

In France, the Supreme Court reviewed the legality of a Court of Appeal case dealing with a resigned director setting up a company competing with the incumbent one in the distribution and maintenance of fire-fighting equipment.[160] The employees of the incumbent company had resigned together with the director and were re-employed in the newly established competing company. The Supreme Court reproached the Court of Appeal for not having verified whether the former director of a company had breached his duty of loyalty. From the wording, it is not clear whether the breach of the duty of loyalty consisted in

[155] See text at ch 1.VII and accompanying notes.

[156] See the case as described in L Zingales, 'In Search of New Foundations' (2000) 55 *The Journal of Finance* 1623, 1641; R Rajan and L Zingales, 'The Influence of the Financial Revolution on the Nature of Firms' (2011) 91 *American Economic Review* 206.

[157] Zingales, 'New Foundations' (2000) and Rajan and Zingales, 'Financial Revolution' (2011).

[158] See Zingales (n 156) 1641.

[159] See text and ch 5.VI and VIII and accompanying notes.

[160] Cass Com 24 février 1998, [1988] *Bulletin Joly* 813.

setting up a competing business or in the (unproved, according to the Supreme Court) embezzlement of employees.[161] Regardless of the rationale of the decision, this case unfortunately does not help in explaining how exactly a French court would deal with a resigning director's preparatory acts.

A situation that looks much more similar to those that may typically arise in highly technologically innovative environments was dealt with under German law, in a case decided by the Court of Appeal of Stuttgart in the 1980s. The defendant was a managing director of a *Gesellschaft mit beschränkter Haftung* (GmbH), which in turn was the plaintiff. The GmbH was active in the production and sale of rodless pressure cylinders. The defendant was approached by an engineer ('K') who offered to develop a novel sealing system that was more cost-effective than the seals employed by the plaintiff. The defendant decided to terminate his employment relationship with the plaintiff GmbH at the time he received K's offer. The defendant and plaintiff agreed to waive any claim eventually arising from the contractual relationship. K eventually developed the novel sealing system, which was employed within a company directed by the defendant. The Court of Appeal of Stuttgart had decided that if the director is not prevented from making any change in employment, he should not disclose offers made to him in person to his employer in the case that he decides to resign. Hence, it went on to decide that any compensation claim was covered by the above-mentioned mutual waiver agreed by the parties.

The *Bundesgerichtshof* (BGH) quashed the decision by the Stuttgart Court of Appeal, stating that it had to be considered as irrelevant that K had offered the opportunity to the defendant privately, ie outside his capacity as managing director. In fact, the BGH stressed that as long as the defendant was a managing director of the company, his duty of loyalty was indivisible. The BGH went on to conclude that the above-mentioned waiver of claims arising from the contractual relationship with the corporation could not be considered as covering a grossly intentional breach of duty, such as the misappropriation of a corporate opportunity.

The decision was heavily criticised by German jurisprudence. Professor Klaus Hopt very clearly explained the negative policy implications of the decision:

> The German Federal Court of Justice (Bundesgerichtshof) squashed this decision, not appreciating the negative overall consequences: Directors who have expertise, but not enough capital of their own, are prevented from opening their own business which is negative for themselves and the market as a whole.[162]

This shows that, although the decision of the BGH was highly unsatisfactory, at least German academics have been aware of the dynamics surrounding innovative corporate opportunities for a long time.

[161] A Brès, 'L'Obligation de Non-Concurrence de Plein Droit de l'Associé' (2011) *RTDCom. Revue Trimestrielle de Droit Commercial et de Droit Economique* 463, fn 236.

[162] K Hopt, 'Conflict of Interest, Secrecy and Insider Information of Directors, A Comparative Analysis' (2013) 10 *European Corporate and Financial Law Review* 167, 179.

The examples dealt with above in this section show that a fine-tuning of the application of the corporate opportunity doctrine to resigning directors may grant the possibility of pursuing policy objectives that go beyond the mere protection of the corporate proprietary boundaries. This renders this legal tool particularly relevant.[163]

VII. REMEDIES IN CIVIL LAW: HOW TO OVERCOME THE INTRINSIC WEAKNESS OF A REMEDIAL SYSTEM LACKING EQUITY REMEDIES

If the remedial system can be seen as the linchpin around which bargaining over corporate opportunities can be organised, the substantive differences between common law and civil law remedies may contain an illustration of a significantly different set of costs and incentives surrounding bargaining on corporate opportunities in civil law and common law jurisdictions.[164]

As already noted, when it comes to forcing disclosure, the behavioural effects of a disgorgement of profits assisted by a constructive trust in its proprietary form can be particularly effective.[165] Now, let us imagine that civil law jurisdictions' lawmakers – instead of trying to introduce alternative remedies such as punitive damages – decide to introduce a disgorgement of profits assisted by a proprietary constructive trust in their jurisdictions. The easier way to introduce rules that are similar in function to those that exist in the Anglo-American systems would be by way of statutory reforms. Trust law has become part of the civil law traditions after the Hague Convention on the Law Applicable to Trusts and on their Recognition of 1 July 1985.[166] But the constructive trust is something completely different from the trusts referred to in the Hague Convention – as it is a form of remedial trust – and it is possible that civil law courts would need many trials to understand how to use it.[167] This branch of

[163] Further policy insights can be gained through analysis of the US 'preparation to compete' doctrine, which, as described by Charles Graves, 'provides latitude for employees – including top executives – to plan new jobs, to take meaningful steps to start a new business before leaving the current job, and to conceal such plans from the employer'. See C Graves, 'Preparing to Quit: Employee Competition versus Corporate Opportunity' (2020) 41 *Berkeley Journal of Employment & Labour Law* 333, 335. Nonetheless, the author notes that in the present (unsatisfactory) state of the art, courts often conflate the 'corporate opportunity' and the 'preparation to compete' doctrines, with the result of introducing elements of rigidity in the latter. See ibid 361ff.

[164] See text at ch 4.II and accompanying notes.

[165] See text at ch 4.IV and accompanying notes.

[166] D Hayton, 'The Hague Convention on the Law Applicable to Trusts and on their Recognition' (1987) 36 *The International and Comparative Law Quarterly* 260. For a comparative perspective, see M Lupoi, *Trusts: A Comparative Study* (Cambridge University Press, 2000).

[167] Part of the difficulty may result from the fact that civil law jurisdictions have developed directors' fiduciary duties but have not delved into the intricacies of fiduciary relationships. See P Lepaulle, 'Civil Law Substitutes for Trusts' (1927) 36 *The Yale Law Journal* 1126, 1131: 'If the person in whom faith has been placed has committed a breach of duty, the person for whose benefit the relation has been established will always have some remedy. In such cases trusts are created only to afford better protection against the fiduciary; they create a preference over creditors; and that is why we do not

the law of remedies is extremely refined in legal terms and would require a full immersion in equity law in order to be applied properly.[168] So, while courts may well be able to apply a rule on disgorgement of profits, they might get tangled with constructive trusts.

Even without the potential applicative problems, introducing such new rules may not be easy in civil law countries. In civil law countries, introducing a new statute can often require a long process of approval through procedures that are regulated by rigid constitutions. It has been noted that in countries such as France, the courts have started to play a creative role that is more commonly seen in common law countries. Deducing the corporate opportunity doctrine from the duty of loyalty was a very significant step, especially for the country that first affirmed the function of the judge as *la bouche de la loi*; that is, merely involved in applying predetermined concepts contained in statutory law.[169] But thinking that French courts will introduce a remedy such as the constructive trust may be a step too far. Therefore, one may wonder whether there are alternative ways to achieve results similar to the ones obtained through the use of disgorgement of profits. Punitive damages were discussed in chapter three,[170] and there seems to be no indication that they will soon be adopted as general remedies in civil law.

In the spirit of this chapter, and focusing mostly on private ordering, a potential contractual remedy similar in its effects to disgorgement of profits might be corporate clawbacks – as far as the insider who appropriates the corporate opportunity is a director. Corporate clawbacks – also known as 'compensation recovery provisions' – are 'provisions that authorise the board to recover compensation paid to executives when the company restates its financial reports',[171] so far employed mostly in cases of accounting irregularities.[172] Clawbacks have emerged in recent corporate contractual praxis[173] as a way to mitigate agency costs[174] and have been increasingly required by institutional investors after

find any civil law substitutes for such trusts. This is particularly true in the present case, since the civil law has not developed the notion of a fiduciary relation'.

[168] E Rock and M Watcher, 'Dangerous Liaisons: Corporate Law, Trust Law, and Inter-Doctrinal Legal Transplants' (2002) 96 *Northwestern University Law Review* 651 show that internal transplant of trust law within the US system can be problematic. Imagine such a transplant into a remedial system which is completely alien to it.

[169] This bears witness to the great transformation that has taken place in the French judicial system over recent decades. See M Renoux-Zagamé, 'Juger selon d'Aguesseau: le Magistrat "Loi Vivante"' (2009) 19 *Histoire de la Justice* 57.

[170] See text at ch 3.VI and accompanying notes.

[171] L Chan, K Chen and T Chen, 'The Effects of Firm-initiated Clawback Provisions on Bank loan Contracting' (2013) 110 *Journal of Financial Economics* 659.

[172] ibid.

[173] S Huang, C Lim and J Ng, 'Not Clawing the Hand that Feeds You: The Case of Co-opted Boards and Clawbacks' (2019) 28 *European Accounting Review* 101.

[174] P Velte, 'Determinants and Consequences of Clawback Provisions in Management Compensation Contracts: A Structured Literature Review on Empirical Evidence (2020) 13 *Business Research* 1417, 1420.

the 2008–09 crisis.[175] Although such remedies are so far mostly employed for preventing accounting irregularities, this does not mean that they cannot be employed successfully in other areas of corporate law.

The possibility of courts granting an allowance to directors who have committed to the exploitation of a corporate opportunity and upon whose business is later declared a constructive trust followed by a transfer order and/or a disgorgement of profits has already been discussed in the context of bargaining.[176] In such a situation, the use of clawbacks would follow exactly the reverse rationale and therefore would not be the right remedy. By contrast, clawbacks could be a precious contractual tool for forcing disclosure: as a matter of fact, one may intuitively identify in a lack of disclosure an attitude similar to the one that underlies fraudulent reports, ie an avoidance of the duty to be loyal and truthful to one's corporation.[177] Hence, I do not see a problem with the idea of identifying lack of disclosure of a corporate opportunity as a possible trigger for a clawback; and, as a matter of fact, at least in the US, clawbacks have already been used for sanctioning a breach of the duty of loyalty.[178]

Literature shows that for a clawback to be taken seriously by directors, it needs to be drafted in a detailed way.[179] For instance, Fried has stressed the importance of selecting a correct form of words, as there may a substantive difference of cogency between the expressions 'the company will seek to recover' and 'permits the company to recoup', and likewise between the use of 'may' or 'will' recover.[180]

Finally, it goes without saying that such provisions may set a strong incentive for disclosure where a director is highly remunerated for their job. Hence, again, there is a strong relationship between 'stick' and 'carrot' rationales.

VIII. CONCLUSIONS

Corporate opportunity rules may be applied to a variety of corporations in which the public and private dimensions are intertwined in different ways. Such intertwining of different dimensions may also evolve throughout the development of a particular corporation; once transitioned from a start-up to a unicorn, a company may at times carry out services of public utility. Because the protection of corporate proprietary boundaries, with reference to business opportunities,

[175] B Hirsch, B Reichert and M Sohn, 'The Impact of Clawback Provisions on Information Processing and Investment Behaviour' (2017) 37 *Management Accounting Research* 1.

[176] See text at ch 4.V and accompanying notes.

[177] M Erkens, Y Gan and B Yurtoglu, 'Not All Clawbacks Are the Same: Consequences of Strong versus Weak Clawback Provisions' (2018) 66 *Journal of Accounting and Economics* 291, 293.

[178] M Warren III, 'Equitable Clawback: An Essay on Restoration of Executive Compensation' (2009) 12 *University of Pennsylvania Journal of Business Law* 1135, 1137, 1141ff.

[179] Erkens, Gan and Yurtoglu, 'Not All Clawbacks Are the Same' (2018) 292.

[180] J Fried, 'Excess-pay Clawbacks' (2010) 36 *Journal of Corporation Law* 721, 738.

must be adaptable to the kind of business opportunities at issue, to the economic environment in which the corporation operates, and to the stage of the corporation's development, the best way to achieve efficient law-making is to grant adequate space to private ordering. Courts can adjust a corporate opportunity doctrine to a varied range of policy objectives by way of manipulating the test for the identification of a corporate opportunity, through the treatment of resigning directors, and by granting effectiveness to contractual arrangement such as clawbacks. Nonetheless, efficient solutions may especially benefit from the introduction of the possibility of a corporate opportunity waiver.

Conclusions

SOMETIMES ETYMOLOGY NOT only explains the past but also predicts the future. The word 'opportunity' derives from the Latin phrase *ob portum veniens* – 'coming toward a port'. Sailors used the expression when the wind shifted and began blowing toward a safe harbour, where profitable (or exciting) business awaited the captain, crew and merchants aboard.

Today, corporate opportunity rules have become the sails and rigging that harness invisible forces and propel ideas from the laboratory to the market. Innovative founders, like ship captains of old, may take command of new vessels, but the success of each voyage still depends on their skills, vision and courage. These captains of industry must also resolve conflicts that break out among the officers, crew and backers. How can they assuage the worried bankers who have financed the journey and are scanning the horizon, hopefully awaiting their share of profits?

Chapter one showed that the vessel of innovation has sailed through all kinds of waters. In Italy, the ship powered through the country's once-roaring industrial districts, where the absence of corporate opportunity rules and the mobility of employees, managers and directors may have prompted innovation spillovers. It then struggled through state-owned companies, where business opportunities at times became stuck in muddy shoals. The navigation also proved tricky in the UK. In London's financial district, the City, tight corporate opportunity rules may have instilled in directors a sense of righteousness and undivided loyalty. But in the UK's celebrated low-tech districts, such as the Staffordshire Potteries ceramic centre, strict corporate opportunity rules may have made fiduciaries too loyal. In California, we saw high-tech clusters where the non-enforceability of rules functionally similar to corporate opportunity rules – employees' covenants not to compete – may have driven a creative recombination of the building blocks of knowledge. That transformation did not emerge along Massachusetts Route 128 – America's Technology Highway – where non-compete covenants were strictly enforced.

These strikingly different circumstances reflect varied economic systems and industries, which may emphasise strict or loose corporate opportunity rules. But what about the *average* economic environment – if there is such a thing? What would foster the maximum amount of innovation in the average economy?

Chapter four reviewed some well-known policy suggestions, such as forcing the full disclosure of corporate opportunities and facilitating bargaining, to allow the value of business opportunities to emerge through private contracting. In the light of what was explained about the differences between common law and civil law corporate opportunity remedies in chapter three, we may have reason to conclude that the Anglo-American system – with its wide variety of common law and equitable remedies – may be best equipped to enforce disclosure and efficient bargaining, thus bolstering innovation and minimising conflicts inside the corporate ship.

But if our future welfare and the health of Planet Earth itself depend on sound innovation, perhaps our eyes should not be fixed on 'average'. When it comes to economic environments that produce groundbreaking innovation, the variables at play seem to be complex and anything but average, as chapters five and six showed. Founders may desire the freedom to leave a company where they no longer fit in, but their co-founders and financers may want to hold them back. The reverse is also possible, of course, as happened when Steve Jobs' co-founders gave him the boot. Nor is it necessarily true that venture capital investors 'take care of the cow' (the entrepreneur) only as long as its creative thinking is required and quickly put it out to pasture when the business takes off and finance-based calculations prevail over creation. To further complicate matters, different kinds of financers – including venture capital funds acting in syndication – may have completely different thoughts on what constitutes an innovative business opportunity.

How, then, can we strike a balance to reconcile, if not resolve, such conflicts? Social constraints may foster respect among crew members, as happens when they need to maintain their reputations inside an established technology hub. But such non-legal constraints are less effective in more nascent clusters, where the crew can get wild – if not downright mutinous.

Carefully drafting waivers (where legal) or income claw-back provisions can help to adapt corporate opportunity rules to some economic environments. Elsewhere, a strong default remedial protection may be required to tighten the proprietary boundaries of the corporation. Legal rules can play a part in regulating the centrifugal and centripetal forces that either drive founders away from a corporation or keep them there, though we must be aware that the centripetal forces often serve finance while the centrifugal forces may spur innovation.

A wise tuning of the tests that courts have adopted for identifying corporate opportunities together with well-crafted rules for how to treat resigning directors could help transform a foreseeable punch-up among crew members into an elegant dance. As suggested in chapter seven, the law of corporate opportunities could ease the emersion of creativity, reconciling the interests of everyone at the ball – financers and innovators alike.

Bibliography

Abernathy, W and Clark, K, 'Innovation: Mapping the Winds of Creative Destruction' (1985) 14 *Research Policy* 3.

Abowd, J and Bognanno, M, 'International Differences in Executive Managerial Compensation' in R Freeman and L Katz (eds), *Differences and Changes in Wage Structures* (University of Chicago Press, 1995) 67.

Acharya, V, Baghai, R and Subramanian, K, 'Labor Laws and Innovation (2013) 56 *The Journal of Law and Economics* 997.

Acocella, N, *L'impresa Pubblica Italiana e la Dimensione Internazionale: il Caso dell'IRI* (Einaudi, 1983).

Agarwal R et al, 'Knowledge Transfer through Inheritance: Spin-out Generation, Development, and Survival (2004) 47 *Academy of Management Journal*, 501.

Aghion, P, Dewatripont, M and Rey, P, 'Corporate Governance, Competition Policy and Industrial Policy' (1997) 41 *European Economic Review* 797.

Aghion, P and Tirole, J, 'Formal and Real Authority in Organizations' (1997) 105 *Journal of Political Economy* 1.

Ahlstrom, D, Bruton, G and Yeh, K, 'Venture Capital in China: Past, Present, and Future' (2007) 24 *Asia Pacific Journal of Management* 247.

Aiello, M, 'Gli Amministratori di Societa per Azioni' in P Rescigno (ed), *Trattato di Diritto Privato*, 2nd edn (UTET, 2013) tomo 6, vol 16, 1.

Aitken, L, 'Developments in Equitable Compensation: Opportunity or Danger?' (1993) 67 *Australian Law Journal* 596.

Akerloff, G, 'Loyalty Filters' (1983) 73 *American Economic Review* 54.

Alexander R, *Insider Dealing and Money Laundering in the EU: Law and Regulation* (Ashgate, 2007).

Alchian A, 'Vertical Integration, Appropriable Rents, and the Competitive Contracting Process' (1978) 21 *Journal of Law and Economics* 297.

Allen W, Kraakman, R and Subramanian, G, *Commentaries and Cases on the Law of Business Organization*, 2nd edn (Aspen Publishers, 2009).

Alli, I, *101 Selected Sayings of Mahatma Gandhi* (eBookIt, 2013).

Altenburg, T and Meyer-Stamer, J, 'How to Promote Clusters: Policy Experiences from Latin America' (1999) 27 *World Development* 1693.

Alvarez, I and Molero, J, 'Technology and the Generation of International Knowledge Spillovers: An Application to Spanish Manufacturing Firms' (2005) 34 *Research Policy* 1440.

Amable, B, 'Institutional Complementarity and Diversity of Social Systems of Innovation and Production' (2000) 7 *Review of International Political Economy* 645.

Aminadav, G and Papaioannou, E, 'Corporate Control around the World' (2020) 75 *The Journal of Finance* 1191.

Amit R, Glosten, L and Muller, E, 'Entrepreneurial Ability, Venture Investments, and Risk Sharing' (1990) 36 *Management Science* 1233.

Anderson, A and Gupta, P, 'Corporate Governance: Does One Size Fit All?' (2013) 24 *Journal of Corporate Accounting & Finance* 51.

Anderson M, Banker, R and Ravindran, S, 'Executive Compensation in the Information Technology Industry' (2000) 46 *Management Science* 4530.

Anderson, R, Duru, A, and Reeb, D, 'Founders, Heirs, and Corporate Opacity in the United States' (2009) 92 *Journal of Financial Economics* 205.

Andersson, M and Koster, S, 'Sources of Persistence in Regional Start-up Rates – Evidence from Sweden (2010) 11 *Journal of Economic Geography* 179.

Andhov, A, *Start-up Law* (Edward Elgar, 2020).

Antonelli, C, 'Technological Districts Localized Spillovers and Productivity Growth. The Italian Evidence on Technological Externalities in the Core Regions' (1994) 8 *International Review of Applied Economics* 18.

Antonucci, T and Pianta, M, 'Employment Effects of Product and Process Innovation in Europe' (2002) 16 *International Review of Applied Economics* 295.

Arlen J, Spitzer, M and Talley, E, 'Endowment Effects within Corporate Agency Relationships' (2002) 31 *Journal of Legal Studies* 1.

Armour, J, 'Corporate Opportunities: If in Doubt, Disclose (but how?)' (2004) 63 *Cambridge Law Journal* 33.

—— 'Who Should Make Corporate Law? EC Legislation versus Regulatory Competition' (2005) 58 *Current Legal Problems* 369.

Armour, J and Cheffins, B, 'The Past, Present and Future of Shareholder Activism by Hedge Funds' (2011) 37 *Journal of Corporation Law* 5.

—— 'The Rise and Fall of Shareholder Activism by Hedge Funds' (2012) *Journal of Alternative Investments* 17.

Armour, J and Cumming, D, 'The Legislative Road to Silicon Valley' (2006) 58 *Oxford Economic Papers* 596.

Armour, J and Eidenmuller, H, 'Self-Driving Corporations?' (2020) 10 *Harvard Business Law Review* 87.

Armour, J and McCahery, J (eds), *After Enron: Improving Corporate Law and Modernising Securities Regulation in Europe and the US* (Hart Publishing, 2006).

Armour J, Hansmann, H and Kraakman, R, 'Agency Problems and Legal Strategies in R Kraakman et al, *The Anatomy of Corporate Law: A Comparative and Functional Approach*. (Oxford University Press, 2017) 29.

Armour J, Hertig, G and Kanda, H, 'Transactions with Creditors' in R Kraakman et al (eds), *The Anatomy of Corporate Law: A Comparative and Functional Approach* (Oxford University Press, 2017) 109.

Armour, J et al, 'Beyond the Anatomy' in R Kraakman et al (eds), *The Anatomy of Corporate Law: A Comparative and Functional Approach*. (Oxford University Press, 2017) 267.

—— 'How Do Legal Rules Evolve? A Cross-Country Comparison of Shareholder, Creditor and Worker Protection' (2009) 57 *American Journal of Comparative Law* 579.

—— 'Private Enforcement of Corporate Law: An Empirical Comparison of the UK and US' (2009) 6 *Journal of Empirical Legal Studies* 701.

—— 'Shareholder Protection and Stock Market Development: An Empirical Test of the Legal Origins Hypothesis' (2009) 6 *Journal of Empirical Legal Studies* 343.

—— 'Law and Financial Development: What We are Learning from Time Series Evidence' (2010) *Brigham Young University Law Review* 1435.

—— 'Putting Technology to Good Use for Society: The Role of Corporate, Competition and Tax Law' (2018) European Corporate Governance Institute (ECGI)-Law Working Paper, 427.

Arsht, S, 'A History of Delaware Corporation Law' (1976) 1 *Delaware Journal of corporate Law* 1.

Arthur, B, *The Nature of Technology: What it Is and How it Evolves* (The Free Press, 2009).

Arundale, K, 'Syndication and Cross-border Collaboration by Venture Capital Firms in Europe and the USA: A Comparative Study' (2020) 22 *Venture Capital* 355.

Asoni, A, 'Protection of Property Rights and Growth as Political Equilibria' (2008) 22 *Journal of Economic Surveys* 953.

Asquini, A, *I battelli del Reno* (Giuffre, 1959).

Assimakopoulos, D, Everton, S and Tsutsui, K, 'The Semiconductor Community in the Silicon Valley: A Network Analysis of the SEMI Genealogy Chart (1947–1986)' (2003) 25 *International Journal of Technology Management* 181.

Atanasov, J, 'Conflicts of Interest and Litigation in the Venture Capital Industry' in D Cumming (ed), *Venture Capital: Investment Strategies, Structures, and Policies* (Wiley & Sons, 2010) 365.

Atanasov J, Ivanov, V and Litvak, K, 'Does Reputation Limit Opportunistic Behavior in the VC Industry? Evidence from Litigation Against VCs' (2012) 67 *Journal of Finance* 2215.

Atanasov V, Black, B and Ciccotello, C, 'Unbundling and Measuring Tunneling' (2014) *University of Illinois Law Review* 1697.

Atanassov, J, 'Do Hostile Takeovers Stifle Innovation? Evidence from Antitakeover Legislation and Corporate Patenting' (2013) 68 *Journal of Finance* 1097.

Athey, S and Roberts, J, 'Organizational Design: Decision Rights and Incentive Contracts' (2001) 91 *American Economic Review* (Papers and Proceedings) 200.

Audia, P and Rider, C, 'A Garage and an Idea: What More Does an Entrepreneur Need?' (2005) 48 *California Management Review* 6.

Austin, C and Gottlieb, D, 'Renouncing Corporate Opportunities in Spin-Offs, Carve-Out IPOs, and Private Equity Investments' (2003) 17 *Corporate & Securities Law Advisor* 2.

Awrey, D, Blair, W and Kershaw, D, 'Between Law and Market: Is There a Role for Culture and Ethics in Financial Regulation?' (2013–2014) 38 *Delaware Journal of Corporate Law* 191.

Ayres, A (ed), *Quotable Edison* (Quotable Wisdom Books, 2016).

Ayres, I and Balkin, J, 'Legal Entitlements as Auctions: Property Rules, Liability Rules, and Beyond' (1996) 106 *Yale Law Journal* 703.

Ayres, I and Gertner, R, 'Filling Gaps in Incomplete Contracts: An Economic Theory of Default Rules' (1989) 99 *Yale Law Journal* 87.

—— 'Strategic Contractual Inefficiency and the Optimal Choice of Legal Rules' (1992) 101 *Yale Law Journal* 729.

Ayres, I and Talley, E, 'Solomonic Bargaining: Dividing an Entitlement to Facilitate Coasean Trade' (1995) 104 *Yale Law Journal* 1027.

Azar, J, 'The Common Ownership Trilemma' (2020) 87 *The University of Chicago Law Review* 263.

Azar, J, Schmalz, M and Tecu, I, 'Anticompetitive Effects of Common Ownership' (2018) 73 *The Journal of Finance* 1513.

Azzariti, F, *I Percorsi di Crescita delle Piccole e Medie Imprese. Teorie, Modelli e Casi Aziendali* (Franco Angeli, 2002).

Bade, R and Parkin, M, *Foundations of Economics* (Pearson Education, 2011).

Baer, M, 'Governing Corporate Compliance' (2009) 50 *Boston College Law Review* 949.

Baker, D, 'The Political Economy of Fascism: Myth *or* Reality, or Myth *and* Reality? (2006) 11 *New Political Economy* 227.

Baker, M and Gompers, P, 'The Determinants of Board Structure at the Initial Public Offering' (2003) 46 *The Journal of Law and Economics* 569.

Baker, T, Harel, A and Kugler, T, 'The Virtues of Uncertainty in Law: An Experimental Approach' (2003) 89 *Iowa Law Review* 443.

Balkin, D, Markman, G and Gomez-Mejia, L, 'Is CEO Pay in High-technology Firms Related to Innovation?' (2000) 43 *Academy of Management Journal* 1118.

Balsmeier, B, Buchwald, A and Stiebale, J, 'Outside Directors on the Board and Innovative Firm Performance' (2014) 4 *Research Policy* 1800.

Bammens, Y and Collewaert, V, 'Trust between Entrepreneurs and Angel Investors: Exploring Positive and Negative Implications for Venture Performance Assessments' (2014) 40 *Journal of Management* 1980.

Barachini, F, 'L'Appropriazione delle *Corporate Opportunities*' in P Abbadessa and G Portale (eds), *Il Nuovo Diritto delle Società, Liber amicorum Gian Franco Campobasso* (UTET, 2006) 608.

Barca, F, *Il Capitalismo Italiano: Storia di un Compromesso Senza Riforme* (Donzelli, 1999).

Barca, F and Becht, M (eds), *The Control of Corporate Europe* (Oxford University Press, 2001).

Barca, F and Trento, S, 'State Ownership and the Evolution of Italian Corporate Governance' (1997) 6 *Industrial and Corporate Change* 533.

Bareghen, A, Rowley, J and Sambrook, S, 'Towards a Multidisciplinary Definition of Innovation' (2009) 47 *Management Decision* 1323.

Baron, J and Dunoff, J, 'Against Market Rationality: Moral Critiques of Economic Analysis in Legal Theory' (1995) 17 *Cardozo Law Review* 431.

Barras, R, 'Interactive Innovation in Financial and Business Services: The Vanguard of the Service Revolution' (1990) 19 *Research Policy* 215.

Barringer, B, Jones, J and Neubaum, D, 'A Quantitative Content Analysis of the Characteristics of Rapid-growth Firms and Their Founders' (2005) 20 *Journal of Business Venturing* 663.

Bartlett, R, 'Venture Capital, Agency Costs, and the False Dichotomy of the Corporation' (2006) 54 *UCLA Law Review* 37.

Bast, C, 'At What Price Silence: Are Confidentiality Agreements Enforceable?' (1999) 25 *William Mitchell Law Review* 627.

Bator, F, 'The Simple Analytics of Welfare Maximization' (1957) 47 *The American Economic Review* 22.

Baum, J, Frese, M and Baron, R (eds), *The Psychology of Entrepreneurship* (Lawrence Erlbaum, 2007).

Baysinger, B, Kosnik, R and Turk, T, 'Effects of Board and Ownership Structure on Corporate R&D Strategy' (1991) 34 *Academy of Management Journal* 205.

Beale Jr, J, 'Contempt of Court: Criminal and Civil' (1908) 21 *Harvard Law Review* 161.

Bebchuk, L, 'Federalism and the Corporation: The Desirable Limits' (1992) 105 *Harvard Law Review* 1435.

—— 'The Myth that Insulating Boards Serves Long-term Value' (2013) 113 *Columbia Law Review* 163.

Bebchuk, L and Cohen, A, 'Firms' Decisions Where to Incorporate' (2003) 46 *Journal of Law and Economics* 383.

—— 'The Costs of Entrenched Boards' (2005) 78 *Journal of Financial Economics* 409.

Bebchuk L, Cohen, A and Ferrell, A, 'Does the Evidence Favour State Competition in Corporate Law?' (2002) 90 *California Law Review* 1775.

Bebchuk, L and Ferrell, A, 'Federalism and Corporate Law, The Race to Protect Managers from Takeovers' (1999) 99 *Columbia Law Review* 1168.

Bebchuk, L and Tallarita, R, 'The Illusory Promise of Stakeholder Governance', available at papers.ssrn.com/sol3/papers.cfm?abstract_id=3544978

Bebchuk, L, Coates IV, J and Subramanian. G, 'The Powerful Antitakeover Force of Staggered Boards: Further Findings and a Reply to Symposium Participants' (2002) 55 *Stanford Law Review* 885.

Beccaria, C, *Dei Delitti e Delle Pene*, Chapter XXIII, trans J Farrer, *Crimes and Punishment, Including a New Translation of Beccaria's Dei Delitti e delle Pene* (Chatto and Windus, 1880) 196.

Beccattini, G, 'Il Distretto Industriale Marshalliano come Concetto Socio-Economico' in F Pyke et al (eds), *Distretti Industriali e Cooperazione tra Imprese in Italia* (Banca Toscana 1991) 51.

Becchetti, L and Rossi, S, 'The positive effect of industrial district on the export performance of Italian firms' (2000) 16 *Review of Industrial Organization* 53.

Becker-Blease, J, 'Governance and Innovation' (2011) 17 *Journal of Corporate Finance* 947.

Begert, M, 'The Corporate Opportunity Doctrine and Outside Business Interests' (1989) 56 *University of Chicago Law Review* 827.

Behr, V, 'Punitive Damages in American and German Law – Tendencies Towards Approximation of Apparently Irreconcilable Concepts' (2003) 78 *Chicago-Kent Law Review* 105.

Belderbos, R, Jacob, J and Lokshin, B, 'Corporate Venture Capital (CVC) Investments and Technological Performance: Geographic Diversity and the Interplay with Technology Alliances' (2018) 33 *Journal of Business Venturing* 20.

Belinfanti, T and Stout, L, 'Contested Visions: The value of Systems Theory for Corporate Law' (2017) 166 *University of Pennsylvania Law Review* 579.

Bell, E and Scott, T, 'Vernacular Mourning and Corporate Memorialization in Framing the Death of Steve Jobs' (2016) 23 *Organization* 114.

Bellelli, A, 'L'Inibitoria come Strumento Generale di Tutela contro l'Illecito' [2004] *Rivista di Diritto Civile* (I) 607.

Belussi, F and Pilotti, L, 'Knowledge Creation, Learning and Innovation in Italian Industrial Districts' (2002) 84 *Geografiska Annaler* 125.

Benner, C, 'Learning Communities in a Learning Region: The Soft Infrastructure of Cross-firm Learning Networks in Silicon Valley' (2003) 35 *Environment and Planning* 1809.

Berkhout, G et al, 'Innovating the Innovation Process' (2006) 34 *International Journal of Technology Management* 390.

Berryman, J, 'Equitable Compensation for Breach by Fact-Based Fiduciaries: Tentative Thoughts on Clarifying Remedial Goals' (1999) 37 *Alberta Law Review* 95.

Bernstein, L, 'The Silicon Valley Lawyer as Transaction Cost Engineer' (1995) 74 *Oregon Law Review* 239.

Bertoni, F, Colombo, M and Quas, A, 'The Patterns of Venture Capital Investment in Europe (2015) 45 *Small Business Economics* 543.

Beyer, J, 'The Same or not the Same-on the Variety of Mechanisms of Path Dependence' (2010) 5 *International Journal of Social Sciences* 1.

Bhattacharya, B and Ritter, J, 'Innovation and Communication: Signalling with Partial Disclosure' (1983) 50 *Review of Economic Studies* 331.

Bhojraj, S et al, 'Effect of Corporate Governance on Bond Ratings and Yields: The Role of Institutional Investors and Outside Directors' (2003) 76 *Journal of Business Law* 455.

Bhoovaraghavan, S et al, 'Resolving the Process vs. Product Innovation Dilemma: A Consumer Choice Theoretic Approach' (1996) 42 *Management Science* 232).

Biekpe, N, 'Financing Small Businesses in Sub-Saharan Africa: Review of Some Key Credit Lending Models and Impact of Venture Capital Provision' (2004) 5 *Journal of African Business* 29–44.

Biermeyer, T and Meyer, M, 'Cross-border Corporate Mobility in the EU: Empirical Findings 2020 (Edition 1)', available at papers.ssrn.com/sol3/papers.cfm?abstract_id=3674089, 2.

Binda, V and Colli, A, 'Changing Big Business in Italy and Spain, 1973–2003: Strategic Responses to a New Context' (2011) 53 *Business History* 14.

Birdsall, N and Nellis, J, 'Winners and Losers: Assessing the Distributional Impact of Privatization' (2003) 31 *World Development* 1617.

Birren, J and Svensson, C, 'Wisdom in History' in R Sternberg and J Jordan (eds), *A Handbook of Wisdom: Psychological Perspectives* (Cambridge University Press, 2005) 3.

Bishara, N, Martin, K and Thomas, R, 'When Do CEOs Have Covenants not to Compete in their Employment Contracts?' (2015) 68 *Vanderbilt Law Review* 12.

Bjørst, B, 'Restrictive Covenants in Employment Contracts – an Unnoticed Hindrance to Growth in Europe' [on file with the author]

Black, B, 'Shareholder Activism and Corporate Governance in the United States' in P Newman (ed), *The New Palgrave Dictionary of Economics and the Law* (Palgrave Macmillan, 1998).

Black, B and Gilson, R, 'Venture Capital and the Structure of Capital Markets: Banks Versus Stock Markets' (1998) 47 *Journal of Financial Economics* 243.

Blair, M and Stout, L, 'A Team Production Theory of Corporate Law' (1999) 85 *Virginia Law Review* 247.

Blind, K et al, 'Motives to Patent: Empirical Evidence from Germany' (2006) 35 *Research Policy* 655.

Boix, R and Galletto, V, 'Marshallian Industrial Districts in Spain' (2008) 7 *Scienze Regionali* 29.

Bös, D, 'Privatization in Europe: A Comparison of Approaches' (1993) 9 *Oxford Review of Economic Policy* 95.

Boschma, R and Ter Wal, A, 'Knowledge Networks and Innovative Performance in an Industrial District: The Case of a Footwear District in the South of Italy' (2007) 14 *Industry and Innovation* 177.

Bottazzi, L and Da Rin, M, 'Venture Capital in Europe and the Financing of Innovative Companies' (2002) 17 *Economic Policy* 229.

Bottazzi, L, Da Rin, M and Hellmann, T, 'The Changing Face of the European Venture Capital Industry: Facts and Analysis' (2004) 7 *Journal of Private Equity* 26.

—— 'The Importance of Trust for Investment: Evidence from Venture Capital' (2016) 29 *The Review of Financial Studies* 2283.

Bower, J and Christensen, C, 'Disruptive Technologies: Catching the Wave' (1995) 73 *Harvard Business Review* 43.

Boyer, R, 'Coherence, Diversity, and the Evolution of Capitalisms – The Institutional Complementarity Hypothesis' (2005) 2 *Evolutionary & Institutional Economic Review* 43.

Bradley, W et al, 'Cross-Border Venture Capital Investments: what is the Role of Public Policy?' (2019) 12 *Journal of Risk and Financial Management* 112.

Braithwaite, J, 'Minimally Sufficient Deterrence' (2018) 47 *Crime and Justice* 69.

Bramanti, A and Senn, L, 'Product Innovation and Strategic Patterns of Firms in a Diversified Local Economy: The Case of Bergamo' (1990) 2 *Entrepreneurship & Regional Development* 153.

Brander J, Amit, R and Antweiler, W, 'Venture Capital Syndication: Improved Venture Selection versus the Value-Added Hypothesis' (2002) 11 *Journal of Economics and Management Strategy* 423.

Branson, D, 'The Very Uncertain Prospect of "Global" Convergence in Corporate Governance' (2001) 34 *Cornell International Law Journal* 321.

Bratton, W and McCahery, J, 'Comparative Corporate Governance and the Theory of the Firm: The Case Against Global Cross Reference' (1999) 38 *Columbia Journal of Transnational Law* 213.

Bray, S, 'Fiduciary Remedies' in E Criddle, P Miller and R Sitkoff (eds), *The Oxford Handbook of Fiduciary Law* (Oxford University Press, 2019) 449.

Brès, 'L'Obligation de Non-Concurrence de Plein Droit de l'Associé' (2011) *RTDCom. Revue Trimestrielle de Droit Commercial et de Droit Economique* 463, fn 236.

Brick I, Palmon, O and Wald, J, 'CEO Compensation, Director Compensation, and Firm Performance: Evidence of Cronyism?' (2006) 12 *Journal of Corporate Finance* (2006) 403.

Briggs, T, 'Corporate Governance and the New Hedge Fund Activism: An Empirical Analysis' (2007) 31 *Journal of Corporation Law* 681.

Brioschi, F, Brioschi, M and Cainelli, G, 'From the Industrial District to the District Group: An Insight into the Evolution of Capitalism in Italy' (2002) 36 *Regional Studies* 1037.

The British Academy, 'Principles for Purposeful Business' (2019) www.thebritishacademy.ac.uk/publications/future-of-the-corporation-principles-for-purposeful-business.

Broughman, B, 'Investor Opportunism, and Governance in Venture Capital' in D Cumming, *Venture Capital: Investment Strategies, Structures, and Policies* (Wiley & Sons, 2010).

Brouwer, M, 'Managing Uncertainty Through Profit Sharing Contracts from Medieval Italy to Silicon Valley' (2005) 9 *Journal of Management and Governance* 237.

Brudney, V, 'Insider Securities Dealing During Corporate Crisis' (1962) 61 *Michigan Law Review* 1.

Brudney, V and Clark, R, 'A New Look at Corporate Opportunities' (1980–81) 94 *Harvard Law Review* 997.

Bruner, C, 'Opting Out of Fiduciary Duties and Liabilities in US and UK Business Entities' in G Smith and A Gold, *Research Handbook on Fiduciary Law* (Edward Elgar, 2018).

Brusco, S and Pezzini, M, 'La Piccola Impresa nell'Ideologia della Sinistra in Italia' in F Pyke et al (eds), *Distretti Industriali e Cooperazione tra Imprese in Italia* (Banca Toscana, 1991) 155.

Bruton, G and Ahlstrom, D, 'An Institutional View of China's Venture Capital Industry: Explaining the Differences between China and the West' (2003) 18 *Journal of Business Venturing* 233.

Bruton, G, Fried, V and Manigart, S, 'Institutional Influences on the Worldwide Expansion of Venture Capital' (2005) 29 *Entrepreneurship Theory and Practice* 737.

Buccafusco, C and Sprigman, C, 'Valuing Intellectual Property: An Experiment (2010) 96 *Cornell Law Review* 1.

Burgel, O and Murray, G, 'The International Market Entry Choices of Start-up Companies in High-Technology Industries' (2000) 8 *Journal of International Marketing* 33.

Burk, D and McDonnell, B, 'The Goldilocks Hypothesis: Balancing Intellectual Property Rights at the Boundary of the firm (2007) *University of Illinois Law Review* 575.

Burrows, A, 'We Do This at Common Law but That in Equity' (2002) 22 *Oxford Journal of Legal Studies* 1.

—— *English Private Law*, 3rd edn (Oxford University Press, 2013).

Bushee, B, 'The Influence of Institutional Investors on Myopic R&D Investment Behaviour' (1998) 73 *Accounting Review* 305.

Butler, H, 'Nineteenth-century Jurisdictional Competition in the Granting of Corporate Privileges' (1985) 14 *Journal of Legal Studies* 129.

Bygrave, W, 'Syndicated Investments by Venture Capital Firms: A Networking Perspective' (1987) 2 *Journal of Business Venturing* 139.

Cable, D and Shane, S, 'A Prisoner's Dilemma Approach to Entrepreneur-Venture Capitalist Relationships' (1997) 22 *Academy of Management Review* 142.

Cainelli G, Iacobucci, D and Morganti, E, 'Spatial Agglomeration and Business Groups: New Evidence from Italian Industrial Districts' (2007) 40 *Regional Studies* 507.

Cainelli, G, Mancinelli, S and Mazzanti, M, 'Social Capital and Innovation Dynamics in District-based Local Systems' (2007) 36 *Journal of Socio-Economics* 932.

Calabresi, G, 'Transaction Costs, Resource Allocation and Liability Rules – A Comment' (1968) 11 *Journal of Law and Economics* 67.

Calabresi, G and Melamed, D, 'Property Rules, Liability Rules, and Inalienability: One View of the Cathedral' (1972) 85 *Harvard Law Review* 1089.

Calandra Buonaura, V, 'Potere di Gestione e Potere di Rappresentanza degli Amministratori'in GE Colombo and GB Portale (eds), *Trattato delle Società per Azioni*, vol 4 (UTET, 1991) 237.

Calderini, M et al, *Corporate Governance, Market Structure and Innovation* (Edward Elgar, 2003).

Cameron, R, *Banking in the Early Stages of Industrialization* (Oxford University Press, 1967).

Cantanessa, M et al, 'Startups' Road to Failure' (2018) 10 *Sustainability* 2346.

Capecchi, V, 'Una Storia della Specializzazione Flessibile e dei Distretti Industriali in Emilia-Romagna' in F Pyke et al (eds), *Distretti Industriali e Cooperazione tra Imprese in Italia* (Banca Toscana, 1991) 35.

Capelleras, J-L et al, 'Venture Creation Speed and Subsequent Growth: Evidence from South America' (2010) 48 *Journal of Small Business Management* 302.

Carlin, W and Mayer, C, 'How Do Financial Systems Affect Economic Performance?' in J McCahery et al (eds), *Corporate Governance Regimes: Convergence and Diversity* (Oxford University Press, 2002) 325.

Carlos, A and Nicholas, S, 'Managing the Manager: An Application of the Principal Agent Model to the Hudson's Bay Company' (1993) *Oxford Economic Papers* 243.

Carney, W and Shepherd, G, 'The Mystery of Delaware Law's Continuing Success' (2009) *University of Illinois Law Review* 1.

Carter, R, 'Corporate Opportunity' (1977–1978) 3 *Journal of Corporation Law* 422.

Caselli, S, *Private Equity and Venture Capital in Europe: Markets, Techniques, and Deals* (Elsevier, 2010).

Cassim, R, 'Post-resignation Duties of Directors: The Application of the Fiduciary Duty not to Misappropriate Corporate Opportunities' (2008) 125 *South African Law Journal* 731.

Cavanaugh, J, 'Asset-Specific Investment and Unionized Labor' (1998) 37 *Industrial Relations* 35.

Chahine, S, Filatotchev, I and Zhara, S, 'Building Perceived Quality of Founder–Involved IPO Firms: Founders' Effects on Board Selection and Stock Market Performance' (2011) 35 *Entrepreneurship Theory and Practice* 319.

Chan, L, Chen, K, and Chen, T, 'The Effects of Firm-initiated Clawback Provisions on Bank loan Contracting' (2013) 110 *Journal of Financial Economics* 659.

Chander, A, 'How Law Made Silicon Valley' (2013) 63 *Emory Law Journal* 639.

—— *Scale and Scope* (Harvard University Press, 1990).

Charny, D, 'Hypothetical Bargains: The Normative Structure of Contract Interpretation (1991) 89 *Michigan Law Review* 1815.

Cheffins, B, 'Does Law Matter? The Separation of Ownership and Control in the United Kingdom' (2001) 30 *Journal of Legal Studies* 459.

—— *Corporate Ownership and Control: British Business Transformed* (Oxford University Press, 2008).

—— 'The Rise and Fall of Shareholder Activism by Hedge Funds' (2012) *Journal of Alternative Investments* 17.

Cheh, M, 'Constitutional Limits on Using Civil Remedies to Achieve Criminal Law Objectives: Understanding and Transcending the Criminal-Civil Law Distinction' (1990–1991) 42 *Hastings Law Journal* 1325.

Cherensky, S, 'A Penny for Their Thoughts: Employee-Inventors, Preinvention Assignment Agreements, Property, and Personhood' (1993) 81 *California Law Review* 595.

Chesbrough, H, 'Making Sense of Corporate Venture Capital' (2002) 80 *Harvard Business Review* 9.

Chirico, M et al, 'An Experimental Evaluation of Notification Strategies to Increase Property Tax Compliance: Free-riding in the City of Brotherly Love' (2016) 30 *Tax Policy and the Economy* (2016) 129.

Christensen, C, *The Innovator's Dilemma* (Harper Business, 2000).

Christensen, C and Raynor, M, *The Innovator's Solution* (Harvard Business School Press, 2003).

Christensen, C, Anthony, S and Roth, E, *Seeing What's Next* (Harvard Business School Press, 2004).

Ciepley, D, *Beyond Public and Private: Toward a Political Theory of the Corporation* (2013) 107 *American Political Science Review* 139.

Claessens, S and Laeven, L, 'Financial Development, Property Rights, and Growth' (2003) 58 *Journal of Finance* 2401.

Clark, M, *Modern Italy: 1871 to Present* (Pearson, 2008).

Clarke, R, *Industrial Economics* (Blackwell, 1985).

Coase, R, 'The Problem of Social Cost' (1960) 3 *Journal of Law and Economics* 1.

—— 'The Nature of the Firm: Origin' in O Williamson and S Winter (eds), *The Nature of the Firm* (Oxford University Press, 1993) 34.

—— '1991 Nobel Lecture: The Institutional Structure of Production' in O Williamson and S Winter (eds), *The Nature of the Firm* (Oxford University Press, 1993) 227.

Coelli, T et al, *An Introduction to Efficiency and Productivity Analysis* (Springer, 2005).

Coffee Jr, J, 'The Future as History: The Prospects for Global Convergence in Corporate Governance and its Implications' (1999) 93 *Northwestern University Law Review* 641.

Cohen, M, 'Ecological Modernization and its Discontents: The American Environmental Movement's Resistance to an Innovation-driven Future' (2006) 38 *Futures* 528.

Cohen, S, 'What do Accelerators Do? Insights from Incubators and Angels' (2013) 8 *Innovations: Technology, Governance, Globalization* 19.

Cohen, W and Levinthal, D, 'Innovation and Learning: The Two Faces of R&D' (1989) 99 *Economic Journal* 569.

Cohen, W and Levinthal, D, 'Absorptive Capacity: A New Perspective on Learning and Innovation' (1990) 36 *Administrative Science Quarterly* 128.

Collewaert, V and Fassin, Y, 'Conflicts between Entrepreneurs and Investors: The Impact of Perceived Unethical Behavior' (2013) 40 *Small Business Economics* 635.

Colombo, M and Shafi, K, 'Swimming with Sharks in Europe: When Are They Dangerous and What Can New Ventures Do to Defend Themselves?' (2016) 37 *Strategic Management Journal* 2307.

Conaglen, M, *Fiduciary Loyalty* (Hart Publishing, 2010).

Connor, G et al, *Portfolio Risk Analysis* (Princeton University Press, 2010).

Conyon, M and Murphy, K, 'Stock-Based Executive Compensation' in J McCahery et al (eds), *Corporate Governance Regimes* (Oxford University Press, 2002) 625.

Cooke, P, 'Regional Innovation Systems, Clusters, and the Knowledge Economy' (2001) 10 *Industrial and Corporate Change* 945.

Cooter, R and Freedman, B, 'The Fiduciary Relationship: Its Economic Character and Legal Consequences' (1991) 66 *New York University Law Review* 1045.

Cooter, R and Parisi, F (eds), *Recent Developments in Law and Economics* (Edward Elgar, 2009).

Cooter, R and Ulen, T, *Law and Economics* (Harper Collins, 1988).

Corradi, M, 'Le Opportunità di Affari all'Ultimo Comma dell'Art. 2391 cc: Profili Interpretativi tra "Società" ed "Impresa"' [2011] *Giurisprudenza Commerciale* (I) 597.

—— 'Les Opportunités d'Affaires Saisies par les Administrateurs de la Société en Violation du Devoir de Loyauté' [2011] *Bulletin Joly Sociétés* 157.

—— 'Agency Costs in the Shadow of the European Stock Exchanges: A Comparative Assessment of the British and Italian Law on Related Party Transactions and Corporate Opportunities' (2012) 6 *Journal of Comparative Law* 23.

—— 'Corporate Opportunities Doctrines Tested in the Light of the Theory of the Firm – A European (and US) Comparative Perspective' (2016) 27 *European Business Law Review* 755.

—— 'Securing Corporate Opportunities in Europe – Comparative Notes on Monetary Remedies and on their Potential Evolution' (2018) 18 *Journal of Corporate Law Studies* 439.

Corradi, M and Helleringer, G, 'Board Duties: The Duty of Loyalty and Self-Dealing' in A Afsharipour and M Gelter (eds) *Comparative Corporate Governance* (Edward Elgar, 2021).

Crepax, N, *Storia dell'Industria Italiana* (Il Mulino, 2002).

Crespi, R, Gispert, C and Rennebog, L, 'Cash-Based Executive Compensation in Spain and in the UK' in J McCahery et al (eds), *Corporate Governance Regimes* (Oxford University Press, 2002) 677.

Crouch, C et al, 'Dialogue on 'Institutional Complementarity and Political Economy' (2005) 3 *Socio-Economic Review* 359.

Cumming, D, 'The Determinants of Venture Capital Portfolio Size: Empirical Evidence' (2006) 79 *Journal of Business* 1083.

—— (ed), *Venture Capital: Investment Strategies, Structures, and Policies*, Vol 9 (John Wiley & Sons, 2010).

Cumming, D and MacIntosh, J, 'A Cross-country Comparison of Full and Partial Venture Capital Exits' (2003) 27 *Journal of Banking & Finance* 511.

Cumming, D, Fleming, G and Schwienbacher, A, 'Legality and Venture Capital Exits' (2006) 12 *Journal of Corporate Finance* 214.

Dahl, M and Pedersen, C, 'Knowledge Flows Through Informal Contacts in Industrial Clusters: Myth or Reality?' (2004) 33 *Research Policy* 1673.

Dakolias M, *Court Performance Around the World: A Comparative Perspective* (The World Bank, 1999).

d'Alessandro, F, 'Il Diritto delle Società da i «Battelli del Reno» alle «Navi Vichinghe»' (1988) 111 *Il Foro Italiano* 47.

Dalziel T, Gentry, R and Bowerman, M, 'An Integrated Agency–Resource Dependence View of the Influence of Directors' Human and Relational Capital on Firms' R&D Spending' (2011) 48 *Journal of Management Studies* 1217.

Damanpour F and Gopalakrishnan, S, 'The Dynamics of the Adoption of Product and Process Innovations in Organizations' (2001) 38 *Journal of Management Studies* 45.

Danielson, M and Karpoff, J, 'On the Uses of Corporate Governance Provisions' (1998) 4 *Journal of Corporate Finance* 347.

Dannemann, G, *The German Law of Unjustified Enrichment and Restitution: A Comparative Introduction* (Oxford University Press, 2009).

Davenport, T and Prusak, L, *Working Knowledge: How Organizations Manage What They Know* (Harvard Business Press, 1998).

Davidson, I, 'The Equitable Remedy of Compensation' (1982) 13 *Melbourne University Law Review* 349.

Davies, D, 'Equitable Compensation: "Causation, Foreseeability and Remoteness"' in D Waters (ed), *Equity, Fiduciaries and Trusts* (Carswell, 1993) 297.

Davoudi L, McKenna, C and Olegario, R, 'The Historical Role of the Corporation in Society' (2018) 6 *Journal of the British Academy* 17.

Dessi, R, 'Venture Capitalists, Monitoring and Advising' in D Cumming (ed), *Venture Capital: Investment Strategies, Structures, and Policies* (Wiley & Sons, 2010) 169.

Davies, P, 'Remedies for Breach of Trust' (2015) 78 *Modern Law Review* 681.

Davies, P and Worthington, S (eds), *Gower and Davies' Principles of Modern Company Law*, 9th edn (Sweet & Maxwell, 2012).

Deakin S, Johnston, C and Markesinis, B, *Markesinis and Deakin's Tort Law*, 7th edn (Oxford University Press, 2012).

de Roover, R, *The Rise and Decline of the Medici Bank* (Beard Books, 1999).

Diamond Jr, A, 'Schumpeter's Creative Destruction: A Review of the Evidence' (2006) 22 *Journal of Private Enterprise* 120.

Dickson, B, 'Unjust Enrichment Claims: A Comparative Overview' (1995) 54 *Cambridge Law Journal* 100.

Didier, P, 'La Théorie Contractualiste de la Société' (2000) II *Revue des sociétés* 95.

Ding Z, Au, K and Chiang, F, 'Social Trust and Angel Investors' Decisions: A Multilevel Analysis across Nations' (2015) 30 *Journal of Business Venturing* 307.

Dixit, A and Pindyck, R, *Investment under Uncertainty* (Princeton University Press, 1994).

Dobbs, D, 'Contempt of Court: A Survey' (1971) 56 *Cornell Law Review* 183.

—— 'Ending Punishment in "Punitive" Damages: Deterrence-Measured Remedies' (1988) 40 *Alabama Law Review* 831.

Doidge, C et al, 'Eclipse of the Public Corporation or Eclipse of the Public Markets?' (2018) 30 *Journal of Applied Corporate Finance* 8.

Dörrenbächer, C and Geppert, M, *Politics and Power in the Multinational Corporation* (Cambridge University Press, 2011).

Drach-Zahavy, A and Somech, A, 'Understanding Team Innovation: The Role of Team Processes and Structures' (2011) 5 *Group Dynamics: Theory, Research, and Practice* 111.

Dushnitsky, G and Lenox, M, 'When Do Incumbents Learn from Entrepreneurial Ventures?: Corporate Venture Capital and Investing Firm Innovation Rates' (2005) 34 *Research Policy* 615.

Dushnitsky, G and Shaver, J, 'Limitations to Interorganizational Knowledge Acquisition: The Paradox of Corporate Venture Capital' (2009) 30 *Strategic Management Journal* 1045.

Dyck, A and Zingales, L, 'Private Benefits of Control: An International Comparison' (2004) 59 *Journal of Finance* 537.

Dyer, J, Gregersen, H and Christensen, C, 'The Innovator's DNA' (2009) 87 *Harvard Business Review* 60.

Easterbrook, F and Fischel, D, 'The Corporate Contract' (1989) 89 *Columbia Law Review* 1416.

—— *The Economic Structure of Corporate Law* (Harvard University Press, 1996).

Edquist C, Hommen, L and McKelvey, M, 'Product Versus Process Innovation: Implications for Employment' in J Michie and A Reati, *Employment, Technology and Economic Needs* (Edward Elgar, 1998).

Ehrlich, I and Liu, Z, 'Sensitive Analysis of the Deterrence Hypothesis: Let's Keep the Econ in Econometrics' (1999) 42 *Journal of Law and Economics* 455.

Eisenberg, C, 'Embedding Markets in Temporal Structures: A Challenge to Economic Sociology and History' in K Nathaus and D Gilgen (eds), 'Change of Markets and Market Societies: Concepts and Case Studies (Wandel von Märkten und Marktgesellschaften: Konzepte und Fallstudien)' (2011) 36 *Historical Social Research (Historische Sozialforschung)* 55.

Eisenberg, M, 'The Structure of Corporation Law' (1989) 89 *Columbia Law Review* 1461.

—— 'Actual and Virtual Specific Performance, the Theory of Efficient Breach, and the Indifference Principle in Contract Law' (2005) 93 *California Law Review* 975.

Eisenberg, T, 'The Predictability of Punitive Damages' (1997) 26 *Journal of Legal Studies* 623.

Eisner, S, 'The "In-Factor": Signature Traits of Innovation's Leaders' (2016) 32 *Journal of Applied Business Research* 185.

Enriques, L, 'The Law on Company Directors' Self-Dealing: A Comparative Analysis' (2000) 2 *International and Comparative Corporate Law Journal* 297.

—— 'Do Corporate Law Judges Matter? Some Evidence from Milan' (2002) 3 *European Business Organization Law Review* 765.

—— 'EC Company Law Directives and Regulations: How Trivial Are They?' (2006) 27 *University of Pennsylvania Journal of International Economic Law* 1.

—— 'Pandemic-Resistant Corporate Law: How to Help Companies Cope with Existential Threats and Extreme Uncertainty During the Covid-19 Crisis (2020) 17 *European Company and Financial Law Review* 257.

Enriques, L and Volpin, P, 'Corporate Governance Reforms in Continental Europe' (2007) 21 *Journal of Economic Perspectives* 117.
Enriques, L, Hertig, G and Kanda, H, 'Related-party Transactions' in R Kraakman et al, *The Anatomy of Corporate Law* (Oxford University Press, 2009).
Epstein, R, 'Contract and Trust in Corporate Law: The Case of Corporate Opportunity' (1996) 21 *Delaware Journal of Corporate Law* 1.
Erkens, M, Gan, Y and Yurtoglu, B, Not all Clawbacks are the Same: Consequences of Strong versus Weak Clawback Provisions' (2018) 66 *Journal of Accounting and Economics* 291.
Evangelista, R and Savona, M, 'The Impact of Innovation on Employment in Services: Evidence from Italy (2002) 16 *International Review of Applied Economics* 309.
Evangelista, R et al, 'Looking for Regional Systems of Innovation: Evidence from the Italian Innovation Survey' (2002) 36 *Regional Studies* 173.
Federico, G and Toninelli, P, 'Business Strategies from Unification up to the 1970s' in R Giannetti and M Vasta (eds), *Evolution of Italian Enterprises in the 20th Century* (Physica-Verlag, 2006) 191.
Feldman, M, 'The New Economics of Innovation, Spillovers and Agglomeration: A Review of Empirical Studies' (1999) 8 *Economics of Innovation and New Technology* 5.
Fenwick, M and McCahery, J, and Vermeulen, EPM 'The End of "Corporate" Governance: Hello "Platform" Governance' (2019) 20 *European Business Organization Law Review* 171.
Fenwick, M and Vermeulen, E, 'The End of the Corporation: Transformation in Corporate Governance' (2020) *Challenges and Opportunities of Corporate Governance Transformation in the Digital Era*. IGI Global, 1.
Fichtner, J, Heemskerk, E and Garcia-Bernardo, J, 'Hidden Power of the Big Three? Passive Index Funds, Re-concentration of Corporate Ownership, and New Financial Risk' (2017) 19 *Business and Politics* 298.
Fierstein, R, *A Triumph of Genius: Edwin Land, Polaroid, and the Kodak Patent War* (Ankerwycke Publications, 2015).
Fiet, J, 'Reliance upon Informants in the Venture Capital Industry (1995) 10 *Journal of Business Venturing* 195.
Fingleton, J and Raith, M, 'Career Concerns of Bargainers' (2005) 21 *Journal of Law, Economics, and Organization* 179.
Fisch, J, Hamdani, A and Solomon, S, 'The New Titans of Wall Street: A Theoretical Framework for Passive Investors' (2019) 168 *University of Pennsylvania Law Review* 17.
Fisk, C, 'Removing the "Fuel of Interest" from the "Fire of Genius": Law and the Employee-Inventor, 1830-1930' (1998) 65 *University of Chicago Law Review* 1127.
Fleischer, H, 'Gelöste und Ungelöste Probleme der Gesellschaftsrechtlichen Geschäftschancenlehre' (2003) *Neue Zeitschrift für Gesellschaftsrecht* 985.
—— 'Gegenwartsfragen der Geschäftschancenlehre im Englischen und Deutschen Gesellschaftsrecht' in J Taeger and A Wiebe (eds), *Informatik – Wirtschaft – Recht. Regulierung in der Wissensgesellschaft: Festschrift für Wolfgang Kilian* (Nomos, 2004).
—— 'Legal Transplant in European Company Law – The Case of Fiduciary Duties' (2005) 2 *European Company Financial Law Review* 378.
Foge, Z, 'American Oligarchy: How the Enfeebling of Antitrust Law Corrodes the Republic' (2019) 12 *Journal of Business Entrepreneurship & Law* 119.
Fombrun, C and Wally, S, 'Structuring Small Firms for Rapid Growth' (1989) 4 *Journal of Business Venturing* 107.
Foss, N and Mahnke, V, 'Advancing Research on Competence, Governance, and Entrepreneurship' in N Foss and V Mahnke (eds), *Competence, Governance and Entrepreneurship* (Oxford University Press, 2000) 1–20.
Francis, J and Smith, A, 'Agency Costs and Innovation: Some Empirical Evidence' (1995) 19 *Journal of Accounting & Economics* 383.
Freeman, J and Engel, J, 'Models of Innovation: Start-ups and Mature Corporations' (2007) 50 *California Management Review* 94.
Fried, J, 'Excess-pay Clawbacks' (2010) 36 *Journal of Corporation Law* 721.

Fried, J and Ganor, M, 'Agency Costs of Venture Capitalist Control in Start–ups (2006) 81 *NYU Law Review* 967, 977.

Friedman, D, 'Why not Hang Them All?' (1999) 107 *Journal of Political Economy* 259.

Friedman, L and Scheiber, H (eds), *Legal Culture and the Legal Profession* (Westview Press, 1996) 146.

Friedman, W and Jones, G, *Business History and Varieties of Capitalism* (Cambridge University Press, 2010).

Friedrichs, D, *Trusted Criminals: White-Collar Criminals in Contemporary Society* (Belmont, 1996).

—— 'Enron Et Al.: Paradigmatic White-Collar Crime Cases for the New Century' (2004) 12 *Critical Criminology* 112.

Fu, P, 'Developing Venture Capital Laws in China: Lessons Learned from the United States, Germany, and Japan' (2001) 23 *Loyola of Los Angeles International & Comparative Law Review* 487.

Fu, P, Tsui, A, and Dess, G, 'The Dynamics of Guanxi in Chinese Hightech Firms: Implications for Knowledge Management and Decision Making (2006) 46 *Management International Review* 277.

Fukuyama, F, *The End of History and the Last Man* (Penguin, 1992).

Fukuyama F, Richman, B and Goel, A, 'How to Save Democracy from Technology: Ending Big Tech's Information Monopoly' (2021) 100 *Foreign Affairs* 98.

Funk, P, 'On the Effective Use of Stigma as a Crime-deterrent' (2004) 48 *European Economic Review* 715.

Gallo, P, 'Unjust Enrichment: A Comparative Analysis' (1992) 40 *American Journal of Comparative Law* 431.

Garber, P, *Famous First Bubbles: The Fundamentals of Early Manias* (Massachusetts Institute of Technology Press, 2001).

Gardner, J, 'What is Tort Law For? Part I. The Place of Corrective Justice' (2011) 30 *Law & Philosophy* 1.

Garita, M and Martinez, S, 'A Sociological Approach Concerning Leadership: How CEO and the Masses Behave' (2016) 2 *Nile Journal of Business and Economics* 15.

Gelter, M, 'The Dark Side of Shareholder Influence: Toward a Holdup Theory of Stakeholders in Comparative Corporate Governance' (2009) 50 *Harvard International Law Journal* 129.

—— 'Taming or Protecting the Modern Corporation? Shareholder–Stakeholder Debates in a Comparative Light' (2011) 7 *New York University Journal of Law and Business* 641.

Gelter, M and Helleringer, G, 'Opportunity Makes a Thief: Corporate Opportunities as Legal Transplant and Convergence in Corporate Law' (2018) 15 *Berkeley Business Law Journal* 92.

—— 'Fiduciary Principles in European Civil Law Systems' in E Criddle, P Miller and R Sitkoff (eds), *The Oxford Handbook of Fiduciary Law* (Oxford University Press, 2019) 600.

Gerner-Beuerle, C and Schillig, M, *Comparative Company Law* (Oxford University Press, 2019).

Getzler, J, 'Equitable Compensation and the Regulation of Fiduciary Relationships' in P Birks and F Rose (eds), *Restitution and Equity* (Informa, 2000) 235.

Gillan, S and Starks, L, 'Corporate Governance Proposals and Shareholder Activism: The Role of Institutional Investors' (2000) 57 *Journal of Financial Economics* 275.

Gilson, R, 'The Legal Infrastructure of High Technology Industrial Districts: Silicon Valley, Route 128 and Covenants Not to Compete' (1999) 74 *New York University Law Review* 575.

—— 'Globalizing Corporate Governance: Convergence of Form or Function' (2001) 49 *American Journal of Comparative Law* 329.

—— 'Engineering a Venture Capital Market: Lessons from the American Experience' (2003) 55 *Stanford Law Review* 1067.

—— 'Controlling Shareholders and Corporate Governance: Complicating the Comparative Taxonomy' (2006) 119 *Harvard Law Review* 1641.

Gilson R, Sabel, C and Scott, R, 'Contracting for Innovation: Vertical Disintegration and Interfirm Collaboration' (2009) 109 *Columbia Law Review* 431.

Giummo, J, 'German Employee Inventors' Compensation Records: A Window into the Returns to Patented Inventions' (2010) 39 *Research Policy* 969.

Glaeser, E and Kerr, W, 'Local Industrial Conditions and Entrepreneurship: How Much of the Spatial Distribution Can We Explain?' (2009) 18 *Journal of Economics & Management Strategy* 623.

Glücksman, S, 'Entrepreneurial Experiences from Venture Capital Funding: Exploring two-sided Information Asymmetry' (2020) 22 *Venture Capital* 331.

Golash, D, *The Case Against Punishment: Retribution, Crime Prevention, and the Law* (New York University New York University Press, 2005).

Golden, J, 'Patentable Subject Matter and Institutional Choice' (2010) 89 *Texas Law Review* 1041.

Goldstein, A, 'Privatization in Italy, 1993–2003: Goals, Institutions, Outcomes and Outstanding Issues' in H Sinn and J Walley (eds), *Privatization Experiences in the European Union* (Massachusetts Institute of Technology Press, 2006).

Gomes, V and Manuel, J, 'Unjust Enrichment: A Few Comparative Remarks' (2001) 9 *European Review of Private Law* 449.

Gompers, P, 'The Rise and Fall of Venture Capital' (1994) 23 *Business and Economic History* 1.

Gompers, P and Lerner, J, 'The Use of Covenants: An Empirical Analysis of Venture Partnership Agreements' (1996) 39 *The Journal of Law and Economics* 463.

—— 'The Venture Capital Revolution' (2001) 15 *The Journal of Economic Perspectives* 145.

Gompers P, Kovner, A and Lerner, J, 'Specialization and Success: Evidence from Venture Capital' (2009) 18 *Journal of Economics & Management Strategy* 817.

Goode, R, 'Proprietary Liability for Secret Profits – A Reply' (2011) 127 *Law Quarterly Review* 493.

Gordon, R, 'Declining American Economic Growth Despite Ongoing Innovation' (2018) 69 *Explorations in Economic History* 1.

Gorman, M and Sahlman, W, 'What Do Venture Capitalists Do?' (1989) 4 *Journal of Business Venturing* 231.

Goshen, Z, 'The Efficiency of Controlling Corporate Self-Dealing: Theory Meets Reality' (2003) 91 *California Law Review* 393.

Goshen, Z and Squire, R, 'Principal Costs: A New Theory for Corporate Law and Governance' (2017) 117 *Columbia Law Review* 767.

Goudkamp, J, 'Exemplary Damages' in G Virgo and S Worthington (eds), *Commercial Remedies: Resolving Controversies* (Cambridge University Press, 2016).

Gourevitch, P and Shinn, J, *Political Power and Corporate Control* (Princeton University Press, 2005).

Graff, M, 'Law and Finance: Common Law and Civil Law Countries Compared – An Empirical Critique' (2008) 75 *Economica* 60.

Grandori, A and Furlotti, M, 'Contracting for the Unknown and the Logic of Innovation (2009) 16 *European Management Review* 413.

Graves, C, 'Preparing to Quit: Employee Competition versus Corporate Opportunity' (2020) 41 *Berkeley Journal of Employment & Labour Law* 333.

Gregoriou, G, Kooli, M and Kraeussl, R, *Venture Capital in Europe* (Butterworth-Heinemann, 2011).

Greif, A, 'The Study of Organizations and Evolving Organizational Forms Through History' in G Carroll and D Teece (eds), *Firms, Markets and Hierarchies* (Oxford University Press, 1999) 338.

Grossi, G and Richard, C, 'Municipal Corporatization in Germany and Italy' (2008) 10 *Public Management Review* 597.

Grunwald, A, 'Diverging Pathways to Overcoming the Environmental Crisis: A critique of Eco-modernism from a Technology Assessment Perspective' (2018) 197 *Journal of Cleaner Production* 1854.

Gulati, R and Singh, H, 'The Architecture of Cooperation: Managing Coordination Costs and Appropriation Concerns in Strategic Alliances' (1998) 43 *Administrative Science Quarterly* 781.

Guler, I and Guillén, M, 'Institutions and the Internationalization of U.S. Venture Capital Firms' (2010) 41 *Journal of International Business Studies* 185.

Guo, R-J, Kruse, T and Nohel, T, 'Undoing the Powerful Anti-Takeover Force of Staggered Boards' (2008) 14 *Journal of Corporate Finance* 274.

Habbakuk, H and Postan, M (eds), *The Cambridge Economic History of Europe* (Cambridge University Press, 1965), vol 4.

Haenlein, M and Kaplan, A, 'A Brief History of Artificial Intelligence: On the Past, Present, and Future of Artificial Intelligence' (2019) 61 *California Management Review* 5.

Hain D, Johan, S and Wang, D, 'Determinants of Cross-Border Venture Capital Investments in Emerging and Developed Economies: The Effects of Relational and Institutional Trust' (2016) 138 *Journal of Business Ethics* 743.

Hall, P and Gingerich, D, 'Varieties of Capitalism and Institutional Complementarities in the Political Economy: An Empirical Analysis' (2009) 39 *British Journal of Political Science* 449.

Hall, P and Soskice, D (eds), *Varieties of Capitalism* (Oxford University Press, 2001).

Hallen, B, Katila, R and Rosenberger, J, 'How Do Social Defenses Work? A Resource-Dependence Lens on Technology Ventures, Venture Capital Investors, and Corporate Relationships' (2014) 57 *Academy of Management Journal* 1078.

Hancké, B (ed), *Debating Varieties of Capitalism* (Oxford University Press, 2009).

Hancké, B, Rhodes, M, and Thatcher, M (eds), *Beyond Varieties of Capitalism: Conflict, Contradictions and Complementarities in the European Economy* (Oxford University Press, 2007).

Hanft, F, 'Control of Public Utilities in Minnesota' (1931) 16 *Minnesota Law Review* 457.

Hansmann, H and Kraakman, R, 'The End of the History of Corporate Law' (2000–01) 89 *Georgetown Law Journal* 439.

Harper, R (ed), *The Code of Hammurabi* (University of Chicago Press, 1904) 11.

Harris, L, 'A Critical Theory of Private Equity' (2010) 35 *Delaware Journal of Corporate Law* 259.

Harrison, L and Huntington, S, *Culture Matters: How Values Shape Human Progress* (Basic Books, 2000).

Harrison, R and Mason, C, 'Backing the Horse or the Jockey? Due Diligence, Agency Costs, Information and the Evaluation of Risk by Business Angel Investors' (2017) 15 *International Review of Entrepreneurship* 269.

Hart, O and Moore, J, 'Foundations of Incomplete Contracts' (1999) 66 *Review of Economic Studies* 115.

Hay, M and Kimya, K, 'Small Firm Growth: Intentions, Implementation and Impediments' (1994) 5 *Business Strategy Review* 49.

Hayton, D, 'The Hague Convention on the Law Applicable to Trusts and on their Recognition' (1987) 36 *The International and Comparative Law Quarterly* 260.

—— 'Proprietary Liability for Secret Profits' (2011) 127 *Law Quarterly Review* 487.

Hazen, T, 'The Short-Term/Long-Term Dichotomy and Investment Theory: Implications for Securities Market Regulation and for Corporate Law' (1991) 70 *North Carolina Law Review* 137.

Headd, B, 'Redefining Business Success: Distinguishing between Closure and Failure' (2003) 21 *Small Business Economics* 51.

Heckscher, E, *Mercantilism* (Routledge, 2013).

Hege, U, Palomino, F and Schwienbacher, A, 'Venture Capital Performance: The Disparity between Europe and the United States' (2009) 30 *Finance* 7.

Helleringer, G, 'Le Dirigeant à l'Epreuve des Opportunités d'Affaires' (2012) 24 *Recueil Dalloz* 1560.

Hellgardt, A, 'Abdingbarkeit der Gesellschaftsrechtlichen Treuepflicht' in S Grundmann et al (eds), *Unternehmen, Markt und Verantwortung: Festschrift für Klaus J. Hopt zum 70. Geburtstag am 24. August 2010* (DeGruyter, 2010) 765.

Hellmann, T, 'The Allocation of Control Rights in Venture Capital Contracts' (1998) 29 *The Rand Journal of Economics* 57.

—— 'IPOs, Acquisitions, and the Use of Convertible Securities in Venture Capital' (2006) 81 *Journal of Financial Economics* 649.

Hellmann T and Puri, M, 'Venture Capital and the Professionalization of Start-up Firms: Empirical Evidence' (2002) 57 *Journal of Finance* 169.

Hellmann, T and Thiele, V, 'Contracting Among Founders' (2015) 31 *The Journal of Law, Economics, and Organization* 629.

Hemphill, S and Kahan, M, 'The Strategies of Anticompetitive Common Ownership' (2019) 129 *Yale Law Journal* 1392.

Henry, D, 'Agency Costs, 'Ownership Structure and Corporate Governance Compliance: A Private Contracting Perspective' (2010) 18 *Pacific-Basin Finance Journal* 24.

Hershovitz, S, 'Tort as a Substitute for Revenge' in J Oberdiek (ed), *Philosophical Foundations of the Law of Torts* (Oxford University Press, 2014).

Hicks, A, 'The Remedial Principle in *Keech v Sandford* Reconsidered' (2010) 69 *Cambridge Law Journal* 287.

—— 'Do Constructive Trusts Deter Disloyalty?' (2018) 69 *Northern Ireland Legal Quarterly* 147.

Hill, C and Rothaermel, F, 'The Performance of Incumbent Firms in the Face of Radical Technological Innovation' (2003) 28 *Academy of Management Review* 257.

Hirsch, B, Reichert, B and Sohn, M, 'The Impact of Clawback Provisions on Information Processing and Investment Behaviour' (2017) 37 *Management Accounting Research* 1.

Hirte, H, Mülbert, P and Roth, M, *Grosskommentar zum Aktiengesetz*, vol 1, 5th edn (DeGruyter, 2015).

Hochner, N, 'Machiavelli: Love and the Economy of Emotions' (2014) 32 *Italian Culture* (2014) 122.

Holthausen, R, Larcker, D and Sloan, R, 'Business Unit Innovation and the Structure of Executive Compensation' (1995) 19 *Journal of Accounting and Economics* 279.

Honjo, Y et al, 'R&D Investment of Start-up Firms: Does Founders' Human Capital Matter?' (2014) 42 *Small Business Economics* 207.

Hopt, K, 'Conflict of Interest, Secrecy and Insider Information of Directors, A Comparative Analysis' (2013) 10 *European Company and Financial Law Review* 167.

Horwitz, MJ, 'Law and Economics: Science or Politics?' (1980) 8 *Hofstra Law Review* 905.

Hounshell, D, 'Invention in the Industrial Research Laboratory: Individual Act or Collective Process?' in R Perkins and D Weber (eds), *Inventive Minds: Creativity in Technology* (Oxford University Press, 1992) 273.

Hovenkamp, H, 'The Monopolization Offense' (2000) 61 *Ohio State Law Journal* 61 1035.

Hsu, D, 'What Do Entrepreneurs Pay for Venture Capital Affiliation?' (2004) 59 *Journal of Finance* 1805.

Hsu, D and Kenney, M, 'Organizing Venture Capital: The Rise and Demise of American Research & Development Corporation, 1946–1973' (2005) 14 *Industrial and Corporate Change* 579.

Hu, H and Westbrook, JL, 'Abolition of the Corporate Duty to Creditors' (2007) 107 *Columbia Law Review* 1321.

Huang, S, Lim, C and Ng, J, 'Not Clawing the Hand that Feeds you: The Case of Co-opted Boards and Clawbacks' (2019) 28 *European Accounting Review* 101.

Hughes, T, *American Genesis: A Century of Invention and Technological Enthusiasm, 1870–1970* (Penguin Books, 1989).

Iacobucci, E, 'On the Interaction between Legal and Reputational Sanctions' (2014) 43 *Journal of Legal Studies* 189.

Iammarino, S and McCann, P, 'The Structure and Evolution of Industrial Clusters: Transactions, Technology and Knowledge Spillovers' (2006) 35 *Research Policy* 1018.

Ibrahim, D, 'The (Not So) Puzzling Behavior of Angel Investors' (2008) 61 *Vanderbilt Law Review* 1405.

Invernizzi, B and Revelli, R, 'Small Firms and the Italian Economy: Structural Changes and Evidence of Turbulence' in Z Acs and D Audretsch (eds), *Small Firms and Entrepreneurship: An East–West Perspective* (Cambridge University Press, 1993) 123.

Irwin, D, 'Mercantilism as Strategic Trade Policy: the Anglo-Dutch Rivalry for the East India Trade' (1991) 99 *Journal of Political Economy* 1296.

—— 'Strategic Trade Policy and Mercantilist Trade Rivalries' (1992) 82*The American Economic Review* 134.

Isaacson, W, 'The Real Leadership Lessons of Steve Jobs (2012) 90 *Harvard Business Review* 92.

Ivanov, V and Xie, F, 'Do Corporate Venture Capitalists Add Value to Start-up Firms? Evidence from IPOs and Acquisitions of VC-backed Companies' (2010) 39 *Financial Management* 129.

Jacobs, L, 'Business Ethics and the Law: Obligations of a Corporate Executive' (1972) 28 *Business Law* 1063.

Jaeger, P, *L'Interesse Sociale* (Giuffre, 1964).
James, H, 'Deglobalization: The Rise of Disembedded Unilateralism (2018) 10 *Annual Review of Financial Economics* 219.
Jayawardhena, C and Foley, P, 'Changes in the Banking Sector – The Case of Internet Banking in the UK' (2000) 10 *Internet Research* 19.
Jeng, L and Wells, P, 'The Determinants of Venture Capital Funding: Evidence across Countries (2000) 6 *Journal of Corporate Finance* 241.
Jensen, M, 'Eclipse of the Public Corporation' (1989) 67 *Harvard Business Review* 61.
Jensen, M and Meckling, W, 'Theory of the Firm: Managerial Behaviour, Agency Costs and Ownership Structure' (1976) 3 *Journal of Financial Economics* 305.
Johnson, S et al, 'Tunneling' (2000) 90 *American Economic Review* 22.
Johnson, S, McMillan, J and Woodruff, C, 'Property Rights and Finance' (2002) 92 *American Economic Review* 1335.
Johnston, A, 'Company Law and Corporate Governance After Brexit: From Short-term Disruption to Long-term Sustainability?' (2020) 8 ETUI Research Paper-Policy Brief.
Joia, L, 'Measuring Intangible Corporate Assets' (2000) 1 *Journal of Intellectual Capital* 68.
Jolls, C, Sunstein, C and Thaler, R, 'A Behavioral Approach to Law and Economics (1998) 50 *Stanford Law Review* 1471.
Jones, P, 'Sanctions, Incentives, and Corporate Behavior' (1985) 27 *California Management Review* 122.
Jonson, C, 'The Effects of Imprisonments' in F Cullen and P Wilcox (eds), *The Oxford Handbook of Criminological Theory* (Oxford University Press, 2013) 672.
Kaab, A et al, 'Combined Life Cycle Assessment and Artificial Intelligence for Prediction of Output Energy and Environmental Impacts of Sugarcane Production' (2019) 664 *Science of the Total Environment* 1005.
Kahneman, D, Knetsch, J and Thaler, R, 'Experimental Tests of the Endowment Effect and the Coase Theorem' (1990) 98 *Journal of Political Economy* 1325.
Kahn-Freund, O, 'On Uses and Misuses of Comparative Law' (1974) 37 *Modern Law Review* 1.
Kang, E, 'Director Interlocks and Spillover Effects of Reputational Penalties from Financial Reporting Fraud' (2008) 51 *Academy of Management Journal* 537.
Kaplan, S and Strömberg, P, 'Venture Capitals as Principals: Contracting, Screening, and Monitoring' (2001) 91 *American Economic Review* 426.
—— 'Financial Contracting Theory Meets the Real World: An Empirical Analysis of Venture Capital Contracts' (2003) 70 *The Review of Economic Studies* 281.
—— 'Characteristics, Contracts, and Actions: Evidence from Venture Capitalist Analyses' (2004) 59 *Journal of Finance* 2177.
Kaplan S, Martel, F and Strömberg, P, 'How do Legal Differences and Experience Affect Financial Contracts? (2007) 16 *Journal of Financial Intermediation* 273.
Kash, D and Rycroft, R, 'To Manage Complex Innovation You Need to Ask the Right Questions' (2003) 46 *Research-Technology Management* 29.
Katila, R, Rosenberger, J and Eisenhardt, K, 'Swimming with Sharks: Technology Ventures, Defense Mechanisms and Corporate Relationships' (2008) 53 *Administrative Science Quarterly* 295.
Katz, M and Shapiro, C, 'Systems Competition and Network Effects' (1994) 8 *Journal of Economic Perspectives* 93.
Keay, A, 'Tackling the Issue of the Corporate Objective: An Analysis of the United Kingdom's Enlightened Shareholder Value Approach' (2007) 29 *Sydney Law Review* 577.
—— 'The Authorising of Directors' Conflicts of Interest: Getting a Balance?' (2012) 12 *Journal of Corporate Law Studies* 129.
Kelsen, H, *Introduction to the Problems of Legal Theory* (Oxford University Press, 1992).
Kenney, M and Zysman, J, 'Unicorns, Cheshire Cats, and the New Dilemmas of Entrepreneurial Finance' (2019) 21 *Venture Capital* 35.
Kershaw, D, 'Does it Matter how the Law Thinks about Corporate Opportunities?' (2005) 25 *Oxford Journal of Legal Studies* 533.

—— 'Lost in Translation: Corporate Opportunities in Comparative Perspective' (2005) 25 *Oxford Journal of Legal Studies* 603.

—— *The Foundations of Anglo-American Corporate Fiduciary Law* (Cambridge University Press, 2018).

—— *Company Law in Context* (Oxford University Press, 2012).

Keuschnigg, C and Nielsen, S, 'Public Policy for Venture Capital' (2001) 8 *International Tax and Public Finance* 557.

—— 'Start-ups, Venture Capitalists, and the Capital Gains Tax' (2004) 88 *Journal of Public Economics* 1011.

Kim, M and Stepchenkova, S, 'Examining the Impact of Experiential Value on Emotions, Self-connective Attachment, and Brand Loyalty in Korean Family Restaurants' (2018) 19 *Journal of Quality Assurance in Hospitality & Tourism* 298.

King, B, 'Strategizing at Leading Venture Capital Firms: Of Planning, Opportunism and Deliberate Emergence' (2008) 41 *Long Range Planning* 345.

Kirkpatrick, D, *The Facebook Effect: The Inside Story of the Company that is Connecting the World* (Simon and Schuster, 2011).

Kirzner, J, *Competition and Entrepreneurship* (University of Chicago Press, 1973).

Knight, G and Cavusgil, T, 'The Born Global Firm: A Challenge to Traditional Internationalization Theory' (1996) 8 *Advances in International Marketing* 11.

Ko, E-J and McKelvie, A, 'Signaling for More Money: The Roles of Founders' Human Capital and Investor Prominence in Resource Acquisition across Different Stages of Firm Development' (2018) 33 *Journal of Business Venturing* 438.

Kor, Y, 'Direct and Interaction Effects of Top Management Team and Board Compositions on R&D Investment Strategy' (2006) 27 *Strategic Management Journal* 1081.

Kornhauser, L, 'The Nexus of Contracts Approach to Corporations: A Comment on Easterbrook and Fischel' (1989) 89 *Columbia Law Review* 1449.

Korobkin, R, *Negotiation Theory and Strategy* (Aspen Publishers, 2009).

Korobkin, R and Ulen, T, 'Law and Behavioral Science: Removing the Rationality Assumption from Law and Economics' (2000) 88 *California Law Review* 1051.

Koziol, H, 'Punitive Damages – A European Perspective' (2007–08) 68 *Louisiana Law Review* 741.

—— 'Comparative Conclusions' in H Koziol (ed), *Basic Question of Tort Law from a Comparative Perspective* (Jan Sramek Verlag, 2015) 685.

Kraakman, R et al, *The Anatomy of Corporate Law* (Oxford University Press, 2009).

—— *The Anatomy of Corporate Law: A Comparative and Functional Approach* (Oxford University Press, 2017).

Kritikos, A, 'Berlin: A Hub for Startups but not (yet) for Fast-growing Companies' (2016) 6 *DIW Economic Bulletin* 339.

Krotov, V, 'The Internet of Things and New Business Opportunities (2017) 60 *Business Horizons* 831.

Krugman, P, *Geography and Trade* (Massachusetts Institute of Technology Press, 1991).

Krygier, M, 'Law as Tradition' (1986) 5 *Law and Philosophy* 237.

Lane, C, 'Globalization and the German Model of Capitalism – Erosion or Survival?' (2000) 51 *The British Journal of Sociology* 207.

Lang, L and Stulz, R, 'Tobin's Q, Corporate Diversification and Firm Performance' (1994) 102 *Journal of Political Economy* 1248.

Langevoort, D, 'Monitoring: The Behavorial Economics of Corporate Compliance with Law' (2002) 71 *Columbia Business Law Review* 71.

La Porta, R, Lopez-de-Silanes, F and Shleifer, A, 'Corporate Ownership around the World' (1999) 54 *Journal of Finance* 471.

—— 'Government Ownership of Banks' (2002) 57 *Journal of Finance* 265.

—— 'What Works in Securities Laws?' (2006) 61 *Journal of Finance* 1.

—— 'The Economic Consequences of Legal Origins' (2008) 46 *Journal of Economic Literature* 285.

La Porta R et al, 'Legal Determinants of External Finance' (1997) 52 *Journal of Finance* 1131.

—— 'Law and Finance' (1998) 106 *Journal of Political Economy* 1113.

—— 'The Quality of Government' (1999) 15 *Journal of Law Economics and Organization* 222.
—— 'Agency Problems and Dividend Policies around the World' (2000) 55 *Journal of Finance* 1.
Lattes, A, *Il Diritto Commerciale nella Legislazione Statutaria delle Città Italiane* (Hoepli, 1884).
Lao, T, *Tao Te Ching* (e-artnow, 2013) ch 38.
Lazonick, W, 'The Theory of Market Economy and the Market Foundations of Innovative Enterprise' (2003) 24 *Economic and Industrial Democracy* 9.
Lee, H and Park, D, '*Post-Covid Asia: Deglobalization, Fourth Industrial Revolution, and Sustainable Development* (World Scientific, 2020).
Lee, S, Park, G and Kang, J, 'The Double-Edged Effects of the Corporate Venture Capital Unit's Structural Autonomy on Corporate Investors' Explorative and Exploitative Innovation' (2018) 88 *Journal of Business Research* 141.
Lehrer, M, Tylecote, A and Conesa, E, 'Corporate Governance, Innovation Systems and Industrial Performance' (1999) 6 *Industry and Innovation* 25.
Le Kama, A and Ayong, D, 'Sustainable Growth, Renewable Resources and Pollution' (2001) 25 *Journal of Economic Dynamics and Control* 1911.
Leknes, S and Tracey, I, 'A Common Neurobiology for Pain and Pleasure' (2008) 9 *Nature Reviews Neuroscience* (2008) 314.
—— 'Pain and Pleasure: Masters of Mankind' in M Kringelbach and K Berridge (eds), *Pleasures of the Brain* (Oxford University Press, 2010) 320.
Leleux, B and Surlemont, B, 'Public Versus Private Venture Capital: Seeding or Crowding Out? A Pan-European Analysis' (2003) 18 *Journal of Business Venturing* 81.
Lemley, M, 'Reconceiving Patents in the Age of Venture Capital' (2000) 4 *Journal of Small and Emerging Business Law* 137.
—— 'The Myth of the Sole Inventor' (2012) 110 *Michigan Law Review* 709.
Lepaulle, P, 'Civil Law Substitutes for Trusts' (1927) 36 *The Yale Law Journal* 1126.
Leptien, C, 'Incentives for Employed Inventors: an Empirical Analysis with Special Emphasis on the German Law for Employee's Inventions' (1995) 25 *R&D Management* 213.
Lerner, J, 'The Syndication of Venture Capital Investments' (1994) 23 *Financial Management* 16.
Lerner, J and Schoar, A, 'Does Legal Enforcement Affect Financial Transactions? The Contractual Channel in Private Equity' (2005) 120 *The Quarterly Journal of Economics* 223.
Lev, B and Daum, J, 'The Dominance of Intangible Assets: Consequences for Enterprise Management and Corporate Reporting' (2004) 8 *Measuring Business Excellence* 6.
Li, F and Srinivasan, S, 'Corporate Governance when Founders are Directors (2011) 102 *Journal of Financial Economics* 454.
Liang, H and Renneboog, L, 'On the Foundations of Corporate Social Responsibility' (2017) 72 *Journal of Finance* 853.
Lieberman, S, *Growth and Crisis in the Spanish Economy: 1940–1993* (Routledge, 1995).
Light, D and Warburton, R, 'Demythologizing the High Costs of Pharmaceutical Research' (2011) 6 *BioSocieties* 34.
Lindsey, L, 'Blurring Firm Boundaries: The Role of Venture Capital in Strategic Alliances' (2008) 63 *Journal of Finance* 1137.
Lins, K, Servaes, H and Tamayo, A, 'Social Capital, Trust, and Firm Performance: The Value of Corporate Social Responsibility During the Financial Crisis' (2017) 72 *Journal of Finance* 1785.
Lipinski, T and Britz, J, 'Rethinking the Ownership of Information in the 21st Century: Ethical Implications' (2000) 2 *Ethics and Information Technology* 49.
Liu, S, 'Law's Social Forms: A Powerless Approach to the Sociology of Law' (2015) 40 *Law and Social Inquiry* 1.
Liu, Y and Markku, M, 'Local Partnering in Foreign Ventures: Uncertainty, Experiential Learning, and Syndication in Cross-border Venture Capital Investments (2016) 59 *Academy of Management Journal* 1407.
Lockett, A and Wright, M, 'The Syndication of Venture Capital Investments' (2001) 29 *Omega* 375.
Lopez, R, 'The Trade of Medieval Europe: The South' in C Postan, M Postan and E Miller (eds), *The Cambridge Economic History of Europe*, 2nd edn (Cambridge University Press, 1987) vol 2.

Lowry, J, 'The Codification of Directors' Duties: Capturing the Essence of the Corporate Opportunity Doctrine' (2006) 2 *Ownership and Control* 22.
Lowry, J and Edmunds, R, 'The Corporate Opportunity Doctrine: The Shifting Boundaries of the Duty and its Remedies' (1998) 61 *Modern Law Review* 515.
Lu, H, Solt, M and Tan, Y, 'Do Foreign and Local Venture Capitalists Behave Alike in Transitional Economies? Evidence from China' (2010) 10 *Journal of International Business and Economics* 68.
Lundvall, B et al, 'National Systems of Production, Innovation and Competence Building' (2002) 31 *Research Policy* 213.
Lupoi, M, *Trusts: A Comparative Study* (Cambridge University Press, 2000).
Luo, J et al, 'Syndication Through Social Embeddedness: A Comparison of Foreign, Private and State-owned Venture Capital (VC) Firms' (2019) 36 *Asia Pacific Journal of Management* 499.
Ma, F, 'Business Integrity v. Business Efficiency: The Corporate Opportunity Doctrine in China (2015) 23 *Journal of Financial Crime* 201.
Macey, J, 'Fiduciary Duties as Residual Claims: Obligations to Nonshareholder Constituencies from a Theory of the Firm Perspective' (1998) 84 *Cornell Law Review* 1266.
Madhavan, R and Iriyama, A, 'Understanding Global Flows of Venture Capital: Human Networks as the "Carrier Wave" of Globalization' (2009) 40 *Journal of International Business Studies* 1241.
Maffei, A (ed), *Commentario Breve al Diritto delle Società* (CEDAM, 1997) 744.
Magnus, U, 'Punitive Damages in German Law' in L Meurkens and E Nordin (eds), *The Power of Punitive Damages – Is Europe Missing Out?* (Intersentia, 2012) 245.
Mahe, C, 'Punitive Damages in the Competing Reform Drafts of the French Civil Code' in L Meurkens and E Nordin (eds), *The Power of Punitive Damages – Is Europe Missing Out?* (Intersentia, 2012) 261–82.
Malmgren, H, 'Information, Expectations and the Theory of the Firm' (1961) 75 *Quarterly Journal of Economics* 399.
Manigart, S, 'The Founding Rate of Venture Capital Firms in Three European Countries (1970–1990)' (1994) 9 *Journal of Business Venturing* 525.
Markovits, D, 'Sharing Ex Ante and Sharing Ex Post: The Non-Contractual Basis of Fiduciary Relations' in A Gold and P Miller (eds), *Philosophical Foundations of Fiduciary Law* (Oxford University Press, 2014) 210.
Marshall, A, *Industry and Trade* (Macmillan, 1919).
Martin, M, 'Keeping it Real: Debunking the Deglobalization Myth, Brexit and Trump: "Lessons" on Integration' (2018) 17 *Journal of International Trade Law and Policy* 62.
Massart, T, 'Note to Cass Com 18 December 2012' [2013] *Revue des Sociétés* 262.
—— Note to Cass Com 12 March 2013' [2013] *Revue des Sociétés* 689.
Mate-Sanchez-Val, M and Harris, R, 'Differential Empirical Innovation Factors for Spain and the UK' (2014) 43 *Research Policy* 451.
Maula, M, Autio, E and Murray, G, 'Corporate Venture Capitalists and Independent Venture Capitalists: What Do They Know, Who Do They Know and Should Entrepreneurs Care?' (2005) 7 *Venture Capital: An International Journal of Entrepreneurial Finance* 3.
Maula, M, Keil, T and Zahra, S, 'Top Management's Attention to Discontinuous Technological Change: Corporate Venture Capital as an Alert Mechanism' (2013) 24 *Organization Science* 926.
Mayer, C, *Prosperity: Better Business Makes the Greater Good* (Oxford University Press, 2018).
—— 'Shareholderism Versus Stakeholderism – A Misconceived Contradiction. A Comment on "The Illusory Promise of Stakeholder Governance" by Lucian Bebchuk and Roberto Tallarita', European Corporate Governance Institute-Law Working Paper 522 (2020).
—— 'The Future of the Corporation and the Economics of Purpose', ECGI Finance Working Paper 710/2020.
Mazerolle, L and Roehl, J, *Civil remedies and crime prevention* (Criminal Justice Press, 1998).
McCluskey, M, 'Defining the Economic Pie, Not Dividing or Maximizing It' (2018) 5 *Critical Analysis of the Law* 78.
McIvor, G, 'Reparative and Restorative Approaches' in A Bottoms, S Rex and G Robinson (eds), *Alternatives to Prison* (Willan, 2004).

Mercuro, N and Medema, S, *Economics and the Law* (Princeton University Press, 1997).
Merges, R, 'The Law and Economics of Employee Inventions' (1999) 13 *Harvard Journal of Law & Technology* 1.
Mestmäcker, E-J, *Verwaltung, Konzerngewalt und Recht der Aktionare* (Müller, 1958).
Meurkens, R, *Punitive Damages* (Kluwer, 2014).
Meyer-Thurow, G, 'The Industrialization of Invention: A Case Study from the German Chemical Industry' (1982) 73 *Isis* 363.
Miao, E and Helwig, B, 'Avoiding Common IP Pitfalls: What Every Startup Needs to Know' (2018) 16 *Snippets* 1.
Milhaupt, C, 'Market for Innovation in the United States and Japan: Venture Capital and the Comparative Corporate Governance Debate' (1996) 91 *Northwestern University Law Review* 865.
Mill, J, *Principles of Political Economy* (Longmans, 1909).
Miller, C, *Contempt of Court*, 3rd edn (Oxford University Press, 2000).
Milosevic, M and Fendt, J, 'Venture Capital and its French Exception: Explaining Performance through Human Capital, Policy and Institutional Failures' (2016) 43 *Science and Public Policy* 660.
Misa, T, *Leonardo to the Internet: Technology and Culture from the Renaissance to the Present* (John Hopkins University Press, 2013).
Mitchell, G and Hamilton, W, 'Managing R&D as a Strategic Option' (1998) 31 *Research-Technology Management* 15.
Mitnick, B, 'The Theory of Agency' (1975) 24 *Public Choice* 27.
Molina-Morales, X, 'Industrial Districts and Innovation: The Case of the Spanish Ceramic Tiles Industry' (2002) 14 *Entrepreneurship & Regional Development: An International Journal* 317.
Molk, P, 'How do LLC Owners Contract Around Default Statutory Protections' (2016) 42 *Journal of Corporation Law* 503.
Mommsen, T and Kruger, P, *The Digest of Justininan*, vol II (University of Pennsylvania, 1985).
Moore, M, *Corporate Governance in the Shadow of the State* (Hart Publishing, 2013).
—— 'Private Ordering and Public Policy: The Paradoxical Foundations of Corporate Contractarianism' (2014) 34 *Oxford Journal of Legal Studies* 693.
More, T, *Utopia* (Yale University Press, 2014).
Morris, M, Watling, J and Schindehutte, M, 'Venture Capitalist Involvement in Portfolio Companies: Insights from South Africa' (2000) 38 *Journal of Small Business Management* 68.
Mosca, M and Bradley, M, 'Perfect Competition According to Enrico Barone' (2013) 64 *Cahiers d'économie politique/Papers in Political Economy* 9.
Möslein, F, 'Robots in the Boardroom: Artificial Intelligence and Corporate Law' in W Barfield and U Pagallo (eds), *Research Handbook on the Law of Artificial Intelligence* (Edward Elgar, 2018).
Motta, M and Peitz, M, 'Big Tech Mergers' (2020) Information Economics and Policy, CEPR Discussion Paper No. DP14353, ssrn.com/abstract=3526079.
Murphy, K, 'Executive Compensation' in O Ashenfelter and D Card (eds), *Handbook of Labor Economics* (Elsevier, 1999) 2485.
Nahata, R, Hazarika, S and Tandon, K, 'Success in Global Venture Capital Investing: Do Institutional and Cultural Differences Matter?' (2014) 49 *Journal of Financial and Quantitative Analysis* 1039.
Neher, D, 'Staged financing: an agency perspective (1999) 66 *The Review of Economic Studies* 255.
Nir, S, 'One Duty to All: The Fiduciary Duty of Impartiality and Stockholders' Conflict of Interest' (2020) 16 *Hastings Business Law Journal* 1.
Nenova, T, 'The Value of Corporate Voting Rights and Control: A Cross-country Analysis' (2003) 68 *Journal of Financial Economics* 325.
Nguyen, H and Bui, X-N, 'Predicting Blast-induced Air Overpressure: a Robust Artificial Intelligence System Based on Artificial Neural Networks and Random Forest' (2019) 28 *Natural Resources Research* 893.
Noack, U and Zöllner, W (eds), *Kölner Kommentar zum Aktiengesetz* (Carl Heymanns, 2010).
Noble, D, *America by Design: Science, Technology and the Rise of Corporate Capitalism* (Oxford University Press, 1977).

Nolan, R, 'Enacting Civil Remedies in Company Law' (2001) 1 *Journal of Corporate Law Studies* 245.
Nonala, I and Kenney, M, 'Towards a New Theory of Innovation Management: A Case Study Comparing Canon, Inc. and Apple Computer, Inc.' (1991) 8 *Journal of Engineering and Technology Management* 67.
North, D, *Structure and Change in Economic History* (Norton, 1981).
Nussbaum, M, 'Flawed Foundations: The Philosophical Critique of (a Particular Type of) Economics (1997) 64 *University of Chicago Law Review* 1197.
O'Brien, J, 'The Paypal Mafia' (2007) 11 *Fortune* 26.
O'Connor, M, 'How Should We Talk about Duty – Directors' Conflict-of-Interest Transactions and the ALI's Principles of Corporate Governance' (1992) 61 *George Washington University Law Review* 954.
O'Connor, M and Rafferty, M, 'Corporate Governance and Innovation' (2012) 47 *Journal of Financial and Quantitative Analysis* 397.
Orlandini, G, 'Diritto del Lavoro e Regolazioni delle Reti' in F Cafaggi (ed), *Reti di Imprese tra Regolazione e Norme Sociali* (Il Mulino, 2004) 281.
Orlinsky, E, 'Corporate Opportunity Doctrine and Interested Director Transactions: A Framework for Analysis in an Attempt to Restore Predictability' (1999) 24 *Delaware Journal of Corporate Law* 451.
Östberg, J, *Styrelseledamöters Lojalitetsplikt – Särskilt om Förbudet att Utnyttja Affärsmöjligheter* (Jure AB, 2016).
O'Sullivan, M, 'The Innovative Enterprise and Corporate Governance' (2000) 24 *Cambridge Journal of Economics* 393.
Otero Crespo, M, 'Punitive Damages under Spanish Law: A Subtle Recognition?' in L Meurkens and E Nordin (eds), *The Power of Punitive Damages – Is Europe Missing Out?* (Intersentia, 2012) 283–310.
Ouellette, L, 'Patentable Subject Matter and Nonpatent Innovation Incentives' (2015) 5 *University of California Irvine Law Review* 1115.
Owen, D, 'Punitive Damages Overview: Functions, Problems and Reform' (1994) 39 *Villanova Law Review* 363.
Özyurt, S, 'Bargaining, Reputation and Competition' (2015) 119 *Journal of Economic Behavior & Organization* 1.
Panda, S, Srivastava, S and Pandey, S, 'Nature and Evolution of Trust in Business-to-Business Settings: Insights from VC-Entrepreneur Relationships' (2020) 91 *Industrial Marketing Management* 246.
Paniccia, I, *Italian Districts: Evolution and Competitiveness in Italian Firms* (Edward Elgar, 2002).
Parhankangas, A and Arenius, P, 'From a Corporate Venture to an Independent Company: A Base for a Taxonomy for Corporate Spin-off Firms' (2003) 32 *Research Policy* 463.
Parisi, F, 'Positive, Normative and Functional Schools in Law and Economics' (2004) 18 *European Journal of Law and Economics* 259.
Parker, M, 'Changing Tides: The Introduction of Punitive Damages into the French Legal System' (2013) 41 *Georgia Journal of International and Comparative Law* 390.
Parsons, T, *Social System* (Routledge, 2005).
—— 'An Outline of the Social System' in C Calhoun (ed), *Classical Sociological Theory* (Blackwell, 2007).
Parthiban, D, Hitt, M and Gimeno, J, 'The Influence of Activism by Institutional Investors on R&D' (2001) 44 *Academy of Management Journal* 144.
Patton, C and Balakrishnan, S, 'The Impact of Expectation of Future Negotiation Interaction on Bargaining Processes and Outcomes' (2010) 63 *Journal of Business Research* 809.
Payne, S, *The Franco Regime: 1936–1975* (University of Wisconsin Press, 1988).
Paz-Ares, C, 'La Sociedad Colectiva: Posicion del Socio y Distribucion de Resultados' in R Uria and A Mendez, *Curso de Derecho Mercantil*, 2nd edn (Civitas, 2006) 639.
—— 'Anatomía del Deber de Lealtad' (2015) 39 *Actualidad Jurídica Uría Menéndez* 43.

Penning, J and Harianto, F, 'The Diffusion of Technological Innovation in the Commercial Banking Industry' (1992) 13 *Strategic Management Journal* 29.

Petri, R, *Storia Economica d'Italia* (Il Mulino, 2002).

Pfotenhauer, S and Jasanoff, S, 'The "Practice Turn" in Innovation Policy and the Global Circulation of Innovation Models' in D Tyfield et al (eds), *The Routledge Handbook of the Political Economy of Science* (Taylor & Francis, 2017) 416.

Pinkley, R, Neale, M and Bennett, R, 'The Impact of Alternatives to Settlement in Dyadic Negotiation' (1994) 57 *Organizational Behavior and Human Decision Processes* 97.

Pistor, K and Xu, C, 'Fiduciary Duties in Transitional Civil Law Jurisdiction: Lessons from the Incompleteness of Law Theory' in C Milhaupt (ed), *Global Markets, Domestic Institutions: Corporate Law and Governance in a New Era of Cross-Border Deals* (Columbia University Press, 2003) 77.

Plaza, M, Ngwenyama, O and Rohlf, K, 'A Comparative Analysis of Learning Curves: Implications for New Technology Implementation Management' (2010) 200 *European Journal of Operational Research* 518.

Plehn-Dujowich, J, 'A Theory of Serial Entrepreneurship' (2010) 35 *Small Business Economics* 377.

Polinsky, M, *An Introduction to Law and Economics* (Walter Kluwers, 2011).

Polinsky, M and Shavell, S, 'Punitive Damages: An Economic Analysis' (1997–1998) 111 *Harvard Law Review* 869.

Popofsky, J, 'Corporate Opportunity and Corporate Competition: a Double-Barreled Theory of Fiduciary Liability' (1982) 10 *Hofstra Law Review* 1193.

Portellano Diez, P, *Deber de Fidelidad de los Administradores de Sociedades Mercantiles y Oportunidades de Negocio* (Civitas, 1996).

Posner, R, 'Some Uses and Abuses of Economics in Law' (1979) 46 *University of Chicago Law Review* 281.

—— 'Optimal Sentences for White Collar Crimes' (1979–1980) 17 *American Criminal Law Review* 409.

—— 'An Economic Approach to the Law of Evidence' (1999) 51 *Stanford Law Review* 1477.

Pransky, J, 'The Pransky interview: Helen Greiner, Serial Robotics Entrepreneur, Founder and CEO of CyPhy Works, CoFounder iRobot Corporation' (2005) 42 *Industrial Robot: An International Journal* 181.

—— 'The Pransky Interview: Melonee Wise, CEO, Fetch Robotics' (2016) 43 *Industrial Robot: An International Journal* 253.

—— 'The Pransky Interview: Dr Cory Kidd, Founder and CEO at Catalia Health' (2017) 44 *Industrial Robot: An International Journal* 259.

—— 'The Pransky interview: Gianmarco Veruggio, Director of Research, CNR-IEIIT, Genoa Branch; Robotics Pioneer and Inventor' (2017) 44 *Industrial Robot: An International Journal* 6.

Quadrio Curzio, A and Fortis, M (eds), *Complessità e Distretti Industriali. Dinamiche, Modelli e Casi Reali* (Il Mulino, 2002).

Querzola, L, *La Tutela Anticipatoria fra Procedimento Cautelare e Giudizio di Merito* (Bononia University Press, 2006).

Rachlinsky, J, 'New Law and Psychology: A Reply to Critics, Skeptics, and Cautious Supporters' (1990–2000) 85 *Cornell Law Review* 739.

Rahman, S, 'The New Utilities: Private Power, Social Infrastructure, and the Revival of the Public Utility Concept' (2017) 39 *Cardozo Law Review* 1621.

Rajan, R and Zingales, L, 'The Influence of the Financial Revolution on the Nature of Firms' (2011) 91 *American Economic Review* 206.

Ranft, A and O'Neill, H, 'Board Composition and High-Flying Founders: Hints of Trouble to Come?' (2001) 15 *Academy of Management Perspectives* 126.

Rasmusen, E, 'Stigma and Self-fulfilling Expectations of Criminality' (1996) 39 *Journal of Law and Economics* 519.

Rauterberg, G and Talley, E, 'Contracting Out of the Fiduciary Duty of Loyalty: An Empirical Analysis of Corporate Opportunity Waivers' (2017) 117 *Columbia Law Review* 1075.

Rias, N, 'L'Amende Civile: une Fausse Bonne Idée' [2016] *Receuil Dalloz* 2072.
Reder, M and O'Brien, C, 'Managing the Risk of Trade Secret Loss Due to Job Mobility in an Innovation Economy with the Theory of Inevitable Disclosure' (2012) 12 *Journal of High Technology Law* 373.
Renoux-Zagamé, M, 'Juger selon d'Aguesseau: le Magistrat "Loi Vivante"' (2009) 19 *Histoire de la Justice* 57.
Ribstein, L, 'Partnership Governance of Large Firms' (2009) 76 *The University of Chicago Law Review* 289.
Rice, M et al, 'Corporate Venture Capital Models for Promoting Radical Innovation' (2000) 8 *Journal of Marketing Theory and Practice* 1.
Rickett, C, 'Compensating for Loss in Equity: Choosing the Right Horse for Each Course' in P Birks and F Rose (eds), *Restitution and Equity* (Informa Law, 2000) 173.
Rickett, C and Gardner, T, 'Compensating for Loss in Equity: The Evolution of a Remedy' (1994) 24 *Victoria University of Wellington Law Review* 19.
Ringe, G, 'Hedge Funds and Risk-Decoupling – The Empty Voting Problem in the European Union' (2013) 36 *Seattle University Law Review* 1027.
Roberts, J, *The Modern Firm* (Oxford University Press, 2007).
Robinson, P and Darley, J, 'Does Criminal Law Deter? A Behavioural Science Investigation' (2004) 24 *Oxford Journal of Legal Studies* 173.
Rock, E, 'Greenhorns, Yankees, and Cosmopolitans: Venture Capital, IPOs, Foreign Firms, and U.S. Markets (2001) 2 *Theoretical Inquiries in Law* 711.
Rock, E and Rubinfeld, D, 'Common Ownership and Coordinated Effects (2020) 83 *Antitrust Law Journal* 201.
Rock, E and Watcher, M, 'Dangerous Liaisons: Corporate Law, Trust Law, and Inter-Doctrinal Legal Transplants' (2002) 96 *Northwestern University Law Review* 651.
Roe, M, *Strong Managers, Weak Owners* (Princeton University Press, 1994).
—— 'Delaware's Competition' (2003) 117 *Harvard Law Review* 588.
—— *Political Determinants of Corporate Governance* (Oxford University Press, 2003).
—— 'Delaware's Politics' (2005) 118 *Harvard Law Review* 2491.
Romano, R, *The Genius of American Corporate Law* (American Enterprise Institute Press, 1993).
—— 'Public Pension Fund Activism in Corporate Governance Reconsidered' (1993) 93 *Columbia Law Review* 795.
Romeo, G, *La Finanza dei Distretti Industriali* (Franco Angeli, 2007).
Rosell-Martınez, J and Sanchez-Sellero, P, 'Foreign Direct Investment and Technical Progress in Spanish Manufacturing' (2012) 44 *Applied Economics* 2473.
Rosenberg, D, *Cloning Silicon Valley* (Pearson Education, 2002).
Rosenberg, N, 'Why Do Firms Do Basic Research (With Their Own Money)?' (1990) 19 *Research Policy* 165.
Rosenstein, S and Wyatt, J, 'Outside Directors, Board Independence, and Shareholder Wealth' (1990) 26 *Journal of Financial Economics* 175.
Ross, S, 'The Economic Theory of Agency: The Principal's Problem' (1973) 63 *The American Economic Review* (1973) 134.
Rossi, A, 'Società con Partecipazione pubblica' in *Enciclopedia Giuridica* (Treccani, 1993) vol 29.
Rossman, J, *Industrial Creativity; the Psychology of the Inventor* (University Books, 1964).
Russo, M, 'Technical Change and the Industrial District: The Role of Interfirm Relations in the Growth and Transformation of Ceramic Tile Production' (1985) 14 *Italy Research Policy* 329.
Ryan Jr, H and Wiggins III, R, 'The Interactions Between R&D Investment Decisions and Compensation Policy' (2002) 31 *Financial Management* 5.
Ryan, R (ed), *The Oxford Handbook of Human Motivation* (Oxford University Press, 2012).
Sahlman, W, 'The Structure and Governance of Venture-Capital Organizations' (1990) 27 *Journal of Financial Economics* 473.
Salzwedel, M, 'A Contractual Theory of Corporate Opportunity and a Proposed Statute' (2002) 23 *Pace Law Review* 83.

Samila, S and Sorenson, O, 'Noncompete Covenants: Incentives to Innovate or Impediments to Growth' (2011) 57 *Management Science* 425.
—— 'Venture Capital, Entrepreneurship, and Economic Growth (2011) 93 *The Review of Economics and Statistics* 338.
Sassoon, D, *Contemporary Italy: Politics, Economy and Society Since 1945* (Routledge, 2014).
Saxenian, A, *Regional Advantage. Culture and Competition in Silicon Valley and Route 128* (Harvard University Press, 1994).
—— 'Brain Circulation. How High-Skill Immigration Makes Everyone Better Off' (2002) 20 *Brookings Review* 28.
—— 'From Brain Drain to Brain Circulation: Transnational Communities and Regional Upgrading in India and China' (2005) 40 *Studies in Comparative International Development* 35.
Saxenian, A, Motoyama, Y and Quan, X, *Local and Global Networks of Immigrant Professionals in Silicon Valley* (Public Policy Institute of CA, 2002).
Schaller, W, 'Corporate Opportunities and Corporate Competition in Illinois: A Comparative Discussion of Fiduciary Duties' (2012) 46 *John Marshall Law Review* 1.
Scheuer, S, *Social and Economic Motivation at Work: Theories of Motivation Reassessed* (Copenhagen Business School Press, 2000).
Schinkel, M and LaRouche, P, 'Continental Drift in the Treatment of Dominant Firms' in R Blair and D Sokol, *The Oxford Handbook of International Antitrust Economics* (Oxford University Press, 2014) vol 2.
Schmidt, K, 'The Costs and Benefits of Privatization: An Incomplete Contracts Approach (1996) 12 *Journal of Law, Economics, and Organization* 1.
—— 'Convertible Securities and Venture Capital Finance' (2003) 58 *Journal of Finance* 1139.
Schmidt, K and Lutter, M, *Aktiengesetz Kommentar*, 3rd edn (Ottoschmidt, 2015) vol 1, 1353.
Schmidt, R and Spindler, G, 'Path Dependence and Complementarity in Corporate Governance' in J Gordon and M Roe (eds), *Convergence and Persistence in Corporate Governance* (Cambridge University Press, 2004) 114.
Schwartz, E, *The Last Lone Inventor: A Tale of Genius, Deceit, and the Birth of Television* (Harper-Collins, 2002).
Schwartz, R and Orleans, S, 'On Legal Sanctions' (1967) 34 *The University of Chicago Law Review* 274.
Sealy, L, 'The Director as Trustee' [1967] *Cambridge Law Journal* 83.
Sejean, M, 'The Disgorgement of Illicit Profits in French Law' in E Hondius and A Janssen, *Disgorgement of Profits* (Springer, 2015) 121–38.
Shapiro, N, 'Ownership and Management' in P Davidson and J Kregel (eds), *Employment, Growth and Finance* (Edward Elgar, 1994) 84.
Shapiro, S, 'Agency Theory' (2005) 31 *Annual Review of Sociology* 263.
Shepherd, D and Zacharakis, A, 'The Venture Capitalist-Entrepreneur Relationship: Control, Trust and Confidence in Co-operative Behaviour' (2001) 3 *Venture Capital: An International Journal of Entrepreneurial Finance* 129.
Shleifer, A and Vishny, R, 'A Survey of Corporate Governance' (1997) 52 *Journal of Finance* 737.
Siems, M, 'Convergence in Corporate Governance: A Leximetric Approach' (2009) 35 *Journal of Corporation Law* 729.
Sitkoff, R, 'The Economic Structure of Fiduciary Law' (2013) 91 *Boston University Law Review* 1039.
Skawińska, E and Zalewski, R, 'Success Factors of Startups in the EU – A Comparative Study' (2020) 12 *Sustainability* 8200.
Son, J-Y, 'Out of Fear or Desire? Toward a Better Understanding of Employees' Motivation to Follow IS Security Policies' (2011) 48 *Information & Management* 296.
Soskice, D and Hall, P, *Varieties of Capitalism: The Institutional Foundations of Comparative Advantage* (Oxford University Press, 2001).
Spolidoro, M, 'Il Divieto di Concorrenza per gli Amministratori di Società di Capitali' [1983] *Rivista Dir Soc* 1314.

Steinwart, M and Ziegler, J, 'Remembering Apple CEO Steve Jobs as a "Transformational Leader": Implications for Pedagogy' (2014) 13 *Journal of Leadership Education* 52.
Stevens, R, *Torts and Rights* (Oxford University Press, 2007).
Stigler, G, 'The Origin of the Sherman Act' (1985) 14 *The Journal of Legal Studies* 1.
Stitt, A, *Mediating Commercial Disputes* (Canada Law Book, 2003).
Stout, L, 'On the Export of U.S. Style Corporate Fiduciary Duties to other Cultures' in C Milhaupt (ed), *Global Markets, Domestic Institutions* (Columbia University Press, 2003).
—— 'On the Proper Motives of Corporate Directors (or, Why You Don't Want to Invite Homo Economicus to Join your Board)' (2003) 28 *Delaware Journal of Corporate Law* 1.
—— *The Shareholder Value Myth: How Putting Shareholders First Harms Investors, Corporations, and the Public* (Berrett-Koehler, 2012).
Strader, K, 'White-Collar Crime and Punishment: Reflection on Michael, Martha, and Milberg Weiss' (2007) 15 *George Mason Law Review* 45.
Suchman, M and Cahill, M, 'The Hired Gun as Facilitator: Lawyers and the Suppression of Business Disputes in Silicon Valley' (1996) 21 *Law & Social Inquiry* 679.
Sutherland, E, *White-Collar Crime* (Holt, 1949).
Swadling, W, 'Constructive Trusts and Breach of Fiduciary Duty' (2012) 18 *Trust & Trustees* 98.
Talley, E, 'Turning Servile Opportunities to Gold: A Strategic Analysis of the Corporate Opportunities Doctrine' (1998–99) 108 *Yale Law Journal* 277.
Tamanaha, B, *On the Rule of Law: History, Politics, Theory* (Cambridge University Press, 2006).
Tambini, D, 'What are Financial Journalist for?' (2010) 11 *Journalism Studies* 158.
Teece, D, 'Economies of Scope and the Scope of the Enterprise' (1980) 1 *Journal of Economic Behavior & Organizations* 223.
Tian, X, 'The Causes and Consequences of Venture Capital Stage Financing' (2011) 10 *Journal of Financial Economics* 132.
Trask, A and De Guire, A, *Betting the Company: Complex Negotiation Strategies for Law and Business* (Oxford University Press, 2013).
Tur-Sinai, O, 'The Endowment Effect in IP Transactions: The Case against Debiasing' (2011) 18 *Michigan Telecommunication & Technology Law Review* 117.
Tykvova, T, 'German Banks as Venture Capitalists' in G Gregoriou (ed), *Venture Capital in Europe* (Butterworth-Heinemann, 2007) 331.
—— 'Legal Framework Quality and Success of (Different Types of) Venture Capital Investments' (2018) 87 *Journal of Banking & Finance* 333.
Tykvova, T and Schertler, A, 'Does Syndication with Local Venture Capitalists Moderate the Effects of Geographical and Institutional Distance?' (2014) 20 *Journal of International Management* 406.
Tyler, T, *Why People Obey the Law* (Oxford University Press, 2006).
Ueda, M, 'Banks Versus Venture Capital: Project Evaluation, Screening, and Expropriation' (2004) 59 *Journal of Finance* 601.
Utset, M, 'Reciprocal Fairness, Strategic Behavior and Venture Survival: A Theory of Venture Capital-Financed Firms' (2002) *Wisconsin Law Review* 45.
Vagts, D, 'Reforming the Modern Corporation: Perspectives from the German' (1996) *80 Harvard Law Review* 23.
Vaidhyanathan, S, '*Antisocial Media: How Facebook Disconnects us and Undermines Democracy* (Oxford University Press, 2018).
Van Osnabrugge, M, 'A Comparison of Business Angel and Venture Capitalist Investment Procedures: An Agency Theory-based Analysis (2000) 2 *Venture Capital: An International Journal of Entrepreneurial Finance* 91.
Van Slyke, P and Friedman, M, 'Employer's Rights to Inventions and Patents of Its Officers, Directors and Employees' (1990) 18 *American Intellectual Property Law Association Quarterly Journal* 127.
Velasco, J, 'The Diminishing Duty of Loyalty' (2018) 75 *Washington & Lee Law Review* 1035.
Velte, P, 'Determinants and Consequences of Clawback Provisions in Management Compensation Contracts: a Structured Literature Review on Empirical Evidence (2020) 13 *Business Research* 1417, 1420.

Ventoruzzo, M, 'Commento all'Articolo 2391 del Codice Civile' in P Marchetti et al (eds), *Commentario alla Riforma delle Societa*' (Giuffre, 2006) 490.

Verdam, A, 'Corporate Opportunities: The Appropriation by Company Officers of Business Opportunities Belonging to the Company (1998) 45 *Netherlands International Law Review* 233.

Vermeulen, F and Barkema, H, 'Learning through Acquisitions' (2001) 44 *Academy of Management Journal* 457.

Viesti, G, *Come Nascono i Distretti Industriali* (Laterza, 2000).

Ville, S, 'Efficient Transactors or Rent-seeking Monopolists? The Rationale for Early Chartered Trading Companies' (1996) 56 *Journal of Economic History* 898.

Virgo, G, 'Profits obtained in Breach of Fiduciary Duty: Personal or Proprietary Claim?' (2011) 70 *Cambridge Law Journal* 502.

Viscusi, K, 'The Challenge of Punitive Damages Mathematics' (2001) 30 *Journal of Legal Studies* 313.

Wachter, T, *Kommentar zum Aktiengesetz*, 2nd edn (RWS, 2014).

Wacquant, L, 'The Great Penal Leap Backward: Incarceration in America from Nixon to Clinton' in J Pratt et al (eds), *The New Punitiveness* (Willan, 2005) 3.

Wadhwa, A, Phelps, C and Kotha, S, 'Corporate Venture Capital Portfolios and Firm Innovation' (2016) 31 *Journal of Business Venturing* 95.

Wallace, J and Erickson, J, *Hard Drive: Bill Gates and the Making of the Microsoft Empire* (Wiley, 1992).

Wallbank, F, 'Trade and Industry under the Later Roman Empire in the West' in M Postan and E Miller (eds), *The Cambridge Economic History of Europe*, 2nd edn (Cambridge University Press, 1987) vol 2, 74.

Wang, H and Barney, J, 'Employees Incentives to Make Firm-Specific Investments: Implications for Resource-based Theories of Corporate Diversification' (2006) 31 *Academy of Management Review* 466.

Warren III, M, 'Equitable Clawback: An Essay on Restoration of Executive Compensation' (2009) 12 *University of Pennsylvania Journal of Business Law* 1135.

Wasserman, N, 'The Throne vs. the Kingdom: Founder Control and Value Creation in Startups' (2017) 38 *Strategic Management Journal* 255.

Weinrib, E, *The Idea of Private Law* (Harvard University Press, 1995).

Weiss, L, 'The Structure-Conduct-Performance Paradigm and Antitrust' (1979) 127 *University of Pennsylvania Law Review* 1104.

Whincop, M, 'Painting the Corporate Cathedral: The Protection of Entitlements in Corporate Law' (1999) 19 *Oxford Journal of Legal Studies* 19.

Wiegand, W, 'Americanization of Law: Reception or Convergence?' in L Friedman and H Scheiber (eds), *Legal Culture and the Legal Profession* (Westview Press, 1996) 146.

Williams, S, 'Venture Capital Contract Design: An Empirical Analysis of the Connection Between Bargaining Power and Venture Financing Contract Terms' (2017) 23 *Fordham Journal of Corporate & Financial Law* 105.

Williamson, O, 'Credible Commitments: Using Hostages to Support Exchange' (1983) 73 *American Economic Review* 519.

—— 'Transaction-Cost Economics: The Governance of Contractual Relations' (1979) 22 *Journal of Law and Economics* 233.

—— 'Strategy Research: Governance and Competence Perspectives' in N Foss and V Mahnke (eds), *Competence, Governance and Entrepreneurship* (Oxford University Press, 2000) 21.

Wilson, R, 'The Theory of Syndicates' (1968) 36 *Econometrica* 119.

Wilson, S, *The Origins of Modern Financial Crime: Historical Foundations and Current Problems in Britain* (Routledge, 2014).

Winseck, D, 'The Geopolitical Economy of the Global Internet Infrastructure' (2017) 7 *Journal of Information Policy* 228.

Winter, R, 'State Law, Shareholder Protection and the Theory of the Corporation' (1977) 6 *Journal of Legal Studies* 251.

Winters, T and Murfin, D, 'Venture Capital Investing for Corporate Development Objectives (1998) 3 *Journal of Business Venturing* 207.

Wise, G, 'Inventors and Corporations in the Maturing Electrical Industry, 1890–1940' in R Perkins and D Weber (eds), *Inventive Minds: Creativity in Technology* (Oxford University Press, 1992) 291.

Witney, S, 'Corporate Opportunities Law and the Non-executive Director' (2016) 16 *Journal of Corporate Law Studies* 145.

Wojciky, D and MacDonald-Korth, D, 'The British and the German Financial Sectors in the Wake of the Crisis: Size, Structure and Spatial Concentration' (2015) *Journal of Economic Geography* 1.

Woolf, T, 'The Venture Capitalist's Corporate Opportunity Problem' (2001) *Columbia Business Law Review* 473.

Wong, A, 'Angel Finance. The Other Venture Capital' in D Cumming (ed), *Venture Capital: Investment Strategies, Structures, and Policies* (Wiley & Sons, 2010) 71.

Worthington, S, 'Reconsidering disgorgement for wrongs' (1999) 62 *Modern Law Review* 218.

—— 'Fiduciary Duties and Proprietary Remedies: Addressing the Failure of Equitable Formulae' (2013) 72 *Cambridge Law Journal* 720.

Wright, M, Pruthi, S and Lockett, A, 'International Venture Capital Research: From Cross Country Comparisons to Crossing Borders' (2005) 7 *International Journal of Management Reviews* 135.

Wymeersch, E, 'Comparative Studies of the Company Types in Selected EU States' (2009) 6 *European Company and Financial Law Review* 71.

Yan, X and Huang, J, 'Navigating Unknown Waters: The Chinese Communist Party's New Presence in the Private Sector' (2017) 17 *The China Review* 37.

Zacharakis, A, 'Venture Capital Decision Making' in D Cumming (ed), *Venture Capital: Investment Strategies, Structures, and Policies* (Wiley & Sons, 2010) 9.

Zamagni, V, *The Economic History of Italy 1860–1990* (Clarendon Press, 1993).

Zetzsche, D, 'Shareholder Passivity, Cross-Border Voting and the Shareholder Rights Directive' (2008) 8 *Journal of Corporate Law Studies* 289.

—— 'Shareholder Interaction Preceding Shareholder Meetings of Public Corporations – A Six Country Comparison' (2012) 2 *European Company and Financial Law Review* 105.

Zider, B, 'How Venture Capital Works' (1998) 76 *Harvard Business Review* 131.

Zimmermann, R, 'Unjustified Enrichment: The Modern Civilian Approach' (1995) 15 *Oxford Journal of Legal Studies* 403.

Zingales, L, 'In Search of New Foundations' (2000) 55 *The Journal of Finance* 1623.

Zipursky, B, 'A Theory of Punitive Damages' (2005) 84 *Texas Law Review* 105.

Zwick, T, 'Employee Resistance against Innovations' (2002) 23 *International Journal of Manpower* 542.

Index

www.ingramcontent.com/pod-product-compliance
Lightning Source LLC
Chambersburg PA
CBHW071352220926
51613CB00008B/109